AWAKENING THE GIANT WITHIN

—Claire Hastain—

About The Author

Claire retired from her role as a teacher of Metaphysics and Expansion of Consciousness to focus on new methods of learning which offered safe ways to exit the matrix, and safe ways to connect to the Heart of Creation, without the barriers to Truth that the satanic cult and ET groups have created: all designed to suppress the giant within you all.

The giant, that once awakened: the dark cult are no match for, and once you realise the power is all within you to create, to re-imagine your preferred reality, and once you become aware that it is they that fear your power — your inner giant — then, the journey can become joyful, peaceful, and enlightening; the power to create the optimal outcome that best serves all life and which secures the children's brightest future.

The opportunity for change is knocking at your door.

Will you listen?

The children hope so, because the danger they are facing if you ignore the warnings will spell disaster for all life, and an end to life as you know it.

Do the right thing, and step forward to assist now. The help has been here since 2012, and yet, very few have attempted to help; using their giant within.

Claire's role has always been to encourage you all that you have everything you need within your heart to help yourselves, your loved ones and pets, the voiceless, and the children.

They are the reason you came.

It is time to awaken now.

It is time to help them get home.

BOOKS BY THE SAME AUTHOR

ELF Waves, How They Harm Humanity,

Paperback – 18 April 2017

EBOOK, 2024

'ELF Waves: How They Harm Humanity,' is a companion guide that takes the reader into the deeper regions of expanding consciousness.

It is to be read alongside Claire Hastain's previous work, and acts as a reminder to the Divine Aspect of Self. Its purpose is to remind humanity of their ability to end suffering and create Peace.

Its goal is to awaken those who came in to protect a sleeping humanity, with the Divine purpose of collapsing the False Light Programs of limitation, suffering, and needless hardships.

This is a must read for all newly awakened souls, and for those who are advancing with their meditation practices.

WHAT ON EARTH IS HAPPENING?

Paperback – 1 Jan. 2021

For Your Heart's Discernment

PLEASE BE ADVISED THAT THIS BOOK SHARES THE AUTHOR'S METAPHYSICAL PERCEPTIONS OF REALITY AS SEEN THROUGH THE LENS OF THEIR INFINITE SELF AND THE HEART OF CREATION. IT IS THE TRUTH; AS PRESENTED TO THE AUTHOR THROUGH DILIGENT INNER RESEARCH; TO SEEK PEACEFUL SOLUTIONS FOR HUMANITY AND ALL PRECIOUS LIFE.

ALWAYS USE DISCERNMENT WHEN CHOOSING TO PARTICIPATE IN ANY TYPE OF RELAXATION.

USE YOUR HEART (YOUR INFINITE SELF) TO DISCERN ALL THE TRUTHS SHARED HERE. DO NOT GIVE YOUR POWER TO THE WRITINGS: SIMPLY, USE THEM AS A MIRROR AND SEE IF THEY REFLECT LIFE AS SEEN THROUGH YOUR OWN HEART CENTRE.

THE INFORMATION WITHIN THE BOOK IS BOLD, AND SOME READERS MAY FIND IT DIFFICULT TO DIGEST. CLAIRE HAS TRIED HER BEST TO REACH TRUTH, HOWEVER, ULTIMATELY, YOUR INFINITE SELF MUST BECOME YOUR GUIDING LIGHT AND TEACHER.

IT MAY TRIGGER A 'REBELLION' OF SORTS WITHIN YOU. IF SO, IT IS A GOOD IDEA TO LOOK WITHIN YOURSELF, TO ASK YOUR INFINITE SELF WHY THE REBELLION IS PRESENT. QUITE OFTEN, IT IS BECAUSE A REBELLIOUS ENERGY, OR ADDICTIVE FREQUENCY, OR A MIND CONTROL TECHNOLOGY IS WITHIN YOUR LADDER OF CONSCIOUSNESS AND DOES NOT WANT TO BE DISCOVERED OR REMOVED.

IT IS *REBELLING* AGAINST ANY TRUTH WHICH MAY *HIGHLIGHT* ITS PRESENCE AND USUALLY WANTS TO MOVE AWAY FROM THE 'LIGHT OF TRUTH' AS IT IS TOO BRIGHT.

SOME OF THE INFORMATION MAY TRIGGER STRONG FEELINGS. YOU MAY STRONGLY DISAGREE WITH WHAT THE AUTHOR SHARES ABOUT YOGA, REIKI, FREEMASONS, HALLOWEEN, CHRISTMAS, SOLSTICE CELEBRATIONS, ETC. THIS IS NOT ABOUT THE AUTHOR'S 'OPINION' OR JUDGMENTS, IT IS ABOUT THE DESIRE TO REACH TRUTH; WHATEVER THAT TRUTH MIGHT BE AND HAVING THE COURAGE TO LOOK IS ESSENTIAL TO OUR SURVIVAL.

MANY THINGS WE BELIEVE TO BE TRUE ARE NOT TRUE AT ALL.

MUCH OF OUR THINKING IS AFFECTED BY THE MIND CONTROL AND INGRAINED EGO-LED PROGRAMMING.

WE HAVE TO PUSH PAST ALL PRECONCEIVED THOUGHTS, ALL INGRAINED TEACHINGS, TO REACH FULLEST TRUTH.

READING THIS BOOK THIS MAY CAUSE DISTRESS. YOU MAY BE DEEPLY SUFFERING YOURSELF,

AND THEREFORE, IT MAY BE BEST TO CONCENTRATE ON SELF HEALING UNTIL YOU FEEL RESTORED.

OTHERS MAY NOT BE READY TO READ ANOTHER'S PERCEPTIONS THROUGH THEIR OWN INFINITE SELF.

DO NOT READ THE BOOK IF YOU SENSE YOUR HEART IS NOT YET OPEN TO DEEPER TRUTHS.

AN OPEN HEART THAT IS FOCUSED ON HELPING THE CHILDREN AND ALL LIFE IS REQUIRED.

A BRAVE HEART. ONE THAT HAS COMPASSION FOR OTHER'S SUFFERING: ONE THAT IS DRIVEN BY COMPASSION AND CONCERN, NOT BY OPINION, FAULTY THINKING, OR EGO-LED CHOICES.

MY INFINITE SELF HAS SET OUT THE TRUE CAUSE — THE TRUE ISSUES — IN ORDER TO GET THE HELP TO THE CHILDREN.

IF WE DO NOT **SEEK THE TRUE CAUSE** OF HUMANITY'S SUFFERING, WE CANNOT RESOLVE THE ISSUES — **THE EFFECTS** — NOR CAN WE HELP **TO PEACEFULLY PREVENT MORE SUFFERING.**

MANY INNOCENT LIFE FORMS ARE SUFFERING ON OUR PLANET.

THE HATRED AND VIOLENCE IS TANGIBLE AND IS INCREASING EVERY SECOND OF EVERY DAY.

THIS BOOK IS FOR THOSE WHO ARE BRAVE ENOUGH TO WANT TO LOOK AT THE PROBLEMS: TO HELP FIND PEACEFUL, CREATIVE SOLUTIONS TO HELP PROTECT ALL LIFE.

POSITIVE SELF HELP:

THE RELAXATION ROUTINES OFFER THE OPPORTUNITY TO STILL THE BUSY 'MIND-CONTROLLED' MIND, AND TO CONNECT MORE DEEPLY TO ONE'S INFINITE SELF.

HEART CONNECTION DOES NOT REPLACE MEDICAL ADVICE.

THE BOOK DOES NOT OFFER MEDICAL SOLUTIONS.

IF YOU DO HAVE MEDICAL CHALLENGES THEN, IT IS ALWAYS ADVISABLE TO CONSULT WITH YOUR HEALTH CARE PROFESSIONAL, ESPECIALLY IF YOU ARE FEELING UNWELL AND ALWAYS, BEFORE COMMENCING ANY NEW RELAXATION ROUTINES.

THE ROUTINES MAY TIRE YOU AND THEY MAY ENERGISE YOU.

CLEARING AWAY TOXIC ENERGY CAN CAUSE FEELINGS OF SADNESS, OR IRRITABILITY, HOWEVER, THESE ARE USUALLY SHORT LIVED AND EASILY MANAGED THROUGH POSITIVE SELF CARE.

CONSULT YOUR MEDICAL PROFESSIONAL BEFORE EMBARKING ON ANY NEW METHOD OF RELAXATION IF YOU ARE IN ANY DOUBT.

THE HEART CONNECTION AND MIND CALMING RELAXATION ROUTINES REQUIRE A QUIET PLACE WHERE ONE CAN SAFELY RELAX UNDISTURBED AND SAFELY CLOSE ONE'S EYES.

THE BEDROOM AND THE BED THAT ONE SLEEPS IN AT NIGHT IS RECOMMENDED BECAUSE IT IS A FAMILIAR, SAFE PLACE TO RELAX — EVERYONE IS USED TO THEIR OWN BEDROOM, AND SLEEPING ROUTINES.

IF YOU DO DECIDE TO PARTICIPATE IN ANY RELAXATION EVENT, COMMON SENSE ADVISES US ALL THAT **THESE ARE NOT SUITABLE FOR THE WORK PLACE, OR WHILST DRIVING OR OPERATING MACHINERY.**

A QUIET BEDROOM AND THE BED THAT WE SAFELY SLEEP IN AT NIGHT IS THE RECOMMENDED PLACE.

COMMON SENSE ALSO ADVISES US TO USE OUR DISCERNMENT AT ALL TIMES, TO ENSURE WE TAKE RESPONSIBILITY FOR OUR OWN CHOICES.

YOUR CHOICE TO PARTAKE IN ANY RELAXATION ROUTINE SHARED IN THE BOOK, WHILE RELAXING AT HOME ON THE BED THAT YOU SLEEP IN AT NIGHT INDICATES YOU HAVE CONSULTED YOUR HEALTH CARE PROFESSIONAL BEFORE YOU COMMENCED READING THE BOOK AND BEFORE YOU EMBARKED ON ANY RELAXATION ROUTINES SHARED HERE AND INDICATES THAT YOU AGREE TO RELEASE AND DISCHARGE C. HASTAIN FROM ALL LIABILITY THAT MIGHT ARISE AND INDICATES YOUR AGREEMENT TO BE BOUND BY THESE TERMS, WHICH MAY BE MODIFIED IN WRITING BY C. HASTAIN IN FUTURE PUBLICATIONS.

ANY DISPUTE ARISING UNDER THESE TERMS OR ARISING FROM THE INFORMATION SHARED IN THIS BOOK, SHALL BE RESOLVED EXCLUSIVELY IN A MANCHESTER UK LAW COURT, OR OTHER UK LAW COURT AS CHOSEN BY C. HASTAIN.

IN SUMMARY, YOUR CHOICE TO READ THIS BOOK RELEASES C.HASTAIN FROM ALL RESPONSIBILITY.

YOU HEREBY AGREE TO THESE TERMS.

...

THE MOST IMPORTANT LAWS ARE THE LAWS OF CREATION:

WE ARE ALL BOUND BY THE LAWS OF CREATION WHICH ARE NOW FULLY OPERATIONAL ON THE EARTH PLANE.

TO BREAK THESE LAWS IS TO CREATE KARMIC CYCLES FOR OURSELVES AND IT IS INADVISABLE, AT THIS TIME, BECAUSE THEY ARE WORKING SO RAPIDLY NOW, THAT ANY MISTAKES WE MAKE THAT ARE LEFT UNCHECKED, UN-REPAIRED AND UNHEALED ARE BEING RETURNED TO US IN THEIR MAGNIFIED STATE, FOR OUR OWN LEARNING.

THIS IS THE CYLCE OF LOVE AND LIFE AND UNITY: THE TRUE LAWS THAT BIND US ALL TO LOVE ONE ANOTHER AND HELP EACH OTHER TO EVOLVE OUT OF DENSITY, AND TO GET HELP FOR THE CHILDREN AND INNOCENT LIFE FORMS WHO ARE TRAPPED IN FALSE LIGHT FREQUENCY BANDS, AND ARE BEING HARMED BY CONTRIVED, POINTLESS WARS, HARMFUL A.I. TECHNOLOGY AND MOBILE FREQUENCIES/ELF WAVES/EMF'S AND SO FORTH.

THE AUTHOR HAS LISTENED TO HER GIANT WITHIN AND SHARED ONLY WHAT THE LAWS OF CREATION HAVE PERMITTED HER TO SHARE.

WE ARE ALL BEING CALLED UPON TO HEAL ALL ERRORS WE MAY HAVE MADE, WHICH MAY HAVE ACCIDENTALLY CAUSED HARM TO ALL LIFE.

WE ARE ALSO BEING ADVISED THAT WE CAN PEACEFULLY ASK FOR:

ALL MALICIOUS, MAGNIFIED HARM, ALL INTENTIONS TO CAUSE HARM, AND ALL HARM CAUSED THROUGH IGNORANCE, OR THE CHOICE TO STAND BY AND DO NOTHING TO HELP THOSE WHO ARE SUFFERING, TO BE GATHERED UP NOW, BY LOVE AND THE LAWS OF CREATION, AND RETURNED IMMEDIATELY TO ALL THOSE RESPONSIBLE FOR THE HARM.

ALL ERRORS MUST BE RETURNED TO THE ORIGINATORS AND PERPETRATORS OF THE HARM,

(FOR THEIR LEARNING: TO GIVE THEM THE OPPORTUNITY TO EVOLVE OUT OF DENSITY; SHOULD THEY WISH TO ADDRESS THE HARM AND CALL ON LOVE TO REMEDY THEIR ERRORS; AND BECAUSE THOSE WHO HAVE CALLED FOR RESCUE ARE BEING CLEARED OF THE HARM CAUSED BY OTHERS.

IT HAS TO GO BACK TO THE SENDER.

WE ARE ALL BOUND BY THESE LAWS WHICH WE ALL HELPED TO CREATE, SO THAT WHEN WE REACHED CERTAIN LEVELS OF EVOLUTION AND LEARNING IN DENSITY, THE LAWS WOULD COME INTO PLAY.

THAT TIME IS NOW.

PEACEFULLY RETURN ALL HARM THAT IS NOT YOURS AND ASK LOVE TO REPAIR YOUR OWN ERRORS.)

THIS IS THE TRUE MEANING OF HEALING: TO RETURN TO BALANCE

THE FOLLOWING MESSAGES ARE SHARED HERE WITH LOVE.

THE AUTHOR HAS HOPE, TRUST, AND FAITH THAT ALL WHO READ THIS BOOK WILL STEP FORWARD TO

PEACEFULLY PROTECT ALL PRECIOUS LIFE, ESPECIALLY THE CHILDREN, BECAUSE THEY ARE THE QUARRY OF THOSE WHO LIKE TO HUNT, RAPE, MAIM AND KILL.

THANK YOU FOR HELPING ALL INNOCENT LIFE.

MAY YOUR GIANT AWAKEN AND MAY YOUR JOURNEY BECOME PEACEFUL, JOYFUL AND FULL OF HOPE FOR THE FUTURE.

In 2014...

I started to realise that the dark elite had infiltrated every aspect of our lives, and they continue to do so, unchallenged as they are, by a sleeping humanity.

KARMA, UNDERSTANDING COSMIC LAW,
Claire Hastain © 2014

Prologue

Dear Reader,

Today, whilst standing at "The Outer Waves of Infinite Possibilities," my heart guided me that the best way that I could serve all precious life was to start collating the many messages of hope and wisdom that I have been asked to share on:

LOVE's Heart Plan, www.substack.com

and

Searching For The Evidence channel

on

www.bitchute.com

and

Deeper Truths Channel, @truelightessence, Odysee.com;

to create a book, whereby the newly awakened can easily source and reference information.

I have been given very little time to do this. I am often guided that perfection is not important owing to the urgency of the hour to get information to others and to help them to strengthen their heart connection. This appears especially true today and I ask you to forgive any errors and to focus on absorbing the codes that will enable the giant within you to awaken.

I will be blunt. The children are in danger. All life is in danger.

You are all being called to assist because you all came here to help and because you carry the codes of Knowledge to protect and defend all life.

There are many awakening giants who do not realise why they are here, or how to connect safely, or how to proceed when dealing with the enormity of the danger that humanity are now facing. Many see it as futile. I do not believe that for one instance.

I re-published my previous five books from 2014/15/16 in 2020 as one title, "***What On Earth Is Happening?***", and unfortunately, because the energy contained within the books was not being utilised by a large enough group, the energy procured from the Heart of Creation was recalled and I was guided to withdraw the information.

I have witnessed this throughout the publications of my books.

I feel saddened by this. So much help is available to us. We do not use it.

Many misuse energy, and many are being badly taught by those who are driven by self-serving agendas.

I explored Holistic Energy healing practices and trained in many, before I grew and learned that they were flawed.

Once a human is attuned to energy from outside of self, they are already lost in the programs of False Light.

The Healing Community came here to help humanity, yet, most are lost in False Light teachings, and most refuse to stop practices that are obsolete and incompatible with the planetary changes and other significant changes in the Greater Cosmos.

This has placed the children in terrible danger, and all innocent life has been harmed by humanity in various ways, however, I have to be honest: my greatest disappointment has been to witness the stubborn refusal of the Healing Community to stop the very activities which have now destroyed the protection from the Galactic Grids, the

Planetary Grids, and worse still, destroyed humanity's shared Cosmic Shield of protection, which offered a level of protection that prevented technologically advanced forces from 'piercing' our twelve levels of consciousness that are trapped inside the False Light programs.

Those twelve levels of protection have since collapsed due to the unwillingness of others to stop and change direction.

We are now facing a worse scenario than the pandemic crisis of 2020.

All protection of the planet, humanity's shared shield of protection, and the individual shield of protection of each human has been destroyed by these activities and the stubborn refusal to go deeper, and stop harming.

Reiki and Yoga groups, 5G technology, and Free Masonry are the leading culprits. The very groups of souls who could be helping are the ones being used to destroy our protection and expose us all to satanic frequencies.

We are all being called to go deeper, and to stand firm together because the world's children are facing a life time of slavery if we allow any more harm to be caused by our poor practices, our poor choices and the selfish decisions to ignore the outcome of those poor choices.

I have tried to wake others up to the dangers. Many others are trying too.

The best way to help protect the children and all life is to ask for help and to ask our hearts to show us the way.

The gateway to our hearts is now under attack — the last bastion to safety and our gateway to Truth.

Many souls are coming into this reality to help us, and many are ending up being sacrificed and trafficked, abused and tortured. They carry the codes that many humans have already given to the dark, you see.

The dark want those codes of Knowledge to feed off and to weaponise against us.

What do you think 5G truly is? Ask your heart, and you will see.

The children are the target of this dark group, and the children are totally exposed, thanks to those who chose to ignore LOVE's guidance.

As LOVE has already shared in one of my messages, *"If a dead infant and suffering newborn will not change your mind, what will?"*

I cannot bare to witness anymore suffering — suffering that is easily preventable by every human who each carry codes of Knowledge to end the game.

Many of my transcripts were made into audio recordings which I have also shared online. The audio versions offer the reader a greater opportunity to relax and listen through their own heart centres whilst resting at home in a quiet environment.

The audio versions help to still the busy mind and they provide a set of easy to follow steps to ensure the heart is engaged and the protection of LOVE/Creator and LOVE's Purest Light frequencies are surrounding the listener. The Laws of Creation must be utilised and questioned also, to ensure that all our actions and intentions are pure and safe, and provide the optimal outcome that best serves all life.

I have had just a few days to collate the work. The fact that I have not been given time to fully edit and proof-read the work, means that something is brewing.

A dark plan is in motion.

You are all being called upon as a matter of urgency to use "The Outer Waves Of Infinite Possibilities" audio version, because your gift of Creativity is our most powerful defence against all evil plans to annihilate humanity and LOVE's children.

Protect the children, focus on listening to your own heart's guidance — utilising LOVE and the Laws of Creation to protect your connection to Truth.

You do have the authority and the power within your hearts to call on LOVE/Creator for help for the voiceless, including the homeless, elderly, vulnerable, newborns and infants, pregnant mothers carrying new souls into this place and all life throughout existence that has been hit badly by the shock waves of the culmination of all our errors.

Let your compassion and love for others be your guiding light and driving force, and be fearless against this dark cult.

They have no power over you when you call on LOVE/Creator for help.

Always remember, we are not being asked to 'do' anything necessarily, except to ask our hearts each day, what is the optimal thing we could ask for to best serve all life, and what could we focus on to create our preferred reality?

Use your gifts wisely. Forgive those who cannot, or do not wish to help.

There are very few working safely with energy. Be aware of this fact, and learn to listen to that still small voice within you who has the full Knowledge and Wisdom to keep you safe.

Your pets are suffering too when you spend too much time using the internet, social media sites which strip you of your life force and mind control you, apps, mobiles, and especially, when using 5G, SMART technology, StarLink, and Sky Net.

Think about your daily activities...how much Artificial Intelligence, EMF'S, ELF WAVES, microwaves and SMART technology are you exposing yourself to that is harming you? Guard your life force at all times.

If humans are not clearing their energy fields each day — at least three times daily — they are exposed to the satanic frequencies which are swarming throughout the planet via this technology, and their consciousness is being 'hacked' by demonic forces and higher levels of our AWOL soul fragments.

A full on attack on our consciousness and a planetary take-over is in full swing.

I will sign off now, and collate the messages.

Thank you for caring and for helping humanity's children.

They are the currency.

Remember this truth, and when you see fires raging, trains crashing, weather engineering, chemicals spilling, planes vanishing, wars raging, chickens dying, businesses closing, cameras everywhere, wind turbines, mobile phone masts, ULEZ cameras, 15 Minute Cities and Clean Air Zones, pandemics manifesting from mystery diseases, and humans suffering, Digital ID, SMART devices, brain chipping, tracking devices and nano technologies, you are seeing the outcome of humanity manifesting The Great Reset Agenda 2030 and reality of choice for those who serve Lucifer and the Trans-human Agenda: the plan to destroy the biological human via genetic modification vaccines, and enslave humanity via injectable nano-technology.

Many do not even know about these plans by the UN, WHO, WEF, Vatican, Royal Family, Big Banks, Big Corp, Big Food and certain agents; strategically placed within your town councils, along with world global leaders, all bought and paid for by Bill Gates to overthrow humanity and enslave them, and so that they can access the children.

They are all 'friends of Jimmy Saville and Jeffrey Epstein' — two men who procured children to abuse for the rich and famous. They all keep each other's secrets.

Most of them have visited Jeffrey Epstein's Island and flown on his 'Lolitta Express' plane.

You can easily view the United Nations and World Economic Forum websites online. "You will be happy and own nothing", "You will eat bugs."

They do not hide these facts. Listen to Yuval Harrari to glean elements of their madness, or research the famous Fauci, planning to introduce a worldwide pandemic and flu vaccine, and discussing how to do it in 2019.

Or, listen to them plotting Event 201, just months before they introduced the pandemic story.

If you are reading the book version, kindly visit: Searching For The Evidence channel on www.bitchute.com, and type "Searching For The Evidence" in the search box, along with the video title, then select the links, or, do a quick search on the alternative channels, Bitchute.com, Odysee.com, t.me, Substack.com etc., as many others are sharing these links too:

Watch **MONOPOLY — WHO OWNS THE WORLD?** | Tim Gielin.

Listen to them laughing and plotting to control the media to cause as much fear as possible.

PURE EVIL IN A NEEDLE | DAVID ICKE/CELESTE SOLUM EXPOSES VACCINE INGREDIENTS TO THE WORLD, 2020

2021: AUSTRALIA: SENIOR NURSE - "THE HOSPITALS ARE FULL OF VACCINATED PATIENTS." TEENS DROP DEAD, MYOCARDITIS

YOU MAY NEVER TRUST A CELEBRITY AGAIN AFTER WATCHING THIS

CHECKUR6: YOUNG HEARTS PART 55 - 16TH JUNE 2024 | HUMANS DROPPING LIKE FLIES AFTER VACCINATION

MARCH OF THE VACCINE DEAD PROTEST IN ITALY

LEFT TO ROT, CHECKUR6 | BITCHUTE.COM AND

ODYSEE.COM | VACCINE INJURED LIST THEIR SYMPTOMS

THE SPIDER'S WEB: BRITAIN'S SECOND EMPIRE | DOCUMENTARY FILM - SEP 14 2018

STRAWMAN - THE NATURE OF THE CAGE (REMASTERED) [2023 - JOHN K WEBSTER]

THE KILL GRID - MARK STEELE | TUNGSTEN IN VAX MAKES HUMANS 'DORMANT RADIATION TRANSMITTERS'

GUINEA KID PIGS | BBC 2004 DOCUMENTARY - HOW FAUCI AND ACS FORCED EXPERIMENTATION ON 'HIV' CHILDREN

BILL GATES | DELETED DOCUMENTARY | "A 20 : 1 RETURN" | WHY HE SWITCHED FROM MICROSOFT TO VACCINES

They rely on your ignorance and your apathy. The parties at Downing Street during the 'deadly pandemic' should have been the last straw for humanity, but they hardly batted an eye.

Finally, kindly listen to this message regarding controlled opposition.

The Controllers | https://truelightessence.substack.com/p/the-controllers| The Controllers, Chapter 22

This group are the ones to watch, and the ones to be most wary of. It is all unfolding as I was guided and I sense that is why this book has to go in such a hurried manner.

Do not be swayed by any 'cure all' or snake oil remedies from the 'saviours'. Don't get led down any more false pathways of needless suffering, especially, by the 'saviour vaccines' and snake oil potions. Use your heart and it will steer you away from harm. Watch their hand shaping, not their faces, and look out for the rings on the men's fingers. This message will help you to peacefully protect all life here.

DIAMOND/PYRAMID HAND SHAPING —COLLAPSE THE SATANIC GRIDS— USE "THE OUTER WAVES OF INFINITE POSSIBILITIES" | https://truelightessence.substack.com/p/diamondpyramid-hand-shaping-collapse | Chapter 51

Look at the background of video interviews, and study what pictures are in view. I have witnessed the star, stone tower pictures, starfish pictures, pyramids, the Caduceus and Rod Of Asclepius (used prolifically by the saviour doctors) and all sorts of satanic symbolism: It is all in plain sight, if you care to look closely. Ask your heart to help you read the energy of others to help you detect dark motives. You are all more than capable.

Currently, along with implementing the Social Credit System via the Digital ID as per communist China, they are also about to legalise pedophilia in order to secure easier access to abusing the children, which is, unfortunately, what this dark cabal seem to enjoy, above all things.

They want you to obey, comply, submit.

This may seem too much to take in, but for those who have taken the time to study this group, it is evident that The Great Reset Agenda 2030 provides nothing beneficial for humanity, except slavery, child abuse, totalitarian control, and loss of everything we hold dear.

You have to be brave to look at these things. The children need our courage.

It is hoped that the messages will spur the reader onwards, to set to work to bring about positive, peaceful change.

It is so serious now, I pray more will listen and take time to help.

The time for planning your holidays, thinking about your TV viewing and other projects is over.

All your spare energy needs to go into saving the children from this dark cult.

You have everything inside you to peacefully bring about change.

The outcome for all of us, especially the voiceless, rests with us.

There is hardly any time left to choose.

Choose wisely.

...

This body of work can be found at these key online channels:

Full Audio Experience:

@Loves Heart Plan | substack.com (transcripts and audio)

Searching For The Evidence, bitchute.com

and t.me.com

@truelightessence, odysee.com

These recordings offer the best way to experience heart connection.

Each new message carries updated codes of Remembrance to help you on your soul evolution and the latest heart connection routine will always carry the most advanced upgrades.

Let your heart guide you what messages will help you the most to best serve all in optimal ways.

Contents

Chapter One

THE OUTER WAVES OF INFINITE POSSIBILITIES

9 May 2024

Full Audio Experience:

"The Outer Waves of Infinite Possibilities"
HEART CONNECTION:

END ALL SUFFERING; USE YOUR POWER OF CREATIVITY

@Loves Heart Plan substack.com | Searching For The Evidence, bitchute.com | @truelightessence, odysee.com

Hello, My name is Claire. I am a retired teacher of Holistic's, specialising in the areas of consciousness and metaphysics — the unknown and unexplored areas of consciousness, and our connectivity to the Greater Cosmos.

My experiences throughout my learning has led me to where I am today, and that place is a place of deep knowing that something greater than ourselves exists — something that is permanent and fixed — and in spite of all experiences in this space that we call Earth, I firmly believe that we have yet to tap into our true potential as a family of Humanity.

My yearning has always been to help humanity and all precious life, to protect all from harm and suffering, and to help others discover their true potential, so that they can also help others and protect all life from harm.

There are deeper teachings that run along side what I am going to share today, but for now, I wish to share with you a beautiful heart connection routine that is for all of humanity, and which holds no impurities, only, a connection to the deepest part of your very selves and the purity of LOVE, however you wish to perceive this.

I prefer to avoid labels and simply use these words because, to me, they cannot carry anything other than Unconditional LOVE from the Heart of Creation.

It is my belief that we all came here to help each other to end all suffering. I believe that you have the power to play your part in creating a peaceful world: free from suffering and free from hardship.

Creativity is key in helping to end suffering.

Others use energy in ways which are creating chaos on our planet.

The aim today is to invite you all to help to create a vision of the world that would truly bring you the most joy and happiness — in ways which best help all life in optimal ways, which are in alignment with the governing laws of all life — the Laws of Creation, and together, my aim is to encourage you all to utilise this powerful help to influence positive, peaceful change.

It can be done.

You are so powerful when you use Creativity to influence change for the better, and this can help with disease, illness, war zones, and all types of suffering, including mental and emotional trauma.

Common sense reminds us that this is not suitable to use at work, or while driving or operating machinery.

Your bedroom is the preferred place. It is a familiar space and the creative energy can grow into a powerful force for goodness that starts to expand around your home, your garden, your neighbourhood and eventually, your planet and infinitely beyond.

Make yourself comfortable by lying down on the bed that you sleep in at night, at home.

Set an alarm clock in case you need to be awake for a certain time, and have a drink of water nearby.

Allow plenty of time for this, initially, because the set-up routine needs time and patience to 'bed into' your reality.

Repeating the routine strengthens its effectiveness.

Repetition and daily practice makes things happen.

The more of you who participate, the quicker the preferred outcome that best serves all life in optimal ways, in alignment with the Laws of Creation and the Laws of LOVE.

We will not be calling on any other energy except Purest Light Frequencies from the Heart of Creation and infinitely beyond.

We are going to connect to our hearts and then, we are going to ask the deepest part of ourselves to help us to clear all suffering and all negativity for all who can be assisted.

We will end with standing at the edge of Creation: the place where the future is not written, and it is here that we will write our preferred future and seek help from the Outer Waves of Infinite Possibilities to help us create our preferred outcome.

In between all this, we will receive clearing and repair, and some gifts to help us overcome adversity in humanity's hour of need.

It may tire you, and it may energise you... Be aware that much is going to be cleared away for those of you who wish to help.

Your sincere desire to help is required. If you have no wish to help, then please move on now, and make way for those with hearts that care.

We will begin...

...

Full Transcript and Audio Experience Available:

LINK:

LOVE's Heart Plan Channel, Substack.com

Full audio to download:

@truelightessence, Deeper Truths Channel, Odysee.com

...

OTHER AUDIO LINKS:

Searching For The Evidence Channel, Bitchute.com

Searching For The Evidence Channel, T.me.com

https://t.me/TrueLightEssence

Chapter Two

'X' DENOTES THE SIGNAL FOR WAR ON ALL LIFE

Will you listen? The children hope so. Their souls are calling out for assistance. Their souls see the danger you have placed them in.

Full Audio Version:
'X' Denotes The Signal For War on All Life:
@Loves Heart Plan, Substack.com
Searching For The Evidence, Bitchute.com
and
@truelightessence, ODYSEE.COM

Please use your own heart intelligence and use full discernment when listening to this message.

This is what my heart and Infinite Love have been telling me.

"Claire, the X signals war on all life especially humanity: who the Cult plan to annihilate.

Humanity need to wake up quickly and to start to understand why X is used by the global cabal and those they serve.

Why Disease X? Why is NHS X coming soon to the UK?

Why X, formally known as Twitter? Why Space-X?

For those who are paying attention, do you recall the World Health Organisation's symbol of death? The cross wires over the planet? The snake sliding down a pole?

It is staring you all in there face, and yet, you have not noticed. And why is this?

It is because of many facets of deception, many layers of dishonest intent to harm all life, especially humanity.

And why humanity? Why would anything or anyone wish to harm humanity?

Claire, everyone needs to sit up and wake up because the warning signs are glaringly obvious, once you understand that X denotes death, control, annihilation.

Those who have designed your demise snigger at your stupidity, your lack of awareness, your ostrich-like head burying, your unwillingness to look.

And that is all they need to harm humanity and all life, because they need your tacit agreement, and so far, most of the planet's occupants have willingly ignored the signals that danger is facing them, and it is about to start in earnest, now that the World Health Organisation have nearly secured their 'trump card' — the power given to them by those who will vote to give your power — your sovereignty — away to one group:

controlled by those who love to maim, and hunt, and kill innocent lives, all under the guise of a 'respectable' organisation that has your health and well being at heart.

This organisation, the World Health Organisation is run and overshadowed by a dangerous entity, one who is placed there to control outcomes that secure your death and annihilation, and which secure your precious life force energy — a prize possession, in order for those who serve Lucifer to maintain their existence away from the Heart of Creation and away from LOVE; Peace; Unity.

This group will not stop unless you stop them, and it all can be done, yet, many of you still think that mentally processing the issues and forming protest groups will prevent the war to annihilate you all.

You are dealing with Lucifer entities, and demonic forces. You are not dealing with rational beings.

They are dangerous and they have their eyes on the children.

How many of you are defending them using the most powerful force in existence, namely, LOVE?

This has gone on for over four years now. The group who could help: the ones who see the issues; know the plans; understand the genocide of 2020 and the climate emergency that followed; those of you battling away on your computers...how many of you have yet to work out that if you are dealing with Luciferians and satanists, other worldly entities and Annunaki blood line entities, if you know this, then, why don't you know that the opposing energy needs to be called upon to help defend humanity and all life?

Why have you not yet worked out that the power lies within you to overpower these forces with your heart intelligence and your love for others?

The children need more of you to step forward because presently, a virtual handful of humans are trying to keep a door closed that is weighted on the other side by Lucifer and demonic forces, and while many plan their holidays, secure their online clothing purchases, check out their Next-fix viewing itinerary, look everywhere — except at the mounting problems on your planet, and expose the children to more danger every day...while you do this, the Luciferian Agenda and those who serve it have had a field day, with virtually no opposition to their plans.

Space-X denotes the war on you from space.

X formerly known as Twitter denotes the war on you through the internet.

NHS X denotes the war on the United Kingdom by the Royal family and the government who they control, who all serve the New World Order Agenda of annihilation and domination: the end to your health care. The end to jobs in the NHS.

Disease X denotes the disease pandemic on the World Health Organisation's death watch list. A mystery disease that does not yet exist, but will exist, once it is announced and once the WHO gain power to control.

It is all coming from May onwards and why is that?

Because humanity stood back and did absolutely nothing to prevent the carnage that will follow.

The war on your life force is above you in space.

Even Virgin mobile and Tricky Dicky Branson are telling you their plans and telling you the part they are playing in this.

Look at their symbol: the twisted circle — made into a wonky number eight, placed on its side and emitting toxic frequencies in the form of ELF waves, Extremely Low Frequency vibrations, which lower your protection — which is already compromised, and for many, your protection from this 'energetic' attack, and it is all energetic: an energetic war to steal your life force codes of knowledge and to murder you on the spot, if they choose.

It all depends what the 'AI god' determines. Everyone is contaminated with metallics and control mechanisms.

The internet of things is up and running. You are all 'nodes in the interface of things.' Many have already become one with the Metaverse, and for them, it is possibly too late — they are too immersed in artificial life to be concerned enough about why the technology is so advanced, why are they so addicted...they can no longer think, you see.

They are lost in the lower programs of false light, and in order for all to be set free, some of you are going to have to step forward and do what you came here to do, which is to connect to your Infinite Self and call on LOVE for help.

Will you listen? The children hope so. Their souls are calling out for assistance. Their souls see the danger you have placed them in.

Tacit agreement means to agree to something which you are aware of.

Those who serve Lucifer avoid being 'hit' by their karmic actions to harm you by manipulating the Laws of Creation to work in their favour.

They show you their plans in plain sight. You see the signals but your conscience cannot get you to acknowledge the danger. Therefore, you cause karma because you ignored a threat to the safety of humanity and all life.

You are all bound by these laws and when you choose to ignore a threat to life, you break the laws.

The circle of energy that protects you weakens and as you watch this circle deflate, watch it become the number eight on it's side.

Often mistaken as the 'infinity' symbol, this does not denote infinity. It denotes the ***eternal cross wire effect****...the circle of LOVE that protects you has been broken by yourself because you broke the Laws of Creation and allowed Lucifer to harm you.*

The eight on its side, look at the cross it makes in the middle... ***the cross wire effect:*** *the way the dark manipulate LOVE's protection and cross* *it to create a false doorway, and preventing the infinite possibilities of* ***Creativity.***

The cross — the X, in this instance, denotes an ending; death; falsehood; false pathways of learning; entrapment and worst of all...death of the soul.

Why did Richard Branson pick this symbol, of all symbols? Someone should ask him. And while they are asking him, perhaps they could enquire as to why his island is so close to Jeffrey Epstein's island...the one that trafficked young women and children to satisfy the appetite for brutality that the global corporations and Hollywood elites have become famous for...

Another overlooked issue that left the world's children in danger, and now, you are all soon to become prisoners in your open-air '15 minute cities', your 'clean air' zones: designed to restrict movement of adults, and increase the trafficking of children.

Your town councils are well in position now to install these systems. Those who serve Lucifer (and there are far too many installed in key positions of power in your neighbourhoods) were the ones who permitted the installation of 5G technology in your lampposts and cameras, and why is the surveillance so important, even in tiny UK villages with low crime rates?

The plan is ***control*** *while enough of you remain alive, but once they have got the whole technological van load of high tech. up and fully operational, the plan is to collapse that circle of LOVE and protection around you all, and to allow a walk-in of your bodies by AI and demonic entities.*

They want your planet.

Many of you will not believe this. You cannot look. You have no courage. Because of this, the children are exposed.

The children, the children, the children.

Will you care about the children once this group have annihilated most of you and left them to the wolves?

You still have time to peacefully stop this. If you take time to still your busy mind, you can powerfully protect them and yourselves, and pets.

All life on your planet is in danger. How easy is it to protect the children and all life?

Humanity, you came here to protect them because you have the ability inside your hearts to be concerned about the plight of others.

If you help in a half-hearted way, nothing will change and that is why Claire is being asked to call upon you all, once again, to do your job and fulfil your debt to the children and all life.

You promised to help them, and yet, many still do not.

You help occasionally or intermittently, and you think that will protect humanity and all life from those who plan and plot every second of every day to create your demise?

This group who harm have limited ability. Everything they do that is advanced has been stolen from you. You have not tapped into this knowledge and they have stolen it to weaponise it against you.

They harm you with your own energy. If you want the harm to stop, then stop giving it away freely, understand what they do to cause you harm, and learn how easy it is to use heart connection to recall all that has been lost and peacefully send back all harm.

When you connect to heart, your heart can guide you each day on what you can do to help all life and how to protect the children.

Your creative ability is also incredibly important. They cannot create. Remember this truth.

They manipulate you to accept their version of reality by subliminal thinking, TV, adverts, marketing, branding, poisoning, prolific use of symbols on your food, drink and medicine.

Look at the medical symbol, the Caduceus or Rod Of Asclepius...look at the snake...the snake represents Lucifer.

Look at the streets of London. Look at the snakes and dragons wrapped around the lamp posts, the statues, the architecture.

Every city and village has an obelisk in its square.

Or a crown, and always, a church.

An obelisk, and now, a 5G mast placed on the church towers strategically to harm you; because you see these things and you ignore them.

You do not protest. You break the Laws of Creation and create a karmic cycle of learning for yourself and if you still do nothing and do not learn, that karmic cycle of learning which is meant to rejoin and become a circle of protection of LOVE, instead, becomes a spiral of never ending descent.

The spiral. Another satanic symbol placed strategically everywhere, and yet, many do not see it.

And then, there is the pyramid with the eye on top. One of the most harmful symbols, along with the star that mothers love to clothe their children in, and conversely, adults like to wear on their shoes.

The pyramid...symbol of Satan, symbol of Lucifer, the Freemasons, and many others. It is all over your food and drink packaging. All over your computer and smart phones. All over the TV and in films, especially, and worn on TV by stars who love to tell their little secrets to their other secret-loving friends — that they serve Lucifer and they are a star.

Do you ask for protection when you see all these things? Do you object at all that this symbol or another symbol is harming all life?

There goes your circle of LOVE surrounding and protecting you and shielding you from all harm. The circle of protection that is always there, unless you break it, and how many times in your life have you broken the Laws of Creation by ignoring the danger to humanity when you see a wrong-doing, a lie, a death, a genocide, a symbol?

How much of that circle is gone? Can you see the circle of protection around you? Is it broken, collapsed, damaged, at all?

If you ask your heart it will show you and help you learn, and if you like to be creative, you can ask your heart how you could create the perfect circle of protection for the children and all life too, because currently, the Earth's circle of protection for humanity is gone, the circle of protection that humanity jointly shared is gone and your circle of protection may also be in tatters.

*This leaves you exposed to **X**, which denotes death.*

*Each time you see a symbol, each time you see them use **X**.*

Remember this message. Remember the children.

*Think about what you can peacefully draw upon to help all life, and then, set to work, because you came here for a purpose and you have a **job** to do."*

...

"Suggested Self Help For Beginners" (Learn through your inner classroom model — Beginners and Advanced)

"Heart Connection For Beginners" (A gentle way to begin)

Full Audio HEART CONNECTION EXPERIENCE

Available To Download:

@truelightessence, Deeper Truths Channel, Odysee

www.odysee.com

Searching For The Evidence Channel, Bitchute

LOVE's Heart Plan Channel, Substack

YouTube.com

Chapter Three

PART TWO: UPDATED MESSAGE FOR HUMANITY AND THE TRUTHERS; "TIME IS RUNNING OUT TO LEAVE THIS MATRIX"

Initially shared in May 2023 and reposted for those awakening in October 2023

Podcast audio link:

PART TWO:

UPDATED MESSAGE FOR HUMANITY AND THE TRUTHERS:

"TIME IS RUNNING OUT TO LEAVE THIS MATRIX"

Hello Everyone,

It's the 14th May 2023, today, and this is Claire, with Part Two of the message for the truth community, and all those wishing to protect and defend humanity and all precious life on Earth.

I include the original message at the end of this podcast, for those who may have missed the original, and may wish to help.

All contributions of help are vital at this time and today, my aim is to give you an update, alongside a deeper explanation, which my heart and LOVE have requested because your vital assistance has already brought dividends, and I wish to explain why that is and how vitally important your contributions are.

So now, I will share the routine I use to access my heart knowledge and connect outside of the False Light Matrix, with the assistance of LOVE and the Cosmic Laws (Laws of Creation), who oversee the safe expansion of consciousness along a truthful pathway of exploration and deeper learning while keeping all safe, in alignment with LOVE and the Cosmic Laws, in service to all.

If you wish to help, all are welcome to join us, however, may I imprint the importance of moving out of the mind control and your mind processes, in order to hear your own heart's guidance?

I may share information which does not resonate and if I do, please ensure you use your connection to your heart and LOVE and the Cosmic Laws to question more fully, and ask lots of questions until you are satisfied with your heart's guidance.

I cannot guarantee that my information is accurate and no one should rely on my message. I share it because I believe others can connect to their own hearts and can help humanity.

If you plan to listen while casually sitting with eyes open whilst being in mind, you will not benefit and you will not perceive the bigger picture.

It is simply not possible, until you go into the silence and ask your heart and LOVE to help you.

This is the routine I have worked to secure for my inner expansion and connection to LOVE at the Heart of Creation through my gatekeeper - my Infinite Self:

I set an alarm in case I fall asleep and need to be awake by a certain time for appointments, or similar.

I lie down flat on the bed that I sleep in at night, at home, and make myself comfortable, as I would for sleep each night.

I keep my legs straight and gently together, my palms are facing down and resting on the tops of my thighs.

If it is safe to do so, I close my eyes, as I do for sleep each night and I gently take my closed eyes down towards my chest area.

I focus on the air going in and out of my chest area, keeping my eyes gently looking down.

I make a decision that I wish to help all life here in optimum ways, in alignment with LOVE and the Cosmic Laws.

I ask my Infinite Self and Infinite LOVE to surround and protect me, and to help me reach truth at the Heart of Creation and Infinitely beyond.

I press an imaginary switch in the centre of my chest, which I call my True POWER Switch.

This switch has been set up and overseen by LOVE to ensure I can safely be escorted outside of the False Light Matrix to see the bigger picture unfolding and to retrieve vital assistance for humanity.

We all have the natural ability to do this if we wish to help all.

It is innate within us, a natural gift that all have, and if LOVE sees we are sincere and will work with integrity, then all assistance is given that can help us to best help all, in alignment with LOVE and the Cosmic Laws.

These are the teachings that I have worked towards simplifying, over a 13 year period of inner exploration on understanding how Earth energy works, why it is harmful to all life, how light is distorted, why it is distorted, and how to work with Purest Light energy from the heart of Creation, in alignment with LOVE and the Cosmic Laws (Laws of Creation), in ways that provide the optimum outcome for all.

Find a way that helps you reach truth, and for example, if you are from a religious faith, then pray for assistance, as you normally do, and ask to be assisted to see the bigger picture through your deep faith.

This message is all inclusive and welcomes all who wish to best help all.

So, by now, hopefully, we are all relaxing and focusing on our breathing as my words float over you and I share a new message, but just before I continue, we need to press our True Power Switch once more - as an indication that we wish to hear truth from the heart of Creation, as a group who will use our own heart discernment and also will listen inwardly for guidance, in case we are being called upon - as we may start receiving new teachings after the message has been relayed, and you may need to pause the recording after the message to tune in more deeply still.

Here is the message my heart and LOVE are guiding me to share:

"Claire, you need to thank the group for all they have done so far. They have worked very hard. Those who have stepped up have already displayed excellent service work because a miraculous issue that was threatening many has been completely averted.

Not so for those who have not asked for help, who are looking the other way.

But for those who have no voice, for the group and their pets and loved ones, children, newborns and innocent souls a huge problem has been averted and Claire will now explain what you have managed to achieve. It really is quite incredible how much you have done to help all vulnerable life.

Claire, will you explain to the group what has happened concerning the old system matrix which is collapsing in on itself, in terms of the old decks of the 'Sinking Ship' analogy?"

[Claire] Ok. The version of the old Earth matrix and False Light Construct was explained to me as an imaginary 'sinking ship' in the middle of a vast ocean of turmoil and chaos.

An SOS call was put out and a fleet of helpers had set sail and were waiting to assist those trapped on the sinking ship. There is a huge barrier of rocks that stand between the ocean with the sinking ship in it and the fleet of helpers that are waiting beyond the rocks, who sailed to assist from the heart of Creation.

The ship had twelve decks on it. The lifeboats are on the top of the upper deck - Deck 12 - and humanity are below decks on the third deck which is rapidly filling with water.

During the last ten 'Earth' years, some of the decks above the third deck have collapsed in on themselves.

Many in humanity think that they need to get to Deck 5 to secure rescue, which many term, the '5th Dimension', however, in terms of vibrational shifts, this is but one tiny step of learning on the ladder of consciousness which has billions of steps, and therefore, Deck 3 and Deck 5 are not good places to be because the whole ship is sinking, not just the third deck or 'third dimension,' in Earth terms.

The name of the game for all souls who are learning how a False Light Construct works is to climb the decks of the ship, whilst collecting vital learning, healing, and repair as they make their way up to the twelfth deck, also known as the 12th Dimension or Planetary Grids, and make their way to the lifeboats at the Galactic level.

They then need to launch their lifeboats and get guidance from the purest light SOS helpers; to navigate their way through the stormy, choppy waters to get beyond the rocks to a place of safety, and retrieve vital teachings from the purest light rescuers on how to help secure the safe evacuation of all those souls still stranded on the decks of the sinking ship before it sinks and they are lost forever.

Some have managed to sail past the rocks and have secured vital teachings, but not enough have launched their lifeboats, and some are still on Deck 5 because they were told it was the best place to go, but this was a deliberate deception; placed into the consciousness to prevent these souls leaving the ship.

On the decks of the sinking ship, there are many different life forms moving up and down the decks of the ship as they learn either through love, or, they drop back down the decks - through breaking Cosmic Laws or harming others.

The ship could be likened to the game of 'Snakes and Ladders': Making wise choices and moving up, only to become attacked by the snakes, or, making poor choices and falling back down to the lower decks.

The dark forces on the decks are soul fragments and fragmented aspects of higher levels of awareness who have gone AWOL and started destroying other's chances of leaving the ship by stealing their life force energy.

This is because AWOL souls do not seek out LOVE's assistance.

They go AWOL and turn their backs on LOVE.

LOVE is the fuel that enables us to exist. LOVE keeps us connected to the heart of Creation, and infinitely alive.

When a soul goes AWOL and rejects LOVE's embrace, they have to find a different power source in order to exist, and so, they use the codes of knowledge that they have retained in their own DNA - to harm others on the same decks as themselves, or on the decks below them, in order to steal life force energy, which they convert and use as their power source.

Without LOVE and without an alternative power source in the form of stolen life force energy to live off, they could not exist.

We are at the stage now, when an In Breath is completing, meaning: that all souls are being called back to the Heart of Creation in preparation for their next, new, exciting cycle of evolution, called here: The Out Breath.

All souls on the sinking ship are being called to climb their ladder of consciousness, to heal and repair any harm they may have caused others, and any harm that may have been caused to them, and return home - to be present and correct - for the next, big, exciting new cycle of evolution.

This return is also known as 'Ascension'.

Humanity have the opportunity in this lifetime to achieve Cosmic Ascension.

During the last ten 'Earth' years, many dimensions or ships decks have collapsed as Infinite LOVE has been offering all souls on those particular decks the opportunity to choose whether to come home or remain on the decks of the sinking ship, because of the next Out Breath,

There have been many who refused to stop harming and Cosmic Laws are very strict at this stage of evolution. It is the final opportunity to repair and make good all harm done and all harm received.

Infinite LOVE does not impose, and all souls make their own choice.

If a soul chooses to come home and wishes to make good - all harm is forgiven and forgotten, meaning: deleted, and this removes all harm that has affected other souls, too. The slate is 'wiped clean' when a soul seeks to remedy their errors.

LOVE loves us all, unconditionally and there is no judgement.

The Cosmic Laws work to keep all safe, and all souls knew this when they came here: that LOVE would remind them that it was time to come home and the soul is offered a choice.

When Cosmic Laws are broken to such a degree that the soul has caused untold destruction, a decision is reached and the Infinite Self will be instructed to sever the ladder at the level of growth where the intention to redeem oneself is present.

Anything below that level that does not wish to stop harming is left behind as the ladder is withdrawn past the rocks and back to the Heart of Creation where the precious knowledge is securely returned, to best help all.

Meanwhile, those aspects of self who refused to stop harming on the severed ladder will be left defenceless on the sinking ship, and all alone, without LOVE to call upon because by this time, it is too late.

The choice is made and once made, it cannot be reversed.

We are at that stage now, when the In breath has practically completed and the Heart of Creation is preparing to expand into a new Out Breath cycle of evolution.

Many on the ship's decks have fallen into this trap, and some were innocently out exploring when they were enticed in and could not find their way out.

Others have climbed their ladder and got to the the twelfth deck of knowledge only to fall down the 'snake's ladder'.

Very few reach the lifeboats, and very few secure help from the beyond the rocks.

During this time on the ship, I am being asked to think of the twelfth deck as the Planetary grids, and the lifeboats as the Galactic grids.

The ship represents our individual ladder of consciousness within the False Light Construct and the ladder of humanity's consciousness, as a group who deliberately 'fell' into this place on a 'mercy mission' to help all souls trapped here to return safely to the heart of Creation.

As humanity descended into the decks of the ship, they were pelted with 'cabbages and eggs' by the dark, who stripped them of as many DNA light codes of knowledge - to use for their own sorry ends - to harm others on the decks of the ship.

Humanity had already come in with less light codes remembered because they could not come in on full power.

This ship represents the one 'juggernaut' from my previous message and each human represents millions of 'juggernauts' of energy, which would collapse the programs, without any lessons being learned of how Earth energy is being used in a distorted way, to harm all life here.

Therefore, each human came in with very little knowledge or codes, and a few humans came in with more.

The name of the game was for those who came in with more codes remembered, to help those who had given up many codes of knowledge and who were therefore, extremely vulnerable because they did not remember they were from the heart of Creation.

All that knowledge was given up - to give those who came in with a higher quota of help, and it was a very brave thing to do because these souls knew they might never return if they did not wake up in time, before the completion of the In Breath.

Those who came in with more codes remembered were entrusted to climb the decks of the ship and to gather up all that they had lost on the way down to the third deck - to get to the lifeboats and launch the lifeboats, and navigate their way past the rocks to reach the team of rescuers in order to get help for those still stranded on the sinking ship.

This plan failed - some got on board in 2012 and were aware of the issues, but they fell under the spell of mind control and the rescue plan collapsed.

Since then, many more projects have been launched and failed as the mind control technologies were upscaled.

I do not know the full details but I understand from my inner teachings that when the purest light waves were at their peek, the dark were able to steal this light, to divert it away from humanity, using advanced technologies that they had prepared for this time, because they know all about the In Breath and Out Breath cycles and how to harm others, as their very existence depends on it.

The convergence of the light waves meant the dark could operate stealthily and out of sight from humanity and start to plot against them to foil any plan to rescue the occupants of the sinking ship, who the dark want to enslave, in order to maintain an existence away from the Heart of Creation and LOVE.

The rejection of their need for LOVE has worked so far and the dark always thought they had a 'win-win' situation, but what they had not counted on was on any humans waking up sufficiently, to secure any fruitful assistance.

The public have been involved, and 'used' in all innocence, to take part in activities that have collapsed the twelfth deck and destroyed the lifeboats on the sinking ship.

These were known as the Planetary and Galactic Grids, as I previously mentioned.

These grids are a vital resource and lifeline for all souls to utilise, and a vital step that all must evolve through before departing the False Light Matrix and evolving along a safer pathway.

The systems used to entice the populous into collapsing these grids were YOGA and REIKI.

Yoga collapsed the Planetary Grids, and Reiki collapsed the Galactic Grids.

Therefore, the two vital steps of evolution, the '12th deck' and the 'lifeboats' were gone and lost to all life.

This ensured that all souls left on the sinking ship could not escape.

Some of humanity noticed these issues and sought to remedy it.

They rebuilt the grids twice, from 2020 onwards.

Unfortunately, the innocent use of these systems by those who believe them to be beneficial continued.

These groups are unaware that these systems have been satanically hijacked and distorted, to ensure that when a person chooses to participate in, or teach a class in these systems, their choice to do so is all that is needed by the dark to infiltrate their ladder of knowledge and steal vast amounts of the person's life-force energy.

These stolen codes of knowledge are then replaced with fake codes of false knowledge and fake feelings of false peace and well being, so that the person never notices.

Those who do notice, no longer participate in these systems because they have realised that harm is occurring at higher levels of consciousness.

Some have sought to remedy their errors and repair all harm received and caused, because these choices to participate in satanically corrupted systems have wreaked havoc for humanity who are still largely unaware of the capacity of the dark to cause untold harm.

Reiki is the same.

I am hearing my heart and LOVE say:

"Claire put several calls out recently to these two communities to ask for assistance - to stop the attack in these areas.

The Yoga groups have largely rejected the information and have now destroyed the only way out of the ship's decks for all life forms, however, enough Reiki people did respond to the call, not many, but enough to secure repair of the lifeboats, but without a twelfth deck, they could not be reached and so, humanity and all life on this ship were stranded as potential slaves.

The dark were very pleased with their plan, however, they often forget the tenacity of a human heart who cares about others and so, even though this did spell disaster, more in humanity - who's souls and higher levels of awareness saw the problem - stepped forward and called to LOVE for help.

Many in the religious community have helped also, because prayer and calls for help are powerful. LOVE always promised that for every ounce of calls for help, millions of ounces of help would be offered by LOVE.

Not just the religious communities, many in humanity saw the evil on the planet and turned inwards, and found that help came when one called for help, and so now, an awakening is happening which the dark cannot seem to put a lid on.

They have tried pandemics, vaccination programs, spraying poison in the skies, poisoning the food and water, creating fear, wars, death and destruction but humanity just seem to be bouncing back and the dark are now on the back foot.

And now, a small group of individuals have helped, once more, with this satanic evil juggernaut and placed millions of juggernauts in the way of this destroying force.

Meanwhile, LOVE heard humanity's call for help and new purest light grids have been built that cannot be tampered with or destroyed by the dark.

And those who have asked for help will be able to continue their evolution on a safe path of peaceful and exciting evolution.

During this time, many calls have been put out from LOVE, reminding souls who are trapped on the sinking ship to, "Make the request. LOVE does the rest", if they wish to grow in LOVE and be rescued from the sinking ship before it eventually sinks, in order to return home to the Heart of Creation and continue their soul evolution.

It is a simple choice to call for help.

For those who choose to stay on this ship, Claire has already explained that the twelfth deck is gone: You cannot reach the lifeboats, and if you don't ask LOVE to help you, you will have made the free will choice to remain trapped.

And even if you change your mind, by the time you realise, it will be too late because at a certain time, the Infinite Self will sever the ladder - to protect the knowledge, and withdraw what can be salvaged - to serve all.

Something miraculous has happened, for those who requested rescue from LOVE.

The group who answered the call for help in the message to the truth community, have launched their lifeboats, because their calls for help ensured LOVE placed them in them and helped them navigate through the choppy waters, past the rocks, and to make contact with the divine fleet of rescuers, and to retrieve solutions and activate their inner gifts, which have helped - as a joint group - to create a bridge on the sinking ship that leads to the lifeboats and therefore, those who were trapped and stuck have been able to escape and return home.

Please ask about this and retrieve deeper insights.

That is what can be achieved when hearts unite and call to LOVE for help.

There are many more plans by the dark to entrap all remaining life on this sinking ship and it is hoped that more will participate, to unlock the codes that they came here with - to help humanity.

Every person on the planet carried a code or two, and some have more."

Remember, those who are asleep were very brave...they came into this place 'naked and unclothed', in complete trust that those of us who came in with more, would care enough and love our family of humanity enough, to make our way to the lifeboats and get past the rocks so that we could retrieve vital codes of knowledge and seek the solutions, because no matter what the dark throw at us inside this False Light Matrix, all the answers are available to us, if we ask for help.

All of humanity came here as a family group because we have the ability to LOVE unconditionally, and although we are not fully awake in this place, many more of us understand that the problem is mounting, and we are leaving it very late in the day to secure humanity's rescue.

We need to focus as much time as possible, to help all souls become aware that they have a choice: to call for help, or remain on this ship.

We cannot interfere with the free will choice of any soul.

It is against Cosmic Law, however, we are here as an act of service to all - to highlight the issues, and once the issues have been highlighted, we must step back and allow others to make their free will choices.

If others are looking the other way, that is a free will choice, too, and it is not our place to force the issue, however, many are starting to question and are looking for help and direction, and it is this group of souls who we can help, if they ask us.

It is important to share information, and many share videos to help raise awareness, and that is important, too. Those in the truth community are being asked to ensure that they have secured their own rescue, because many have been immersed in highlighting the issues, but many are not aware of the bigger picture unfolding.

They have been critical to raising awareness. Some have done this with very few codes of remembrance of their true origins, and it would be a calamity if they did not secure their own rescue, in the process of awakening others to the danger they are in.

The biggest danger and calamity would be to remain on this sinking ship because they did not realise that there was a rescue plan available, if they wanted it, and for many, they have been taught that the 5th Deck or 5th Dimension is our next evolutionary step, when, it is a tiny step in vibration and is part of the sinking False Light Construct.

All the decks of the sinking ship collapsed in on themselves in recent years, and so now, the Third Deck occupants are swimming in the choppy waters of a 'cosmic soup' of satanic attack from all the remaining decks - with all the occupants of higher awareness - who are on the side of destroyer force energy, and all the aspects of their own ladder that has fragmented and gone AWOL, which is now attacking each person and all life here, and trying to suck as much life force energy out of them, in order to try and maintain their existence away from LOVE.

The higher technologies are being used to harm humanity and all life that existed on the third deck of this ship.

There are no 'barriers' of the higher deck walls to protect them from the higher technologies.

And 5G radiation is deadly as it is all our 'heartache energy' and all the 'heartache energy' from the Earth, as she watched her Galactic and Planetary grids 'raped and sucked dry' of her vital life force energy, and so, you can imagine why the radiation from 5G, Wi-Fi, and other microwave technology is so deadly to us...the soul recoils in horror and shock that we would use the equipment, or ignore a mobile mast, or deadly street light without uttering a cry of outrage to those responsible, nor asking LOVE for protection.

Protection and defence is the name of the game.

There is much more to share. I have tried to simplify things as much as possible and recommend you keep the 'Sinking Ship' analogy in mind, because it keeps things simple.

I am sure that your Infinite Self will have teachings for you, to help you retrieve further assistance for all life here.

I have always said, we are not the weaker side, and I am deeply grateful to those who have helped thus far.

It is incredible - what has been achieved in such a short time, which is why the dark are on the back-foot.

We must keep up the pressure now, and work diligently, as we must secure as much help as possible, before June 2023.

Each time I listen to the following recording, I am getting new insights.

Keep all teachings to yourself. Don't let the dark know what you are doing.

Silence is best. Keep them guessing.

Your heart is your teacher, no one else, and so, any questions must be directed within, where the knowledge is and where your evolution is dependent upon.

I will be in touch again when I get more guidance.

Keep up the excellent work and thank you, on behalf of humanity and the new borns who are still coming onto this planet, because their future is our duty to secure, and we must keep these special and very brave souls in our hearts and minds, as we keep our promise - to do our best for all -and to remember that those who came in with less codes, those who rigidly refuse to see, are like that because they gave you more; in complete trust that when the whistle blew for the final time, that you would have done your very best to remind them that is it time to call for help, to 'request rescue', and come home.

"Make the request LOVE will do the rest."

That is all they need to do, because LOVE knew they would be running late for the bus and knew it would be a 'close call' before the whistle blew, and that if those of us who came in with more light remembered could secure as much help as possible... that even in a false light program...if we could raise the vibration enough, we would enable them to remember - to make the choice to come home.

We must do our very best for all these souls because that is the promise we made before we came here and I know that we would never want to break a promise like this, not when so much was given at our disposal which we have failed to use, and with so little time left to remedy our own errors, I know, that we all know, a promise is a promise...

We simply cannot fail these souls.

Chapter Four

THEY CANNOT OVERPOWER LOVE

They know that. It is time for humanity to fully awaken to this truth, too.

This is the world that we have helped the demonic cult create. They could not have created such a dark place without humanity. Do you like what we have allowed to be created?

Here is a message from my Infinite Self and LOVE:

"Claire, they (the dark elite and dark forces they serve) are nothing without humanity's acquiescence. This group have no ability to create. They do not have the codes. When a soul destroys as much as this group have destroyed, their connection to the Heart of Creation becomes so badly damaged, their ability to create is the first thing to go. It is Cosmic Law.

So, the first step to losing power when one persistently destroys is, loss of ability to create.

Everything must be in balance:

'An eye for an eye' relates to this Cosmic Law.

The ability to create is a precious gift and an important one not to lose. Therefore, creativity is key to setting yourselves free from this 'mind-prison.'

The best way to use creativity and your personal allocation of creative power is to request for an increase of creative power each day. This may sound whimsical, however, once you start to see results, you will feel encouraged to do more, because the results will be profound.

Claire, we will use your situation as an example of using creative power to get the best outcome for your husband's soul evolution: You were persistently guided during his illness, last year, to focus on asking for help in ways that best helped his soul evolution in "optimal ways, in ways that best helped all."

This request created an opening of opportunity that surpassed the dark attack on you both.

An open heart that places faith, hope and trust in a perfect outcome that best helps all, created the outcome that ensured your husband survived, as he was meant to, and did not die from 5G Direct Energy Weaponry attack or from attacks at higher levels of awareness, because you were also guided to

ask LOVE and the Cosmic Laws to "SEND BACK ALL MALICIOUS HARM TO ALL THOSE RESPONSIBLE."

This utilised the power of Creativity in subtle ways.

Your hearts have taught you both to always seek guidance on "how to best serve all in order to

gain optimum outcome for all innocent life and those protecting the innocent."

It is why we always advise you to seek counsel through heart before taking action.

That way, you use Creativity without placing a restriction on outcomes that best help you and all life.

When you listen to heart; when you ask LOVE for help; when you hand over the reins, LOVE can set to work to create the best outcome.

Creativity is, therefore, not about controlling outcome.

Creativity is about creating an opportunity for LOVE to set about to secure the perfect result for everyone and all life, everywhere.

You have the power to create when you ask LOVE for help.

We guide you to utilise this gift to defeat the demonic plans of the World Economic Forum, your councillors, and politicians.

They cannot overpower LOVE. They know that. It is time for humanity to fully awaken to this truth, too."

Chapter Five

HOW TO AVOID A SOUL HARVEST, OCT 15, 2023

"There are easy solutions even for targeted individuals, even against those who use their keyboards as weapons, and remotes to directly harm you."

AUDIO: HOW TO AVOID A SOUL HARVEST

"Claire, we said the biggest soul harvest is upon you all, and it has started in earnest. You have been asking for assistance; to pass on helpful methods and techniques for targeted individuals of Havana Syndrome and we have made it clear that these souls are experiencing the 'effects' of what is a broad spectrum attack on all life here.

It will not stop, not now it is in full swing and has largely gone unimpeded by a sleeping humanity. For those who want protection, they only have to ask LOVE at the Heart of Creation for protection and it is given. It is the Law. Meaning: that it is the law of Creation to honour all sincere requests for help that best serve all life, and it does serve all life to ask for help when one is being attacked at multiple levels of awareness, as you all are.

Of course, the issues you raised are valid. What about those who, like many of your dear friends, have no belief system that would fuel their faith, or give them hope, or trust that powerful technologies exist and are at their disposal to help all life?

You have friends who are very dear to you who empower all that is goodness, and yet, they hold no beliefs, but they must be protected, surely, you asked, because of their goodness and clean life-style? Meaning: they treat others around them with kindness and respect, and appreciate their life...You asked for a method for people like that who may turn away from the message because they hold no religious or spiritual beliefs.

We say all life can be assisted, and those who live a good life, who treat others with kindness, who love and care for others have a natural protection, but this will only protect them to a certain degree, because the level of attack on humanity and all life on your planet is at a critical 'point of no return,' and the chaos being engineered currently is a deliberate act to gather more souls to harvest.

The dark elite and ET groups aim to create as much chaos and hardship as possible, to stir up as much hatred as possible, and sadly for humanity, they are being played again and walking into nothing more than a 'soul harvesting trap'.

The more who choose to retaliate, stir up hatred, stay angry and full of vengeful feelings... those who take matters into their own hands will rue the day they allowed the ET groups and dark ones on your planet to play them like well-known strings of a violin.

The melody is so well known now: AI, ETs, political leaders and your authority figures at higher levels all know how to get you to open your door to the Grim Reaper, and we guide all of you who want protection, to consider how well you are being played by this group.

For example, where are your weaknesses, in terms of your 'castle and moat' protection?

Is the castle gangway open?

Have you blocked all your exits?

Have you defended your weak points?

Is the moat full of deep water and is the gangway up or down?

We will show you a simple routine to use each day to check your energy and ladder of consciousness, and this is being shared because you all need to 'up your game' and move forward, and this is a simple means to an end.

The end being: keeping the dark forces and Grim Reaper out of your energy fields, and learning how to return the attack without lifting a finger and doing it in a way which is peaceful and loving towards yourself, and from a place of non anger, or malice, or judgement towards those humans and other entities who are directing energy weapons at you.

The harm has to go back to them now, and you can help and will be helped, but you all need to understand that LOVE does not attack or harm. Never. It is not in LOVE's remit to do so, nor is it necessary.

You all need to become aware that this is a 'redistribution of malicious harm', which has become magnified and is gathering speed because those who created or took part in this harm have never tried to stop it, repair it, or heal the damage they have inflicted on themselves and others.

These groups are so stupid really, if you try to look at them with clear eyes, without fear distorting your view of them as 'powerful beings', and we say 'stupid', not through cruelty, it is to jar your brains out of the mind control sufficiently, to help you see these entities and humans who are harming you as weak and pathetic creatures.

They lack love; have no warmth or affection given to them; they have lost so much of their purest light codes they are truly pitiful, and these codes have been taken and replaced with False Light codes.

It is why they are soulless, heartless and cruel. But they are not strong.

They are weak, vulnerable little entities and you need to start seeing them as 'midges', as flies that would easily die if you swatted them, however, we say this to help you see them for what they are, but we are not and never would advocate violence.

Why? Because it is against the Laws of Creation/Cosmic Law.

If you use violence, you lose vital purest light codes and get them replaced with False Light codes. Those who are religious, or spiritual, or believe in something greater that is good came with more codes of purest light that enable them to remember and so, it is easier to love, to have faith, hope, and trust in your prayers being answered.

Those who gave you their measure of codes of remembrance so that you could come in with more, are the ones who hold no beliefs, and for some, they have fallen in density through their love for you all and all precious life that now, they are harming the most.

To judge someone else for not being religious, or believing in God, or LOVE, or a Creator is a sign of immense ignorance when you look at the reasons why they are less connected. They gave you their codes to help you rescue trapped souls here. None of you could come in with the same measure of remembrance.

Purest light is powerful: it would have collapsed the False Light grids, and vital lessons of learning need to take place for all those who found themselves trapped here in the first place. So, you all came in with more or less remembrance on the understanding, the promise, that those who gave up their codes would be helped by those who came in with more.

And what has happened?

Many religious and spiritual folk see themselves as superior and see themselves as 'saved' by their badge of honour; by their belief system.

Do you see how wrong this is? Do you think God/LOVE loves the ones less who came in with less codes?

You are all being asked to respect every soul and their belief system or lack of belief because your religion is not going to save you, nor is your spiritual belief system, not if it involves low vibrational thoughts of superiority or judgement. You are all going to have to work equally as hard as those without their codes if you plan on continuing with thoughts like that. You are all loved unconditionally.

LOVE knows your story, knows your hardships and what you have endured before you came to this time and place. LOVE sent you all because LOVE believed in you and trusted that when the time came to make ready and prepare, and help the others who are stranded here with no remembrance, that you would fulfil your promise.

That time is now.

You all need to start the process of ensuring your 'castle and moat' is fully protected each day, from here on in. If you hold a deep faith and trust in GOD, it gives you protection.

If you hold a deep spiritual belief and deep faith, it gives you protection. If you have no faith and treat others kindly and are loving and balanced in your thoughts, it gives you protection. Yet, we are at a cataclysmic time on the Earth, whereby many in society are being stirred into angry violence, hatred, division, and fear.

There has been violent death and this has caused deep, deep heartache. What happens to the groups who have deep faith or natural protection through their kind thoughts, actions, words, and deeds?

Even those who have a nominal protection, are left exposed. The dark are generating as much low vibrational energy from humanity because they need the 'fuel in their tanks' that this offers them, and they use it to survive because they cannot live off purest light. They need energy in the form of fear, in order to exist.

They need heartache and deep sadness because they use these elements as weapons to use against humanity. They can only steal energy from you that you give to them. They strip that energy down, exist off some of it, and weaponise the rest. Targeted individuals are sensitive to the attack that is happening to everyone because the attack has crept inside their castle walls under the cover of darkness, so to speak, and you have noticed it is there.

It has crept in more easily now because humans have made some very poor choices, and unfortunately, the consequences of their choices have affected others in the group. Regardless of how much you try to balance, the issues are that humanity, as a group, are not defending each other from the dark attack.

They are in ignorance that it is taking place, or that their 'castle' has been infiltrated. They have no method that is working to secure their 'castle' and clear out the inner attack. They do not do a daily check of their 'perimeter fence', or their boundaries, or their inner castle and so, the attack is becoming a full on take-over, and soon, their castle will be taken by the dark and all the energy, all the codes of remembrance that they can loot from each castle will be stripped down, used as fuel for their existence, and the rest will be weaponised against humanity and all precious life.

Do you see the cycle of harm occurring, here?

How do you plan to defend your castle when so many humans are being played into letting the dark attack their inner walls and take over their prized possessions, their codes of remembrance, to weaponise against you?

Do you see, the attack on you will get worse as more of humanity's codes are looted from within their castle walls?

There are easy solutions even for targeted individuals, even against those who use their keyboards as weapons, and remotes to directly harm you. All is possible.

How to go about defending your inner and outer castle wall?

Each day, upon awakening you need to check your castle. You all have imagination. If you find it hard to imagine things, pretend you can see your castle.

Claire cannot recommend that her routine will be best for you, however, she will share her simple routine and you can ask your inner heart intelligence what routine would best help you and best help all, and you will get help.

It is the law. Remember this. If you ask for help. It has to come.

Claire, can you share your routine?"

I say, I only use this when I can safely relax undisturbed and close my eyes.

Common sense highlights this is unsuitable for use while driving, working, or operating machinery.

I set an alarm, in case I fall asleep, and I always have a drink of water to hand, and I ensure the room is shaded from bright sunlight.

I lie down on the bed that I sleep in at night, at home, flat on my back, legs straight, and lightly touching, but never crossed, I rest with my palms facing down, and placed flat on the tops of my thighs.

If it is safe to do so, I close my eyes.

I take my closed eyes and look gently downwards, towards my chest area.

I keep my closed eyes softly focused there, and I focus on the air going in and out of my chest.

I allow myself to relax, and keep my closed eyes focused on the air going in and out of my lungs. I pretend I have an imaginary switch in the centre of my chest which I call, my TRUE POWER SWITCH.

I imagine I press it, or I physically press my chest to switch my True Power Switch ON.

I pretend that I am connected to a super power - a power so strong, that nothing else can attack it. It is all loving, all knowing, all intelligent, and it is far superior to any other living thing. I ask this super power for help and I trust that it will help me. I ask for protection of my castle and moat, and for all airspace above it.

I rest, I relax, I imagine and pretend I am receiving powerful healing and repair of my castle and moat, and I pretend that all satellites/all ET technologies are being wiped off the board with an invisible board wipe.

All attack from deep space is being deleted, and it disappears.

Then, I focus on my castle and I ask my True Power Switch to show me a picture on my inner heart screen. I look downwards with closed eyes focused on my chest area, and I pretend that my True Power Switch is showing me areas where my castle walls are weak, and whether my moat gate and bridge is down or up. I ask for repair. I imagine this is done instantly. Next, I pretend my inner heart screen is showing me the inside of my castle walls and where any looting might be taking place. If I want to know how this has happened, I pause the recording here and take time to get information on how this attack got in. Otherwise, I ask my True Power Switch to reset, and delete all attack, and I ask for repair from any harm done. I also ask that any errors I may have made are deleted.

Then, with a neutral heart, with no anger or malice, I ask my True Power Switch to gather up all malicious, magnified harm and send it back to all those responsible for ensuring it harmed my inner and outer castle walls.

This is for their learning. The more neutral I am, the more I stay peaceful, the more powerful this is. It does not work with anger or malice. Next, I ask that if any looting has taken place, for the codes to be found, healed and repaired, and returned to me in the form of purest light codes that can never be looted by any person, place, or thing. This builds a strong inner layer of additional protection and there is less to steal as these purest light codes are returned in their original, powerful, 'nonlootable' form.

Then, I rest. Before I stir, I always ask how I can best help myself and all precious life, in optimal ways, in alignment with the Laws of Creation and LOVE.

I listen to any guidance and always follow it. **I do this every day, upon awakening, midway through the day and at night, before sleep.** If I have ever forgotten, the attack is horrendous. I understand that with many in humanity not doing anything to protect their own castle, the more we are all exposed as targeted individuals, and so, I follow the inner guidance to do this unfailingly each day. I know that the dark technologies are just waiting outside my castle, waiting for me to make a mistake and let my guard down, and as I am a perfectly imperfect human who makes mistakes, if I do make errors, I try to rectify my mistakes by asking my True Power Switch for help.

The more I have used this method, the quicker I can take my attention down to my heart to ask my True Power Switch for help. It only takes a few minutes with practice. I use a quicker version during the day. The morning requires the most effort. Every energy exchange we make, whether through food, drink, air, energy, consciousness, people, technology, etc., contains attack of some sort, so this True Power Switch routine covers all those things, and for those who wish to strengthen it further, it can be used to energetically purify food, drink and medicine before ingesting it. That may be a step too far for those who do not perceive things as energy.

It helps me and I hope that it may help others too.

Links:

Full Audio Messages:
To Assist Others To Experience Leaving The Matrix To Reach Their Heart:
Free Teachings Available At:
@Loves Heart Plan | substack.com | Searching For The Evidence, bitchute.com and t.me | @trueliightessence, Odysee.com

HOW TO AVOID A SOUL HARVEST

THE KILL GRID - MARK STEELE |
TUNGSTEN IN VAX MAKES HUMANS 'DORMANT RADIATION TRANSMITTERS'

"ZOMBIE BLOOD" -
Self-Assembled Quantum Dots or Kinetically Active Microstructures? (SHARE) |

YOUR COSMIC SHIELD:
DEFEND YOURSELVES AGAINST ELECTROMAGNETIC AND ELECTROPLATONIC ATTACK | 13 AUGUST 2023

HELP FOR HUMANITY - 18 JULY 2023

DR. MIHALCEA – THEY HAVE PUT ARTIFICIAL LIFE INSIDE HUMANS, LEGAL ACTION COMMENCES
https://www.bitchute.com/video/QKY7IeXzjpG2/

Relaxation Audio:

https://odysee.com/@TrueLightEssence:dRELAXATION-AUDIO
:b

AN EMPTY VESSEL

Chapter Six

MESSAGE FOR TARGETED INDIVIDUALS

No matter how ill you may be feeling, no matter how scared you might be right now, there is help available.

Audio Link:
Searching For The Evidence, Bitchute.com
THE ET AGENDA FOR NON HUMANISM BY 'HUMANOID' LEADERS OF NON HUMAN ORIGIN

...

My name is Claire. I have been working with Purest Light frequencies from the Heart of Creation through use of my heart (my inner intelligence) and through LOVE.

I hold a deep respect for all belief systems that lead to loving goodness.

I am not Christian, however, I was raised as a Christian. I am not Spiritual, yet, I have explored spirituality.

I am none of those things because I am not a label. I have no status. I am just me. I wish to help others who are struggling with directed energy weaponry.

I have been working diligently for over ten years now to try to get information to others on how to protect themselves. I have been blocked from getting this information out at every turn. I have knocked on many doors and I have had many doors slammed in my face.

I keep going because I trust what my heart has been telling me for all these years. I have written books warning humanity on what was coming. Very few have read them and even fewer used the recommendations to help others.

We are in this mess, not because it cannot be solved. It can. Easily. It is not being resolved because if any information is presented to a targeted individual, they may glance in its direction briefly, however, soon enough, the mind control programs kick in, or someone is sent to 'put-off' the target from looking to help themselves, and so, the help that is available is blocked.

My computer plays up. Things stop working. I know this is all deliberate.

But the one thing they can never have from me is my concern to get the help to you. It drives me forwards every day. I look at the world we have all created and wonder if anyone will ever look up from their mind controlled state and take responsibility, and then take the time to undo what they, themselves have created?

The children are facing a lifetime of digital slavery. A digital hell where only their avatar, their digital twin will be targeted. The 'real human' will be long gone and with that loss, there will be eventual death of the soul.

Others may not realise how important this risk is to their onward evolution. Quite literally, it means that if we do nothing to stop this, our soul will see the harm we are doing and will be either, recalled if it calls for help, or if it is severely damaged, it may not know it can call for help and therefore, the dark will destroy it. But not before it has been hunted: over, and over, and over again.

It will be a huge game to the dark ones. This is what they love to do: Hunt; chase; destroy; burn; harm; mutilate.

And they get to do this, because of our apathy?

Really?

Are you going to allow this to happen to yourself, just because your handlers and mind control technologists are using their keyboards to control you?

You do have a choice. You have always had a choice.

You can play the helpless victim, or you can ask your heart for help.

Many do not understand what happens when a human calls for help.

Let me explain.

The Laws of Creation state that it is against the law to interfere with another soul's free will choices.

Just let that sink in for a moment.

The laws cannot interfere with our free will. However, when a human asks for help, the laws are permitted to assist you in whatever way 'best serves all life throughout the whole of existence.'

Essentially, if you are not getting help of any sort, it is because you have not asked for the help.

"Make the request. LOVE does the rest."

Once you have made this request, things will start to shift. It may not be overnight, but things will shift.

No one needs to know you called through your heart for help. You can just say inwardly and silently, something like:

"Please can you help me?"

Your heart starts the process of surrounding and protecting you with LOVE frequencies.

LOVE burns the dark. They cannot go near you when you are surrounded by LOVE.

If you ask every day in the morning for help, then at lunchtime, then before sleep at night, the protection gets stronger, and LOVE will do the rest.

You do not need the scientific explanation; the data; the full discourse on how or why this is possible.

That is a distraction to keep you all in the mind control and away from your heart connection, where the help is to be found.

It is frightening being a targeted individual. All of humanity are also being targeted, but for many, the direct attack is deliberate on their person, and it is because you have the gifts inside your heart to help humanity.

No matter how ill you may be feeling, no matter how scared you might be right now, there is help available.

It has to start with you.

You have to use your free will to ask your heart for help.

The laws start up then and the help can come in.

If you only ask once, you get help for the next few hours.

If you ask throughout the day, you get help for the day.

If you ask three times daily, AM, PM, and midway through your day, you get a lot more help.

If you stop, the protection stops.

If you stop asking each day, the attack starts up again.

The dark troops wait for us to 'slip-up', to forget to ask, and it may be odd that asking for help is all we need to do, yet, how many out there never feel drawn to ask, or inclined to ask, or cannot be bothered, or do not believe it would work?

This is the mind control at play. The mind control kicks in hard when a human looks like they may be a threat, and asking for help is the biggest threat to the ETs and dark ones on the ground.

Those computer operators and handset humans who get paid lots of money to harm you and control you, too?

How do you deal with this unseen attack?

The answer is, you don't deal with their attack.

You peacefully sit quietly and you ask LOVE and the Laws of Creation to do this for you.

You also ask for any errors you have made that day to be deleted. Because the dark ones rely on you making choices that harm, and these are mostly tricks they play on you, such as placing satanic symbols on the TV, in advertising and marketing, on your clothes, on the brands, the food and drink packaging, and on the starred reviews of your purchases on websites.

Has anyone noticed how many times these topics display the star? The star that you place on your Christmas tree, for example? Did you know that all the Christmas tree represents is a pyramid, with a satanic star on top, with 'snaking lights around it in a spiral' and 'spheres' dotted about randomly.

Did you know that all that is, is an obelisk;: a ritual; a tool that acts as a receiver of satanic energy and fallen planets energy, like Saturn, and that it is also a receiver of destroyer force frequencies into your home?

This antennae, which we are encouraged to build each year is also a sender of energy, and it is a satellite, of sorts. It steals your life force energy, and that is taken this way, but there are a myriad of others ways your life force is stolen.

Wind turbines are receivers and transmitters. They are capable of sending 'virus type symptoms' and 'illnesses' because they are Luciferian by design.

Our life force is stolen that way.

You go to the fairground and go on the big wheel.

The wheel rides have gone up worldwide in cities everywhere.

Ask your heart why this is and what they do.

And because we engage in these things without protecting our life force energy, and our 'castle and moat', we break the Laws of Creation: the protection we may have had, dwindles.

So, the dark trick us into breaking the Laws of Creation by manipulating us into giving our ATTENTION to these things, or, we do not notice the harm they are doing and, therefore, we do not stop what we are doing — to ask our hearts for protection, and because we haven't asked, our hearts cannot interfere.

This is not 'wishy washy' stuff. This is how the Laws of Creation work.

If we can learn to understand how they work, we can learn how to avoid being tricked into creating karmic cycles that trap us in the pyramid structure of the mind control and False Light programs.

The pyramid. What do others perceive about the pyramid? Many new age practitioners think that ancient Egyptian energy is beneficial.

Really?

Why?

Because, one, they have never gone deeply into heart to ask.

And two, they do not perceive ancient energy as 'a threat'.

It is perceived as 'mysterious,' and, therefore, must be powerful.

It is powerful: it is destroyer force energy; wrapped up as 'earth' energy and 'healing' energy.

Those who fall for this clap-trap have not asked deeply enough, and we are at the time when those who could be helping others to wake up from the mind control are so immersed in it themselves, they cannot get to truth, they have lost their ability to discern wisely, because the more one focuses on destroyer force frequencies and structures like pyramids, stars, snakes, the caduceus, (used by the new age healing industry), the Rod of Asclepius (used prolifically by the medical industries and military industries, including those purporting to be informing humanity of the genocide) the more we are losing valuable time to help others.

We are sabotaging LOVE's plan. And I wonder, how long it will take before these groups will stop?

I started sharing information in 2011. Nothing much has changed since then. Except new generations of badly trained healers and teachers have emerged to continue the cycle of preventing humanity exiting this False Light trap.

It means that, quite simply, each person has to be their OWN RESCUE PARTY, now, more than ever and I wish to share information that my heart and LOVE have prompted me to type out today.

This is the information I have retrieved. You must all discern wisely. I try my best to get the fullest truth information. Your hearts have the knowledge and the ability to discern truth.

Please lie down or sit quietly AT HOME. Your bed is ideal, and let the words flow over you as you take your focus down to your chest area.

If you ask your heart to help you hear truth, the laws can come into play and help you.

Here we go:

"Claire, thank you for the introduction. It leads into the message we shared earlier about IMAGINATION and CREATIVITY, and how everyone can utilise the 'castle and moat' metaphor as a way of listening to their heart centre each day and getting the protection up and running, and then powered up by regular daily connection.

The energy from the Heart of Creation is to be used wisely and not squandered. It leads to repercussions, in the sense that the dark can use 'squandered help' against you, by weaponising it.

See this help from the Heart of Creation as a battlefield supply of defences and medical assistance.

You are not in a war against the dark.

They are in a war against you.

Your biggest way to defend and protect, and to defeat this dark group is not by violence.

This is a mind war. A war on your spirit. It is a war where different factions of dark forces are fighting against each other because they all want to get to the 'honey pot' and steal it. That honey pot is your knowledge and codes of wisdom from the Heart of Creation which are secreted within deep chambers inside your heart centre.

A human cannot defeat the dark armies. Your spirit can. Your spirit is vast and is barely here. If it were, it would burn through the darkness and they would not exist.

This is a place for learning and you all came in with your life force/your purest light codes diminished.

Claire has shared more about this, and we recommend you listen to her previous podcasts if you want deeper understanding.

The purpose of today's message is to encourage you all to see that you can turn this around in an instant.

It is all easily resolved.

The only reason it has not been dealt with is the reluctance in many, to call for help to activate the Laws of Creation, and to enable your heart/your Infinite Self to get involved in helping you.

When you stop asking. They have to stop helping.

And so, even though some have asked for help, they stop, and the help stops, and it means that LOVE's plan is constantly having to be readjusted and fine tuned, and a lot of good energy gets wasted, stolen by the dark armies and used as weaponry against humanity.

A calamitous cycle of harm is ongoing, and we need people on the ground to help to stop this cycle, because a lot of energy is being squandered.

Have you noticed how things have ramped up around the world, the Middle East, presently; Russia and the Ukraine before; Paris riots; worldwide fires; flooding; poverty; food shortages?

None of this is possible when more call on LOVE of help. This is not part of LOVE's plan; all this suffering.

This has been created by two factions: humanity and the dark armies.

We have said before, and we will repeat this because it is crucial, and many overlook its potential: CREATIVITY is a huge threat to the dark armies and A.I technologies.

These groups cannot create. The power to create gives others the power to re-imagine a world full of peace, love, and unity.

Claire's group were asked, some time ago, to focus on the pharmaceutical companies going bust and to ask LOVE for a fair redistribution of funds.

Have you noticed what is happening with various companies? It has taken longer, simply because few made the effort to re-imagine this event.

Had more got involved, it would have happened sooner.

Everything is given by LOVE in equal measure to the efforts of the individual/group.

If more focused on asking for all those who have harmed in politics, government, medical industry, military, big Pharma, big banking and big corporations to be held accountable, and if more imagined all the people being arrested and fairly tried by an honest jury and judges, then, it would happen.

Why hasn't it happened, you may ask?

Are you creating this reality, yet?

We say the best way forward for targeted individuals is to keep asking "for all your own errors (including those caused by 'tricks' being played on you) to be deleted,"

Then, from a peaceful, neutral heart, without anger or malice, "ask LOVE and the Laws of Creation to gather up all magnified, malicious harm and send it back to all those responsible for the harm."

Then, to "ask LOVE and the Laws of Creation to find all that you have lost, and return it to the Heart of Creation and then, return it to you in the purest, original form that can never be corrupted or infiltrated by the dark."

It needs to be followed each day: morning, lunch time, before sleep.

Otherwise, it stops and the attack starts up. That is why we are asking you all to be committed to your own rescue from targeting.

When you are strong enough, you can start to help others too, but first, we recommend you build this powerful protection of LOVE around you.

Have Hope, Trust and Faith that LOVE will help you.

That concludes the message for targeted individuals and those in society who wish to protect themselves more powerfully.

Of course, a group effort will give you all more protection. Remember this: it may help you to stay committed to helping yourself when you know that others who are suffering in your group get the help, through your own effort to help yourself.

For now, we have more information, and this is happening because those who Claire has been asked to reach out to are putting in tremendous effort to help themselves and humanity, and this beautiful exchange of love is helping Claire to retrieve more guidance to help you all.

Do you remember, Claire mentioned karmic cycles and how the dark ones are trying to trick you all into creating karmic cycles which trap you in avenues of learning in a spiral that pivots downwards and away from your original path?

This is how the mind control was created.

Claire is going to share with you how they are trapping you all, and how they use this to keep you locked down in a mind prison.

Your hearts can break you out of the mind prison. The dark fear this information because if enough of you realise that you can ask for help, the help will come and with that, the prison they have created around you weakens and if you step out of that prison... they are terrified of your power. You have to wake up to this fact. You are being played and made to look weak and vulnerable, and unable to address the technological attack on your person.

This is all a lie. It is not true at all.

Your power is feared by those who like to hunt and destroy.

Claire, tell them about the one who anchored in the Cosmic Laws into the Earth grids."

A lovely soul who I was guided to connect with, started to listen to my information and applied the teachings to help them get deeper inside their heart centre.

They took part in a 'heart call' podcast that I had put out online to ask for other's hearts to help humanity.

I was unaware of how many took part, however, I felt the change of frequencies. Each day, I notice the vibrations of the planet as a whole, and somedays are better than others. After others had helped, I noticed things felt better energetically.

I was subsequently guided that the reason why the dark armies were harming humanity so readily was because the Cosmic Laws (Laws of Creation) were not operating fully on the Earth plane.

The Cosmic Laws/Laws of Creation are in place to help all souls avoid causing harm to all life.

When we make poor choices. We harm all life. We are all connected, like frogspawn in a lake.

If a stone is thrown on a mill pond, it sends ripples out into the calm water, and when a human makes an error, and does not try to correct it, the shock waves move outwards and start harming all life everywhere.

If a human realises that they have made an error and calls to heart and LOVE for help to correct their mistakes, the Cosmic Laws set to work to calm the waters and to recall all 'magnified' harm. LOVE sets to work to help heal and repair any harm done and if any souls have lost codes as a result of these errors, LOVE finds the codes, heals and repairs them, and returns them in their true, original state of purity.

"Claire this is part of evolution and we wish to jump in here to help Claire summarise what is a complex set of steps. We will simplify further.

Claire said that when a mill pond which is calm and still and has a stone thrown in it's middle, the result is waves of motion as the water moves outwards from the centre.

This can be likened to the harm that the False Light frequencies and poor choices of humans make when they do not call on LOVE to help correct their errors.

The harm becomes 'magnified' if it is not stopped, and by the time the waves of magnified harm reach the banks of the mill pond, the waves lap up against the banks and if the force of the wave is strong enough and has not been addressed, the waves rebound back and move back towards the centre.

However, if lots of stones are being thrown into this mill pond by many poor choices, left unchecked, what do you think the result is?

The mill pond turns into choppy, disturbed waters. The reflection of calmness and stillness is lost. You can no longer see the mirror of the sky. All is disturbance, as if the wind has started to roughen the waves, and the short answer is: calamity.

Calamity, because what was once peaceful and calm, quiet and in balance is being rocked and pitched, and waves of distortion have been created so that humans can never see the peace or the calm of that mill pond.

They cannot perceive the purity or still, clear water reflecting peace and calm around it. All becomes distortion.

And in similar ways, the dark armies who held remembrances of knowledge at higher levels of consciousness have used their knowledge to ensure that humanity never get to see the calm waters, the reflections of peace and tranquility.

The dark armies perpetually trick humanity to throw stones into the water, and yet, if humanity took a deep breath and stood back, they might realise that they are being played. The only reason the water is unclear and choppy is because they perpetually pick up stones and throw them in.

We think it is about time that you stopped, don't you?

All we are asking those of you who want to help yourselves is to stop picking up the stones that the dark armies are handing you to throw, and call on your heart and LOVE to surround and protect you.

The soul who took part in the heart call message, brought gifts in their heart centre that they were unaware of. They did not need to know the specifics to activate them. They simply asked that if they had any gifts or codes to help humanity that they had carried in their hearts into this place, could they be activated.

The whole group had asked and the whole group assisted each other at deeper levels of awareness.

As a result, of this soul's willingness to help, the Laws of Creation were brought fully into this space. We need you all to be here to physically bring in these codes of help for humanity.

This soul was unaware of their immense ability and immense gifts. They have been targeted and been very ill with life threatening illness. Claire was able to share this with the person who brought it in. They are so under-confident with their gifts and ability, they were unsure they could possibly have achieved that.

But the thing is, this soul is being attacked so heavily - to feel 'less than', 'no good', 'unable to achieve anything' and yet, their huge heart and willingness to want to help humanity meant that they activated this vital component.

Without the Cosmic Laws/Laws of Creation anchored physically into the Earth grids, you would not be able to call on LOVE and ask the Laws of Creation to gather up all magnified, malicious harm and return it to those responsible.

One soul did that. A very ill, attacked, targeted individual. Picked on and made very ill because the dark armies knew who were coming, who had the gifts and they are using your own energy as weaponry against you.

Send it all back!

Claire has been guided that cancer can be assisted by calling on the frequencies of HOPE, FAITH, and TRUST.

These frequencies; the Laws of Creation; the power of CREATIVITY are like keys in a lock that open humanity up to avenues of assistance that take you away from the mill pond, away from the disturbances and offer a safe place for others to find stillness and relief from the onslaught of the False Light programs.

The pyramid structure is the False Light program.

It is satanic in nature and holds no benefits for soul evolution.

The pyramid system is the prison around you that the dark forces trap you into creating, by making you create karmic cycles and before the Cosmic Laws/ Laws of Creation were anchored into the Earth plane they were using their dark knowledge to deflect their own karmic debt and place it around you, to hold you in a 'mind prison' and keep you locked out of getting help.

With the arrival of the Cosmic Laws/Laws of Creation, the bars that they had used to imprison you that really belonged to them, are now being slowly returned to them and imprisoning them because now, their poor choices are being returned to them.

The mill pond that we talked about, where they were handing you stones to throw? That is your mill pond that they deliberately 'roughed up' to keep you stuck in a spiralling, karmic cycle of harm and retribution.

Up until that point, they had been largely living, 'scot-free', on your energy and DNA codes of knowledge. And all their karmic mistakes were being placed around your pyramid prison to further contain you.

That time is over. With the arrival of these laws, all that these groups have done to cause harm, the magnified malicious harm that they created and did nothing to stop or heal or repair? It is all being returned, according to the Laws of Creation and LOVE's plan, and that is why those who profited from this genocide and from their plans to destroy LOVE's/God's creation are receiving back all magnified, malicious harm.

Of course, it would happen faster if humans cottoned on that the more they request this, the quicker these companies, entities, authorities and deceivers will fail and lose.

LOVE has warned them many times, particularly in ZOMBIE APOCALYPSE - BY JUNE 2023, ALL WILL KNOW | 7 MAY2023, and various more recent recordings that all is being returned and it is unstoppable, now the tide is turning.

This is happening because a few brave souls decided to help themselves. They really could do with more help because they need your loving support.

There are souls around the world who are asking everyday for help and the more who join in this call for help, the sooner the dark armies will fall.

That is all for now Claire, please post this as soon as possible so that those who are willing to help will start the process of making that call and drop those stones that the dark armies wish them to throw to imprison them in their pyramid structures of lockdown, heart shock, and death.

It will not happen as they plan, however, it needs more to get on board now.

And we are asking you all, to make that call."

...

Full Audio Messages:

To Assist Others To Experience Leaving The Matrix To Reach Their Heart:

Free Teachings Available At:

@Loves Heart Plan | substack.com | Searching For The Evidence, bitchute.com

and telegram.com | @trueliightessenceOdysee.com

...

ZOMBIE APOCALYPSE - BY JUNE 2023, ALL WILL KNOW | 7 MAY2023 |

BY JUNE 2023, ALL WILL KNOW |

A SINKING SHIP, THE WAR FOR YOUR CONSCIOUSNESS, THE FREQUENCY OF PEACE | 2 DECEMBER 2022 | (CONSCIOUSNESS AND THE FREQUENCY OF PEACE) DEW, PROTESTS, FIREWALL

THE CLOCK IS TICKING...TICK.TOCK. (PART ONE)
(A personal story about cancer, courage and compassion...Have hope. Find out how you can help yourself when diagnosed with cancer and how to handle medical staff...)

Chapter Seven

EXIT THE MATRIX

Audio:

EXIT THE MATRIX —

WHAT FOUNDATION STONE DID YOU BRING?

@truelightessence, Odysee.com

GOOD MORNING EVERYONE,

I hope this podcast finds you all well and thriving, and I truly mean, thriving, as we are all starting to benefit from the fruits of our labour, and the birthing pains are subsiding as the help from the Heart of Creation comes flooding in to those with hearts that listen and are making that call for help, each and every day now.

I do have information to share. I am told there is a lot to unpack and download.

Here goes:

"Claire you need to get the group of individuals who are all helping as sovereign beings to understand that the worst thing they can do at present is form groups.

It simply will not work in this environment which is unstable and unreliable.

We guide you all, to steadfastly work within the parameters of sovereign beings, using their heart centre - their Infinite Self - as their sole resource and 'go to' teacher.

Your hearts have all the answers and must be utilised fully now, and if you are seeking teachings or have questions, whatever those questions may be, for example, about feelings of strong emotions, extreme fatigue, sense of anxiety, forgetfulness, or, more complex teachings, for example, the energy felt powerful but has waned, why? The energy feels less powerful on my own, why? They can all be answered and addressed from within.

We promise you that every change that you notice that you subconsciously question requires inner exploration.

Claire grew in knowledge through self enquiry between her heart centre and LOVE at the heart of Creation.

The same knowledge and understanding is available to all of you and simply requires a measure of your time and energy to get you through the doorways of the Cosmic Libraries of Knowledge and Wisdom.

We say, LOVE is inviting you in. Any willing soul who has been motivated by the inner heart assistance is encouraged to continue to work diligently with this vital piece of technology, your heart, your Infinite Self. There is nothing and no one who can guide you better. Your Infinite Self knows you in your entirety. It works with LOVE's plan and is bound by the conditions of the Laws of Creation/the Cosmic Laws to help you as much as you help yourself.

Some of you are being targeted more profoundly and personally than the bulk of humanity.

This energy from your heart will feel very powerful at first. It is because your sincere requests for help, and your effort to ask for help on a daily basis: AM, PM, and midway through your day is providing your Infinite Self the opportunity to work with LOVE's plan; to help surround and protect you; to get your boundaries strong, and when we think about your boundaries, we will consider your 'castle and moat' as the metaphor, to simplify the many complex manoeuvres which your Infinite Self is overseeing.

There is no thing outside of your 'castle and moat' that has the authority to help you or to interfere with your soul evolution.

Do you see, that to look outside of yourself wastes so much time and energy?

And to form groups at this stage is most unwise.

Not enough are working in a responsible manner with their 'castle and moat'. Many are not even connected at this late stage.

The codes were given by LOVE's plan to those who are calling for help and these codes are helping you all to connect very deeply to your heart's inner sanctum, where truth is found.

Many are mistaken in other groups, that they are hearing truth, yet they fail to understand that as soon as they use an outside force, such as a healing system, or they let in dark energy from social media platforms, because they are not protecting their castle and moat sufficiently well enough to prevent attack.

The dark technologies of mind control programs and ego programs are set up to prevent a human moving forward on their journey of growth, and we say, that it is sheer folly at this time to be using any other method except asking through heart as your gatekeeper to ensure you safely connect and accurately connect to LOVE/God at the heart of Creation.

There are many routes to the inner sanctum of the heart centre and to LOVE/GOD.

This means that you all have choices on how you travel to that destination.

However, whatever choice that is, you must ensure that it is robust enough and accurate enough, that you never miss the target.

When you ask your guardian - your teacher - A.K.A., your Infinite Self to help you, you no longer have to worry about how, what, when, or where, etc., in the sense that your Infinite Self is completely capable of overseeing your safety, and because you are calling on your Infinite Self and LOVE at the heart of Creation, together with the Laws of Creation, you have tripled your safety by using clear, concise instructions, and these are directions; codes that work to unlock the doors that lead out of the matrix and to safety.

Why do you think the attack is so heavy when you forget to use the routine?

This is a huge threat to the dark. Claire has already been advised that it has ruffled their feathers because many more are using these directions to safety.

You must check everything through your heart, though, and you must be fully confident with this process because these are your decisions and your choices.

Everything has to come from within you.

It is beautiful, isn't it, when the help comes in after an age in the wilderness? The sense of relief and freedom, the lightening of spirit, the faith that grows and the gratitude of feeling LOVE's embrace...?

Such a long time in the making. So much heartache, as many of you have suffered considerably.

And yet, you have bravely kept going against all odds.

That is why LOVE sent you because LOVE knew you had it in you to last the distance.

And the race is nearly at its final conclusion.

Who will win, you might be wondering?

There are no winners in this race. The race to the finish is primarily about you and your soul evolution, and where you finish in this race is solely down to how much effort you put into growing your light quotient, forgiving yourself of all errors, and sending back all the harmful attack that has hit your energy body and has magnified itself, causing you untold harm and suffering, and it has deterred you from growing your light.

Sending back all this harm returns the errors to those responsible for their own learning, and may be able to help them have a change of heart before it is too late.

For some, it is already too late. Some have already ended their evolution for eternity. They are now lost in the black hole of eternal suffering and 'harvesting'. There will be no respite. They have entered the gates of hell, and it is too late for those who would not stop harming.

You have also been requesting for all that has been lost to be found and restored to you as purest light codes.

These three steps will be bearing fruits for many, if not already, and we do wish to offer some crucial advice for you all who are at this stage.

The energy that has been 'deposited' in the podcasts are codes of Knowledge and Remembrance. Listening to the podcasts and utilising the information has been bringing dividends to those who have regularly listened and worked with their heart's guidance.

Because a group of individuals are joining in with LOVE's assistance also, the energy will feel powerful, but these are carefully measured codes of assistance and they have a time limit.

Once the codes have been absorbed or used up, there may be a sense of 'loss of power' and the inner heart work may feel less powerful; you may notice the dark attack; or perceive the frequencies of the planet are 'low', and this often leads individuals to think that the help from heart and LOVE has stopped working.

Be aware of this, when this happens. If something changes, you must go in and ask your Infinite Self for guidance.

Very often, what has happened is the energy measure given to you has been fully absorbed, so to speak, and you need to ask for an 'energy upgrade', or you may need to activate gifts that you brought in.

When energetic changes occur, or, if things happen that cause you to be concerned or question, try not to worry, you will never lose your connection as long as you stay connecting: AM, PM and midway through your day.

However, this is not a time to rest on one's laurels. This is a time to be diligently and silently working with your Infinite Self, LOVE's plan and the Laws of Creation to secure your future and ensure you are doing your level best each day to restore all that was lost.

The help comes in equal measure to your efforts. If you are working, this can be problematic. We suggest you find at least one time in your day where you can lie quietly and receive deeper teachings. It does not have to take long. It simply requires you to be focusing on your inner heart area, and not in mind, where the programs kick in and send you on a detour.

It is why your eyes need to be looking down when closed, to keep your attention on your chest area, and heart area.

That concludes the message for today, however, Claire is being asked to share other information and this will follow..."

What other information is there to share today? I ask.

"Claire, there is coming a time when gateways to new realities will close for good. You need to advise the group that these new realities are the ones they have been creating through their imagination.

We advise you all today, to draw a picture on a piece of paper, draw the world you truly dream of. What does it look like, who is there, who do you share this reality with?

Draw a peaceful place, where unity thrives and where all are free.

Draw awakened souls who look happy and free.

Think of what you wish, for the world's children.

There is nothing in this space that harms.

Draw only good things. Draw your dreams, your hopes, and pencil-in sentences that mirror your drawing.

Put the drawing somewhere prominent, your bathroom mirror where you brush your teeth, or your fridge; anywhere, where you will see it throughout your day, to remind you of your ability to imagine, to dream, and to recreate.

A rare window of opportunity has opened, thanks to a very special soul who has jumped on board with helping through their heart centre, and through their deep ability to love and to want to help, through their enthusiastic desire to do the right thing, they have activated their gifts and these gifts are rather miraculous.

Many of you have suffered untold hardship and heartache, and yet, your love for humanity and all precious life has not wavered.

You all have gifts and codes that are miraculous, and we repeat, that are MIRACULOUS.

Claire mentioned the dear soul who thought so little of themselves, and yet, had carried the codes of the Cosmic Laws that grounded them into this reality.

Without their help, you would not be benefiting from many things. These codes of the Cosmic Laws were critical to humanity leaving the matrix.

And here we are again, to be the bearers of the good news: That more miraculous codes have been activated, and now, you can anchor these dreams fully into this place, and this does not mean they will stay here, rather, that in order to get out of this space you needed to physically start the process off at the lowest point of your descent, and it had to be the foundation stone laid before you could all fully create your liberation from this place, in powerful ways.

Is it any wonder you have all been so suppressed?

Another beautiful soul has given you all, this foundation stone on which to build your new reality.

The other soul built the foundation stone on which the Laws of Creation could fully start operating in this space so that those who harm received back their own errors, which had been deflected by the dark ones and used to imprison you.

They have lost this game, and you must focus now on drawing, dreaming, creating your new, beautiful, peaceful reality.

What foundation stone did you bring to help humanity?

You are all carrying miracles, and if you ask, you will be shown how you can help to further advance the soul evolution of all those who wish to exit the matrix.

Claire, we need this posting, as soon as you are able."

I say, **"May I ask, you mentioned in past teachings that we need to be silent with our work, in order to protect the help coming in. Is it still the case, that you are advising individuals to work diligently and silently? I have had a few enquiries and I am unsure how to proceed with helping individuals, without seeming aloof, or unconcerned about their progress. Do you have any advice for us?"**

"Claire, you are better to post publicly and leave the personal contact to a minimum, because the more you get involved outside of these parameters, the more you expose yourself and those who need the protection. The work can be shared and the help given, however, we guide all of you: To remain working silently and diligently is the biggest threat to the dark. They cannot get through with any technology when you keep up your inner work practises. Try to keep comments short and sweet, and keep using heart connection to seek answers within, not without."

Q. How can I best support vulnerable souls who are just waking up?

"Claire, we guide you, as we have often guided you in the past, this work has to go 'broad-spectrum' now - to reach as many souls as possible. Others can best help by getting strong themselves, by getting used to the rise and fall of the power of the 'measures of energy', and get used to asking lots of questions inside their heart centre. Their Infinite Self is their sole teacher. Nothing outside of self must be used at this stage.

You are here to guide and support through your messages, and we guide you to encourage all those who are partaking in their heart connection, to maintain that connection by regular questioning. It keeps the doorways open to the libraries of knowledge and wisdom. No one can take you there, only yourself. We say again. The answers are all inside of you. That is all, Claire."

I would like to thank each and every one of you all, for all you are doing to help yourselves, and each one of you is helping everyone else who is participating, to get the foundation stones laid to higher learning which is quite literally building a ladder out of this reality.

This is the true meaning of 'group work'.

In my experience, when I worked with others in the physical, things always went wrong. Things got sabotaged. It has been a continual cycle of sabotage. And so, my inner wisdom advises that we are already working as a team at higher levels of awareness.

This is where the true meeting of hearts and divine minds occurs.

I have witnessed controlled ops destroying groups throughout my work, and more recently, I have benefited from the wisdom and experience of others who have also had their hard work sabotaged. Groups simply do not work in the current environment.

Staying sovereign; being an individual, while at the same time working with unseen individuals who also share the same goal offers many benefits.

The most important thing to me is protecting LOVE's plan and ensuring we secure our dream reality.

Thank you to the soul, who by miraculous circumstances, has gifted us all with a way to finally exit the matrix.

What an incredible gift.

It must not be squandered by us all. This gift must be appreciated and valued in every sense of the word, because this soul suffered to bring this in, not just in this lifetime, but every lifetime.

I am deeply grateful, and I know, everyone who understands what tremendous courage and determination it has taken to bring this in, will be deeply moved by the hardships and trials this soul has endured during their arduous sojourns during their fall into this place.

This is what you are all capable of.

It is indeed a freeing frequency, liberating and magnificent!

Thank you! Happy drawing, everyone!

...

Audio Link:

Exit The Matrix —
@truelightessence, Odysee.com

Chapter Eight

PART TWO: UPDATED MESSAGE FOR HUMANITY AND THE TRUTHERS

Audio Links: Initially shared in May 2023. Reposted for those awakening in October 2023.

...

Hello Everyone,

It's the 14th May 2023, today, and this is Claire, with Part Two of the message for the truth community, and all those wishing to protect and defend humanity and all precious life on Earth. I include the original message at the end of this podcast, for those who may have missed the original, and may wish to help.

All contributions of help are vital at this time and today, my aim is to give you an update, alongside a deeper explanation, which my heart and LOVE have requested because your vital assistance has already brought dividends, and I wish to explain why that is and how vitally important your contributions are.

So now, I will share the routine I use to access my heart knowledge and connect outside of the False Light Matrix, with the assistance of LOVE and the Cosmic Laws (LAWS OF CREATION), who oversee the safe expansion of consciousness along a truthful pathway of exploration and deeper learning while keeping all safe, in alignment with LOVE and the Cosmic Laws, in service to all.

If you wish to help, all are welcome to join us, however, may I imprint the importance of moving out of the mind control and your mind processes, in order to hear your own heart's guidance?

I may share information which does not resonate and if I do, please ensure you use your connection to your heart and LOVE and the Cosmic Laws to question more fully, and ask lots of questions until you are satisfied with your heart's guidance. I cannot guarantee that my information is accurate and no one should rely on my message. I share it because I believe others can connect to their own hearts and can help humanity.

If you plan to listen while casually sitting with eyes open whilst being in mind, you will not benefit and you will not perceive the bigger picture. It is simply not possible, until you go into the silence and ask your heart and LOVE to help you.

This is the routine I have worked to secure for my inner expansion and connection to LOVE at the Heart of Creation through my gatekeeper - my Infinite Self:

I set an alarm in case I fall asleep and need to be awake by a certain time for appointments, or similar.

I lie down flat on the bed that I sleep in at night, at home, and make myself comfortable, as I would for sleep each night.

I keep my legs straight and gently together, my palms are facing down and resting on the tops of my thighs.

If it is safe to do so, I close my eyes, as I do for sleep each night and I gently take my closed eyes down towards my chest area.

I focus on the air going in and out of my chest area, keeping my eyes gently looking down.

I make a decision that I wish to help all life here in optimum ways, in alignment with LOVE and the Cosmic Laws.

I ask my Infinite Self and Infinite LOVE to surround and protect me, and to help me reach truth at the Heart of Creation and Infinitely beyond.

I press an imaginary switch in the centre of my chest, which I call my True POWER Switch.

This switch has been set up and overseen by LOVE to ensure I can safely be escorted outside of the False Light Matrix to see the bigger picture unfolding and to retrieve vital assistance for humanity.

We all have the natural ability to do this if we wish to help all. It is innate within us, a natural gift that all have, and if LOVE sees we are sincere and will work with integrity, then all assistance is given that can help us to best help all, in alignment with LOVE and the Cosmic Laws.

These are the teachings that I have worked towards simplifying, over a 13 year period of inner exploration on understanding how Earth energy works, why it is harmful to all life, how light is distorted, why it is distorted, and how to work with Purest Light energy from the heart of Creation, in alignment with LOVE and the Cosmic Laws (Laws of Creation), in ways that provide the optimum outcome for all.

Find a way that helps you reach truth, and for example, if you are from a religious faith, then pray for assistance, as you normally do, and ask to be assisted to see the bigger picture through your deep faith.

This message is all inclusive and welcomes all who wish to best help all.

So, by now, hopefully, we are all relaxing and focusing on our breathing as my words float over you and I share a new message, but just before I continue, we need to press our True Power Switch once more - as an indication that we wish to hear truth from the heart of Creation, as a group who will use our own heart discernment and also will listen inwardly for guidance, in case we are being called upon - as we may start receiving new teachings after the message has been relayed, and you may need to pause the recording after the message to tune in more deeply still.

Here is the message my heart and LOVE are guiding me to share:

"Claire, you need to thank the group for all they have done so far. They have worked very hard. Those who have stepped up have already displayed excellent service work because a miraculous issue that was threatening many has been completely averted.

Not so for those who have not asked for help, who are looking the other way.

But for those who have no voice, for the group and their pets and loved ones, children, newborns and innocent souls a huge problem has been averted and Claire will now explain what you have managed to achieve. It really is quite incredible how much you have done to help all vulnerable life.

Claire, will you explain to the group what has happened concerning the old system matrix which is collapsing in on itself, in terms of the old decks of the 'Sinking Ship' analogy?"

[Claire] OK. The version of the old Earth matrix and False Light Construct was explained to me as an imaginary 'sinking ship' in the middle of a vast ocean of turmoil and chaos.

An SOS call was put out and a fleet of helpers had set sail and were waiting to assist those trapped on the sinking ship. There is a huge barrier of rocks that stand between the ocean with the sinking ship in it and the fleet of helpers that are waiting beyond the rocks, who sailed to assist from the heart of Creation.

The ship had twelve decks on it. The lifeboats are on the top of the upper deck - Deck 12 - and humanity are below decks on the third deck which is rapidly filling with water.

During the last ten 'Earth' years, some of the decks above the third deck have collapsed in on themselves.

Many in humanity think that they need to get to Deck 5 to secure rescue, which many term, the '5th Dimension', however, in terms of vibrational shifts, this is but one tiny step of learning on the ladder of consciousness which has billions of steps, and therefore, Deck 3 and Deck 5 are not good places to be because the whole ship is sinking, not just the third deck or 'third dimension,' in Earth terms.

The name of the game for all souls who are learning how a False Light Construct works is to climb the decks of the ship, whilst collecting vital learning, healing, and repair as they make their way up to the twelfth deck, also known as the 12th Dimension or Planetary Grids, and make their way to the lifeboats at the Galactic level.

They then need to launch their lifeboats and get guidance from the purest light SOS helpers; to navigate their way through the stormy, choppy waters to get beyond the rocks to a place of safety, and retrieve vital teachings from the purest light rescuers on how to help secure the safe evacuation of all those souls still stranded on the decks of the sinking ship before it sinks and they are lost forever.

Some have managed to sail past the rocks and have secured vital teachings, but not enough have launched their lifeboats, and some are still on Deck 5 because they were told it was the best place to go, but this was a deliberate deception; placed into the consciousness to prevent these souls leaving the ship.

On the decks of the sinking ship, there are many different life forms moving up and down the decks of the ship as they learn either through love, or, they drop back down the decks - through breaking Cosmic Laws or harming others.

The ship could be likened to the game of 'Snakes and Ladders': Making wise choices and moving up, only to become attacked by the snakes, or, making poor choices and falling back down to the lower decks.

The dark forces on the decks are soul fragments and fragmented aspects of higher levels of awareness who have gone AWOL and started destroying other's chances of leaving the ship by stealing their life force energy.

This is because AWOL souls do not seek out LOVE's assistance.

They go AWOL and turn their backs on LOVE.

LOVE is the fuel that enables us to exist. LOVE keeps us connected to the heart of Creation, and infinitely alive.

When a soul goes AWOL and rejects LOVE's embrace, they have to find a different power source in order to exist, and so, they use the codes of knowledge that they have retained in their own DNA - to harm others on the same decks as themselves, or on the decks below them, in order to steal life force energy, which they convert and use as their power source.

Without LOVE and without an alternative power source in the form of stolen life force energy to live off, they could not exist.

We are at the stage now, when an In Breath is completing, meaning: that all souls are being called back to the Heart of Creation in preparation for their next, new, exciting cycle of evolution, called here: The Out Breath.

All souls on the sinking ship are being called to climb their ladder of consciousness, to heal and repair any harm they may have caused others, and any harm that may have been caused to them, and return home - to be present and correct - for the next, big, exciting new cycle of evolution.

This return is also known as 'Ascension'.

Humanity have the opportunity in this lifetime to achieve Cosmic Ascension.

During the last ten 'Earth' years, many dimensions or ships decks have collapsed as Infinite LOVE has been offering all souls on those particular decks the opportunity to choose whether to come home or remain on the decks of the sinking ship, because of the next Out Breath,

There have been many who refused to stop harming and Cosmic Laws are very strict at this stage of evolution. It is the final opportunity to repair and make good all harm done and all harm received.

Infinite LOVE does not impose, and all souls make their own choice.

If a soul chooses to come home and wishes to make good - all harm is forgiven and forgotten, meaning: deleted, and this removes all harm that has affected other souls, too. The slate is 'wiped clean' when a soul seeks to remedy their errors.

LOVE loves us all, unconditionally and there is no judgement.

The Cosmic Laws work to keep all safe, and all souls knew this when they came here: that LOVE would remind them that it was time to come home and the soul is offered a choice.

When Cosmic Laws are broken to such a degree that the soul has caused untold destruction, a decision is reached and the Infinite Self will be instructed to sever the ladder at the level of growth where the intention to redeem oneself is present.

Anything below that level that does not wish to stop harming is left behind as the ladder is withdrawn past the rocks and back to the Heart of Creation where the precious knowledge is securely returned, to best help all.

Meanwhile, those aspects of self who refused to stop harming on the severed ladder will be left defenceless on the sinking ship, and all alone, without LOVE to call upon because by this time, it is too late.

The choice is made and once made, it cannot be reversed.

We are at that stage now, when the In breath has practically completed and the Heart of Creation is preparing to expand into a new Out Breath cycle of evolution.

Many on the ship's decks have fallen into this trap, and some were innocently out exploring when they were enticed in and could not find their way out.

Others have climbed their ladder and got to the the twelfth deck of knowledge only to fall down the 'snake's ladder'.

Very few reach the lifeboats, and very few secure help from the beyond the rocks.

During this time on the ship, I am being asked to think of the twelfth deck as the Planetary grids, and the lifeboats as the Galactic grids.

The ship represents our individual ladder of consciousness within the False Light Construct and the ladder of humanity's consciousness, as a group who deliberately 'fell' into this place on a 'mercy mission' to help all souls trapped here to return safely to the heart of Creation.

As humanity descended into the decks of the ship, they were pelted with 'cabbages and eggs' by the dark, who stripped them of as many DNA light codes of knowledge - to use for their own sorry ends - to harm others on the decks of the ship.

Humanity had already come in with less light codes remembered because they could not come in on full power.

This ship represents the one 'juggernaut' from my previous message and each human represents millions of 'juggernauts' of energy, which would collapse the programs, without any lessons being learned of how Earth energy is being used in a distorted way, to harm all life here.

Therefore, each human came in with very little knowledge or codes, and a few humans came in with more.

The name of the game was for those who came in with more codes remembered, to help those who had given up many codes of knowledge and who were therefore, extremely vulnerable because they did not remember they were from the heart of Creation.

All that knowledge was given up - to give those who came in with a higher quota of help, and it was a very brave thing to do because these souls knew they might never return if they did not wake up in time, before the completion of the In Breath.

Those who came in with more codes remembered were entrusted to climb the decks of the ship and to gather up all that they had lost on the way down to the third deck - to get to the lifeboats and launch the lifeboats, and navigate their way past the rocks to reach the team of rescuers in order to get help for those still stranded on the sinking ship.

This plan failed - some got on board in 2012 and were aware of the issues, but they fell under the spell of mind control and the rescue plan collapsed.

Since then, many more projects have been launched and failed as the mind control technologies were upscaled.

I do not know the full details but I understand from my inner teachings that when the purest light waves were at their peak, the dark were able to steal this light, to divert it away from humanity, using advanced technologies that they had prepared for this time, because they know all about the In Breath and Out Breath cycles and how to harm others, as their very existence depends on it.

The convergence of the light waves meant the dark could operate stealthily and out of sight from humanity and start to plot against them to foil any plan to rescue the occupants of the sinking ship, who the dark want to enslave, in order to maintain an existence away from the Heart of Creation and LOVE.

The rejection of their need for LOVE has worked so far and the dark always thought they had a 'win-win' situation, but what they had not counted on was on any humans waking up sufficiently, to secure any fruitful assistance.

The public have been involved, and 'used' in all innocence, to take part in activities that have collapsed the twelfth deck and destroyed the lifeboats on the sinking ship.

These were known as the Planetary and Galactic Grids, as I previously mentioned.

These grids are a vital resource and lifeline for all souls to utilise, and a vital step that all must evolve through before departing the False Light Matrix and evolving along a safer pathway.

The systems used to entice the populous into collapsing these grids were YOGA and REIKI.

Yoga collapsed the Planetary Grids, and Reiki collapsed the Galactic Grids.

Therefore, the two vital steps of evolution, the '12th deck' and the 'lifeboats' were gone and lost to all life.

This ensured that all souls left on the sinking ship could not escape.

Some of humanity noticed these issues and sought to remedy it.

They rebuilt the grids twice, from 2020 onwards.

Unfortunately, the innocent use of these systems by those who believe them to be beneficial continued.

These groups are unaware that these systems have been satanically hijacked and distorted, to ensure that when a person chooses to participate in, or teach a class in these systems, their choice to do so is all that is needed by the dark to infiltrate their ladder of knowledge and steal vast amounts of the person's life-force energy.

These stolen codes of knowledge are then replaced with fake codes of false knowledge and fake feelings of false peace and well being, so that the person never notices.

Those who do notice, no longer participate in these systems because they have realised that harm is occurring at higher levels of consciousness.

Some have sought to remedy their errors and repair all harm received and caused, because these choices to participate in satanically corrupted systems have wreaked havoc for humanity who are still largely unaware of the capacity of the dark to cause untold harm.

Reiki is the same.

I am hearing my heart and LOVE say:

"Claire put several calls out recently to these two communities to ask for assistance - to stop the attack in these areas.

The Yoga groups have largely rejected the information and have now destroyed the only way out of the ship's decks for all life forms, however, enough Reiki people did respond to the call, not many, but enough to secure repair of the lifeboats, but without a twelfth deck, they could not be reached and so, humanity and all life on this ship were stranded as potential slaves.

The dark were very pleased with their plan, however, they often forget the tenacity of a human heart who cares about others and so, even though this did spell disaster, more in humanity - who's souls and higher levels of awareness saw the problem - stepped forward and called to LOVE for help.

Many in the religious community have helped also, because prayer and calls for help are powerful. LOVE always promised that for every ounce of calls for help, millions of ounces of help would be offered by LOVE.

Not just the religious communities, many in humanity saw the evil on the planet and turned inwards, and found that help came when one called for help, and so now, an awakening is happening which the dark cannot seem to put a lid on.

They have tried pandemics, vaccination programs, spraying poison in the skies, poisoning the food and water, creating fear, wars, death and destruction but humanity just seem to be bouncing back and the dark are now on the back foot.

And now, a small group of individuals have helped, once more, with this satanic evil juggernaut and placed millions of juggernauts in the way of this destroying force.

Meanwhile, LOVE heard humanity's call for help and new purest light grids have been built that cannot be tampered with or destroyed by the dark.

And those who have asked for help will be able to continue their evolution on a safe path of peaceful and exciting evolution.

During this time, many calls have been put out from LOVE, reminding souls who are trapped on the sinking ship to, "Make the request. LOVE does the rest", if they wish to grow in LOVE and be rescued from the sinking ship before it eventually sinks, in order to return home to the Heart of Creation and continue their soul evolution.

It is a simple choice to call for help.

For those who choose to stay on this ship, Claire has already explained that the twelfth deck is gone: You cannot reach the lifeboats, and if you don't ask LOVE to help you, you will have made the free will choice to remain trapped.

And even if you change your mind, by the time you realise, it will be too late because at a certain time, the Infinite Self will sever the ladder - to protect the knowledge, and withdraw what can be salvaged - to serve all.

Something miraculous has happened, for those who requested rescue from LOVE.

The group who answered the call for help in the message to the truth community, have launched their lifeboats, because their calls for help ensured LOVE placed them in them and helped them navigate through the choppy waters, past the rocks, and to make contact with the divine fleet of rescuers, and to retrieve solutions and activate their inner gifts, which have helped - as a joint group - to create a bridge on the sinking ship that leads to the lifeboats and therefore, those who were trapped and stuck have been able to escape and return home.

Please ask about this and retrieve deeper insights.

That is what can be achieved when hearts unite and call to LOVE for help.

There are many more plans by the dark to entrap all remaining life on this sinking ship and it is hoped that more will participate, to unlock the codes that they came here with - to help humanity.

Every person on the planet carried a code or two, and some have more."

Remember, those who are asleep were very brave...they came into this place 'naked and unclothed', in complete trust that those of us who came in with more, would care enough and love our family of humanity enough, to make our way to the lifeboats and get past the rocks so that we could retrieve vital codes of knowledge and seek the solutions, because no matter what the dark throw at us inside this False Light Matrix, all the answers are available to us, if we ask for help.

All of humanity came here as a family group because we have the ability to LOVE unconditionally, and although we are not fully awake in this place, many more of us understand that the problem is mounting, and we are leaving it very late in the day to secure humanity's rescue.

We need to focus as much time as possible, to help all souls become aware that they have a choice: to call for help, or remain on this ship.

We cannot interfere with the free will choice of any soul.

It is against Cosmic Law, however, we are here as an act of service to all - to highlight the issues, and once the issues have been highlighted, we must step back and allow others to make their free will choices.

If others are looking the other way, that is a free will choice, too, and it is not our place to force the issue, however, many are starting to question and are looking for help and direction, and it is this group of souls who we can help, if they ask us.

It is important to share information, and many share videos to help raise awareness, and that is important, too. Those in the truth community are being asked to ensure that they have secured their own rescue, because many have been immersed in highlighting the issues, but many are not aware of the bigger picture unfolding.

They have been critical to raising awareness. Some have done this with very few codes of remembrance of their true origins, and it would be a calamity if they did not secure their own rescue, in the process of awakening others to the danger they are in.

The biggest danger and calamity would be to remain on this sinking ship because they did not realise that there was a rescue plan available, if they wanted it, and for many, they have been taught that the Fifth Deck or Fifth Dimension is our next evolutionary step, when, it is a tiny step in vibration and is part of the sinking False Light Construct.

All the decks of the sinking ship collapsed in on themselves in recent years, and so now, the Third Deck occupants are swimming in the choppy waters of a 'cosmic soup' of satanic attack from all the remaining decks - with all the occupants of higher awareness - who are on the side of destroyer force energy, and all the aspects of their own ladder that has fragmented and gone AWOL, which is now attacking each person and all life here, and trying to suck as much life force energy out of them, in order to try and maintain their existence away from LOVE.

The higher technologies are being used to harm humanity and all life that existed on the third deck of this ship.

There are no 'barriers' of the higher deck walls to protect them from the higher technologies.

And 5G radiation is deadly as it is all our 'heartache energy' and all the 'heartache energy' from the Earth, as she watched her Galactic and Planetary grids 'raped and sucked dry' of her vital life force energy, and so, you can imagine why the radiation from 5G, Wi-Fi, and other microwave technology is so deadly to us...the soul recoils in horror and shock that we would use the equipment, or ignore a mobile mast, or deadly street light without uttering a cry of outrage to those responsible, nor asking LOVE for protection.

Protection and defence is the name of the game.

There is much more to share. I have tried to simplify things as much as possible and recommend you keep the 'Sinking Ship' analogy in mind, because it keeps things simple.

I am sure that your Infinite Self will have teachings for you, to help you retrieve further assistance for all life here. I have always said, we are not the weaker side, and I am deeply grateful to those who have helped thus far. It is incredible - what has been achieved in such a short time, which is why the dark are on the back-foot.

We must keep up the pressure now, and work diligently, as we must secure as much help as possible, before June 2023.

Each time I listen to the following recording, I am getting new insights.

Keep all teachings to yourself. Don't let the dark know what you are doing.

Silence is best. Keep them guessing.

Your heart is your teacher, no one else, and so, any questions much be directed within, where the knowledge is and where your evolution is dependent upon.

I will be in touch again when I get more guidance.

Keep up the excellent work and thank you, on behalf of humanity and the new borns who are still coming onto this planet, because their future is our duty to secure, and we must keep these special and very brave souls in our hearts and minds, as we keep our promise - to do our best for all -and to remember that those who came in with less codes, those who rigidly refuse to see, are like that because they gave you more; in complete trust that when the whistle blew for the final time, that you would have done your very best to remind them that is it time to call for help, to 'request rescue', and come home.

"Make the request LOVE will do the rest."

That is all they need to do, because LOVE knew they would be running late for the bus and knew it would be a 'close call' before the whistle blew, and that if those of us who came in with more light remembered could secure as much help as possible... that even in a False Light program...if we could raise the vibration enough, we would enable them to remember - to make the choice to come home.

We must do our very best for all these souls because that is the promise we made before we came here and I know that we would never want to break a promise like this, not when so much was given at our disposal which we have failed to use, and with so little time left to remedy our own errors, I know, that we all know, a promise is a promise...

We simply cannot fail these souls.

Chapter Nine

YOU CANNOT STOP WHAT IS COMING, 21 October 2023

"PRAY FOR THE NEWBORNS AND INFANTS.
PRAY FOR THEIR PEACE."

AUDIO LINK:
LOVES HEART PLAN, SUBSTACK.COM
SEARCHING FOR THE EVIDENCE, BITCHUTE.COM
DEEPER TRUTHS CHANNEL,
@TRUELIGHTESSENCE, ODYSEE.COM

...

Q. HOW CAN I BEST SERVE ALL, IN OPTIMUM WAYS, IN ALIGNMENT WITH LOVE'S PLAN AND THE LAWS OF CREATION?

You have asked me to put out a message?

I have no idea what it is, but it feels serious and, therefore, I would ask all those who are using their hearts as the method to connect to

LOVE and the Cosmic Laws; the Laws of Creation to discern wisely, and seek clarity through your own inner heart exploration, where truth is found.

Here we go:

"Claire, you can't do anymore, yet. Not enough are stepping forward to help in ways that will get humanity out of the matrix as a group.

Those who have requested rescue have secured their own rescue, however, that does not mean that the vulnerable are all safe, or that the children will not face an agonising death. And we do say, an 'agonising death'."

Q. Oh dear, what are you going to tell us? I have already had the pictures shown to me on my inner heart screen. I saw young infants, new borns, it was hazy but they were in a sink and the people with them, the adults, were harming them.

Then I sensed I was in a False Light place, I closed the door in a dingy, dark corridor that led to where the babies were and I marked a cross on the door, and I know that the X is linked to Elon and the slides of the microscopy of the blood; the nano 'X' is visible to the eye on the magnified slide samples.

I wondered why I would see myself draw a symbol which I know is dark — they are all corrupted, even the heart harms others.

It's why I never use emoji's, hearts etc., and I never leave X's as kisses on messages.

The X signifies the 'Kiss of Death' in the False Light program.

My inner perceptions took me back to the street I saw in my heart after the earthquake in Turkey..

In my vision, I was with company in a nice place, and I heard a commotion, so I went down from the roof to the ground floor an empty bare room and looked out into the narrow cobbled street.

I saw an army tank in the narrow street to my left, it had a Nazi symbol on it.

The army tank filled the width of the street and it was pushing the dead and the dying down the street beyond where my eyes could see.

But I heard their screams of terror and there was blood everywhere. I heard the sounds of metal as it scraped its way along the cobbled street crushing the dead and dying as it forced its way up the incline of the street, scraping and scarring buildings and clearing everything in its path.

It was as if I was in a place where the streets were very narrow and the buildings were made of stone, all single story, with a roof terrace, and a whole terrace, a whole street, on both sides, were the same.

In my previous vision, an old women stepped partly out of her wooden doorway, just as the tank had passed and the terrified cries of the dead were filling the air, but she did not look, merely threw her dirty water out of her bucket, and she looked resigned to the situation. There was no emotion.

It was very disturbing.

This vision today was also very disturbing. I also saw an eye, as if it was looking through a spy hole and watching things unfold on Earth.

The babies in the sink were blurred, but my heart told me something is happening at present and something big is about to unfold.

I can 'feel' the fear on the planet, like a barometer, and each day, I can sense the fluctuations of this fear.

Our hearts and our souls are trying to tell us something.

It breaks my heart that people will not open their hearts fully to truth, and to seek the truth above all things. I am watching things unfold in the usual pattern that is human behaviour.

We have a group who see themselves as the truth community.

Really?

How much truth is too much truth, for some at least?

People have given their power away to far too many 'saviour' characters in this community.

Did they deliver in the three years of hell that we have endured?

Did anyone steal money and gold, and pay themselves handsomely through public donations?

Are they linked to the Club Of Rome, through their old political ties which everyone has a short memory of, or, is unaware?

And was this hastily hidden from view, to sever the link to Soros?

Did the British parliament respond honestly, three years ago, when the group of concerned scientists approached them?

Does one current 'saviour' serve the people or the Mossad party that all parliamentarians have to join in order to become an MP?

It is called 'Friends of Israel.' And all MPs have to join, otherwise, they cannot be an MP.

It's a big club, this secret club.

Choose the people you put on a pedestal and choose wisely, and do not attack others who may know more than you do.

My question is, if you care so much about humanity, why attack those who hold a different view?

Because my eyes are turning on all those in the truth community, now, and I am starting to question if the most vocal are there to lead the rebels into the same trap as the rest of humanity?

They all profit in some way. Many are selling their wares.

Really?

At a time like this?

When the twin towers were hit, would you all consider it perfectly acceptable to charge everyone trying to exit the building for the privilege of showing them a safe doorway?

So, my eyes are now starting to look more closely at those who purport to be sharing vital knowledge to serve humanity.

The macrocosm of the hate that is rising up, as different peoples of the world gather to swear allegiance to their friends abroad. The hate builds...

The truthers give their power away to any 'saviour.' They must not be knocked down from their pedestal; no matter their connections to Soros or the Club Of Rome, and the 'truthers' attack their own — anyone who questions their opinions on the 'saviours' must be silenced, their comments deleted...

And in the microcosm: I watch the poison, that is 'X', having a 'field day'; destroying life, extracting the life force, and bringing death inside the blood of humanity.

Why am I sharing my perceptions?

A. *"Claire, ask a question"*

Q. **"What question should I be asking now that best serves all, in optimal ways, in alignment with LOVE's plan and the Laws of Creation?**

I am very concerned for the children. Many feel that I am attacking them when I share my teachings about Yoga and Reiki, without understanding that the whole point is to secure a turn around, a change of heart, by those who are capable, but who choose to use outdated methods that harm the children and have, in effect... if they want the truth above all, have placed us in this 'cosmic soup,' without any divide or void to separate out the darkest forces from the False Light program, who now, thanks to the choices of these groups to continue a practice without educating themselves on their consciousness, their ladder of wisdom, or the protective shields of the Galactic and Planetary grids which are now destroyed...

The reason I am being asked to keep sharing is because you have not only placed humanity and all precious life in danger, you have secured your place in hell and unless you ask for rescue and desist from practicing these occult systems, they will destroy you.

It has already started.

I trained in many holistic energy healing practices, including Reiki, and I used to enjoy Yoga and Pilates, etc. When I started connecting to my heart centre, when I stopped using energy healing methods, I started my journey of expansion of consciousness.

I started to enquire and ask for teachings, and I share what I know after thirteen years of daily study.

It must be nice to be popular. I am not here to smooth egos. I am here to help save the children and to help those who are caught up in this False Light Construct to understand that they are trapped, that they can extract themselves with help, but they need to understand the cause and then understand the effects.

No one teaches this in healing circles. The teachings are flawed.

No one understands how energy healing systems get attacked as soon as they are anchored in. Many lack vital knowledge and understanding, but they do have big opinions about things they have never researched themselves.

Everything they know is from a book or from someone else, or a course they paid for that gave them their 'master badge' in a weekend.

I have posted many times about Yoga and Reiki. What I find interesting is that no one comes back with their own research.

When I started to find out that I was making errors, when I was told by someone who was far more knowledgeable than me that the caduceus that I had around my neck was satanic, I took it off and spent the whole day asking other questions, because this person knew a lot about healing systems, about the flaws, about the poor methods of teaching.

Many know it [REIKI] is flawed beyond repair.

Did it ever do any good? It helped people like me become aware of energy and how to perceive things beyond my previous state of awareness.

Why did I stop? Because I started to grow when my heart started teaching me.

I wanted to help humanity. I wanted to do it properly and safely. I always believed we could cure ourselves. I wanted to understand why things had started feeling distorted.

I asked my heart for teachings. The more I wanted to learn, the more my heart taught me.

And that is how I have spent much of my time and energy. It has become my passion and I trust that LOVE has the answers to help us all.

The biggest issue is that the planet is in danger. The children are in danger. Those in the healing world are in danger because they have been deliberately sidetracked.

I am a small voice because my truth threatens those who want control.

A pattern has emerged over the years... People gravitate towards the help because they have put out a heart call for help. LOVE answers the call. They receive the simple teachings on how to connect to heart and ask for help within.

The help comes. It is very strong. They are drawn to it because they have never felt anything so beautiful... Their own heart energy.

Then, they forget to practise as taught, or they start to mix in another system: a bit of Reiki; a workout of Yoga, and all the doors they had shut, open wide, and because they had expanded their Knowledge and learning, they have more light to steal.

The dark use technology to hold humanity in place. As soon as a soul starts to expand, they are in 'emergency mode'.

All the dark attack within you and around you must not be blocked — not for the dark — they exist off your light, and so, you have opened the door to them, and in they walk.

They totally trash all your hard work and efforts, and they steal the codes you had received back to help you remember your true origins. They replace these codes with False Light codes. You won't know they are there.

And you do not notice.

Yet, something has happened, something so sinister: the False Light codes are programmed to stop you seeking help, to deter you from seeking fullest truth, and they put you off using the method that was helping you the most.

Your interest in the Heart Connection wanes. You carry on with your other practices that let the dark steal your light.

You do not notice, and as more Purest Light codes are stolen from you, you stop seeking the truth, or, you are led down false pathways to truth, and when another soul shares fullest truth with you, you are now programmed with False Light codes — to vehemently attack the truth.

The dark have wedged your door open. You no longer see it is open. You do not have the codes. You lost that ability as soon as you gave your attention to a satanic frequency, practice or movement that opened your energy fields up at the BIOFIELD level, to satanic attack.

Bye, bye, help.

Bye, bye, remembering.

And all the while, the codes that the dark stole from you are partly used to sustain them and partly used as a weapon to cause you more harm; to keep you in this False Light matrix.

What happens on the macrocosmic level when someone loses vast amounts of Purest Light remembrances?

Death.

Death of the soul....

And the death of other souls, because your Purest Light codes were not just there to protect you. They were there to protect the children and those souls who are now being harmed by technologies and entities that you cannot perceive, and are unwilling to acknowledge.

I am not here to be your friend to smooth your ego. I am hear to ask you to open your hearts to the harm you are doing to yourself and the children.

They are the currency, and you just sold your soul.

A. *"Claire, we did warn you that the biggest soul harvest is upon you all. It has started now, and it will not stop, not unless more souls turn their backs on old methodologies and purify their practices by keeping it simple.*

Heart is simple and pure. Why would you go elsewhere? And the answer is, because, as the healing system or physical practice has progressed you have had a multifold loss of light codes from your DNA.

It is the same for all humans. It is why the others wont wake up, either. The codes are missing, and they do not think to question.

I say: I see the problems and I am at a loss. To me it is crystal clear that heart connection to LOVE keeps the dark at bay. The world is getting more aggressive and the hatred is rising. I see it happening, even in the groups who are concerned.

What is the true cause and what is the effect? Can you help us all to reach truth, the truth above all, because that is what we need, whether we like the truth or not, and it does hurt, which is why many turn their backs on truth.

It threatens their business, or their kudos, or their insecurities about themselves.

I would expect those in the Healing/Holistic Communities to want the truth above all and yet, I see the corruption — it is a pyramid system, a huge profit-making industry.

That has nothing to do with healing.

It is another false myth that so many cannot let go of. What are they so afraid of? Because they criticise the ones who got vaccinated who want to stay in denial, and yet, they are also in denial about their energy healing modalities being safe. People are in denial about high profile characters who are meant to be on humanity's side.

Many, simply, are Controlled Ops. They serve the Cult.

What are the solutions to all these issues, especially for those of us who are having our lives and our peace disturbed by other people's poor choices?

It is harming all precious life...

Denial...

Deny, refute, dismiss.

It is a pattern that is highly prevalent in humanity at present. Why? I have so many questions...

Please use your own heart discernment. I am guided that a large amount of information is coming in. Let your heart and LOVE be your guiding light. This is aimed at helping, but it may be distressing and so, if your heart advises you to stop listening here, then please do stop, and receive healing.

I am seeing a picture, a drawing, with light coloured areas, and I am seeing a figure stood on the left and a large group of souls sat at their feet and the figure is saying, "Suffer little children to come unto me, for their's is the Kingdom of Heaven," and I see a softly pink, coloured path inside what feels like a brightly lit warm cave and the path in the cave is a soft zig-zag carved out of the rock, and I am hearing;

"Claire, the soul harvest is underway. You cannot stop what is coming. You both sensed it today. Tell the others what you sensed."

I sensed fear. In the pit of my stomach. Deeply entrenched fear. I sensed they are starting something. Something 'big' is coming or has started. It will amplify the soul harvest.

I cannot perceive what is coming. I am not scared. I am afraid for the children and the animals, and nature, and all those who do not want to live like this, who are caught up in this hell on Earth."

A. *"Claire, there are a lot of souls coming into the place. They are being prepared, prior to departure."*

Q. What is this place, and are they safe?

It feels peaceful here. It is peaceful. Is this surrounded by LOVE and the Laws of Creation? I do not feel fear in this place. It feels restful, calm, tranquil. Where is it?

Each time I close my eyes and take them down to my heart, I see this place, the mouth of a cave to the centre and off right, at the back of the picture, the cave mouth is open and there are millions of souls on a really wide flat path walking towards the figure.and I hear:

"Claire, you cannot stop what is coming."

Q. Why did I see myself closing the door in that corridor and drawing an X and saying "ye shall not pass."

I am not religious and yet, it had a religious overtone to the words. Why was I seeing myself doing this? It felt like those who were behind the door harming the babies were being contained and imprisoned by their own actions to cause harm.

The babies in the sink in my heart vision - I could not see, I just knew they were harming these children beyond our ability to comprehend. I do not know what is coming but what can we do to protect the children, the newborns, the innocent.

"Claire, all prayers are heard and all are answered."

Q. I don't seem to be getting far. What question should I be asking now?

I hear,

"Prepare," and I hear more, too, and your heart will be telling you if you ask for the truth, above all things.

Q. How do we prepare? I ask

"Claire, we guide you to go gently from here on in. You have to trust that you all have the tools within you to hear truth - to follow the guidance and to act upon any heart messages as soon as you are guided.

Messages will always be peaceful, loving, and gentle. Those who drew the pictures of their perfect reality are helping to create a safe place for souls to exit the matrix and LOVE is overseeing all departures from here on in.There is nothing to fear.

Many souls are about the exit the planet. You do need to be prepared for that. Claire, you have to post this."

Q. It feels very hazy. I am uncertain about the guidance because I have not secured any details. Why is that?

"Claire, it is past the stage of no return. All free will choices have already been made. It is too late to stop what is coming because many simply did not want to listen, or address the areas where harm is happening.

You pay a huge price spiritually when you refuse to stop harming. It is game over for many, including those who continue to open their door to the destroyer forces and, thereby, expose all precious life on the planet.

It has imprisoned many. It is why you can't get through to many. They are lost in the programs of false light. It is too late.

There is always a time and a place when LOVE steps in to stop the chaos. The chaos will continue but not before the plans of LOVE move full-steam ahead, into action.

Q. Anything else to share here? I must admit I have struggled to hear but I can just glean the message.

The drawing, however, is clear in my mind, and I think someone drew this after hearing the message. I think it is their picture. It is a picture someone drew, and it has helped to create a window of opportunity for souls to leave along a safe pathway, ready for departure from this place.

This drawing - it makes me want to weep tears of relief. The energy is so pure. It is beautiful and calming. It feels so peaceful here. If this is what awaits these souls, then I am relieved because I have spent so much time worrying about all this, the children, the effects of the harm that has made things so dark on our planet.

Those words....

"Suffer little children to come unto me, for their's is the Kingdom of Heaven."

Pray for the world's children and the newborns.

Pray for them, and pray for their peace.

...

AUDIO LINK:
LOVES HEART PLAN, SUBSTACK.COM |
SEARCHING FOR THE EVIDENCE, BITCHUTE.COM
DEEPER TRUTHS CHANNEL,
@TRUELIGHTESSENCE, ODYSEE.COM

Chapter Ten

UNDERSTANDING CONSCIOUSNESS, 25 October 2023

"You are all at the stage when you need to be making choices: to stay in mind ignorance and cause death of the self, or to choose life and love and ask for help."

...

AUDIO LINK

...

Hello, my name is Claire, and I am about to share information and perceptions on consciousness: What it all means; what has been my perception of expansion of consciousness; how has it helped me to see the bigger picture that is unfolding on planet Earth? And why I do not fear death, or fear the dark mafia that are trying to take over humanity's consciousness?

Your consciousness is yours. It cannot be taken or stolen... Not unless you give it away.

So, what is consciousness? My perception is that consciousness is the art of being aware of the deeper truths surrounding 'happenings' on the Earth plane; the ability to access memory banks of data and Knowledge, and the ability to ask questions in order to hear Wisdom and an overview, from higher levels of awareness.

I do not think of it as hard, but in the beginning, it was difficult to keep a steady focus on my heart centre. That is where our consciousness is accessed.

It cannot be accessed by other means, not any more, and so, with the constant shifting of vibration on the planet, and the constant poor choices of humanity, which are giving away their 'consciousness' to a system of Artificial Intelligence, and Extra Terrestrial life forms, and the satanic crowd in politics, governments, pharmaceuticals and big corp., big banks, etc., it is becoming increasingly hard for anyone starting out to explore consciousness, to know how to do it safely, accurately, and with help from higher levels of awareness to ensure one reaches truth.

It is a complex issue - the method of navigation; the method of expanding consciousness in order to reach accurate information, honest data, clarity and direction in ways that best serve all precious life, not just the self.

And that is what I have been exploring for over thirteen years. I cannot have many conversations with friends about this part of me that is very important to me. It is the most important thing I have that guides me and steers me in the right direction.

Everything that I have learned about frequencies, consciousness, false light, the illusionary matrix of suffering that we find ourselves in, and the groups who are out to deliberately ensnare humanity is a story that unfolds every day, as I expand my consciousness through a simple heart connection, using a specific set of instructions which I have inwardly been taught to use, and I leave this place of Earth energy and go off exploring the Greater Cosmos.

Is this possible for everyone? It is an innate part of ourselves; like being able to talk, or see, or hear, it is a 'sense' within all humans and all life that enables each one of us to reach beyond limitation and reach for help; for ourselves, our loved ones and all precious life.

Why am I being asked to talk about consciousness today? The energy has lifted somewhat. Has someone else joined in with helping themselves and humanity through heart connection? I do feel someone or some others have helped today.

What would you like me to convey in this message today?

"Claire, talk about heart call."

I say, "Can you be more specific?"

"About the importance of asking your heart for help, why this is instrumental and why others need to understand that if you do not ask, your heart cannot help, and why that is."

Outside of the False Light Matrix; this illusion in which we find ourselves, there are laws that govern the whole of Creation. They are called by different names. I was taught by my heart to refer to them as 'The Cosmic Laws', or 'The Laws of Creation'.

These laws act as boundaries; to prevent harm being actioned by others that may harm the whole of Creation. The laws work to keep all souls safe and free; to use their free will choices to explore and create, and experience different aspects of Creation.

All life forms have free will and they all have aspects of their consciousness that are more greatly connected to the Heart of Creation from where I was taught, we all originate.

I was taught about free will and our greater aspect of self; the Infinite Self which should always be called upon for help, because the Infinite Self is also bound by these laws, and one of the laws is that it is against the law to interfere with the free will choices of another, no matter the consequences of those choices.

Therefore, the Infinite Self - the most 'aware' part of our consciousness that is fully connected to the Heart of Creation - needs our acquiescence before it can help us, and that requires our free will choice to ask our Infinite Self for help.

Once we ask, the help comes in. The Infinite Self surrounds and protects us, and I was taught to also be extremely specific about where I wanted to connect to because we are immersed in low, dense frequencies of hatred, fear, aggression, anger, sadness etc., and this makes it harder to send a message directly. Therefore, in order to 'hit the target' and ensure I reach the place I wish to connect to before I expand my consciousness, I always ask through my heart for help using specific requests.

My heart call involves me stilling my mind and focusing on my heart area, in my chest area.

I take my closed eyes down to the chest area and I keep my eyes looking softly downwards.

I only tend to do this while at home and for those who are new to this, it is important to get your own space clear and build up the protection that regular heart connection assists with.

What is a heart call, or heart connection? It simply means that while I am focusing my closed eyes down towards my chest area I see my inner heart as a doorway that leads me to a place of safety and to truth, and I see my heart as a conscious part of myself that is advanced and knowledgeable, that helps me to connect accurately to the heart of Creation.

Many years ago, I could clearly hear any guidance, I could see things like I was watching a film, all on an inner screen. Everything was much easier to perceive.

In recent times, the planet has dropped in density, meaning, it is harder to hear accurate guidance or see clearly on my inner screen, and in late

2010, I was guided that anyone who was expanding consciousness, working with energy healing, or connecting to energy and frequencies in any other way needed to change their method of connection because the Heart of Creation knew what was coming.

A few teachers had also received the same guidance and moved on to heart connection. They stopped their teaching practises and advised their students to start going within to get direction through their hearts. They were the few that listened.

Many healers and others connect to the Biofield. This is the part of their physical body that is unseen by most eyes, yet, it is a scientifically proven fact that we have an electrical field.

The problem with this is that many who are looking at the Biofield are unaware that there are twelve other areas above this Biofield, and very few have been working to perceive these other areas, which is a huge sadness because it is delaying the help that humanity and the children need right now.

Those who focus on the Biofield are like a scientist that has discovered fingers and think that the fingers hold all the answers without looking more closely to see what the fingers are attached to, and that there are actually arms, legs, a head and a whole body.

There are twelve levels of our human consciousness within the False Light Matrix. Starting at the very top, where the most knowledge is to be found is the Cosmic Field level or Galactic level.

The Cosmic Field at the Galactic level is a vast area of consciousness. It hold keys to doorways that lead to higher learning.

Below this Cosmic Field level is the Planetary level.

And down it goes, like floors in a lift, descending down to less and less knowledge, until you get to the very thin field of knowledge and protection, the Biofield level.

The attack on humanity's consciousness is taking place at the Cosmic

Level.

It seeps downwards, and eventually, if enough knowledge and codes of remembrance are stolen from the higher levels of awareness that are present in this False Light Matrix, the physical self will present with illness, disease and distortions in the Biofield and this attack at the Cosmic Field Level can lead to possible death if it is not addressed.

For those with cancer, the attack is so severe at the Cosmic Level that if a soul is unaware of the theft of large amounts of data and knowledge from the higher levels, how can a soul possibly defend itself or secure it's own life in the physical body?

I was guided by my Infinite Self and LOVE that cancer is a man-made disease and it should not be happening. It is happening because of the attack on humanity from every angle possible: POISONING OF FOOD, DRINK, AIR, AND METAPHYSICAL ATTACK AT THE COSMIC LEVEL.

I was guided that the frequencies of HOPE, FAITH and TRUST are powerful healing frequencies, and that if more requested help through their hearts for these frequencies to surround and protect them, that they would be supported.

My husband had stage four cancer last year, of the liver, spleen, and all lower organs. It was late stage, he was on death's door by the time he was diagnosed and he was given two months to live on palliative care. We both connect to our heart and to our higher consciousness daily, and regularly: throughout the day, and we used all our inner strength and connection to heart to seek guidance on best ways forward.

My husband was guided by his heart to take the chemotherapy but to ask for all food, drink, air, chemotherapy, blood samples, urine samples, biopsies and tests to all be surrounded and protected, purified and made harmless.

We took practical steps, too, such as buying an expensive fluoride and water filter.

However, I also fed my husband well on puddings and chocolate, along with organic meat, fruit, and vegetables because he was emaciated and extremely weak.

It was a very stressful time, however, this heart connection pulled us through, and my husband drew strength and courage from the guidance his heart gave him.

He was cleared of all cancer in November 2022. We know the risks of chemo, however, everyone is different and that is why heart connection is so important because your own heart knows exactly what is right for you and if you truly listen with a desire to help yourself and others, all assistance comes to you.

It is the Law of Creation.

Remember this, it is the Law that if you ask from a sincere place in your heart, you will get the help for your journey, whatever your destiny is.

I was guided that it was not my husband's destiny to die of cancer and because he had called for help each day for himself and for all life, because he let go of trying to control outcome, because he trusted that he was being helped either to die peacefully or to live, and he let go of what he could not control, his Hope, Faith, and Trust enabled him to receive the optimal assistance from LOVE.

I wish more in humanity understood how much help is out there.

A 'heart call' is simply a sincere effort to focus on your heart centre and make a free will choice to allow your heart to help you by saying something like, "Please can you help me?"

That is the first step.

However, help comes in more powerfully when the one 'gets out of the way' by allowing the mind to go quiet, to stop mentally processing what is happening and just allow the heart to lead the way.

This is the hardest part to expanding consciousness or exploring consciousness. The mind and ego get in the way, and it actually stops a human from hearing their heart.

Exploring consciousness is an 'experience to be had' that cannot be described, it has to be 'experienced' before the human realises that there is something in it.

And if a human has a mind that needs to process everything and put everything into neat little boxes, and has to justify everything by their own limited experience or beliefs of what is possible, then this limits expansion of consciousness.

I would say that most humans do not know how to trust in their innate ability to protect themselves, and let go of trying to control what will happen when they connect to their heart and Infinite Self.

Can expansion of consciousness be dangerous? It can if humans are in ego, or if they are trying to use it for self-serving reasons, or if they cannot follow simple instructions on how to do it safely.

However, humanity has already placed itself in extreme danger. It has already allowed vast amounts of life force and DNA codes of Knowledge to be stolen by the dark, and AI, and ET groups, and that is why we are experiencing chaos on the planet.

When others use consciousness to harm others, there used to be very few barriers to prevent them from harming all life here. However, this has changed, and recently, the Laws of Creation have fully arrived into this space and so now, you are seeing the cycle of magnified malicious harm, being returned to all those who maliciously harmed all life here.

And I hear,

"Claire was warned last year that those who harmed would start dropping like flies. Have you noticed how many newsreaders, sports personalities and journalists have started dropping like flies on TV?

This is the Laws of Creation at work, who have been called upon by those working earnestly with energy to help humanity, for all malicious, magnified harm to be returned to all those who maliciously harmed all life. There is a cut off approaching where it will be too late for those in the healing community, and those trying to awaken humanity to the truth from clearing up their own karmic cycles of harm.

All souls are here to clear up any harm they may have caused themselves, and not just from this lifetime, but from every time they have entered this place. There are timeline switches being made by the dark ones, and when these switches occur, it makes it impossible to clear up any cycles of harm, and it is why Claire had been advised to ask for all errors to be deleted for all those who could be assisted by Infinite LOVE and the Laws of Creation.

The request is said to help the voiceless and those who may not know that they have lost the ability to clear up any harm and to recall lost codes of Knowledge. Infinite LOVE and the Laws of Creation can set to work to help, where necessary, without infringing on the free will of all life. However, when souls have not given full consent because they have been deliberately tricked or harmed by dark forces, it is the Law that if enough souls see this and make requests for help, the LOVE will step in and help. So, many of you who are expanding consciousness are not only being called upon to ensure that your connection is strong and true, but also to ask you to keep using the prayer requests that Claire has shared, unless you are specifically guided otherwise, because your group effort powers up more assistance for all those souls who, through no fault of their own, have been left fragmented, defenceless and unprotected from attack by destroyer force energy. Your role is to keep asking how you can 'best serve all in optimal ways, in alignment with LOVE and the Laws of Creation', because this request secures the purest, optimal assistance for all precious life, while working within the boundaries of the Laws of Creation, and this keeps all souls safe.

It also keeps you safe. And it ensures that those who wish to help humanity

and all life on Earth, that you have a safe, direct, accurate route to truth, and to help from the place that will only provide loving assistance and guidance, because without accurate directions, you can go down false pathways of learning and that is what is happening to many on the Earth plane who have been misdirected in order to keep them from securing humanity and all life on Earth's brightest future.
Claire, can you talk about false pathways of learning?"

Expansion of consciousness via heart connection is the safest route I have experienced, and I have had many lessons along the way in order to understand why we can go off-kilter, and why many seem to be talking nonsense, but think they have connected to truth.
I was witnessing this many years ago and it has not changed. If anything, I think it is worse than ever.
People are practising healing methods that are outdated, and no longer work to help on any level. Once they get attuned to these modalities and start connecting to these distorted frequencies, they become addicted to the frequencies.
At the Biofield level, a doorway of acquiescence opens. The distorted frequencies contain dark energy which walks into the Biofield. It goes in a lift and presses floor Twelve and goes up to the Cosmic level, where it gets it's drill set out and starts creating holes in the Cosmic Field 'perimeter fence'. Codes of Knowledge are stolen from here. The person does not notice. They are busy looking at the Biofield, eleven floors below. They have never asked their heart to show them where the main attack takes place, or they have only been taught about the Biofield, and those who taught them have not known about the Cosmic Field level, and so, all are in blissful ignorance, which is why the dark attack there.
When the codes of Knowledge are stolen, the dark fill the empty

pockets with false light codes and false knowledge that is 'untrue' and 'inaccurate'. It also fills the pockets of the stolen DNA Knowledge with addictive frequencies that keep the person coming back for the healing modality's distorted frequencies.

No one knows. No one notices.

The codes of distorted light that have been allowed in by the person, steadily and stealthily start to penetrate other areas of the person's consciousness, and by the time someone advises them that their healing modality is flawed and causing harm to all, the healer is fuelled with vehement denial and hostility towards the human who told them the truth.

They turn their back on the truth and continue with their practises.

The teachers who train these students are equally, poorly trained. No one has explained to them that their own energy body, their consciousness at all twelve levels is flawed, as is the whole of humanity's.

They have not been trained how to perceive their own twelve decks of consciousness within the False Light Matrix, they are unaware of their existence, and so, they are unaware that the attack is taking place on their energy fields at the higher levels of awareness.

What happens when a person who cannot see their own energy fields - all twelve levels of consciousness, and who does not have the Knowledge to know how to clear the attack on their own consciousness? What happens when they attune another, or hold a meditation class or world peace group meditation? If their consciousness is not clear, if the students do not know how to protect their own twelve levels of awareness, what happens when they all open up their consciousness with each other and those who may join in a world meditation globally?

Do you think they are safe? Do they lose any codes of Knowledge? Does attack on their energy fields go full blast up to their Cosmic

Fields and downwards?

Why do you think humanity are exposed at present?

How many people are taking responsibility, as a whole, for their own twelve levels of awareness, and how many are protecting their own consciousness?

Why is humanity in this mess?

Have we all jointly let something dark into our family of humanity's consciousness?

Who are the biggest culprits?

Anyone who does not take responsibility for their twelve levels of awareness is responsible.

Especially, those who came in with more remembrance, who have squandered the codes of Knowledge that they brought in to secure humanity's rescue, and now, are under such heavy attack that those who are trying to awaken them are attacked, vilified and mocked.

And all the while, the dark are beheading babies, drinking their terrified, adrenochromed blood...

And so, at what point is 'the point of no return,' for these souls?

It is coming.

And I hear:

"All those who turn their backs on their own twelve levels of awareness, their own consciousness, are liable and are breaking the Laws of Creation, because when a soul chooses to ignore the guidance that an attack is ensuing, that it is ongoing and that it is going to get worse, and when a soul dismisses the information as 'poppycock', 'codswallop', then, that soul has broken a very serious law, and that law is that whenever information is presented to us that requires inner heart reflection and inner heart questioning, when a human decides, through ego controlled thinking; through their mind controlled mind to dismiss the information, and

when that information would save lives, and the decision to dismiss it is taken, the threat of death to other souls is worsened, and so, the laws state that to ignore guidance, to avoid asking heart or to refuse to ask heart in order to discern truth, carries the most serious penalties because LOVE gives life, and no soul has the right to end the life of another.
Ignorance, therefore, leads to death, or the threat of death to a soul who needed your help, and so, the law states that ignorance is one of the gravest errors and the penalty for this is death of the self.
The reason? Because to remain in a place where other souls require your heart felt concern, to dismiss their situation as unimportant, to see yourself as the centre of life as opposed to the centre of life being part of you, your ignorance has failed to see the truth, and that truth is, life leads to death when souls choose to save themselves and ignore the need by others to be saved.
It is a heinous crime and results in Karma, and this is not being issued by the Laws of Creation, in the sense, that outside of this reality selfishness does not exist, but the penalties for selfishness and ignorance is, death.
And that is what many are facing, even in the truth community and healing communities because many are wolves in sheep's clothing, and anyone who is profiting from others at this late stage of a planetary shift and the ending of the In Breath cycle are going to pay a heavy price for profiteering from the desperate situation that souls find themselves in."
Claire tell them what you are perceiving."

I am starting to question the doctors and scientists who are the leading voices in the truth community. So many use satanic symbols alongside their work. Many are selling products or pushing their books, and many have positioned themselves in a place whereby it seems they are no longer listening to other voices. I see many who have given their power away to energies and frequencies that I perceive as highly questionable, and I wonder, why don't those who see things through their consciousness, why are they not promoting self- enquiry through inner heart questioning?

If they aren't doing this? Why? Because my learning and inner questioning was always about securing the optimal help for all precious life in alignment with LOVE and the Laws of Creation, because we are all individuals and we all have higher levels of awareness to tap into, and so, why are others encouraging 'mystery schools' or groups, when all the answers are inside each one of us?

Why do they not share this vital teaching that would liberate many, and help many to stand on their own two feet and be sovereign, to make decisions that are fully aligned with LOVE?

Why?

"Claire, they are not here to help. It is a self- serving mission and one seeking recognition. The outcome of humanity swings in the balance as more give their power away to others, and no matter what side of the fence they are on, if you are giving your power away to any other being, you will lose vast amounts of Knowledge and codes which will be replaced with false light codes and which will hold you in this place, and make you the 'quarry' for those who like to hunt.

If you do not choose to be 'hunted', or 'quarry' for the destroyer forces, you need to focus on your own consciousness, on your twelve levels of awareness, and getting them clear of false light, and filled with purest light, and that is why Claire has been utilising the request to ask through her heart to her Infinite Self and Infinite LOVE to find all that has been lost and returned to Wholeness and returned to her in the form of purest light codes that cannot be infiltrated or corrupted by the dark or any other thing."

Claire this needs to go out now. People are starting to stir from their deep coma and need the guidance."

I say, "Can I ask. You guided me to write to someone recently. I am confused as to why. I am now uncertain of their goals. Are they trying to help humanity? I am starting to doubt their motives. Too many satanic symbols used in their work; the use of colour to heal, which is distorted; the mention of mystery schools which do not resonate for me...what is their true motive or agenda, and why was I asked to write to them?"

"Claire, they are being pulled in the wrong direction by those with an agenda. This person does not discern wisely enough, does not go deep enough, has not yet examined or discovered their twelve decks of awareness and therefore, is missing vital codes of Knowledge whilst having vital codes stolen and replaced with false light codes."

I ask,"What was the purpose of the message?"

"It was an attempt to try to steer them in the right direction."

"Did it work?"

"No, it failed."

I ask, "Why did it fail?"

"Because the desire for kudos supersedes the desire for truth."

"Any guidance for those of us who are starting to question this group?"

"Yes, Claire, the whole point of this discourse is to demonstrate to others that no matter how high you hold others in high esteem, you will never really solve the Earth's problems when you look outside of yourself to others who may appear to hold answers.

Your consciousness can rise above the twelve levels of awareness that are stuck inside this false light matrix.

Your mind cannot.

Therefore, if your higher levels of awareness and consciousness hold the solutions and the answers, why would you continue to listen to others outside of self? They do not hold the answers, but, your hearts do, and when a heart is willing to hear the truth above all, LOVE will escort that heart to beyond where the eye can see, to the Heart of Creation to secure the teachings that are held there, waiting for a soul with a heart and a care for others to make the request for help for all life.

You do not need intellect, academia, or degrees. You need a heart that is filled with love and concern for all life. When humanity overcomes this limited aspect of self - of the 'mind knows best' mentality - and starts to use heart, then, miracles happen, because miracles are simply: the sincere request for help to come - from those who care.

No matter who you are, you can do this.

No matter how scared you are, you can do this.

You are all at the stage when you need to be making choices: To stay in mind ignorance and cause death of the self, or to choose life and love, and ask for help.

The choice is yours, and yours alone."

...

Audio Link: Odysee.com:

Chapter Eleven

SOUL HARVEST, 26 OCTOBER 2023

Audio Link:

...

Hello, This is Claire. I was listening to yesterday's message today, as my heart had advised that more are listening and helping.

I had felt the energy drop at a certain point in the late morning and I had felt somewhat irritable. I recognise any low mood as an attack, either on my consciousness or, on the consciousness of humanity and all life on the planet as a whole. As I listened again to the message I perceived the strangest thing...I sensed a really dark, cloaked pirate type figure, as if it was an animation, and I perceived it climbing out of my computer. I had my eyes closed and I was not alarmed, however, I never let this type of thing go. The fact that my consciousness had given me this image meant something was wrong. It was a very dark energy.

I immediately and calmly connected again, to my True Power Switch, to my Infinite Self and Infinite LOVE at the Heart of Creation and infinitely beyond, and to the Laws of Creation to ask for help to protect me and to advise me why I had the image presented to me and what action best served all, in alignment with LOVE's plan and the Laws of Creation.

These teachings above are precious to me. They are very robust, and always help me to learn new things whilst protecting me from dark attack.

My heart and LOVE guided me to ask LOVE and the Laws of Creation to send this dark energy back to the dark black hole from which it has escaped.

I firstly asked if this request best served all life, in optimal ways, including this dark energy's, in alignment with LOVE's plan and the Laws of Creation.

I never jump in and take action without seeking further clarity about any requests that I am advised to make. All actions require a pause for discernment and clarification. Learning always follows this way.

I was guided that it did serve all life in optimal ways in alignment with LOVE's plan and the Laws of Creation. So, I pressed my True Power Switch and made the request for this dark energy to be sent back by LOVE and the Laws of Creation into the black hole of hell from which it had escaped.

I then asked what were my next steps to best serve all in optimal ways, in alignment with LOVE's plan and the Laws of Creation?

I was guided to carry on listening to yesterday's message: "Understanding Consciousness", and to seek the teachings, once I had finished.

This is to demonstrate how specific I am when I question my consciousness and seek clarity. I leave nothing to chance. I make my questioning watertight and incorruptible, to ensure I can hear accurate guidance.

I am not saying that I don't mishear guidance or that I am always right because we are humans living in a False Light Matrix, who are under a constant barrage of attack by destroyer force frequencies. However, I find this route offer's me the best method for securing accurate teachings, in the main.

If a topic is very serious, and perhaps, life threatening, for example, when I was helping my husband to secure accurate guidance on how to help himself through stage four cancer, then, it is prudent to take one's time to double, triple check the guidance, and to do it at different times and over the course of a few days, to ascertain all truth has been validated as best as possible.

We can all make mistakes. It is important to not overburden oneself with the responsibility to reach truth to the point of anxiety. The more relaxed and calm one can be and the more one hands over trust to the Infinite Self and LOVE whilst trusting the route to truth is watertight, then that is doing one's best.

You will never be penalised for sincerely trying to reach truth, and harm will never be caused to others if you make accidental errors because sincerity takes us to the truth, as does a desire to help others, in alignment with LOVE's plan and the Laws of Creation.

And so, this dark energy was lifted by LOVE and the Laws of Creation and sent back to the black hole of hell from where it had escaped.

My question to my heart and my Infinite Self, is:

What was the energy?

How had it escaped, and why was it appearing to climb out of my computer?

And why has the pitch in my ear shot up again today?

Yesterday, when I was recording "Understanding Consciousness", the pitch in my ear went sky-high. It was off-putting, but I asked my heart to send back all malicious harm because it did feel like a beam was being directed at me to stop me from recording.

My movie maker plays up. The recording was not very smooth. Is some kind of new attack happening?

"I have so many questions. Please can you help me hear Truth from the Heart of Creation so that I can share accurate guidance to help others?"

"Claire, the movie maker issue has been going on for some time. You do have interferences that are deliberately activated in order to slow you down."

"What is happening? Where is the pitch in my ear emanating from?"

"Claire it is deep space technology and linked to StarLink and Sky Net. It will not go away now that it has been allowed to go up."

"What question should I be asking now to best serve all in optimal ways, in alignment with LOVE's plan and the Laws of Creation?"

"Claire, it is all linked to StarLink, Sky Net, Neura Link and other off-worldly technologies that are aimed at humanity and planet Earth, and all in position now to do ultimate damage. Ask, why do you think we are sharing this message today, at this precise time?"

I ask, **"Why are you sharing this message at this precise date and time?"**

"Claire, because as more awaken, the dark elite start messing with the timelines, and once again, a timeline switch is upon you all.

We do need your help with this. You all have gifts tucked inside your treasure chest; your heart centre, and for those who sincerely care and wish to do the right thing to help humanity, you are all being called upon to connect via a safe route and ask LOVE and the Laws of Creation, via your Infinite Self, to unlock any gifts which you are carrying to assist to protect all precious life here.

We have previously explained that timeline switches have many purposes.

One purpose is that it starts to dilute Knowledge and Wisdom, and it starts to alter history, and the course of humanity's and all life's future.

It causes soul shock at deeper levels of consciousness, because the soul sees the tremendous damage that will ensue and for a pure part of yourselves to witness this monumental error, this breaking of the Laws of Creation which are respected and valued because they keep all safe, then, to see this happening...it is akin to you all knowing that the vaccines were going to kill people, having availed yourselves of the ingredients in advance, and the horror of knowing that if they started on the children, that the children would also die.

This is how your soul feels when it witnesses monumental errors and when done deliberately to cause harm, it causes fear at soul level and above, at the higher self levels and beyond, and this fear can start to weaken your ladder of consciousness, and once this occurs you are fair game for those who like to hunt, because the dark walk in and start to take your consciousness and replace it with False Light codes.

Higher levels of awareness see this and perceive the bigger picture of the great harm that this will do, and your ladder of awareness higher up despairs at humanity's personality self, the self that never checks their ladder of consciousness or calls on LOVE to surround and protect it. So many aspects of you get harmed by yourself.

So, it is not so much what the dark do to you, it what the dark manipulate you into not doing to help yourself - to protect your consciousness and highly regarded codes of Knowledge.

It is akin to selling your fingers and toes, and to keep chopping off body parts to sling in the dark's direction, without ever questioning the sanity of your poor choices to do absolutely nothing to protect yourselves.

This group of idiots who are harming you, lack Knowledge. It is why they are constantly stealing it from your consciousness.

At what stage is the penny going to drop, and humanity realise that they are powerful, creative beings from the Heart of Creation and all they need to do is call on LOVE and the Laws of Creation for help?

How hard can this be? And yet, it is hard for many to do.

And why is that, you may be wondering? Because the less a human does to help themselves the more of their consciousness is stolen, and the more their codes of Knowledge are replaced by the thieves with False Light codes, and codes that ensure humans are disinterested in finding out how to deal with the war on their consciousness. And it is a war on your consciousness. This is the true cause of all humanity's troubles. The war for your consciousness.And you not only have a group attacking you all, you have groups who are fighting to gain your consciousness before the other groups get to you. This is a war for your spirit. A war for your soul. And the more you remain sitting on the sidelines, watching the show, and scoffing at those who are trying to tell you that you are in danger, your family and pets are in danger, all life is under threat of extinction, but not before they have cut off every bit of you that remained attached to the heart of Creation.

Oh yes. They want those bits, those are the juiciest, most priced 'bits' of you that they want to own, and hunt, and dismantle, and rape and pillage all of your true nature. Your beauty, as a spirit, and the vibrance of your soul...they want all of it and this is the timeline switch attempt of all timeline switch attempts, to have the ultimate of these prized possessions and to undervalue everything that you hold dear. It will be gone - replaced with False Light codes of remembrance, and finally, they will be gone too. You will be nothing and you will be happy because you will have no identity, no soul, no knowledge of your past, present or future.

This timeline switch is the one planned to finish you all off for good."

I say: "I thought LOVE had stepped in to prevent any more timeline switches? How can the dark ones be planning this and how are they able to do it?"

"Claire, you recall the occasions when you put out a call for urgent assistance and the call was answered?"

"Yes."

"Do you recall LOVE advising all that a firewall needed to be built and maintained around the children and all life in order to keep all safe?"

"Yes."

"Claire, not many hold firm when it comes to longevity. They all have False Light codes that keep taking them off-track. The firewall did not hold as strongly as required.

This means: the dark were able to attack and what do they do? They steal consciousness because your consciousness contains the Knowledge that they lack. We referred to them as idiots, not through mean spiritedness, we are trying to draw a clearer picture of your enemy - the ones who are attacking you and who are warring for your consciousness.

We do not use the word 'enemy' because no life form is an 'enemy', however, in the context of this war, we refer to them as your 'enemy' because they are attacking you and harming you, and you are not putting up sufficient levels of assistance to defend and protect.

All that is required, in truth, is a simple call from your heart - to ask your Infinite Self and LOVE, and the Laws of Creation to help you. Why is this so difficult to request?

And there is the cycle repeating itself. Those who do not ask, lack vital codes of remembrance that would drive them to ask and to maintain the firewall.

So, the dark have stolen more of your energy, your DNA, your consciousness and Knowledge, and they have set to work.

The one thing this group do have is determination, and that is because they cannot exist without your consciousness to live off. They are like drug addicts who crave their next 'fix'. This is life or death to them.

What humanity have not realised is that this is life or death to your very selves. If you keep opening your door to this group, they will strip everything that is your life and steal it.

This results in death.

While they are stealing life force, and if a human is making other errors, the risk of death can be speeded up by making poor choices which harm others, such as, dismissing expansion of consciousness as 'poppycock' or 'self hypnosis', and that is the mind-control technology that is already working in the pockets of stolen consciousness inside your ladder of awareness.

Don't you think it is sad that humanity has the power to use their inner might to deal with this group who are powerless without your acquiescence, and yet, are in the process of destroying your beautiful planet and have infiltrated every system, which they are also destroying?

How bad does it have to get before you decide to put a halt to it?

Why, on Earth, have you all allowed it to get so bad, when you have the ultimate power and authority to call on LOVE for help?

Look around you at the suffering and question, why have you waited so long to do something to stop this suffering?

Because, people are dead now, and babies are dead, and no one had to die.

It was not their destiny.

This has occurred because of making poor choices that best harms all life, and it has not best served all in optimal ways, nor have the Laws of Creation been utilised, and LOVE's plan is being continually sabotaged by these poor choices.

Claire, we did warn that the biggest soul harvest is upon you all and it has started. There are many facets and factors to consider that go into the melting pot of damaging harm, drummed up by destroyer force frequencies. We wish you all to focus today on your gifts and whether you truly wish to help and remain vigilant to helping, to prevent further timeline switches, because if you feel you may not be able to commit, it is best to stop the recording now and move on to having healing and repair.

It could do more harm than good if you do not feel strong enough or determined enough to last the distance. And so, we are asking all of you to consider how committed you are to regular daily connection to your heart and your consciousness, because humanity is reliant upon you keeping your promise to ask each day for their protection, not just your own.

The regular requests maintain a strong firewall. When others lose interest, the firewall weakens, and in walk the dark; to steal your consciousness. Not only that, those that you were helping to protect, through your regular requests for their protection, will be harmed immeasurably at higher levels of awareness, because these parts of them can fragment when they witness the protection failing.

When you commit, you all have a great duty and responsibility to helping, because it protects all precious life, and that is why expanding consciousness and working diligently with your Infinite Self, LOVE, and the Laws of Creation carry this extra responsibility; to ensure all are kept safe at all times.

It is the Law, and for those who wish to move out of density, and into higher levels of awareness, the laws work very quickly on any soul who misuses energy in ways that could have devastating effects elsewhere.

We are impressing this upon you because the attack is so severe and what is planned is so severe that we need you to ask your Infinite Self for guidance before you step forwards to assist.

Pause the recording here and follow all guidance from your Infinite Self, and remember, if you are advised that you are not yet ready for this responsibility, there is no judgment.

The aim of this line of inner questioning is to keep all safe at all times, including your very selves...

For now we will continue:

Claire will share her routine with you. If you have a robust routine that takes you to the same place, then use what feels natural and what your Infinite Self has directed you to use.

For those who follow a religious path, a heartfelt prayer to ask for LOVE's/ the God of LOVE's plan and the Laws of Creation to hold you in LOVE's embrace will take you there.

If you are new to all of this and have had the inner direction to help, then perhaps this routine may offer you direction?

Ask your Infinite Self for guidance on your best route to Truth."

I say: "Here we go:

I lie down, flat on my back, on the bed that I sleep in at night, at home, having set an alarm in case I fall asleep, and placed a glass of water nearby.

I have ensured that I am not in bright sunlight and the room is sufficiently shaded to ensure relaxation and inner heart connection.

I have asked my loved ones to allow me some time to remain undisturbed and this room is empty of technology, save the one playing this message.

I relax on the bed, and if it is safe to do so, I close my eyes, placing my palms flat, facing down, and resting them on the tops of my thighs.

I take my closed eyes and gently look down towards my chest area.

I keep my eyes focused down there and I become aware of the rise and fall of my chest. I have made a decision that I wish to help with LOVE's plan,

I am prepared to take action each day to connect to my heart AM, PM, and midway through my day; to connect through my Infinite Self and my consciousness to Infinite LOVE and the Laws of Creation at the Heart of Creation and infinitely beyond.

With that intention, I imagine I am pressing a switch in the centre of my chest, my True POWER Switch, which has been set up by LOVE to provide a powerful, accurate and direct route to Truth. I relax, I focus on heart area, with my closed eyes, softly looking downwards and I allow peace and tranquility to wash over me.

I hold no expectation. I move my natural desire to 'guess' what will happen, to one side.

My closed eyes keep looking towards my chest area, and that helps me leave the mental processes of mind. I focus on my heart and allow things to unfold.

My choice to help stems from somewhere deep within me.

I do not know how or what it is, but ever since I was told that humanity was in danger and that harm was planned that could be prevented, over thirteen years ago, I have felt compelled to keep sowing seeds, to keep sharing information, and there are many like me, silent small voices, trying to be heard above the noise of other's egos, or desire for kudos, or profit or recognition.

And these voices who shout the loudest are not necessarily the voices offering the best solutions for all, and they are not necessarily fully committed to serving others.

For many, it appears to me, that many are serving self under the guise of 'concern'.

"I ask Infinite Self, LOVE's plan and the Laws of Creation to help me ensure that I serve LOVE's plan and abide by the laws that keep all precious life safe and at peace, and I ask, how can I best serve all in optimal ways, in alignment with LOVE's plan and the Laws of Creation?

What can I do to help with the timeline switch?"

And I hear: *"Claire, ask those who wish to best serve all in optimal ways in alignment with LOVE's plan and the Laws of Creation to open the chest that they see in front of them.*

If they cannot see, they may perceive it or feel it, or they can pretend that they have a chest. Creativity and imagination are all key here.

Pause the recording as we go through this and allow yourselves all time to do this in a way which is relaxing and easy.

If you keep your closed eyes softly looking down towards your chest area, you leave the mind control and the focus on your heart area will make things easier.

Please <u>do not look</u> through your third eye.

The third eye was sabotaged and blocked by False Light frequencies a long time ago. It will show you false truths and is not to be used under any circumstances.

Keep your eyes softly focused on the rise and fall of your chest and imagine that inside your chest your imagination can go and inside your heart you can imagine that you are in a very safe place surrounded by LOVE's embrace, and the Laws of Creation and your safety is overseen primarily by your Infinite Self who you have requested to be present, so you are in a very watertight and safe place.

Anything that happens here is for your learning. Anything presented to you requires your inner questioning. Keep going and you will always secure deeper understanding and deeper teachings.

What has you heart shown you from this treasure chest of yours?

Remember to keep pausing the recording to give yourself lots of time to relax and learn in an unpressurised environment.

By now you hopefully will have been shown something and you are now going to ask your Infinite Self and Infinite LOVE, how are you to use it in alignment with the Laws of Creation to best serve all in optimal ways?

Let your heart show you.

We will allow 2 minutes.

2 minutes are now complete.

Pause the recording if you need more time.

We will continue by thanking your Infinite Self for helping you today.

Close the treasure chest and come back each day now to do this routine because each day will be different and if you ask lots of questions, you will be assisted.

If you are stuck on what to do or say, you can simply ask: what question should I be asking now, or what do I do next?

Your Infinite Self will show you the way.

Fear nothing as you go about your day. You are connected to the most powerful force and protector in existence. The more you connect to this powerful protector, the stronger you will feel and the less attack you will suffer from, because this connection to your Infinite Self and the heart of Creation, start to work on you each day to ensure your safety and to help you best serve all life.

If you need help with any issues or problems, this is where you need to go to effect positive, peaceful change. Seek all direction within, even for the most practical issues, because your heart can guide you where to go or who to ask for help. It has the greater picture and it understands what is happening on the Earth Plane and Claire is now going to move on with the message we have to share today, so relax and bathe in peaceful frequencies while she continues to share today's information.

Claire, the attack by StarLink, Sky Net, Neuralink is hotting up. They are engaged in a multi-level war; in space, land, air and sea.

The war for the planet rages on, unnoticed by a sleeping humanity."

I say, **"What questions should I be asking? I have so many, I don't know where you wish me to start?"**

"Claire, worry not, we will give the full discourse now. The individuals who wish to help humanity need to understand that the war for consciousness is reaching a desperate conclusion.

Many in humanity are unaware that a huge cycle of creation is inwardly expanding. The 'In Breath' is the drawing in of all of Creation that has been out exploring for millennia, in Earth terms, and the Creative cycle is at a close.

All is drawn back towards the heart of Creation, which is preparing to expand.

All life forms are recalled from all areas of the Greater Cosmos, and this is how Creation expands and evolves. All cycles of learning are collected and shared, and this helps with the next cycle of learning. The next big 'Out Breath' cycle of Creation is knocking at your door.

The issues lie in the fact that you are all in a False Light Matrix, and this False Light Matrix is collapsing in on itself, because when an In Breath is nearing completion, there is a quickening of every aspect of reality.

Lessons need to be learned and healing of any errors need to take place. But, in a False Light Construct, this becomes impossible at times because the dark have ensnared many life forms, and the dark forces are desperate for fuel which they plan to steal and contain, and recycle in such a way that they think they will maintain their existence away from the Heart of Creation without ever having to repair their own errors, or return to their true origins.

The plan for their immortality involves imprisoning your data banks of Knowledge and keeping your digital twin, in Avatar world, as their new power source.

They think they have found a way. It will not transpire as they have planned yet, in the meantime they are doing a lot of damage to innocent life who have become trapped herein, and your role in being here was to help these souls see:

that they were trapped and,

that if they called on LOVE for help, they could secure their own rescue.

That was your role here: to highlight the issues and to secure their data by calling on LOVE to protect them. It has to be a soul choice — a free will choice — and the personality self needed to be asking too, in order to save themselves and their ladder of consciousness, because that ladder of Knowledge is like 'gold' to the dark ones.

Without your data banks of Knowledge, their plan cannot succeed, at least that is what they think, but it will fail anyway, however, not before they have stolen vast amounts of data and if the personality self refuses to look at this issue and call on LOVE to intercede to prevent this from happening then, the outcome will be death of the self.

Why death of the self, you may ask?

Because a personality self has to make the free will choice to ask for rescue. They are their own rescue party. No one can save them if they choose to ignore the guidance, however, how many of you know anyone who acknowledges that they are in the end cycle of an In Breath; about to be recalled back to the Heart of Creation with all that was lost, found, and all errors that were made; healed and repaired?

How many will balk at this guidance?

And do you see the cycle of harm that the theft of life force codes has had upon the ladder of consciousness?

The False Light codes cause the person to balk at the suggestion that they need to request rescue or face death.

Who will listen?

Who cares? Not many, because they are so immersed in the False Light Construct, and that is where you all come in because we have repeatedly said that when enough start to climb their ladder of consciousness along a safe and protected pathway, when enough start the process of asking LOVE for help, they start to expand their light, and as they ask ***'for all that has been lost to be found and returned as purest light codes that can never be corrupted by the dark',*** *a miracle is in the making.*

A planetary shift is taking place.

Humanity are not in position, nor are they prepared for departure.

No soul can exit this False Light Construct if it has not shown worthy cause to wish to exit the program, meaning, if it has not asked for rescue or shown interest in securing its own rescue. No life form can continue on its journey of evolution if it fails to request exit from this False Light Construct, and therefore, the choice to remain here will result in death.

Death of the self.

And if the soul has fragmented to such a degree as to not know it can call for rescue, the dark forces gather up all these remnants and assist in the destruction of whatever was life, and it results in death.

The soul harvest has started. It is upon you all, as a family of humanity. Many will choose to remain here, simply because they are filled with

False Light codes that prevent them from knowing LOVE exists and that LOVE is waiting for them to call for help.

The soul harvest is being witnessed at home and abroad. The wars are raging. The hostility is rising, and the floods and earthquakes keep on coming. Fires rage, buildings burn, lives are lost and homes are lost forever, and yet, even while the flames are burning, little miracles are happening because all those frightened voices who called for help were heard by LOVE, and when LOVE is powered by many frightened voices, when others who recognise they have the authority and ability to call on LOVE for the innocent and the voiceless, miracles happen, because what the dark can never take away from all precious life is their ability to ask for help.

Each voice that requests help makes the call for the millions who cannot, and so your voice — your powerful voice — can call for help and yet, millions upon millions of tiny frightened voices are joined in unison, and what became a throng of a few, starts to gather speed and we are telling you, humanity, you have the power within you to end all this and if we could ask one thing of you all, it is to have the courage to be the most powerful, authoritative voice and to be bold — to courageously shout from the rooftops what you hear your heart calling you to do.

This is not the time to be silent.

This is the time to shout and ring the bells of alarm, because this soul harvest will take many souls, unless you make your voice heard at the Heart of Creation and through your truth.

And that truth is what?

What is your truth?

Where are you from and where are you planning to go next?

Because the Out Breath is preparing.

The In Breath is quickening.

The False Light Construct is collapsing in on itself and humanity are still immersed in the illusion that this is normal — this world that the dark have made you create.

So many are immersed in this life, they do not perceive what others can see.

You cannot interfere with the free will choices of others, yet, you can still shout from the rooftops that their world is collapsing and that they need to make a choice now before it is too late.

The soul harvest will become apparent for all with eyes to see and hearts that hear.

Make no mistake, it is knocking at humanity's door."

Chapter Twelve

LION'S GATE: GATES OF HELL HAVE OPENED; 'THE LIVING DEAD'

Audio Link: Lion's Gate/Gates of Hell Have Opened - 'The Living Dead': Dark Matter, Feasting On Children And The Innocent. —Can You Help?— 28 OCTOBER 2023

Q. How can I best serve all in optimal ways, in alignment with LOVE's plan and the Laws of Creation? And who is this message for?

"Claire, this message is for the targeted groups, those who wish to help themselves, and for humanity as a whole, because your whole family of humanity is being lulled into another false sense of security as the dreaded 'night of the dead' creeps nearer."

Q. What do you wish me to share here today?

"That you are all being targeted and led down a pathway to suffering, unless you take immediate action to protect your ladder of consciousness.

The children are at the biggest risk, along with those who encourage them to participate in satanic ritual, dressed up as 'entertainment'. You follow that with the Bonfire night, or Guy Fawkes night; another satanic ritual that engages folk in participating in the ritualistic burning of a human body, and follow it with the '11.11.' ritual date, followed quickly by, 'satanic December', under the guise of 'Christmas', and that moves swiftly into January, when the Lion's Gate closes."

Q. "The Lion's Gate?" I ask.

"The gates of Hell - they open wide from October through to January."

Q. "Is that why the Lion's head is seen on Royal insignia and on other paraphernalia across the world?" I ask.

"Claire, the Lion's Gate refers to the black hole we have already shared with the listener about, and the gates of Hell refers to this black hole which is opened up at strategic times, however, this opening is the beginning of the end, for many souls.

This one will produce the biggest soul harvest for the dark ones. They have planned for this for a very long time. The technologies that are up in space now, are so advanced. They are constructed out of your family of humanity's stolen consciousness; their life force energy; DNA codes, and also known as, your Knowledge and Wisdom, which have been handed over to the dark ones by humanity's poor choices.

All this effort on humanity's behalf has created the Black Hole of Hell — Avatar World — the world where those who go there will end up 'owning nothing and being happy', whilst being hunted over, and over, and over again, by those who like to maim and kill, and hunt and beat, and harm, relentlessly, but don't worry, you will be happy, as you go where Klaus wishes you to go.

The gates of Hell opened, recently. Claire, please convey your experiences, recently."

I was connecting to my heart and consciousness the other day and when my eyes were closed my consciousness showed me a picture on my inner heart screen of a very dark energy - a darkly dressed and cloaked pirate-type figure attempting to climb out of my computer.

I sought the inner guidance, and was inwardly advised to ask LOVE and the Laws of Creation **"to send this dark energy back into the black hole from where it had materialised."**

This morning, I sensed a dark energy around my husband, at least, it was trying to get to him, but couldn't. It was seen on my inner heart screen whilst I was connecting inwardly to my heart and my consciousness, using a robust connection routine to the heart of Creation, and I sensed it was a female, ghost-type energy. It was creepy. I followed the inner heart advice to **"call on LOVE and ask for LOVE and the Laws of Creation to send this energy back into the black hole"** as it had also come from there.

My husband woke up just after I had done this. We connected together, to seek further guidance and deeper teachings, and we utilised the help from my previous podcast recording, "Soul Harvest."

I wish I did not have to be making these recordings because it signifies that humanity is not helping itself, and is still being tricked into taking part in satanic rituals, under the guise of 'family fun' and 'entertainment'.

We were guided that the black hole energies have been activated by the advanced technologies that are now in space and fully operational. At this time of year, very dark doorways that should be left shut are opened by satanic rituals, satanic worshippers, the elites, and ET groups, and Artificial Intelligence via higher technologies (which are created out of our stolen consciousness), and when this is coupled with humanity's activities and acquiescence, such as Halloween and

Bonfire night celebrations, more of our consciousness can be stolen to weaponise against us, and to act as the food that keep all dark energies alive, and it means that all those who do not protect themselves will get attacked by dark matter; that emanates out of the black hole: The Lion's Gate, or gates of Hell.

When these gates open, the dark matter that got sucked into the black hole, which contains all the evil actions and wrongdoings that have never been repaired, healed, or called back to remedy and which lack any light or life force as a consequence — this dark matter is released from the gates of hell.

It is why it is known as the **"Night Of The Living Dead."**

This energy is 'hungry' for food, and that food comes in the form of sustenance from unprotected humans, animals, innocent children and babies, and souls who are sick, vulnerable, ill, or in a weakened state.

This is why we are being warned that the biggest soul harvest to end all soul harvests is knocking at humanity's door.

How does this energy manage to get into this reality?

Ritual; repetitive behaviours; poor choices of humanity to neglect looking after their consciousness and their life force energy.

Human behaviour led to ignorant participation in satanic ritual, such as, Guy Fawkes Night and Halloween.

Who is its prime target audience?

The children.

If you have children, the worse thing you can do is get them involved in this satanic ritual of dressing up as ghouls, witches, skull and bones, or headless monsters, etc.

Their participation and your agreement to allow this, is the key that opens the doors of your children's consciousness and life force, to become the 'fuel source' for these energy vampires.

It is a mass feeding frenzy. Nothing more. It is akin to placing one's child on an altar and handing the devil a knife. Why do others participate? Ignorance of the true intentions of these rituals.

Getting you to participate are tricks played on you — to gain your acquiescence, so that the dark entities can walk in, to treat themselves by gorging on your children's life force energy and consciousness.

"Claire, we will take over the reins from here. The very act of participation is enough to open your gateways up to loss of life force. When this is done en masse, as it is in October, early November, 11.11, Christmas and New Year, then these are frequent points of entry for the dark destroyer forces. They rampage through your 'Castle and Moat' that Claire had taught you to defend, and it is a complete 'tear down' of all the good work you may have done at other times.

The dark elite have brought in re-enforcements, in order to secure the maximum 'soul harvest spectacular', and believe us when we say, (and this is not to cause fear, this is being emphasised in order for you all to understand), that you simply, can no longer afford to be slap-dash with your heart connection routine, or your daily prayer routine — however you normally connect to LOVE, it has to be watertight, now, and highly robust at defending yourselves against this attack.

The Heart of Creation is here for you to ensure you are protected, but as Claire has already explained many times, you have to use your free will by asking for help, because neither the Heart of Creation and your Infinite Self, LOVE, or the Laws of Creation have the authority to interfere with your choices.

Therefore, if you want the help you have to ask each time, and that means using a request method each day: Morning; upon awakening, evening; before sleep, and midway through the day even if it is for a few short minutes. You need to keep up the protection now.

We have guided that if you work, then you can ask your Infinite Self and LOVE for quick methods to connect during work time schedules. However, you can always squeeze things in during loo breaks, before you leave the car, when you get back in the car... there are always work arounds, and you need to secure them now, if you want the protection.

Your request starts it off and so, if you don't find time to ask for yourself, LOVE cannot interfere.

If you forget to help yourself, you will start losing vast amounts of life force. Why are we saying this?

Because the destroyer forces have all their technology in place now, to cause maximum harm, and we wish you to ensure you have called in help, so that the Heart of Creation can give you the maximum protection. It does not require fear based motivation to do this. It needs to come from a deep space of love for yourself and your own spiritual and emotional wellbeing, alongside physical and mental wellbeing.

We are attempting to impress upon you all that when the Lion's Gate opens, the level of attack on humanity and all precious life is tripled.

These dark, dead energies, and dark matter have no place in your reality. They have found their way in through satanic ritual, through humanity's acquiescence and through the nano-technologies, alongside the space technologies.

The nano-technologies that came in the vaccines have taken over authority of the physical self, and for many who acquiesced to the False Light vaccines, they have allowed False Light to go straight into the body, directly inside the vessel that contains their spirit in the physical realm, and so, it has been a 'walk in the park' for the dark matter in the black hole - the gates of Hell - to walk right inside your 'Castle'. It did not matter if your drawbridge was up. The nanotechnology was already inside your Castle walls. You let it in via a different doorway.

If humanity wishes to seek the help to get this nanotechnology out of their 'Castle and Moat' space, they will have to work three times as hard — to ensure their Infinite Self and LOVE, and the Laws of Creation can clear it— unhindered by faulty practices; slip ups; irregular spiritual hygiene methods; intermittent prayers, or whatever method you are using which is providing you with a robust method of moving past all restrictions of your twelve levels of consciousness, and moving to the Heart of Creation to get the assistance. No method on Earth can resolve this. We have repeatedly said that this is a spiritual war: a war for your consciousness.

If you wish for your consciousness to be cleared of dark matter and dark attack, it requires three times daily connection, at least, spaced out, as described earlier.

What about the children, you may be wondering? How does this affect the children? We are sorry to advise you that it does not bode well for the children.

They are innocent bystanders in all this. They are not fully aware, and therefore, they are being encouraged to do things by adults who themselves are unaware of the harm these rituals create.

*In **"A Race Against Time"**, we explained what happens to the children when their life force is stolen. The children gave a message to Claire which was very moving and deeply upsetting to hear.*

The children explained that they have "had enough," on a spiritual level: they are fragmenting and losing soul fragments at an alarming rate, owing to humanity's free will choices to participate in vaccine programs, permitting radiation and Wi-Fi in schools, and other poor choices, which are all having a detrimental effect on children at all levels of their consciousness.

The children coming in today, and those under twelve years old, all came in at this stage because humanity was in a terrible mess and had lost many opportunities to resolve issues which were well within their spiritual remit to resolve.

We have explained that Yoga participants collapsed the Planetary Grids and Reiki participants collapsed the Galactic Grids. These are the top levels of consciousness of humanity, that are trapped inside the False Light Construct. The collapse of these grids have ensnared more life forms who could not progress onwards on their evolution, and they became trapped inside the False Light Construct without an exit route.

This meant that all those souls who were trapped, got attacked by dark, destroyer forces who stripped these souls of their life force and consciousness, and fed off it, and used other codes of stolen data to attack humanity with, in the form of higher technological weapons. Star Link, Sky Net and Neuralink are the result of these stolen codes being 'weaponised' against humanity.

The children who came in during the last decade in the main have come because many in the aforementioned groups of Yoga and Reiki, had come in with more light codes of Knowledge. They had squandered the codes of Knowledge and this meant humanity was left completely exposed, especially with two, fundamentally vital grids of higher Knowledge, collapsed.

These brave souls coming in now and in recent years, are carrying the codes that the Yoga and Reiki participants squandered; through outdated practices, which left their consciousness unprotected. It is why their codes were stolen, and more is explained in detail in other discourses.

So, the children are here because of this wastage. They have come in at great risk to their own evolution. They have been vaccinated with nanotech. They are sitting in radiation hot spots at school. They are encouraged to participate in satanic ritual, dressed up as 'entertainment'.

They were forced to wear masks, which are inadvisable on all levels of well being, and especially, spiritually because the dark need acquiescence and they need children to be used to adults wearing masks, because the satanic rituals that will take place over Halloween are being used to also get your children used to satanic masking of the faces by those who like to abuse the children. This is all about abuse at the end of the day, whether humanity wish to see it that way, or not.

You have a World Economic Forum and town councils who are gearing up for 15 minute cities and villages. This is the 'trojan horse' for what is planned as child trafficking routes, which can remain hidden from view, but this is all in the planning by those who like to hunt, maim, and kill.

Humanity has no idea what they are truly up against, and for some, they choose not to look. But many who read this, know this is indeed, true.

Your governments and town councils all serve the World Economic Forum and United Nations, and they bang to the beat of the drum of these organisations. This group hold a large part of themselves separate from humanity. They see themselves as 'better than', and above questioning. They are the ones who see them as 'entitled'; the elites; the 'Royal class' who are above you, and if they can get your children to learn to acquiesce to their demands, it will not be long before pedophilia is made legal and lawful, because so many in this group like children for breakfast, lunch, and dinner.

Many in this group serve Satan and serve their masters. And they have many in society who will do their bidding.

This is frightening, isn't it? It is also true, and everyone reading this would do well to start connecting to their own heart and Infinite Selves to secure the truth of all that we share here.

It is coming...the pedophile agenda. They are testing the waters for your reactions at present, and yet, in California and various countries in Europe, child abuse is legal. When you steal large amounts of an innocent child's life force, how much needs to get lost before the child becomes full of False Light codes, instead of purest light codes of Knowledge?

In "Understanding Consciousness," it was explained how False Light codes are used to replace Truth, and Knowledge, and Remembrance of one's true origins. How much needs to be lost before a child does not recall itself, before a child acquiesces to abuse because it no longer knows how to call for help?

Can you, in good conscience, stand by and do nothing to protect these innocents? We are asking you all to connect deeply within, to seek deeper teachings on all that Claire is sharing here, and to secure help for the children, the innocent participants of this very dark and sinister game, because we have repeatedly told you that the biggest soul harvest is knocking at your door due to the timeline switch.

Despite requesting assistance for help to prevent this, the dark succeeded and it is another reason why this dark matter is escaping from its lair and walking into this reality.

If you want to stop this, there is no time like the present. Claire, that is all. This needs to go as soon as possible."

"Can I ask: what about the animals and other precious life that must also get harmed by the escaping dark matter walking into this reality?

People are promoting Halloween everywhere. We went to a beautiful bird sanctuary recently. They are promoting it there. I think about the poor birds and wild life...this special, peaceful place: being sabotaged by the 'dark matter' black hole energy being stomped in by walkers, and I worry about those who are vulnerable who come here for peace and tranquility, and I feel despair at the harm being done at hidden levels of awareness, but done, none-the-less.

How can we protect the innocent, the vulnerable, sick, and elderly, as well as the children and all precious, innocent life forms such as the otters, birds, insects, and nature?"

"Claire, ask those with hearts that care and eyes that see how dark and deep the harm can go, to seek the teachings and requests that can be made to LOVE and the heart of Creation, that are in alignment with the Laws of Creation. Everyone must be connecting to heart and inwardly considering what they can ask for and how they can best serve all. That is all Claire.

This must go as soon as possible, to reach those who may wish to assist."

UNDERSTANDING CONSCIOUSNESS, 25 OCTOBER 2023

https://www.bitchute.com/video/3cATvoUrIFxA/

SOUL HARVEST, 26 OCTOBER 2023

https://www.bitchute.com/video/9XqOjzaAvXPh/

HOW TO AVOID A SOUL HARVEST

https://www.bitchute.com/video/jkjKrh5icWAJ/

YOUR COSMIC SHIELD: DEFEND YOURSELVES AGAINST ELECTROMAGNETIC AND ELECTROPLATONIC ATTACK | 13 AUGUST 2023

https://www.bitchute.com/video/szz495pFkul5/

HELP FOR HUMANITY - 18 JULY 2023

https://www.bitchute.com/video/COPkNuixzly3/

RELAXATION AUDIO (GOOD FOR BEGINNERS)

https://odysee.com/@TrueLightEssence:d/RELAXATION-AUDIO:b

AN EMPTY VESSEL

https://www.bitchute.com/video/YEIlth0LcA6P/

A RACE AGAINST TIME | A MESSAGE FROM THE CHILDREN'S SOUL FAMILY - "SECURE OUR BRIGHTEST FUTURE" 6 April 2023 |

https://www.bitchute.com/video/QcUc7PB4d9Di/

UNDERSTANDING COSMIC LAW | StarLink KILL-SWITCH | https://www.bitchute.com/video/mKpgG9Pw9zKq/ |

You have the authority and power to ask LOVE to reverse any choices you may have made that you regret. It is the last day to do this. By June 2023, it will be too late. "Make the request Love does the rest." (The information is highly relevant as the Neuralink will go live soon and it will be too late for those who agreed to take the shot to reverse their decision if they regret it.)

THE PROMISE https://www.bitchute.com/video/f4sz8O7TVwwh/

ENVISAGE YOU ARE MIGHTY AND FREE, A 'HARM-DEFLECTING' LIGHTNING BOLT | https://www.bitchute.com/video/cTsNJIGUCySj/

Message For The Truth Community And Those Wishing To Find Solutions: Time is running out to leave this matrix | Bitchute: https://www.bitchute.com/video/SjU5t2iKixpA/

AVAILABLE ON @TRUELIGHTESSENCE,on TELEGRAM, ODYSEE, SUBSTACK, PATRICK.NET

AND SEARCHING FOR THE EVIDENCE, on BITCHUTE, VETERANBRIGADES.COM, TELEGRAM

Chapter Thirteen

DEATH RATES AND DEATH'S DOOR, OCT 30, 2023

"They will not win this war, not in the end, however, they are intent on causing you all harm and therefore, you need to use your 'God given right' to peacefully defend all precious life."

Audio Link

Hi Everyone, This is Claire, and it brings me no joy to be writing this today.

I don't know what message is going to come through, however, judging by the title, it does not bode well. I know there are many more hearts and minds joining in consciousness to try to help limit the damage caused by our many poor choices and acquiescence. I know many of you are concerned about the children and their future if this cabal have their way. It seems so sad, doesn't it, that we have the authority and the ability to call on LOVE and the Laws of Creation for help, and yet, so few in humanity choose this simple option...the option which would best serve all, in optimal ways, in alignment with LOVE's plan and the Laws of Creation?

I understand that new voices have joined those of us who are trying to help ourselves, humanity and all precious life, and I wish to say, "Hello and welcome, and thank you," for all you are doing to help.

Remember, that many tiny frightened voices are joined by LOVE when cries for help are made. It is so simple, "Make the request. LOVE does the rest."

And then, we ask our Infinite Selves "what could we ask for, to gain the optimal help that best serves all, in alignment with LOVE's plan and the Laws of Creation?"

How simple it is, and yet, how few try it to see if it works?

And this dismissal of this technique, this 'wave of the hand' at the possibility that this could, in fact, be the one thing we all need right now, has left us in this mess whereby the children are exposed to a pedophile agenda; the genocide continues as the medical boards fire off their letters - calling vulnerable patients for their booster, and the death rates keep climbing.

Death is knocking at humanity's and all life's door. This death campaign is ongoing, relentless, and in full motion. The technology is going up as we speak, and people are in awe at this: Quicker speed, less time impatiently waiting for our computers to respond, all these 'benefits' while the death rates soar.

In Blackpool, a town on the North West coast of the United Kingdom, there is an unusual spike in deaths, especially among the young.

Children are having heart attacks, dying in their sleep, getting rare, aggressive cancers and dropping like flies. It has made the mainstream newspapers, and I wonder, is this something to be concerned about after three years of propaganda and lies? Or, can't they hide it any longer, so they make a sad story about the deaths, yet still, no one mentions the elephant in the room.

And those of us who were paying attention were told, three years ago, that immortal cancer cells were in the poison shots. This has since been identified through rigorous testing, as SV40. If anyone cares to look on Telegram you will find lots of vaccine damaged groups posting pictures of their loved ones who died after the poison was taken.

It is heartbreaking reading through the ages of those who have died. Many are incredibly young. So many 'Snow Whites' are permanently sleeping now, after taking the poisoned apple that the fairytales warned us all about. The Pied Piper story seems ever more grim too, as a mainstream news article highlights the death of two parents, leaving their three children orphaned. What will happen to these poor souls?

In the UK, the social services is now a private contract, and there are rumours galore that the social services hunt out kids to put through the child trafficking system. Not every one, of course, but enough have infiltrated this private enterprise from the World Economic Forum to ensure that children are highly vulnerable when they get lost in these systems.

Ask Klaus, he has told us many times that he has his servants everywhere to implement his new world order and accessing the children has always been their goal. The children are the currency of this group who like to hunt, maim, rape, and kill.

We did a cursory glance at the criminal records for child abuse online. There are websites that collate the court data and the names of those who have been charged and jailed. And would it surprise you to know that some of those charged, worked in the charities for the homeless, or chaired foster homes, or oversaw council-run care centres and schools for orphaned kids?

They position themselves where they can access the kids. It is eye opening and eye watering to review the posts these criminally charged people had previously held. And it is also worth mentioning that some of your councillors hold criminal records for child abuse, and yet, still hold the job. How does that work, then?

Those who practice 'importunity' in the local town toilets do get reported. If they accept a caution, they get away with it, and keep their jobs. How many MP's are compromised this way? The answer is, more than you think.

Tony Blair, an avid supporter of the Digital ID, and a WEF member, was himself fined (as "Charles Lynton") for importunity in the 1980's for approaching an undercover police officer for sex in a London Men's public toilets.

We've got your number 'Charles Lynton', (Tony's middle names), and then, later, he became Prime Minister.

Have you ever looked to see how many councillors are Freemasons? Should it concern us that they belong to a 'black magic club'? They may raise money for charity and many are innocent participants in all of this, yet, how do they get lured in to a black magic circle? Could it be, because their status and kudos gets the better of them?

I knew someone who was a Freemason. None of my family approved. It seemed to be a very sociable club, however, the secrecy issue bothered us and 'the looking after their own' bothered us more.

Someone told me recently that a crook owes his friend a lot of money and the crook is a Freemason. And because he is a Freemason, his black magic club protect him. They overlook his idiosyncrasies.

So, you have crooks and coppers, all rubbing shoulders...Where is the transparency?

Q. Why am I mentioning all this today?

I wish to reach fullest Truth from the Heart of Creation and I ask for Truth, Knowledge, Wisdom and Clarity to be my guiding lights.

I try my best, however, your heart knows best and so, take what you need from this message today, and question everything through your own heart for that is where the Truth is found.

Here goes:

"Claire, we want you to focus on the StarLink today. Others are stepping forward now to assist and we would ask each of you who are wishing to help to keep up a regular, daily, heart connection routine using the directions from the previous, most recent messages, because they all offer techniques for heart and consciousness connection which help with a robust, direct connection to truth.

You all need to keep this up from here on in. You cannot afford to slip up or be lackadaisical with your inner work. The Black Magicians work tirelessly and relentlessly to keep these gates of Hell open during this period. They are having to work harder because of your assistance, but that does not mean you are winning. This is a 'damage limitation project', in the sense that the death rates are going to keep rising.

It is inevitable if one considers the 'poison apple' and the higher technologies now going up into your atmosphere. Why do humans never question the sanity of wrapping your streets, houses, and now, planet in a 'web' of electrical nodes and interfaces.

It has got so dark because of all this technology which is cloaking the planet and starving all life living on it, of oxygen."

"Oxygen?", I ask...

"I am struggling to hear Truth loud and clear, everything feels faint today, and I also wish to mention, in case others are experiencing this,

I am waking up in the middle of the night, approximately between 2 and 5am, and I have sensed a beam of energy being directed onto me.

I always use my heart connection and ask my Infinite Self, LOVE and the Laws of Creation to surround and protect me, and I ask for all malicious harm to be sent back to those responsible for ensuring the malicious harm reached myself and my husband's door, and the innocent, the children, and all those trying to protect the innocent.

I am very thorough with my connection routine; my inner heart requests, and I always ask for all who can be assisted, because this is affecting many innocent lives."

[And I hear:] *"Claire, the reason why the death rates are going to continue to soar is due to the death stars going up.*

The increase of radiation around your planet is multiplying. However, there is more to the story: Do you recall, many years ago, that we told you about isobars being used to alter the oxygen emissions around the planet?"

I say: "I wish I had kept that discourse. I was advised to destroy it. Can you explain the difference between isobars because one is intangible; in the sense that it is a 'measure', but this was not what you were alluding to, I seem to recall?"

"Claire, we will help you to reach truth at the heart of Creation. Let go of any worry of getting this wrong. We understand that you are not a scientist. We will keep things simple and easy to digest.The isobars that we refer to, are molecules of air. Claire, please trust you are hearing truth. Let go of worry. They are like ampules of droplets found in the atmosphere. The dark have developed a technology that alters the oxygen levels, and when the death stars go up and as more are switched on, this is going to affect breathing in the vulnerable, those who have respiratory issues, and those with asthma, etc.

The children and newborns are at greater risk simply because they have smaller bodies and their systems are still developing. This isobar technology can literally suck the air out of the atmosphere, and it can be controlled over land, sea and air.

It has the ability to cause radiation-type symptoms and hypoxia-type symptoms, however, it also falls neatly into the dark's plans for another 'respiratory pandemic' and the soaring death rates, once they become too difficult to hide from, the previous 'poison apple' will be blamed on this new respiratory virus which, of course, will require Remdesivir and ventilation.

Do you see where we are going with this?"

"Yes, I am not a doctor, but many doctors and scientists have highlighted that Remdesivir should not be given to respiratory patients, and ventilating them actually causes death, it does not prevent it. The information about Remdesivir in the patient insert is compelling reading by itself. It seems to cause many adverse reactions, including renal failure."

"Claire, this methodology is all in the pipeline. It is hoped that by highlighting what they are up to, that at least some aspects can be stopped before they start. ***The dark have to constantly adapt and change their plans as soon as their plans become known.*** *They seek to avoid karmic cycles or having to address their own errors to cause malicious harm, however, they reduce the damage they cause to themselves in a False Light Construct by gaining humanity's acquiescence. This often comes through ignorance and avoidance of looking too closely at the death star technology that is all around you now. The dark avoid karma, or, we should say, they used to avoid karma by gaining humanity's attention on something that they plan to do to them.*

This used to shift the karma onto the human who had given it their attention. Why do you think they show you movies that highlight all their cunning plans to control and harm you?

They avoid karma when you give their plans your attention and do nothing to protect your twelve levels of consciousness. You do not 'report back' to the heart of Creation, or ask your Infinite Self how to address the harm that the dark have planned, and since it is your creativity that creates this world, not the dark's, who lost their ability a long time ago... in order for their world to materialise, they need your attention on what they plan for you, your ignorance in the sense that you do not defend your self, and your acquiescence, by never standing up and refusing to allow these things to happen.

As a whole, humanity have materialised the world the dark want for themselves, and that world involves death of many of you, enslavement of your consciousness and soul, and enslavement of the remaining humans, who will be used as sex slaves, and to be used for hunting parties and 'entertainment' by those in the World Economic Forum and other organisations that serve the Satanic Agenda, the Immortality Agenda, and the Death Star Agenda.

Claire, this isobar technology has been waking you up at night, or should we say in the wee small hours, but we want you to know; it cannot harm you or harm anyone who calls on their Infinite Self, LOVE and the Laws of Creation to surround and protect them from all harm.

What we are asking those who wish to help themselves, and those who may have experienced increased breathlessness at night and in the wee small hours, which then subsides, is to understand that the attack on those calling for help is ongoing and so, you must all keep up your connection; to keep the attack at bay.

You do not need to fear this bunch of 'idiots' as we have fondly referred to them. We say 'idiots' because we wish to keep re-enforcing this point: That you are not the weaker side.

You are the side that connects to LOVE, and the Laws of Creation are working very hard on everyone now, including those who hunt, maim and kill, and in spite of their best efforts and relentless black magic spells, they cannot and will never outshine LOVE and the Laws of Creation.

They do not have the Knowledge or the Wisdom, but you do and so, we are advising you to keep going inside your heart centre and seeking the knowledge and wisdom to find out what your requests need to be, each time you 'report back' on your own experiences, symptoms, mood swings, irritability or feelings of depression, anxiety...anything which is not in balance.

When you ask your Infinite Self — your consciousness — for advice on what to request to best serve all in optimal ways in alignment with LOVE's plan and the Laws of Creation you will get a watertight response, and the request suggested will always cover every aspect of life so that all receive the best help possible.

The isobars ...Claire is wondering about how to address this advanced technology and wondering how they could possibly draw out oxygen from the atmosphere and target humanity. She is wondering if that is why children have died in a 'hotspot'; a target area, perhaps?

Unfortunately, we advise this is the case. They are testing the technology."

I ask, "Who is responsible for this — on the ground and in space?"

"Claire, would it surprise you to know this is a joint operation of many groups across many countries?"

"I do find that hard. Are we dealing with humans or something else? It is not human nature to want control over others like this, to kill innocent children and new borns. What kind of monsters are we dealing with?"

"Claire, you are dealing with Extra Terrestrial technology and Artificial Intelligence. We have explained before, many times, that ETs are your AWOL soul fragments and AI is your mind codes of consciousness that have been stolen and used to create artificial intelligence.

You are all 'facing the devil' in your own mirror, and that is why it is important to keep asking LOVE and the Laws of Creation to call back all that you have lost, and return the lost codes as healed and purified codes in the form of Purest Light codes that can never be infiltrated by the dark or any other thing.

This request strengthens you all, and it weakens the ET and AI because the more of you who ask for your codes back, the less the ET groups and AI have to use against you.

Make no mistake, this whole planet and False Light Construct is made up of stolen consciousness and codes of Knowledge that have been weaponised against you all.

It is time to fight back, but this is not through violence, and we only use the work 'fight' loosely, because LOVE does not need to fight.

LOVE recalls, LOVE finds what you have all lost and weakens the fighter and those who love to harm, by withdrawing all the Knowledge that they are using to harm you all with. The most powerful way to weaken this group is recalling, healing, and sending back all malicious harm, for their learning.

We offer a routine below that Claire uses in case, you need help with securing a robust routine.

Once you are connected to your Infinite Self, you simply have to ask your heart for a simple way to connect each day and what requests best serve your soul evolution and the soul evolution of all in optimal ways in alignment with LOVE's plan and the Laws of Creation.Claire, will you share your routine to help newcomers?"

I say, "No problem,"

I lie down flat on my back on the bed that I sleep in at night, at home. My legs are straight never crossed and slightly touching. My palms are placed flat, facing down, and resting on the tops of my thighs. I have ensured the room is shaded from bright sunlight, that I have set an alarm, in case I need to be awake at a certain time, and I have a glass of water nearby.

If it is safe to do so, I close my eyes, as I do each night for sleep, and I get myself comfortable as I normally would for sleep. I relax and gently take my closed eyes to look in the direction of my chest area, listening to the air going in and out of my chest.

I keep my closed eyes looking down there, noticing the rise and fall of my chest and when I am ready...I imagine that I have a tiny switch inside my chest area where my heart is and I imagine that I can go inside my chest area and press this switch, my True Power Switch, and I trust that is all that is required to connect me safely to my Infinite Self, to LOVE's plan, and to the Laws of Creation at the Heart of Creation and infinitely beyond.

I ask to be surrounded and protected by my True Power Switch — my Infinite Self, LOVE and the Laws of Creation and connected to my infinite consciousness.

On behalf of all who can be assisted, we ask for all errors that we may have made to be deleted.

From a place of peace, without anger or malice, we ask for all magnified malicious harm to be gathered up by LOVE's plan and the Laws of Creation, and returned to all those responsible for ensuring it reached our door, the door of the innocent and those trying to protect all precious life.

May all that has been lost, be found by LOVE's plan and returned to all those who can be assisted, in their true, original form that can never be corrupted or stolen by the dark or any other thing.

May the Frequency of Peace reign supreme and may Infinite LOVE help humanity through these dark days, weeks, and months ahead.

Then, I rest and receive supportive frequencies.

Pause the recording while this continues and come back once your heart and consciousness advise you to.

Now we are ready, we ask, as individuals who are joining as a concerned group with our consciousness, how can we best serve all precious life in optimal ways, in alignment with LOVE's plan and the Laws of Creation?

Listen for inner guidance on what you can request from LOVE to best serve all, and at this point, find out if you are being asked to activate any gifts or codes that you are carrying and how you are to use them to peacefully best serve all precious life.

I will leave links to previous podcasts that share teachings on activating your gifts. Listen to the guidance, pause the recording here to give yourself plenty of time to listen. Then come back when you are ready.

When you have received the teachings and made the requests that you were advised to ask for LOVE's help with, thank all, for all their loving help and support.

AM: This is the most important connection to heart and is best done as soon as you wake up in the morning.

Midway through the day: A simpler, shorter version can be used during the day and working hours, using the routine up to the end of the Frequency of Peace request.

PM: Ensure you connect before sleep each night by using the routine up to the end of the Frequency of Peace request.

Once you get used to this daily connection routine — AM, PM and Midway through your day — it takes about 5-10 minutes, with the morning routine taking slightly longer.

Make it fit into your day and ask for help from your heart to create your own routine that is easy for you to follow.

When you have finished, remember to stir your body slowly and gently, as you do each time you awaken from a deep relaxing sleep.

Take your time getting up out of bed, and have a drink of water to hand.

Trust that you have the power within you and the authority of the Heart of Creation and the Laws of Creation, to ask for help for yourself and others.

This war on our consciousness and war on our children can be dealt with from the comfort of our own home. The more you connect to your consciousness, the less afraid you will feel as you start to perceive the enormity of your own Infinite Consciousness and the support available by the unseen yet, tangible force of LOVE.Remember, you are all deeply loved and supported.

You are not expected to resolve these complex issues or attacks.

All you are being asked to do, is be present in this reality and to 'report back' to the Heart of Creation through your Infinite Self, your Infinite Consciousness and to ask for help that "best serves all in optimal ways, in alignment with LOVE's plan and the Laws of Creation."

We have to trust — LOVE has a plan — and if we listen, truly listen to our deeper heart's guidance, we will always serve all life here, in ways which move mountains and create miracles for all.

The dark have no power over you anymore, not when you call on LOVE for help, and no power on Earth has dominion over LOVE's plan.

They simply do not and will never have the Knowledge, or power, or authority to continue to cause this level of harm.

Keep sending back all malicious harm and watch how things turn around as their empires collapse and their foundries fail.

They will not win this war, not in the end, however, they are intent on causing you all harm and, therefore, you need to use your 'God given right' to peacefully defend all precious life."

LINKS:

https://truelightessence.substack.com/p/understanding-consciousness-25-october

...

https://truelightessence.substack.com/p/how-to-avoid-a-soul-harvest

https://truelightessence.substack.com/p/your-cosmic-shield-defend-yourselves

https://truelightessence.substack.com/p/you-cannot-stop-what-is-coming

...

@covid19vaccinevictims:

https://t.me/covid19vaccinevictims/10010

...

Lancashire coroners dealing with surge in sudden deaths including tragic youngsters
Lancashire is dealing with a tragic increase in deaths among its young people.

https://www.blackpoolgazette.co.uk/news/people/lancashire-coroners-dealing-with-surge-in-sudden-deaths-including-tragic-youngsters-4385454

...

ORPHANED CHILDREN

https://t.me/covid19vaccinevictims/

...

SV40

On contamination, monkey viruses and their parts

Chapter Fourteen

UNITY AND THE FAILURE OF PROJECT IMMORTALITY, 5 NOVEMBER 2023

Your heart knows your optimal path, and LOVE knows where your help is needed.

Audio Version:

UNITY AND THE FAILURE OF PROJECT IMMORTALITY

LOVE'S HEART PLAN, SUBSTACK.COM

Hello Everyone,

I am pleased to say that despite the failure of many plans to help humanity, the greatest failure to date has been the dark's agenda for immortality which has failed miserably, although they are still ignorant of the fact.

However, they will have noticed that several key figures are no longer around to cause as much chaos. It has only kept them quiet for a while. These little devils will stop at nothing to cause mayhem.

Which brings me nicely onto the 'castle and moat' metaphor, and it may well help those of you who are helping yourselves, to connect to your True Power Switch and imagine you are inside your castle and moat, as I have shared in previous podcast recordings.

Once you are inside the safety of your castle, ensure the moat draw-bridge is secured up, and your entry and exit routes securely sealed off, press your True Power Switch, as previously taught, and relax while I type out today's message:

It has been decidedly choppy over the last few days. Last night, I was in a deep state of distress energetically, not because I wasn't protected, I trust I am safe at all times, but the energy of the planet has become so toxic recently, especially with the Halloween activities, as the children have lost vast amounts of their life force — all handed over to the dark to feed off, and this has created a huge soul harvest of their energy and consciousness.

It is distressing to feel the torment of these children at soul level, and not just their torment, but the torment of our family of humanity and all precious life that gets hit with the shock waves of destroyer force attack, as humans open the gates of Hell and let in this attack.

When will humanity learn to stop these activities of mass, satanic ritual which are dressed up as entertainment?

I wish you to imagine that you have pressed your True Power Switch, and now, you are fully connected to your Infinite Self, Infinite LOVE and the Laws of Creation at the heart of Creation, and infinitely beyond. I say 'infinitely beyond,' because Creation is always expanding and we need to be moving forward to keep up with this expansion.

Can you imagine that you are looking out of your castle window and across your moat, to survey the weather and the view?

Pretend you have a barometer on the wall which has 'Fair', at the top and works its way down, from 'Slight Gusts', to 'Strong Winds', and further down, to 'Storm Warning, Hurricane, Tornado', and finally, 'Total Collapse'.

Q. What does your barometer read today, regarding the Earth Plane environment?

Pause the recording to give yourself plenty of time to do this at your own pace.

Do this with each question or step that follows, and come back to join us when you are ready.

Q. Imagine you are looking beyond your moat, and pretend that you are looking at the structure of the Earth Matrix which may look like a huge steel structure, a huge scaffolding going beyond where your eyes can see, and inwardly, take note of whether the structure and scaffolding is steady or starting to collapse in parts. Does it look or sense like a nice place to be?

Imagine you are now back inside the deep heart of your castle, moat draw-bridge is always securely shut, and inside the deepest part of your castle, you are surrounded by the purest part of your Infinite Self and LOVE.

You press your True Power Switch once more, and pretend or imagine that your treasure chest appears in front of you.

The lid is open. You reach inside it, and retrieve a ticket, similar to a plane ticket.

It reads, "Final Destiny, The Heart Of Creation — First Stop, Transiting At Unity."

Pause the recording here and ask your heart — your Infinite Self — does it best serve your soul evolution in optimal ways, and best serve all in optimal ways, in alignment with LOVE's plan and the laws of Creation, to make the move to Unity?

Only your heart can guide you what your next steps are. Your Infinite Self knows your heart's deepest desires. Your free will must decide.

Once you have your answer, come back and join us.

For those who do not wish to move forward, stop the recording here and receive inner teachings on your best steps.

We are all travelling on different paths and we have different roles here on Earth.

Your heart knows your optimal path, and LOVE knows where your help is needed.

For those who do get the guidance that it is time to move forward to Unity, imagine that your True Power Switch is now being renamed 'Unity Switch'.

Press your Unity Switch, and just rest a while.

Pause the recording to receive supportive energies and rejoin us once your heart guides you to.

Imagine you are looking at your castle and moat.

Does it look or feel bigger? Does it feel stronger, more resilient?

Take a peak outside your window at your barometer. What is the weather forecast today?

Have new indicators appeared such as calm, tranquil, peaceful?

How is the view, by comparison to the Earth Matrix view?

How vast has your inner castle become?

There are many more rooms within this upgraded building. You are always surrounded by your castle and moat, and your draw-bridge must remain closed, and all entry/exit points, secured.

Within your castle there are rooms for healing; repair; learning; teaching; there is a vast library of Knowledge to visit, and all sorts of other rooms to visit.

Come back each day, by pressing your Unity Switch and explore this place.

It is a place that all will transit through on their journey home to the heart of Creation.

A place to be still, to unify our actions, thoughts, words, and deeds; to heal, repair, and to cement all that we have learnt on our journey so far.

Welcome.

Chapter Fifteen

THE CHILDREN, 8 NOVEMBER 2023

"THE CHILDREN, THE CHILDREN, THE CHILDREN...UNFORTUNATELY, IT IS ALL ABOUT THE CHILDREN, AND CURRENTLY, AN ARMY IS MARCHING INTO THIS REALITY— THANKS TO THEIR PARENTS —WHO HAVE WILLINGLY OPENED THEIR CHILDREN'S PROTECTIVE SHIELD, AND ALLOWED THE DARK TO WALK RIGHT IN AND STEAL LARGE QUANTITIES OF LIFE FORCE ENERGY, DNA CODES OF REMEMBRANCE AND KNOWLEDGE, AND THEIR ABILITY TO DEFEND THEMSELVES OR CALL FOR HELP."

Audio Message Links:
SEARCHING FOR THE EVIDENCE, BITCHUTE.COM
@TRUELIGHTESSENCE, ODYSEE.COM
LOVE'S HEART PLAN, SUBSTACK.COM

"Claire, has already explained the satanic implications of involving young souls in the celebrations of ritual satanic practices, dressed up as 'entertainment'. As doorways open, the dark can reach inside this reality and steal what they need to exist — life force energies, codes to help humanity leave this False Light Matrix, and defensive protection; to keep the dark forces out of the Earth plane.

The issues with humanity is: they do not listen, and despite repeated warnings coming from all angles, they still go along with these activities without ever questioning the sanity of these events, nor, why churches would encourage such celebrations? It is not 'child's play'.

This is a serious attack on humanity and all precious life here. We will repeat: The dark ones are after humanity's children. They are the currency, and their life force is a precious commodity.

So now, an army is marching onward towards the children, and it is too late to prevent the carnage that is coming because too few cared to help, and too many parents involved their children and exposed them to satanic attack by destroyer forces.

*Claire, tell the others what you have witnessed t*his evening."

I saw dark, black widow spiders and scorpion- type creatures walking into this reality.

My 'castle and moat' had felt extremely peaceful, thanks to the others who are using this method to help themselves and to help protect the defenceless, and it all changed today. Military jets flew close over our house. It has been beautifully sunny but, no doubt, it will rain tomorrow as it always does after they fly over. The weather always deteriorates, and I wondered, what they were up to...?

I was already connecting to my heart and was inside my castle and moat. I repeated the connection routine that I am currently being guided to use, and that includes; asking for all magnified, malicious harm to be returned to all those responsible for the magnified, malicious harm.

I was advised to listen to my previous two podcast messages, and while using my Unity Switch, I had been guided to go to the top floor of my castle and saw the creepy crawly creatures marching in. I also noticed that I had a crown on top of my castle. Crown symbolism is satanic and it had not been there before.

If you notice anything lying about inside or outside your castle or anything that was not there before, you must question it with your Infinite Self, as I have taught you all, by using a robust line of inner heart questioning. Even if you see an innocuous object of animal/bird or a fire extinguisher, a mop bucket, anything at all — it is a sign by your Infinite Self that something is wrong and requires investigation.

I was guided to check the view outside my castle window and perceive the environment. It didn't look or feel bright and clear. I checked my barometer. It said "storm coming".

All these are signs that you need to inwardly question more deeply: "What actions best serve your optimal soul evolution and best serves all in optimal ways in alignment with LOVE's plan and the laws of Creation?"

Take it slowly, step by step, and follow your Infinite Self's guidance.

Use this recoding to help you and pause it while you retrieved deeper teachings then come back and follow each step, plus any additional steps your Infinite Self is asking you to make until you have exhausted all lines of questioning.

So, I went to the top floor of my castle and was shown the black widow spiders and scorpion-type creatures and I was advised that this army was advancing in on the children and all precious, innocent life. I was guided to ask for all who could be uplifted to be uplifted by LOVE and the Laws of Creation to a safer place.

I was told I could not do anything more, except ask LOVE to help the parents to awaken to the danger they have placed the children in, and for humanity to awaken to Truth, and for the children to awaken to the danger they were in.

I have had to accept that I cannot ask for more because we must respect the free will of all and we must not interfere, we can only ask for what we are guided. I tried to ensure that I have covered all possible avenues of securing as much assistance, however, I am sad to tell you that I was advised that unless the parents ask LOVE for their errors to be deleted, and for repair— for the harm done to the children — we are facing a 'mass extinction event'.

How many children are there in the world, I wonder?

How many under the age of twelve attended Halloween events, and Guy Fawkes night or Bonfire events, recently?

How many parents chose to keep their children away from the whole satanic ritual?

How many adults dressed up their houses in Halloween decor and let in destroyer force that way?

How many businesses took part in this satanic ritual event by holding Halloween events or promotions under the guise of entertainment?

How many humans around the world lost life force energy, and how many of their children suffered satanic attack too, do you think?

How many pets were harmed?

How many others got hit by satanic attack because they either walked past a human who had attended a satanic ritual or they received an email/text from someone who had?

How many humans around the world effectively protect their ladder of consciousness from satanic attack?

How many life forms also got hit by this attack, throughout all levels of consciousness, and how much life force were the dark able to steal, harvest, and then weaponise against all precious life here?

We still have Christmas to get through. The same cycle will start all over again. Then, it's the Satanic Spring Equinox, then it's Mayday, and Maypole dancing, and on and on it goes...

All these events are satanically driven, no matter the 'opinion' of others. You have to go deep inside your heart and leave the mind-control behind to secure accurate guidance about these staged, satanic events.

How much time is left before we are all out of options on Planet Earth, given that the In Breath is practically complete?"

"Claire, many have been helping themselves and it has helped a great deal — for their own soul evolution and protection at least — and it has offered a 'buffer zone' for others to try to awaken from their deep sleep, however, the dark never rest; they never stop planning and conniving new ways to secure your life force.

It is food to them, and they are getting hungry for food; like wasps at the end of the summer season and before the winter, they need fuel and your life force is their 'fuel'.

Aside from that, the children are being misled by parents who willingly go along with these events, without ever questioning the moral outcome of these choices, namely that pedophilia is all linked to masking, scaring and frightening children, as is Halloween.

It has only one purpose and that is to dumb-down the rational of getting scared by monsters, skeletons, ghouls and devils, and witches. It is a way of normalising satanism and all satanism stands for — not just for forces outside of this reality — but for those who secretly practice satanism as part of their daily lives.

It won't be too long until satanists demand the right to sacrifice children openly, and will expect a dumbed-down society to meekly accept their demands. It is all building that way and it is why your children are being used now, and their children (if they can still reproduce) will also be used. It is like incest. It is being passed down and conditioning children and the adults of tomorrow— to accept ideologies that would never have been permitted thirty years ago.

This is where it is heading and it is going at a rate of knots. They are still checking out your reactions for legalising pedophilia. They want it because it is what they like. Anyone who pushes this agenda: either through education, science or politics needs scrutinising. They serve the World Economic Forum, and UN, etc., and these elites like to harm children.

As above, so below. And so, what can those of you do to help the children and innocent who are about to be 'hit' by the army of 'dark insects' marching into this reality? The answer is nothing at present. Not while the parents choose to do nothing and not while society chooses to do nothing to help themselves.

The only thing you can do is help yourselves. And this requires you to be using your robust connection routine and a strict line of questioning — to ensure you leave nothing to chance, in order to secure fullest Truth guidance from your Infinite Self, Infinite LOVE and the Laws of Creation from the heart of Creation.

You may find yourself being advised to go to the top floor of your castle (having checked outside of your window and your barometer), and to ask what is happening to the children and what this army looks like that Claire was shown.

You will need to ask if it is time to upgrade your inner heart connection and what action best serves all in optimal ways, in alignment with LOVE's plan and the Laws of Creation to secure this upgrade.

Please have Trust, Hope, and Faith that the Heart of Creation is walking this through with you.

As long as you are using a strict line of questioning and being sensible, you will never fail. It is your desire for Truth and your desire to protect all precious life that secures your help, so worry not.

The Heart of Creation 'has your back', and you must trust that your Infinite Self is your bodyguard and security.

Never move forward until you have received the guidance to do so, and if you do see anything unusual inside your castle, you now know that it is a lesson and must be questioned, because that will bring Knowledge and that will help with your growth.

This has to go.

Claire has had many issues with sound and the simple activity of making videos.

Please include a request for her assistance too, because it helps her to get the advice out to you without untimely delays."

...

Audio Message Links:

THE CHILDREN| SEARCHING FOR THE EVIDENCE,Bitch
ute.com

THE CHILDREN | @truelightessence,Odysee.com

Chapter Sixteen

'BECOMING ONE' WITH THE STARLINK COMPUTER: ASSISTANCE REQUESTED, NOVEMBER 9, 2023

"It is unsustainable to cause this much harm and destroy these many lives without repercussions from the Laws of Creation, and a huge karmic cycle is about to reach humanity; and the story will unfold."

Audio Version:
'Becoming One' With The StarLink Computer — Assistance Requested:

"They are heading for the full-on 'StarLink-Hive-Mind' — the place where the Internet Of Bodies overpowers any 'human' trace, at all. They are about to become mindless morons, incapable of doing anything, other than obey; comply. The dark, dark world of the hive mind awaits humanity, and it is happening for the dark — they don't even need to try.'"

Hello Everyone,

This is Claire and this message follows on from yesterday's, entitled and the previous message. If you wish to help, it is necessary to listen to these, firstly, and then, to follow your inner heart's guidance because your help is needed and time is of the essence.

The thing that saddens me the most is that humanity are more than capable of resolving all errors and mistakes, and yet, as the days progress I am starting to become increasingly concerned for the children, newborns, innocent, vulnerable and elderly who, through no fault of their own, are being laid bare to a massive onslaught of attack unlike anything the planet has ever seen.

Please do listen to the aforementioned messages and come back once you are ready, because this message will make far more sense, hold far more meaning, and offer far greater opportunities for helping — once you have viewed the planet through the lens offered in the last two messages.

I also recommend the following links below in case you wish to explore further, as they offer simple methods for connecting to your own inner conscience — your Infinite Self — to secure deeper understanding through your own inner expansion of consciousness:

...

OTHER LINKS:

THE CHILDREN | 8 NOVEMBER 2023

https://www.bitchute.com/video/QIBFUMYxexo6/

...

UNITY AND THE FAILURE OF PROJECT IMMORTALITY — 5.11.23

https://www.bitchute.com/video/B9LUHB4I0HMR/

...

LION'S GATE OF HELL HAS OPENED | DARK MATTER FEASTING ON CHILDREN AND THE INNOCENT - HELP REQUESTED

https://www.bitchute.com/video/NfGrpR4akNN7/

@truelightessence, Odysee | https://odysee.com/@TrueLightEssence:d

...

SOUL HARVEST | 26 OCTOBER 2023 | (UNLOCKING YOUR GIFTS)

https://truelightessence.substack.com/p/soul-harvest-26-october-2023

...

UNDERSTANDING CONSCIOUSNESS | 25 OCTOBER 2023 | (CONNECTION ROUTINE AND EXPLORING YOUR GIFTS)

https://truelightessence.substack.com/p/understanding-consciousness-25-october

HOW TO AVOID A SOUL HARVEST

https://www.bitchute.com/video/jkjKrh5icWAJ/

...

YOUR COSMIC SHIELD: DEFEND YOURSELVES AGAINST ELECTROMAGNETIC AND ELECTROPLATONIC ATTACK | 13 AUGUST 2023 (HEART CONNECTION ROUTINE)

https://www.bitchute.com/video/szz495pFkul5/

...

HELP FOR HUMANITY - 18 JULY 2023 (HEART CONNECTION ROUTINE)

https://www.bitchute.com/video/COPkNuixzly3/

...

MESSAGE FOR TARGETED INDIVIDUALS |

https://truelightessence.substack.com/p/message-for-targeted-individuals

...

I will move rapidly on now. There is much to cover today, and I am sorry to say, much to be concerned about.

This morning, I was guided to listen to the last two recordings and as I went through my connection routine, I discovered what looked like multiple faint mop buckets inside my castle. Our castle and moat should be completely clear of any items. Nothing should be present — nothing should be visible except bare walls, the building and our own inner presence.

Yesterday, I emphasised the importance of looking out for or perceiving anything innocuous lying around inside your castle and moat, or outside this safe haven.

I had found a crown on top of my castle. I secured deeper teachings and secured an upgrade to my Unity Switch, which was an upgrade from my True Power Switch.

These are all stepping stone teachings to expansion of consciousness for those who feel driven to help in this way.

Many in the religious community are supporting the planet through prayers, and their prayers are vitally important in securing help for the voiceless, the innocent and all precious life.

Each of us has a path to growth. There is no fixed route. Some of us are meant to go via a different path, but it is all working towards helping all precious life to exit this place. This path is about finding a safe way out of the matrix and securing a way out for others who will also walk this way.

The In Breath is nearing completion. It is on finals and with the completion of this huge cycle of creation, the dark are scrabbling to secure all the life force they can harvest from all souls who are trapped inside this False Light Matrix, in the misguided belief that they will achieve immortality and live forever — away from LOVE's light, which is too bright for them.

They are bent on the destruction of all that we value and cherish, and they need our life force energy because this is their food — their 'fuel' that sustains their existence.

Without our life force, they could not exist. And yet, they do exist, because we willingly feed them: We open up our gateways and our doorways and we allow this dark group to walk right in and ransack our precious life force codes.

The dark steal this life force and as I have shared many times, they take some to fuel their existence and the rest is used in a distorted fashion; weaponised and used against us, to cause more ongoing chaos, fear, and heartache, and this is what sustains their existence.

I need to explain this simply, because newcomers often join and may have missed previous podcasts that have shared more information on this issue.

Many are suffering, in great magnitude today, and I am afraid it is about to get a whole lot worse, unless humanity start to protect their life force in a cohesive way.

In the meantime, we are facing a huge major crisis. From my inner perspective, at least, things are not looking great at all. Hopefully, newcomers have caught up by listening to the previous two messages.

Today, I went through my connection routine as we have all be inwardly taught and there were these innocuous and out of place mop buckets floating about my castle.

I went to the top floor, checked the barometer and outside view.

How is yours looking today?

Can you see/sense what is happening below you, at ground level?

What about your barometer?

Pause the recording here, and rejoin us when you are ready.

When I looked down, the entire ground was overrun with a thick covering of black widow spiders and dark scorpion-type creepy crawlies.

A full-on invasion is taking place. I also noticed things dotted about in space, in the higher levels outside of my castle.

I asked about the mop buckets, what they represented and was advised it is all about StarLink.

Currently, StarLink is posing the greatest threat to humanity, the children, and all life here.

I wanted to understand why the StarLink technology was inside my castle, especially considering I am regularly upgrading my connection to my Infinite Self and the heart of Creation, regularly clearing my energy, checking my castle and moat, keeping an eye on my barometer...I am extremely thorough...how had this technology entered my heart space?

This is what they want us all to know:

"Claire, this was a lesson, and you were always safe inside your castle, but we always need to show you what is happening to those who are not protecting themselves and the risks to yourself if you remain in a place too long, because this is all about passing through as quickly as possible, as the In Breath is nearly complete and the dark are working overtime to steal as much life force to trap humanity and all life in this False Light Matrix.

We wanted you to perceive the StarLink technology and a mop bucket was as good a signal as anything that something was present that should not be there.Your castle should be clear, as you previously shared.

The issue with StarLink is the grave danger it truly places humanity's children in, and of course, it places all life in danger, however, the children are more vulnerable because they are not fully able or aware to secure their own rescue; they are reliant on their parents making the best choices for them, and sadly, many parents see no harm in Halloween or the ritualistic burning of a 'human' body on Bonfire night.

They see it as 'entertainment' without understanding how Earth energy truly works. Many don't want to know, and many don't believe in energy being harmful or beneficial. This leaves the children exposed to satanic attack because the parents do not understand why Halloween is satanic, or how it can severely harm children at all levels of consciousness, and therefore, they are unaware of the implications of satanic attack on their off-spring's life force energy.

We will summarise briefly: Placing a poison of unknown origin into a little human body is detrimental to health, it is detrimental to the child's spirit, and it can result in much harm happening to the child.

The 'pot shots' contain pot luck ingredients. More is coming out from America, where many honest, decent doctors and scientists have got hold of large quantities of the 'pot shots' and studied them in depth.

Many are microbiologists and virologists, heart experts and well respected physicians in their field. These are not amateurs. These are well respected professionals. All their findings point to a multitude of ingredients that have no right to be there.

The SV40 ingredient causes turbo cancers. Cancer rates are shooting up, in line with the pot shots being administered.

There are many more ingredients present in the pot shots, and Pfizer is now admitting this because the evidence is so overwhelming, they cannot back away from this, nor can they back away from the fact that the trials were corrupted, flawed, and unprofessionally conducted.

Many babies died in the trials, miscarried by the pregnant mothers who carried their young into this world. In New Zealand, 30 people died in a 'pocket', all of whom attended the same clinic and had the same pot shot, at the same venue, on specific dates.

This is not 'new' news. It is old news.

However, the media black-out on the data is unprecedented in a free world, and so, many are simply not aware of the terrible harm these 'pot shots' are doing to many souls. It is estimated that 1 billion have died as a direct result.

We guide you that by the time these 'pot shots' have done their thing, the death rate will be far, far higher. And yet, despite the unprecedented data — facts that cannot be disputed — the liars keep lying, and the pot shots are being recommended for young babies and infants. We guided you that it is a serious mistake to place an unknown poison into any body, however, a young baby has no defence; no spiritual wisdom awakened; cannot yet utter a call to its parent, let alone, a call to LOVE for help and so, it is completely at the mercy of the parent to seek inner heart guidance on best choices to make for the newborn.

The 'system' is like a hive mind. All minds are working as one. There are few left who have independent thought.

All must do what the others say they must do, without question, without inner-heart-research.

This is the state of the Earth plane energies and it is about to get much worse, and despite those who have prayed for help to come, despite those who are expanding their consciousness, the damage has become untenable, and this is the situation that you will all find yourselves in now — unless you call on LOVE for help — it will be game over.

It is unsustainable to cause this much harm and destroy these many lives without repercussions from the Laws of Creation, and a huge karmic cycle is about to reach humanity; and the story will unfold...

So, what story is going to unfold?

The story of what happens when a human stands by and does nothing to secure their own rescue.

The story of what happens when parents open up their children's protective shield and allow dark, satanic matter to enter the security of their precious heart space.

The story of how expansion of consciousness and/or deep prayer will spare those from the StarLink technology.

And the story of how humanity allowed this to happen, despite having all the tools they needed inside their heart centres — inside their castle walls — which are now going to be overrun with StarLink technology — and the final battle for humanity's heart and soul ensues.

There doesn't seem to be much 'battle', though...

It is more a case of humans lying back and allowing this attack to take place — such is the mind control. They appear incapable of defending themselves, and many are too disinterested to particularly care.

They are heading for the full-on 'StarLink-Hive-Mind', the place where the Internet Of Bodies overpowers any 'human' trace, at all. They are about to become mindless morons, incapable of doing anything, other than obey; comply.

The dark, dark world of the hive mind awaits humanity, and it is happening for the dark — they don't even need to try...

Humanity has made this final battle 'a walk in the park' for the destroyer forces. Not even a baby's whimper will stir them now. They are lost in the programs of false light.

And yet, even in their darkest hour so far, there is always hope, trust and faith, and it is suggested to those who truly care about their own future, to make every attempt to secure your rescue from this place, before it is too late.

It may be too late to bring about change for the majority, but you can still ensure that you secure your own rescue, and if that is your wish, you need to climb your ladder now, and allow your Infinite Self and LOVE to show you the way.

The jets that fly over Claire's area are spraying toxic chemicals and metals. See these metals like iron filings; magnetic by design and capable of creating large areas of False Light grids; through which StarLink energies can transmit.

These iron filing-type compounds link up with every electric contraption in your homes: washing machines; kettles; fridges; smart meters; lamp bases; iPhones and computers, and these act like 'satellites' to help transmit the StarLink signal.

The air is full of the iron filing-type compounds. You breathe them in and they circulate around your body: Depositing themselves en route and via your blood — in your brain; lungs; heart and lower organs.

You now 'become one' with the StarLink computer and the other technologies of 5G and wind turbines, which in themselves are transmitters and receivers of frequencies, and, now, have the complete circuitry in place for the Internet of Bodies, and your bodies are ready to receive and transmit whatever disease-type symptoms, or heart attack, or cancer that the 'chosen ones' at StarLink Head Quarters deem relevant to you — depending on how obedient you have been.

And you will "comply or die", according to Elon's new 'toy'.

What type of entity is he, after all? He is no longer human, not anymore.

It's 'Cyborg Land' on planet Earth, now, and those of you with hearts to see and minds that can still think independently, would do well to play "spot the bot" and "spot the cyborg," because many on your planet are already in key positions to unleash this harm on humanity.

When you connect to your heart and Infinite Self, you can ask for help to move yourself away from the energetic attack.

This power of StarLink operates from stolen, harvested human energy and life force codes of Knowledge. Equally, you have the power and the authority to defend yourselves from this onslaught of attack, and each day, you can ask for Infinite LOVE and the Laws of Creation to:

"Delete any errors you may have made, to gather up all magnified, malicious harm, (and, a new request), all harm directed your way, and for Infinite LOVE and the Laws of Creation to send it back to all those responsible for harming you, and for all that has been lost, to be found, returned to Wholeness for repair, and then, restored to you in the form of Purest Light codes that can never be corrupted by the dark or any other thing."

This is your 'meal-ticket' out of this place, if you choose to secure your own rescue.

However, you must validate all this, and ***YOUR COSMIC SHIELD: DEFEND YOURSELVES AGAINST ELECTRO-***

***MAGNETIC AND ELECTROPLATONIC ATTACK | 13 AUGUST 2023 (HEART CONNECTION ROUTINE)** is highly recommended as a starting block from which to launch your 'lifeboat rescue' campaign.*

It is now a race against time to help yourselves.

Nothing more can be achieved unless more search for help. Therefore, our advice is to keep climbing, and for those who have been diligently working — you need to move forward once again — from Unity, to Wisdom.

Keep asking how you can: "Best serve all in optimal ways, in alignment with LOVE's plan and the Laws of Creation," and secure any requests that you are able to make for the children, the innocent, the vulnerable, and all precious life.

Keep checking your barometer, and the inside and outside of your castle.

Claire saw a swarm of darkness far below her top floor.

She is advised to steadfastly keep climbing when it is suggested, and in that way, it may help some last minute stragglers who may have sensed the imminent danger and decided to seek assistance.

Indeed, it is akin to being in a jungle filled with hostile threats and all pathways are hidden.

Find a safe route, and keep walking it each day, in the hope that others following behind you have a safe route to travel in the quickest time possible — before the False Light Matrix fully collapses in on itself.

The 'name of the game' is to secure a safe exit and to return home, before this place implodes on itself under the weight of the many errors caused by a dumbed-down humanity and hostile forces.

Claire, this must go. Others need the information."

Audio Version

'Becoming One' With The StarLink Computer —

Assistance Requested:

LOVE'S HEART PLAN, SUBSTACK.COM

@truelightessence, Odysee.com

Chapter Seventeen

HEART CONNECTION FOR BEGINNERS, NOV 10, 2023

An easy technique for those new to heart connection - including for parents to use with their children, and those going through cancer, suffering from grief, trauma, illness, or heartache.

Never give up. Never think you are all alone. Never forget to call for help.

Audio Experience:

...

LOVE loves us all, unconditionally. LOVE does not impose, LOVE comes when called upon, and so, it is important to understand that we need to make a decision: a free will choice to call on LOVE for assistance, in order for LOVE to be able to help us."Make the request. LOVE does the rest," is an important message for humanity.

Heart Connection For Beginners

Hello my name is Claire, I am a retired holistic teacher, and my area of interest and learning has been centred around consciousness and metaphysics. The unknown and the unexplored areas of consciousness that we refer to as; our 'intuition' and 'our inner voice of Truth and Reason'. Over the space of 13 years I have been exploring ways to help humanity to connect deeply within, in safe ways, that cause no ill-effects, and which are pure and simple.

The following routine I am now going to share, is one I have found to be highly supportive, my husband too, and when he was diagnosed with stage four cancer of the liver, spleen and all lower organs, with only two months to live, we used everything I had learnt, and all my husband had learned, to seek inner guidance on ways to help ourselves.

There are deeper teachings alongside our approach to helping ourselves, but this recording is for beginners, for those who have not experienced heart connection before, and it is a simple routine that anyone can use.

It does not involve connecting to any other energy except LOVE through your own heart centre.

This is important, and there are deeper teachings about why this is, but for now, we will focus on getting this heart connection strong for yourself because once you have a strong heart connection, it is a useful tool to use alongside all decision making and all approaches that want the best outcome - the optimal outcome for yourself and for all.

When we ask LOVE through our hearts for the best outcome that best serves all, all life in existence receives the best help, including yourselves and it always offers the better outcome than if you just asked for help for yourself.

This approach helped us enormously as we navigated life-threatening illness.

My husband accepted that he may not survive. We held no expectation towards outcome as we knew we could not control outcome. However, we hoped, trusted and had faith that our requests for help were being answered, and we hoped for the best outcome, even though we knew we could not control my husband's destiny. So, we handed all the things we could not control over to LOVE and we focused on listening to our hearts to hear what steps we could take each day to best help all, knowing that those steps would help us too.

My husband survived stage four cancer. Our hearts guided that Hope, Faith, and Trust are frequencies, as is LOVE, which is the overriding, most powerful frequency in existence, and our hearts advised us that if humanity would listen and start to help themselves by asking for Hope, Trust, and Faith to help them, then much help would be made available to all who asked for help.

LOVE loves us all, unconditionally. LOVE does not impose, LOVE comes when called upon, and so, it is important to understand that we need to make a decision: a free will choice to call on LOVE for assistance, in order for LOVE to be able to help us.

"Make the request. LOVE does the rest," is an important message for humanity.

The more we ask for help, the more LOVE will help us.It is 'quid pro quo', in the sense that LOVE's help is dependent on our efforts to ask for help.

LOVE will never override our free will choice to do nothing to help ourselves. But LOVE is always there for us, in case we change our minds and ask for help. Aim for securing the best outcome for yourself and all precious life.

"Make the request. LOVE does the rest."

The following routine requires:an alarm clock, a place to rest quietly, undisturbed, where you can safely close your eyes, an eye mask is useful, and the bed that you sleep in at night, at home, preferably, is the preferred place, because the help you receive can spread throughout your home to your loved ones and pets. LOVE will clear the space for you.

It is portable though, and can be used anywhere where you can quietly relax and safely close your eyes, and remain undisturbed.

Therefore, it is not suitable in the work place, whilst driving, or operating machinery.

This needs a quiet room with a bed in it where you can lie down on the bed and safely close your eyes and remain undisturbed.

Ask your family to allow you some time to remain undisturbed. Switch off all technology that is not required. Try to remove technology from sleeping areas.

The frequencies of Artificial Intelligence do not resonate with LOVE frequencies and they are incompatible with heart connection, so try to keep your sleeping quarters clear.

You may also wish to have a glass of water by the side of your bed.

Set an alarm clock in case you fall asleep, to ensure you are awake for any important appointments.

Make yourself comfortable by lying on your bed as you normally do for sleep each night.

An eye mask is useful to ensure that no bright sunlight is shining in your eyes.

Here is the routine I use to ensure a powerful heart connection:

I lie down, flat on my back, on the bed that I sleep in at night at home. I ensure my legs are straight and slightly touching but never crossed.

I place my palms facing downwards, flat, on the tops of my thighs.

I ensure I am comfortably warm.

I prepare to relax as I normally do before sleep each night.

When it safe to do so, I close my eyes, and pull down my eye mask and breathe normally.

Then, without strain, I gently take my closed eyes downwards, to gaze softly in the direction of my chest area.I keep my closed eyes gently focusing downwards, and I focus on the air going in and out of my chest.I focus on the gentle rise and fall of my chest, and I start to relax.

I make a free will choice to ask my heart to help me by inwardly saying, "Please can you help me?"

Then I say, "I ask my heart to connect me to LOVE, and I ask LOVE for help, in ways that best serve all."

Then, I press an imaginary switch in the centre of my chest, called "My True Power Switch.

Each time I press my True Power Switch, it indicates my commitment to wanting to make a request for help and for my heart to help me make the best choices for myself and all life.

And with that action, LOVE powerfully comes around me and protects me.

I know that when I do this at home, the help spreads to my loved ones, my pets, my livestock, and my entire space. I know the more I do this, the more help comes in and the more this energy of LOVE reaches out to help all who are suffering or who need help.

I relax and breathe normally, and keep my closed eyes gently focused on my chest area. All my concentration is directed towards my heart centre.

I use the time to talk to my heart about things that are worrying me.

While you rest and receive help, I will tell you about my husband.

Just relax and breathe normally and keep your closed eyes gently focused on your chest area.

My husband used the True Power Switch method to make choices regarding his medical health, in addition to consultation with his medical team. When he was diagnosed with stage four cancer of liver, spleen, bowel and all lower organs in March 2022, he only had two months to live without any treatment. His consultant advised that chemotherapy may help him. We knew the risks of chemotherapy and the side effects. We handed over all our worries to LOVE and asked his heart how he should proceed. In this instance, his heart guided he follow his medical team's advice to take the chemotherapy. However, he was advised by his heart to ask for all that entered his body and all that left his body to be made harmless and purified including the chemotherapy.

Each morning, upon awakening, we would connect to our True Power Switch, and we asked LOVE to purify all chemotherapy, and medicines, all food, drink, all scans, any blood and other samples that left his body.

We were even guided to include the air that we breathe. We asked for all exchanges of energy to be purified, and we always asked for peaceful outcomes that best helped all.

We placed all these requests into our True Power Switch, which we used like a 'wishing well' for requests, and we sought guidance on how we could best serve all. We asked for help three times daily minimum, sometimes more if things were bad:

Morning, upon awaking, midway through the day, and at night, before sleep, as we had been guided that it would keep the heart connection strong.

It is never an easy journey dealing with cancer, however, we did our best to connect each day and ask for help, and we always followed any heart guidance we received.

We kept adding the advice, such as making requests, into our True Power Switch so that we did not have to recall all the requests each day. Once a new request was made, we imagined that we had placed it in our True Power Switch, and we always asked that whenever we connected to heart by pressing our True Power Switch, that all our previous requests were automatically included.

Sometimes, we were asked to make requests for others, such as on hospital days, we often asked for help for the medical staff and patients and hospital teams. Sometimes, we were guided to make requests for world events.

Frequently, when things were overwhelming, we used the True Power Switch to receive supportive frequencies.

Every time a new piece of advice was given to us, we placed it into our heart's 'wishing well', our True Power Switch.

So to recap: We connected Morning — upon awakening, Midway through the day and at Night — before sleep.

The morning connection was the important connection because, if it was a hospital day, or a food shop day, it meant that if we were out somewhere or maybe eating at a cafe, everything we ate or drank would be purified and made harmless for us.

Many don't believe in the power of LOVE but what they may not understand is that as the overriding frequency in existence, and as a powerful force of goodness to be reckoned with, LOVE will set to work to clear all negative energy, all harm that has been caused to food, drink, and medicine, that may have made it drop in frequency, because all that exists on planet Earth are distorted frequencies and the only way to purify the distorted frequencies is to call on LOVE to do this.

There is scientific evidence to show that purest Light frequencies can alter the spin of the atom, and many things which are out of alignment with LOVE are in a state of 'energetic spin' that hold the atom in a trance-like state, or holds a food atom in a low vibrational state.

Purest light frequencies do not carry harm or destructive frequencies.

Atoms are altered and harmed by microwaves and other forms of radiation, so it is worth asking your heart for deeper teachings about this because if you are a medical doctor or scientist, there is much knowledge available to you within your heart centre, and making the time to find out and question may help you to help others in profound ways.

I don't take any action without asking my heart each day.

My husband received the all clear from cancer in November 2022. Our hearts guided us that by handing over what he could not control; - by his acceptance that he may die but also by his hope that he may live; - by never giving up, because he felt in his heart that he had more to do here; - by trusting and having faith that his calls for help had been heard and answered, because we were guided that it is not people's destiny to die of cancer — that it is man-made and not part of LOVE's plan for humanity and all life to die of cancer.

Our hearts advised us that Hope, Trust and Faith are powerful healing frequencies and that if more called for help, LOVE would come in to help, and that might be, to help a person to die peacefully without any distress, or, to survive, because it is not their time.

LOVE decides our ultimate destiny but we do have the ability within our hearts to call for help and this permits the help for us personally to come in.

Never give up. Never think you are all alone. Never forget to call for help.

This simple routine of pressing an imaginary switch in the centre of our chest that I will summarise again below can be used by parents with their children, especially if children are suffering, or out of balance, have autism, depression or anxiety.

It is a simple calming tool that be used like prayer, to calm the mind sufficiently, in order to hear our heart's wisdom. Our heart holds so much knowledge. It has the whole overview on what is happening on the planet, and to us, as individuals.

So, when we ask our hearts for help, we get the best advice that best serves all, including ourselves.

Be a force of goodness for yourself and for others.

Here is the easy routine to follow, once you have listened to the above message, once and in full. Lie down, flat on your back, on the bed that you sleep in at night, where you will not be disturbed.

Relax and take your closed eyes down towards your chest area.

Breath normally and allow your body to relax. Keep focusing your closed eyes gently on your chest area.

With your hand, press an imaginary switch, or pretend you have pressed an imaginary switch in the centre of your chest, your True Power Switch.

Keep your focus on your heart area. Imagine you are speaking to your heart and LOVE, and say:

"Please can you help me?"

Then, say,

"I ask for help in ways that best help all. "

Relax, and receive supportive frequencies for 2 minutes here, and pause the recording if you need more time.

When you feel ready to carry on with your day, ever so gently, move a foot, lift one finger then gently, move the rest, wriggle your toes, gently, raise an elbow, then the next, and stir your body ever so gently as you normally do upon awakening, and when you feel ready, open your eyes.

Become aware of your surroundings and as you do when you normally awaken from a good night's sleep, roll over onto your side.

And wait there until you feel ready to sit up at the side of your bed.

Have a drink of water, if you wish. And when you are ready, slowly and ever so gently, stand up.

The True Power Switch method is very simple to use, and if you use it as guided, at least three times daily, AM, PM, and midway through your day, you may find your spirit uplifts and troubles melt away or resolve. Take time to notice any improvements, and when times are challenging, you may find that regular use of your True Power Switch provides comfort.

The more you ask for help, the more help will come. Once you have made a request, trust that the request has been heard.

We all have lessons and growth, we have to accept that LOVE knows what helps us to grow in ways that best help all.

My husband and I have found this is a useful way to support ourselves and our loved ones each day. I have always believed that humans are capable of so much more than we think and I have always believed that goodness exists. Any doubts about my personal beliefs ebbed away as I watched my husband's miraculous return to health.

The journey is not over for us. We still have many hurdles to deal with. However, without the help from our hearts and LOVE, we would not have coped with the stress as well as we did, and we would not have witnessed the evidence — that LOVE moves in mysterious ways, and LOVE can move mountains.

And we would never have fully cemented the understanding that humanity's creative ability, our imagination and ability to 'hope for the best', are powerful forces, for goodness to prevail.

Chapter Eighteen

STARLINK AND THE INTERNET OF THINGS, NOV 14, 2023

ENTRAPMENT OF YOUR 'CONSCIOUSNESS-AND-ESCAPE-FROM-THE-MATRIX' ENERGY

Audio Link:
@truelightessence, Odysee.com
LOVE'S HEART PLAN, SUBSTACK.COM

How has everyone been, the last few days? It certainly has been extremely choppy, from my perspective, and I have been digging deep — to connect with my consciousness through my heart connection routine — which has been changing with the wind, so to speak, and all is well. It is a lot calmer today, and I feel, it is thanks to all those who are helping themselves now.

Many are starting to benefit from connecting to their higher states of awareness and because many have also understood that we are partly trapped, in twelve levels of awareness in this False Light Construct, you are all starting to understand the enormity of disconnecting within this construct and using heart technologies and LOVE's help to move your consciousness to a safe place.

You are being shown the necessity of how and why this is — by your own consciousness — and I wish to impress upon you all that if you wish to succeed with your role here, it is imperative, repeat, imperative that you no longer give your power, your attention, or your focus on any person, place, or thing for any length of time because you will lose vast amounts of precious codes and they are needed to build your escape ladder out of this place.

The dark have been very clever, and we have been very weak, to be honest.

As a group — as a family of humanity — a group that came in with much Knowledge and Wisdom, and an easy method to secure deeper teachings on how to help others leave this place — we have become immersed in the very trap that we came here to help others escape from. We have not tapped into our consciousness. We have remained trapped in ego-led behaviours, and we have tried and failed to use our minds to resolve Earth issues, yet, all to no avail.

Why is that, when we have the technology to defeat the dark? We simply have not remembered that we could ask LOVE for help. It is as simple as that. Yet, in spite of this dilemma, and in spite of the huge harm this has caused many, and in spite of the danger we have all placed the world's children in, and exposed all precious life, a ray of Hope is shimmering on the horizon — as more realise their potential to escape this place via their consciousness — and have recognised that we have the power within our hearts to help others who are trapped here.

If it were not for the monumental efforts of you all, I would not be sitting here typing out another important download of information. I am unable to retrieve unless others are helping.

Worry not, plenty more have joined and it is hoped that as more are shown the truth about our situation — by their own hearts and consciousness — it becomes less about ego-driven 'opinion' and more about an inner heart 'knowing' ... knowing what we are up against and knowing that we can surmount this if enough choose to help themselves too and so, we must press forward.

Important teachings are on my channels but I currently recommend LOVE'S HEART PLAN, Substack.com because the transcripts and the recordings are there, and I recommend you download these and place the audio messages and transcripts on a memory stick, and on paper.

Keep the teachings safe because they are our history of what happened to us in this place, and what we chose to do about it to — resolve it. I also suggest this because if there is an outage, you may find comfort and more teachings in the saved messages.

The information is freely given. It is our work, our efforts. I am just the typist. We all had to make the effort, in order to secure the teachings — to help us, as concerned individuals, and as a large body of consciousness — our family of humanity.

Here is the message for today. Sit tight, rest on your bed and allow the words to be tested inside your own heart and consciousness, where truth is to be found.

I can make mistakes. I try my best to listen, however, you must be discerning and use your own heart to validate, in case I mishear the message and because the attack on us all is so great, I have to concentrate hard to hear LOVE's guidance...

"Claire, it is all about a soul harvest. The whole episode of the last month's activities has handed over large quantities of data to the dark elite and they have utilised this technology as a weapon against humanity.

What do we mean by a weapon against humanity?

We mean that your attention and focus on satanical rituals such as Halloween, which is the night that the children awaken the dead and have large amounts of their precious life force, their life giving energy — is given away to the dark ones.

You have followed this swiftly by the tradition in the UK of celebrating Guy Fawkes night, another satanic ritual, dressed up as 'entertainment' for the kiddies, but really, all this is about is the burning of a man, a human on the fire as a ritual sacrifice.

The simple act of participating in these rituals fuels the dark's armoury with your stolen life force and worse still, the life force of innocent children, infants and new borns — all taken to these events.

A local church held a festival of light for the children during the Halloween rituals and they presented their pumpkins for a competition. What in the devil has Halloween got to do with church activities?

Quite a lot, it seems, and we will share more later in this discourse.

But first, we wish to share that Claire has been having difficulties trying to stay connected to her heart centre to hear LOVE's guidance and to feel LOVE's embrace. She has diligently continued to follow her heart, and used the methods that we have shared here about a 'castle and moat' metaphor, to help her detect when her connection needed to be upgraded.

So now, more are using this method and it is helping you all to climb further towards the Heart of Creation — to hear truthful guidance and to help you to secure enough help for those who remain trapped inside this False Light Construct.

And it is a 'construct' which has been 'constructed' around you.

What is this construct of False Light made from, you may be wondering? It is made from your life force energy which has been stolen and weaponised against you. That is also what we mean by, "weaponised."

The dark have been very clever, like we have said many times, yet, in their stupidity — at times, when their own ego led behaviour has led the way, it has also fuelled their demise.

They will not succeed. LOVE will put a stop to that behaviour, but you all need to be aware, they are bent on harming you all in the process. The level of malevolence that they feel toward you all is off-the-scale.

Perhaps, if more could perceive this hatred they may try to help themselves more? Who knows? So many are trapped inside the programs of False Light.

The False Light being; their own energy which they have given away, which has been harvested, stolen, manipulated away from them, and this is the 'prison' around each human being and each life form, at soul levels and beyond, which have become trapped — caught up in their own spider's web of their own making.

'Of their own making?'

Yes, we say this, because each one of you is only trapped because you helped the dark construct this web around you. You do understand thi s...don't you?

The dark cannot create.

We have repeated this many times. You need to understand their weaknesses. They cannot create.

How have they managed to entrap you all here, you may be wondering? They trap you into giving your attention to the things that open your energy gateways to your own consciousness, and particularly, at the physical level — your BIOFIELD or Auric field.

This is the low level electrical energy around the human physical body. The further this field goes out, the more powerful it should be, and if you can imagine twelve Russian Dolls of consciousness and higher levels of Knowledge wrapped around your physical self, this might help you to see that your consciousness is not only at the biofield level.

It expands out into higher zones of advanced awareness and the last level that is trapped inside this construct is your COSMIC SHIELD or COSMIC FIELD level.

Unfortunately, many in the group of humanity who could be helping others to leave this trap are themselves immersed in the activities at the Biofield level, without understanding that they are looking at a narrow bandwidth of data and technology.

If you want to get help for yourself and for all precious life, you need to start at the COSMIC SHIELD level and work your way down to heal all levels from there.

Think about this rationally. Your Biofield level at the physical level has the least amount of 'charge' in the electrical atoms that surround the body.

The Cosmic Shield level contains more atoms, more electrically charged systems, and more Knowledge and technology about how to exit the matrix. Why is everyone looking at the Biofield level?

Why restrict yourselves to this limitation?

You will not succeed in escaping this place and you will only be able to hold off the attack from StarLink for so long, but as more in humanity continue to give their power away to the TV, to film programming, to satanic ritual, to the groups who we all know are harming, more and more power is given to the groups who know exactly how to extrapolate your data, and the bigger the attack will become, as more fall into the HIVE MIND mentality.

This means that those of you who are ***targeted individuals*** *are more exposed, not less, and this also means that if you are working with consciousness — which is the only way to overcome the attack — you will find it incredibly hard to protect yourself this way, if you choose to give your power away to those who have self-labeled themselves as your 'rescuers'.*

Are they truly going to help you get out of this place?

You must all start to be highly discerning of other's motives. No court case, no rescuer is going to solve this.

Be aware — you have wolves amongst the genuine folk who are trying to help, but some are not being discerning enough themselves to perceive who is deceiving them.

You could all end up being led astray and getting trapped here. If you are awake, you must surely know that the 'name of the game' is to exit this False Light Construct before it collapses in on itself, and before your consciousness is stolen — to such a degree — that you cannot leave because you gave all your 'escape the matrix' power away.

We say again: No one is going to rescue you.

Be aware of the wolves, passing themselves off as 'rescuers' and 'saviours'.

And be aware of who is being misled by their peers, because there are actually, very few genuine 'rescuers' out there, and they must learn to save themselves.

So, here we all are — contemplating life's meaning, and wondering where this guidance is going...

We always allow time for you all to start to relax and get deep into your heart space before we launch into the important advice for today's listeners. The bar codes on your food and drink have started to become permanent markings on glass and jars, bottles and plastic containers.

Have you noticed this transition?

Have you noticed how many symbols are on your food and drink items, your deliveries and greetings cards?

Where is this heading?...

It is referring to QR codes, the Internet of Things, and the ways the dark will steal more of your life giving codes of Knowledge — to speed up the arrival of the Internet of Things.

What about the Internet of Bodies? That is up and ready to go. Not yet, surely? Oh yes. It has been up and running for some time now...

And with the opening of Parliament and the King's speech, more life codes are stolen — as others view this satanic ritual on their TV and computer screens.

Then, it is straight into Christmas. A satanic ritual, not a Christian ritual, as many have deemed it. The ritual of setting up a 'satellite' in your lounge, complete with satanic star on top and 'snaking' twinkly lights — is an 'effigy' to satan — bringer of destruction and stealer of precious life force codes — to keep you bound to this space so that when you die, your soul cannot escape.

You make this soul harvesting tool each year.

You focus much time on this ritual.

You think about your 'satellite pyramid': will it be a real dead tree or will you use a fake?

It matters not to destroyer force energy. What matters is how much ***time,*** *and* ***effort,*** *and* ***focus you give*** *to securing your Christmas 'satellite' and* ***establishing your soul harvesting equipment*** *— in plenty of time for the children to lose vast amounts of their data and life force.*

You think this is untrue?

Have you asked your heart and consciousness about rituals, and how Christmas trees and celebrations are all geared towards loss of your precious life force codes?

Many of you already know this is true.

So, how does one protect oneself during a busy time for the soul harvesters? Stop giving your power away, even to those you trust.

Trust no one, and listen to your heart and inner consciousness first and foremost.

Protect your energy fields — all twelve levels of trapped consciousness, and protect this each and every day, as Claire has shown you — to ensure that you can reach outside of this matrix — this construct of your own making, and secure help for yourselves, primarily, to ask your Infinite Self, and LOVE at the Heart of Creation — to work with the Laws of Creation — to untangle you from the matrix, and to start to recall all that you have lost, by 'releasing' the attack of malicious, magnified harm and all harm that has been aimed at you — to keep you from hearing truth at the Heart of Creation.

You can all come home if you wish — you simply have to ask for help and it is yours for the taking.

Claire, we wish the others to know about the QR codes and bar codes, and what they truly are.

Do you recall, we said earlier that the dark cannot create? They have to steal your codes of creation — your life force and life giving energy — in order to create the reality of their choice, but it is of your own making, not theirs, simply because, you have to volunteer to give your codes away and the dark are adept at tricking you into giving away your life force.

The QR codes and bars codes are a mishmash of your energy — all of you — and this coding is being used to enslave you, because in order to get the Internet of Things up and running, they need you to give your permission away in order for the Internet of Things to go full-speed ahead. You have all given your permission for the Internet of Bodies.

You have partaken in vaccine programs, given samples of your blood and urine, had biopsies, surgeries, etc., throughout your life.

You have been giving the medical industrial complex your samples for decades.

How many of you have asked for these 'donations' to be surrounded and protected and purified by LOVE — to keep those codes safe, so that they could not be used against you to harm you?

How many of you ever ask for your medicine to be purified before you ingest it?

The Internet of Bodies is up and running, you just haven't noticed it yet.

The Internet of Things is waiting for a few more data dumps of human life force, and from various other life forms too, and it will be ready to 'rock and roll'.

Those who work in the corrupt aspects of your government and local town councils are rubbing their hands with glee and feeling very smug about how easy it has been to box you all into your own self-made prison.

Oh, how the Freemasonic black magicians dance with glee at their clever 'astral-travel tricks' and other illusions. They do feel that they are winning, in spite of the fact that it will not bode well for them and we will share more about this shortly. But, these QR codes and bar codes are now evident everywhere, on magazines, newspapers, vouchers, iPhones, packaging, greetings cards, food and drink items, and so forth.

Now that you know that this coding is all your stolen life force, does it make sense to some of you as to why these codes make you feel uneasy, suspicious?

Some of you do notice, that is also true.

How do you protect yourself from losing your life force codes and what happens when they end up as a QR code, mixed in with other stolen fragments of code from other humans and other life forms?

Do you see enslavement here?

What is your heart and consciousness telling you — when viewed from the Heart of Creation's perspective? Pause the recording here, and give yourself plenty of time to research this for yourself.

Come back to join us once you are ready.

Now you are back, and hopefully you have secured deeper truths to enlighten your perspective on this reality.

It is a reality of choice, meaning: humanity chose this reality by doing what the dark wanted, which was — to give away their codes of Knowledge — to create their own enslavement.

Don't you think it is time to break free from these shackles that bind you to this place? If you caused the problem, it makes sense, doesn't it, that you can also uncreate this?

Those codes that form the QR codes and bar codes have been placed in front of you so that you are, in effect, complying with and agreeing with your own enslavement.

If you spotted the harm — spotted the trick — and took steps to defend yourself and ask for help, the dark would be powerless to enslave your codes. They would not be able to use them, LOVE could find all that you have lost and recall them — to be repaired and restored to you as Purest Light that can never be corrupted by the dark or any other thing.

Your acquiescence is what the dark are seeking, and if they place something in front of you and you do nothing, they can steal it because YOU GAVE IT AWAY.

Why the movies about death by cell phone; disasters; viruses; aliens; corrupt governments? Why the adverts and marketing with satanic symbolism? Why TV and comedies designed to distract you? Why Halloween? Why Christmas? Why, why, why?

They place things in front of you and if you do nothing to protect yourself, nothing to defend yourself, meaning: if you do not ensure that your twelve 'Russian Dolls' of your trapped consciousness are protected and all doors closed, the dark can walk right in and the soul harvest begins.

It is a shame that parents do not yet understand what they are doing to their children each year. The children's codes are deemed more valu-

able and children love Disney and the like, don"t they? All those movies with one eyed monsters, fairytales, and princesses.

Parents need to be extra vigilant about what they expose their children to and to not take part or be a party to the child abuse that takes place at higher levels of the 'Russian Dolls' of infants and new borns, all because the parents volunteer to give their life force away.

Who needs satanic ritual in broad day light? Parents are sacrificing their children's soul each day, through activities run by churches and the like, that hold no moral or ethical value when viewed from the Heart of Creation's perspective. And when parents expose their children in this way, their own Russian Doll of higher awareness is also raped and pillaged.

How much life force was stolen between October and November 2023? *Ask your heart, to hear fullest truth about how much has gone, and if not restored soon, will be lost for good.*

The Internet of Things relies on your stolen life force codes. We have explained, that when the stolen codes are presented to you on packaging etc., and when you ignore this, the dark can use the codes of yours that they already have stored in data banks, and they can copy these and copy these, and copy this, and eventually, the copied copies become part of you in AVATAR WORLD.

You recall your supreme 'Annihilator Klaus', saying: ***"You will own nothing, and be happy?"*** *This is because eventually, you that is you now, will not exist at all. That is the plan. The plan is that the* ***AVATAR YOU*** *will supersede any requirement for you, as a human, to exist.*

You will become 'one' with the quantum computer. You will be a 'node in the interface'.

Many of you balk at the absurdity of this possibility, and it just goes to show how fast the technology has gone, and how far behind many are, because they simply cannot conceive why anyone would want this and the truth is, not 'anyone' does.

You are not talking about 'anyone'.

You are talking about a full-blown attack by Artificial Intelligence, A.K.A., Extra Terrestrials (which are AWOL souls and AWOL higher levels of awareness) that are so lost in the programs of false light, they are bent on destruction, not love.

LOVE no longer exists for this group. They are the reason this is happening. Claire has talked about this many times and many do share information about ET's and AI, and the war that is raging in space; as different factions of the aforementioned groups line up to gain complete power and control over humanity and all life here.

You have all been 'copied and pasted' so many times, and it has been relatively easy to create ***AVATAR WORLD*** *with your life force codes and* ***DNA*** *codes.*

You do have the power to turn this around, but it will take an enormous effort to start looking at where your life force is being given away voluntarily — by yourself.

Everything around you is branded; labelled; coded; carries additional mind controlling symbols. Others may say: to ignore these things and to focus on the Biofield.

We say, do that at your peril. You have to look at the bigger picture. This is not just about a body part. That is a nugget of information and can lead to misunderstandings on what is happening to you.

See yourselves as twelve levels of vast consciousness — compartmentalised into higher levels of learning and Knowledge and expanded states of awareness — with solutions and hindrances at every level.

LOVE has the overview. You simply do not.

And you do not have enough time to resolve this by yourself. There is no more time left.

The In Breath is near completion, and all will end where they are, when that completes. The name of the game is to extract all your consciousness from this False Light place and to ask LOVE to help you by finding all the fragments of code that you have lost, because much of the ***QR codes and bar*** *codes contain your* ***"escaping the matrix codes."***

These are the codes that you brought with you and they are your 'emergency ration' because you have squandered all your other codes to escape. All that Knowledge has been stolen and weaponised against you. So, these QR codes and bar codes are your escape codes, stolen and mixed in with other codes from other humans and life forms...

Do you have the Knowledge to retrieve them?

No, you do not. However, your Infinite Self at the Heart of Creation has the Knowledge, along with LOVE and the Laws of Creation, who ensure all actions ensure the safety of all precious life.

That is why we are suggesting that in order to secure your lost codes to exit the matrix, you must give your permission to your Infinite Self and LOVE and the Laws of Creation to help you.

This is LOVE in action and LOVE cannot impose on your free will to do nothing, or to keep giving your power away. It can only intercept what the ET's and AI technologies are doing when you give your permission — by asking for the assistance. "Make the request. LOVE does the rest."

Your Infinite Self has to be engaged in your rescue. It is the part of you that is unhindered by destroyer force; that is connected to LOVE at the heart of Creation. It is there to be your protector, but you have to ask. It will never impose. It can only help you if you ask for help.

And the dark do the opposite, don't they? They trick you into giving your focus, your attention, your PERMISSION for them to step in and start to rape and pillage your Russian Dolls of Knowledge and Wisdom.

Where are you currently giving your power away? Who are you currently giving your power away to? Which rescuer? Which saviour? *No one can save you, except your heart and your Infinite Self. No one. Remember this truth. And so, next time someone raises your hopes that something is being done to stop all this; when they want your signature, your money, your subscription, or a coffee, remember what we guide here: To ask for anyone at this dark, dreadful time for their money, when the role of many is to help others who have become trapped in density — to ask for their palms to be crossed with silver is not in alignment with LOVE's plan. It breaks Cosmic Law — the Laws of Creation.*

It causes untold harm and suffering, and loss of life force. You are all at a critical phase — a stage of learning on the Earth — where it is becoming clear that many in the 'alternative' groups are harming humanity.

Claire is seeing this. Many that she thought were helping are now being called into question. Why do you see some of them, but not all, and why do others see the threat and not you?

You have all lost different codes of Knowledge, and like a faulty computer with a virus, you cannot always see what is glaringly obvious to others, and vice-versa.

Forgive yourselves for all errors of judgement. Those who are deceiving will pay a high price eventually, but not before they have led many good souls who have been shouting about the deceptions into the same trap as the others are already in.

Most are there to steer, and most will turn on you eventually, so, be warned. Do not be as trusting. Some are being misled themselves. Some are seeking fame, kudos, and some are ego-driven. All these traits are damaging to others when they give their power away.

How many have offered solutions?

How much change has honestly been achieved?

In four years, what has been stopped?

This is too big for any group or human to resolve. This is a multi-pronged attack on humanity at every level of awareness. They attack you in the ***physical*** *and manipulate you here because this part of your extensive energy field — those Russian Dolls — this part* ***lacks the most codes,*** *the most* ***Knowledge*** *and is, therefore, easy to use as a way of breaking into your higher decks of Knowledge at the Cosmic Field level, downwards.*

It is a full-scale attack.

How many mention the Extra Terrestrial attack on humanity?

How many advise you that your codes of Remembrance are being stolen?

How many suggest that you can use your own heart and consciousness to exit this space, and secure help for those innocent souls who are still trapped in this matrix?

Too much to take in?

Why would any human want to trap you in the Internet of Things and Bodies?

You are ***not dealing*** *with a* ***human threat.***

You are dealing with a full-scale, full-on attack on your consciousness.

A mass soul harvest is in full swing. Your children are being harmed in extensive ways, and unless you stop giving their power away, they will become trapped when this place implodes.

You have all given too much of your power — your DNA, your life force, life giving energy, and your emergency escape energy away. You will need to get it back, and you need to secure a safe method for doing this that does not risk giving more of your power away.

At this stage, it is all about:

Asking for your mistakes to be corrected and deleted. (Think — overlooking where you volunteer your power away, such as, QR codes),

then,

asking for all magnified, malicious harm, and all harm directed at you to be gathered up by Infinite LOVE and the Laws of Creation, and sent back to all those responsible for ensuring that this magnified, malicious harm and all harm reached your door,

then,

asking Infinite LOVE and the Laws of Creation to find all that has been lost and return it to wholeness — to purity — and to be restored to you as Purest Light codes that can never be infiltrated, harmed, destroyed or corrupted by any other person, place or thing, including destroyer forces, and then: To ask your Infinite Self, Infinite LOVE, and the Laws of Creation from the Heart of Creation to help you understand how you can best help all in optimal ways, in alignment with LOVE and the Laws of Creation.

This prayer can be used three times daily, AM, PM and midway through your day: ***"May the frequency of Peace reign supreme and may Infinite LOVE help humanity in optimal ways that best serve all precious life."***

The prayer is transportable and can be ***used to purify food, drink, medicine, and the very air that you breathe.***

The more you use it, the more powerful it becomes and the more help you 'magnetise' into this reality; to secure help for all the innocent life and those who are trying to protect all innocent life throughout all levels of awareness — all levels that are being harmed within the Russian

Dolls of the children, newborns, infants, and countries — where wars are raging and decimating the populous. This prayer offers powerful assistance to best serve all life.

Look at the world.

Look at the world beyond your TV sets...

Does it look futile?

Does it feel frightening?

This is what happens when the few out-manoeuvre the many. When those with knowledge use it as weapons against those who also have Knowledge but give it away too freely.

Humanity created this world. They helped build the empire that is now destroying them. At some point soon, it will be too late to undo all your errors.

For those who understand that the issues start at the metaphysical and nothing can be resolved until these issues — these open gateways — are closed on the dark, then, more will suffer.

Children will be raped, abused, trafficked and harmed beyond your imagination. If you don't like this world, you have to uncreate it, and this means, asking from heart — to the purest aspects of Creation for help.

Your minds are captured agencies. Their Knowledge is gone. All that is left is your heart Knowledge and that is under attack.

When StarLink gets more advanced aspects of your stolen Knowledge and that of the children then, the soul harvested energy will be weaponised.

You will be enslaved in the Internet of Things and Bodies.

You will "comply or die."

Elon has recently glamourised the future and made it sound very cuddly and warm. He baited you, that is all, and Rushi Sunak helped him.

The interview about the future was simply to gain your attention and, therefore, your compliance and therefore, your permission — for them to use the codes they already have to harm you.

Remember this — they steal your life force and weaponise it against you. They can only harm you with stolen energy. They can only direct this weaponry at you if you have given your permission and attention, and without defending or protecting yourself while listening or watching — that is all they need to break-in further, to other areas of your Russian Doll.

Think:

Where are you giving your energy away?

Who are you giving your energy to?

How much power have you got left to leave the matrix, when you eventually die?

How can you help to expose those who lie?

How can you best serve all in optimal ways, and how can you help to awaken the others to the dangers they are in?

You are all loved. You can all get the help.

Climb your ladder and ask for help. It is here, waiting for you to retrieve it.

Claire, that is enough for today. This must go.

Others need their eyes opening wide before they give their signature, their money, or pointless coffees away to those seeking power-over and/or offering power-stealing 'assistance' to those who are targeted and being harmed the most.

Please post this immediately. Post it now, and pray that the liars are exposed before more lose vast amounts of life force to pointless court cases and power-point presentations."

Chapter Nineteen

FINAL TIME TO CHOOSE LIFE: TIMELINE SWITCH, NOV 15, 2023

"There is very little time left and we wish all groups to be given as much warning as possible because their choices affect their future, or lack of one. This is the final time to choose life. "

LOVE'S HEART PLAN, SUBSTACK.COM

AUDIO LINK

"Claire, we have a huge amount of data to share. It won't be pretty but it has to be said. It is the only way left to wake the others up. They have to know what they are up against if they are to stand a chance at surviving what is coming. Make no mistake, things are grim right now. Many of you must be feeling the descent in frequencies; like a lift descending into the basement, humanity have managed to go further down, into the 'bowels of Hell,' and now, we are unsure of their future. Indeed, it is a grim day for all. But not for the Grim Reaper, who has thoroughly enjoyed and been entertained by his soul harvest this year. This year's soul harvest has proven to be a 'bumper year'.

A year to remember as 'special', because so many souls gave their power away and have got stuck in the deepest recesses of false light. They are so entrapped now, that only LOVE can save them, and yet, LOVE needs them to ask for help. It is the law of Creation that even LOVE cannot and will not interfere with the free will choices of the many who are choosing to try to tackle the Earth's issues with their minds — thinking in some superior fashion — that they have sufficient Knowledge to resolve the many complex issues, and the many layers and levels of unseen attack by unknown forces; unidentified enemies and slayers of men, women and children — many of whom are keeping their lights shining brightly — but only for the Child Catcher and the Grim Reaper to see them.

What we are inferring here, is that these bright lights emit their light for all to see and steal, yet, they do not protect it; they constantly give it away; they do not question the motives of others, and they do not question the part they have played in the downfall of the world's children who are suffering greatly at the hands of these 'evil doers,' and this is about to get a whole lot worse. Nor can those of you who are trying to help others, interfere with the choices made by these bright lights. It is against the law for you to interfere.

What to do, then, to assist without interference? Climb. Climb your ladder of Knowledge and Wisdom. Do not stop, not even for a few hours or more. You have to climb now, higher than you have been before in this life, and you have to hope that your efforts to climb can pull these bright lights up from the bowels of Hell into a finer frequency of light.

It is their only chance now. Your efforts. Your climb. Your heart-felt desire to protect all precious life. You are supported. It may seem difficult at times.

You have been advised to work quietly and diligently to keep the dark from knowing what you are up to. Of course, they know this. They listen and hear the messages, too.

But what they cannot hear, or see, or know is your intentions when you connect to LOVE through your own heart, your expanded states of consciousness, and most importantly, your Infinite Self.

Your Infinite Self is your protector, your friend, the part of you that is all knowing, all loving, all wise. The part that is powerfully connected to LOVE's embrace at the heart of Creation, and the part of you that knows the Laws of Creation — inside and out, and back-to-front.

It knows what is possible and what is not. It knows what you can do and what you must not. It sees the effects of choices and knows the outcome. It can offer the "optimal options — to best serve all precious life, in alignment with LOVE's plan and the Laws of Creation from the heart of Creation. "

It knows how you must climb; where you need to go. And it knows what the dark are doing to try to stop you from helping.

In essence, your Infinite Self has the entire overview and therefore, must be consulted at all times.

We are jumping over now to another issue: "Comply, or die. "

This is the narrative that is being put out over the dark net and we don't mean the 'dark net' of the World Wide Web, although some of it is linked. No. We are talking about the dark, shady world of Avatar World and the place that you all go to at night when you sleep and your consciousness is left unprotected from the harm that happens in this dark place.

They (that is, the dark Extra Terrestrials and Artificial Intelligence groups) are already experimenting on your copied copies of copied life force energy — the life force that they stole from you during lock-downs through your waste water, your sewage waste, your PCR 'DNA procurement test', lateral flow discarded tests and many other methods; used to procure and steal your life force codes — your unique codes of Knowledge and data.

Such a 'prize' for the dark because now that they have the Internet of Bodies up and running, they are intent on executing the Internet of Things in the shortest time possible, because they are in a race against time.

You did know that time is running out, quite literally, didn't you?

TIME is about to end.

Tick, tock, goes the clock...

When TIME ends, what do you think will happen? If you are still stranded in density, or worse still, inside the basement gates leading to Hell and the point of no return, what will happen to all your codes, your life, your soul, your entire ladder of consciousness that is still inside this place?

Climb your ladder.

Climb fast.

Climb like there is a fire burning along your ladder and it must not reach you. *Not before you have exited this place.*

Climb high.

Keep climbing.

This is not just about others, this is about your self, about your journey — your 'fall' into this place. LOVE promised that when the TIME came, when things were looking worse than ever before, when TIME was running out for these other souls, LOVE always promised that if you asked for help, you would be transported away from this place so that when it collapses in on its own errors, none of your life force, none of your valuable Knowledge is lost in this place.

Climb your ladder. Climb high. Climb fast.

Ask LOVE to help you and trust that LOVE's promise will be honoured. The Laws of Creation know no bounds when it comes to helping souls who call for help. Your calls for help need to be regular, persistent, and your heart centre must be frequently monitored for new updates, because as humanity descend rapidly into the StarLink trap and move towards the gates of Hell, the vacuum left from the space they are being manipulated away from, which is causing the descension — that space; that vacuum has to be filled.

Any soul who is not asking LOVE for help will get sucked into the space; the vacuum left by humanity.

If you are working on the BIOFIELD area, if you are ***not*** *looking at your entire ladder of consciousness that is trapped inside the False Light Construct, if you are not asking your Infinite Self for help, not asking LOVE and the Laws of Creation for protection and guidance,* ***you are UNPROTECTED.***

Those who do YOGA, REIKI, PILATES, CIRCLE DANCING etc., are highly vulnerable. We will explain, once more, but we also ask that you use these connections and ask to be shown on your inner heart screen what is happening metaphysically to your ladder of trapped consciousness, and what is happening to your life force when you practice these things.

Yesterday's message will help shed more light. We will summarise here again:

Reiki is a frequency which was procured by sixth dimensional beings — to help others below decks — in the lower dimensions.

Sixth dimensional energies are riddled with corrupted, satanic frequencies.

Thirty years ago, Reiki offered some benefits — in line with the planetary and Greater Cosmos activities. In 2012, things changed so drastically, that all the satanically corrupted aspects of Reiki — the symbols used to attune subjects, for example the spiral, the 'Zonar', etc. , all the toxic, harmful energies became terribly dangerous and when put into a human energy field at the BIOFIELD level — the place that is the weakest part of the human energy fields — the loss of life force became untenable.

Reiki groups were asked to disconnect from Reiki energy to protect themselves, and humanity and all precious life from further loss. Some heard the call. Others chose to ignore it, and many carried on teaching, making money from this practice, and this corrupted it further.

A decade ago, all in the holistic communities were asked to stop using any method that came from outside of self, to use heart connection, and to secure new teachings from their hearts.

Yoga has been corrupted by the same satanic method over millennia of meddling by man's ego-led behaviour. The purity of these teachings were lost, millennia ago, and what is left is a corrupted spiritual exercise that opens the gateways at the BIOFIELD level and allows the Grim Reaper to walk right into your entire ladder of consciousness inside the False Light Construct, and construct a 'web of enslavement' around you with your own, stolen energy which you volunteered freely by giving your permission, by giving your attention to this exercise.

The 'salute to the sun' pose is a classic, satanic 'bait'. You bow to the Sun god energy — Lucifer — your bow indicates that you permit your gateways to be open to Lucifer.

Many other exercises cement your permission to have your life force stolen. Lucifer has done nothing wrong. Lucifer has not broken any Laws of Creation because you gave your attention, your time, your body, your consciousness willingly. No laws were broken by Lucifer. They were broken by you.

Opening your BIOFIELD and your ladder of consciousness that is trapped inside the False Light programs, is akin to murder. You are allowing your life force to be stolen — your life-giving energy. You are also opening a doorway for Lucifer to enter the Earth plane. This means that Lucifer energy can ride rough shod over every person you meet and connect with, including, via email and text.

It is akin to murdering others because they lose vast amounts of life force energy, too.

Pilates. How could Pilates possibly be harmful or detrimental to your health and spiritual well-being?

We have repeatedly said: when you give your attention to anything; when you have not called on LOVE to protect your entire ladder of consciousness; when you go to a classroom where the teacher has no knowledge of this attack; when you spend time with others who also have no idea about their ladder of consciousness or BIOFIELD; when you choose to give your power away — by opening all your gateways while you FOCUS on making small, circular movements and create SINE WAVES inside your BIOFIELD, what do you think happens?

What happens when you volunteer to open your gateway at the BIOFIELD level; what happens to your BIOFIELD when you create SINE WAVES inside an unprotected part of you, that you cannot yet perceive?

That's right.

Vast amounts of life force are stolen — volunteered — by your actions to participate in something without understanding Earth energy, Lucifer energy, Biofield energy, or, your ladder of consciousness — up to the Cosmic Field level.

This is not an attack on your person: This is a warning from LOVE that these methods harm others, not just yourselves, and when you all open your doorway to the Grim Reaper — like 'viral shedding' — you spread this attack to everyone else on the planet.

Who needs depopulation and mass genocide, when the very groups who could be helping to protect are busy facilitating humanity's demise?

That is akin to murder, and we would ask those of you who still are choosing to be hell-bent on harming in this way; who refuse to stop because of kudos; limited, ego-led thinking; a refusal to want to hear the Truth above all, and a refusal to do your job which is to protect and defend the very souls who came in with less codes of protection and remembrance, so that you could have more.

You have squandered this help — this opportunity — and unfortunately, your refusal, at this stage, spells dire consequences because as we have previously shared, you do not have the right to take a life.

LOVE gives life.

LOVE is asking you to save the lives of those who are trapped through no fault of their own.

If a dead infant and suffering newborn will not change your mind, what will?

The Laws of Creation are working hard now on the Earth plane. These laws govern humanity's choices and the individual choices of those who choose to take life, not protect life. Those who could not love will be thrown into the gates of Hell by their own choices, not by LOVE's or anyone else's.

You will do this to yourself, because the vacuum we talked about earlier will be filled by your very selves, and slowly, this vacuum is moving so close to the point of no return that soon, you will have no choice.

"You will own nothing and be happy", because you will end up dead and your soul will be sucked into AVATAR WORLD a. k. a, the Gates of Hell, ready for the Klaus supporters to hunt you down — over, and over, and over again. This is not exaggeration. This is what you are all facing — all who hear this, and choose to do nothing to protect all precious life.

And what about those students, the clients and villagers who continue to attend your classes at your local venues?

Do you even care about what this is doing to their life force?

What will happen to these innocent participants?

Death. And, death of the soul.

The ladder of consciousness is so badly injured and corrupted — from the Cosmic Field level down to the BIOFIELD LEVEL — that, at some point, the soul will either: fragment completely and get sucked into the abyss of Hell; never to return to its true home — to LOVE at the Heart of Creation — or, if parts of the ladder of conscious awareness call for help, at a critical point, the Laws of Creation will decide to withdraw all aspects that can be saved back to the heart of Creation, but not before severing the ladder at the personality level.

There will be a thin Biofield of weak, electrical energy around the person— nothing to protect against StarLink frequencies, which are off-the-scale in terms of the damage they will do to the ladder of unpro-

tected consciousness, and if there is no ladder except the Biofield, there is no protection.

If there is no protection, what do you think will happen to your remaining life force energy?

Lucifer will grab that.

You cannot call on LOVE for help once your entire ladder of consciousness is withdrawn from this place. You have imprisoned yourself, further — given yourself the death sentence — and when Lucifer comes for you, it will not be enjoyable.

It will be a 'feeding frenzy' and we are afraid to tell you — you will suffer. You can either, take offence at this information or you can receive it as it is intended — a message of warning: to tell you that you are in danger of jeopardising your future; your life; your onward journey.

LOVE loves you, and wants you to know, so that you can save yourself.

To dismiss this guidance is a revelation to yourself — of how immersed you are in density, and immersed in the prison of your own making. You have allowed too much of your life force to be stolen and replaced with False Light codes, and this means that you cannot access Truth.

You gave Lucifer those codes and Lucifer gave you False Light. You don't even realise that your codes of Remembrance are gone.

That is all we have to say on the matter. There is much to share and it is hoped that you are all connecting deep inside your heart centres and stilling busy minds, in order to hear Truth from the heart of Creation, nowhere else.

You will not reach Truth inside this False Light Construct. Not at this stage of the game. You have all lost vast amounts of life force. LOVE can be called upon to get this life force back, but you will need to be quick.

Claire, can you expand on what you are perceiving?"

I say: "I have been using my heart connection method — by using my 'Castle and Moat' routine. It has proven to be very helpful. I have been checking in more than three times daily; because my gut and heart respond to planetary changes in frequencies.

This 'early warning alarm system' has been 'going off' very regularly.

For example, I am waking up in the night and needing to check the outside of my castle tower because my heart and gut are feeling the changes; the drop in density.

Even though I may have upgraded, a few hours later, my early warning system is sounding the alarm, again. My gut tightens and sometimes I feel quite nauseous.

I feel pressure on my heart... all these are signs to me that an attack is ensuing and causing harm to all life. It indicates a soul harvest and loss of life force. The sensations calm down once the upgrade is completed.

I feel the trauma that others are feeling. It is not a pleasant experience; it can be heartbreaking to feel this level of their suffering, but at least I know how bad things are and I can take action to help in some way.

So, I am upgrading my heart connection switch and being moved to uplifted levels of awareness very regularly, at present.

It calms down for a while and then the whole thing starts up again: my alarm system warns me; my gut feels like it has a lead weight in it; a sense of dread washes over me; my chest area feels pressure.

I go straight into Heart Routine... I look out of my 'castle tower' window. I check the outside situation and then, check my barometer. Then, I ask my Infinite Self and LOVE for guidance on each step that I need to take.

I use the prayer that was shared yesterday and previously. It feels very powerful and I feel it is helping all precious life. I value the support I am receiving and I value the efforts of you all, because we are all helping each other and we are a strength for each other.

The outside view from my castle tower window is very telling.

Initially, I perceived a dark mass of marching 'scorpion-type' creatures, and black widow spiders, all crawling and swarming over each other at the base of the castle but this has now changed and where it had all been happening at the base, my entire outside view has now become black— pitch black — and the energy is dark, dense, toxic.

My barometer has read "Total Collapse" sometimes, at other times, it has read "Gales", "Stormy", "Rain". Oddly enough, it has matched the real weather that followed the barometer's weather warning. I also noticed that when we had gales, the attack that I was sensing and the help that eventually came to move me out of this dark, metaphysical space and away from the toxic Earth energy coincided with a return to calmer weather and ceasing of rain.

Is it connected? How can I help the listeners today, in ways that best serve all precious life, in alignment with LOVE's plan and the Laws of Creation from the heart of Creation, and infinitely beyond?

"Claire, we wish the group who wish to help humanity and the children, especially, to know that they will have to be extremely vigilant about checking the situation from their castle tower and reading the barometer, and they need to secure a method whereby they are not in distress but can have an 'early warning' that they need to go inside their hearts and check the situation outside their tower.

It can be a song playing in your head — anything at all — ask your Infinite Self to help you secure an 'early warning alarm system' to help you know when your heart connection is required, because we are attempting to help you all move through density and to pioneer a pathway to safety — for others to follow.

You may feel 'blocked' at times. You may feel like you cannot hear your heart guiding you, or you cannot perceive the way forward.

If you stick with the routines and hit a block, ask for help to explain why that might be:

What is happening on the Earth plane?

How is that affecting your climb?

There are always teachings to be had. You will have to 'push' your way past density. Your determination to help others 'pushes' you onwards.

It may not feel an easy climb at times, however, you must Trust that if you have tried your best and cannot move forward, if the block is too great to 'push' past, hand it all over to your Infinite Self and to LOVE, and trust that at the perfect time, you will be assisted.

See the bigger picture. See this like a military operation:

LOVE has many projects on the go.

Sometimes you cannot move forward until others have secured their own rescue package.

Sometimes LOVE is waiting for others to secure a new tool or gift, and until this is discovered and utilised, LOVE has to put things on hold.

The harder you work to help yourself, the harder you try to unlock your own gifts, and to listen to LOVE's guidance on the 'requests' that you are being asked to make to secure the optimal outcome for all precious life, the more you help humanity and the children.

Your hard endeavours are keeping Claire busy typing.

Look how many messages are coming out, as downloads. These 'data packages of Knowledge' cannot be released until you have offered your assistance, and your hard endeavours are securing huge 'data dumps of Knowledge' to be placed in the emergency grids and grids of consciousness, and this offers life-lines of assistance for those awakening, who have called on LOVE for help.

"Make the request. LOVE does the rest. "

Love cannot impose. LOVE comes when called upon and when you ask your heart — your Infinite Self — what request could you make to help humanity in optimal ways that best serve all life, it is your heart that can assess the seriousness of the situation, the outcome if left unattended by LOVE, and therefore, can secure the prayer or heart request that you can make to LOVE, to try to secure the best outcome for all.

Quite often, it is the 'optimal request' that you make to LOVE that is ensuring the most powerful assistance comes through from the heart of Creation.

Question everything and seek clarity on your best actions. If you do not understand why you are being asked to request a certain thing, you must ask your heart for teachings and explanations.

You must ensure that any request "best serves all precious life in optimal ways, in alignment with LOVE's plan and the Laws of Creation. "

This keeps all your actions and prayers working at ***optimal*** *levels to best help all life. Being strict about how you check for clarity brings dividends, and you will gain so much deeper understanding, which can be joyful and enlightening.*

Any Knowledge that helps you grow also helps all precious life, especially, those souls who are trapped in this False Light Construct, through no fault of their own. It is a group effort, and more are being called upon to help because the situation is dire, truly dire on the Earth plane.

Claire, we are going to move on now to another severe warning and this is aimed at those who collaborate and perpetrate.

Claire, your world as you know it is about to change, and not for the better. Another TIMELINE switch is about to take place. It is why we have been encouraging you all to gather up all that you have lost in this place before the vital codes of lost Remembrance are gone for good.

With the switching of the TIMELINES, comes more soul shock, more soul fragmentation and more souls to harvest for the dark. We have put out many warnings about TIMELINE switches and we had previously said that this would not be able to happen again.

A group had been asked to maintain a firewall. The help came in, but the issue is that many are lost in the programs — to the degree that their hearts will answer a call for energetic help and, then, this firewall requires their heart's input each day.

If others wane with their heart connection, if they connect erratically, or haphazardly, this weakens the firewall. LOVE can put a stop to something, but humanity has to contribute — to keep that firewall strong. If not, it weakens, and it means: codes of Remembrance can be stolen.

The TIMELINE switch issue keeps cropping up when it could be prevented. Each time, humanity allow their ***life force energy*** *and* ***codes of DNA*** *(their codes of Knowledge) to be stolen; taken; lost; handed over to the dark, destroyer forces, that energy — those* ***codes of Knowledge*** *— are used to sustain the dark forces, and the rest is used as a weapon against you.*

Stolen codes of Knowledge will hand the dark the information that they need to create a new TIMELINE switch... If humanity understood how dire this situation is... If they knew how exposed this leaves them... If they knew it will cause the soul to go into shock as parts of it witness the switch, and knowing the outcome — the devastation that this switch will create... The soul fragments, and sometimes, it implodes in on itself.

We explained about this 'implosion' a long time ago. To remind those who do not know about the soul imploding in on itself, it is akin to a nuclear explosion of the most delicate aspect of your spirit.

Your poor soul is in a weakened state because you do not protect it sufficiently to stop dark forces attacking it. If the attack on the soul is ongoing; repetitive; torturous and unrelenting, then, it starts to break away... Tiny pieces of itself leave; fragment, and try to go into hiding.

The 'soul fragments' are hunted down; eventually caught; stripped of their purest light codes, and raped and pillaged until there is nothing left of it, except a broken 'bag of bits' — akin to a car being stripped of its engine, tyres, anything of value that can be repurposed, and all that is left is a few nuts and bolts.

The soul no longer knows itself, and the worst is yet to come, as these unwanted parts are thrown into the Gates of Hell — unwanted; discarded; broken. That is one scenario.

There are many other scenarios that cause the soul to fragment. The worst case scenario is a 'nuclear' explosion: An atomic implosion, at nuclear level. This is when the soul can no longer face the onslaught, the repetitive attack; the lack of love from the human who the soul belongs to. It is all too much sometimes, and this fragile creature takes drastic action — it blows itself up to prevent its codes of Knowledge being stolen.

A last act of love to best help all, it mistakenly thinks.

You did this. At certain stages, all of you have caused your soul to implode.

This lifetime, it was hoped that you would peacefully protect this precious part of yourself — in peaceful ways — but at all costs. It was hoped you would save your own soul, at least...

So now, we have souls who are about to implode because they sense what the dark are doing, they perceive the outcome of this crisis, and they know that the Laws of Creation are about to be broken by humanity, once more.

What happens when your soul implodes; when it explodes in on itself?

Death. Death of your soul.

And death of your very selves because when your soul implodes, the ladder of consciousness is broken — it is severed.

A chain reaction starts. The ladder of consciousness is severed between the higher self level and the personality self.

The human does not notice, not unless it connects to its heart, in which case, this would never happen because a heart that is connected to LOVE has protection.

Then, you have the additional ingredient of StarLink. The energy of all your ***heartache*** *is trapped inside* ***StarLink. StarLink*** *is the* ***technology created by Extra Terrestrials and Cyborgs like Elon,*** *and this energy is being used against you,* ***weaponised*** *—to blow huge holes in your Cosmic Shield, the place that holds great Knowledge and the information: the* ***data*** *needed to break into your heart space. That is all that StarLink is for. Forget your faster speeds.*

And if you are thinking of signing up for StarLink, we guide that you are signing your own death warrant because to give your power — your permission — for this technology to reach you directly through your acquiescence will open up the Gates of Hell for you, as the Grim Reaper walks right in to harvest your soul and ladder of consciousness from the top floor down — from the Cosmic Shield down to the BIOFIELD level.

A raping and pillaging is on the cards.

The soul will suffer untold trauma as it witnesses this event. It knows it will become trapped if another timeline switch takes place and it knows that TIME is nearly over, and that there will be no more time to secure rescue.

The outcome is dire. Do you see, now?

When a sleepwalking humanity who do not perceive their heart or soul go unprotected through a timeline switch: How many will lose vast amounts of data? How many will lose soul fragments? How many will experience death of the soul, as the soul feels forced to make an 'emergency implosion' to protect its codes?

Will humanity experience more death, as this takes place?

Will humanity suffer loss within their very selves?

Will unexplained heartache follow? Or, illness — followed by 'sudden' death?

What will happen if this timeline switch completes?

What do we mean by the 'end of TIME is approaching' and what does this mean for you all?

How can you help yourselves and best serve all precious life?

If you cannot interfere with humanity's choice to surrender it's soul to the dark, what can you do to help protect your own life force and consciousness?

Are you protected sufficiently?

Is prayer enough, or do you need a more robust routine?

If you have children, what could you do to help secure their brightest future?

We also repeat this question that follows:

How can you help to expose the liars; the deceivers; those who self-label themselves as your saviours, rescuers, and those who are distracting you with promises that are only being presented to you, to enable more of your power, and attention, and focus to be directed away from your soul evolution and toward their spiders web of deception and extraction of your precious data?

What does this TIMELINE switch plan aim to do?. . .

You all have the means and the tools to secure this information through your Infinite Selves, with LOVE and the Laws of Creation to keep you safe. We repeat once more, the situation is dire on planet Earth and is about to get a whole lot worse.

Climb your ladder.

Climb as often as you are able.

Give yourself the gift of love and life, and be prepared that many are not going to survive this onslaught, not with all the other levels of attack that are taking place unhindered.

Climb your ladder and reach out for safer and safer places to climb through.

The best help you can offer all life at this time is to secure your own rescue.

Claire, we want this to go. There is very little time left and we wish all groups to be given as much warning as possible because their choices affect their future, or lack of one.

This is the final time to choose life".

Chapter Twenty

CONSERVING ENERGY DURING A PLANETARY CRISIS: FULL ON INVASION, NOV 17, 2023

NEW HEART CONNECTION ROUTINE UPGRADE; ET INVASION; PLAY SPOT THE BOT: SPOTTING CONTROLLED OPS AND PIED PIPERS; PROTECTING YOUR CONSCIOUSNESS AND LIFE FORCE — YOUR LIFE-GIVING ENERGY; USING YOUR GIFTS; SECURING A SAFE PLACE TO RETREAT TO.

"If you have LOVE, you have enough

LOVE'S HEART PLAN, SUBSTACK.COM

Audio: @truelightessence, Odysee.com

Get your X- Ray specs. out...

How are you all doing today? I know you are all working hard because so much has already been achieved — for yourselves — for your own evolution and climb out of this place, and for those who are just starting to realise that their consciousness; their hearts will save them, no one else.

Not without LOVE's help. Not without calling on our deepest aspects of Self — our Infinite Self and LOVE, together with the Laws of Creation from the Heart of Creation to help us. . . It will simply be impossible for others to exit the matrix unless they use their own inner resources because no one has authority over others, not even LOVE. However, our Infinite Self works in complete synchronicity with LOVE and the Laws of Creation and the continuation of expansion of Creation, and therefore, our Infinite Selves are the only part of us, of our innate 'knowing' that can direct us safely out of the matrix and to perfect, peaceful safety, eventually.

It is going to take a monumental turn-around to help humanity awaken to what they are facing, and I am concerned about what is happening currently. I have to admit, I am deeply concerned, to be honest. The reasons why are as follows: I am concerned about who is truly helping those who are awake, and who is controlling a narrative that leads to a trap?

I have perceived the importance of the truthful information coming from others, yet, we are also learning, aren't we, that the message can be factual and truthful, but the motives behind that narrative can be the opposite of what we believe.

Who is telling us the truth with a pure heart that serves LOVE? And who is part of a larger group who are playing the part of actor, the 'crisis scientist', the 'honestly baffled doctor', the 'whistleblowing nurse', the lawyers who serve under the BAR?

How do any of us know, truly, who is telling the truth for the right reasons? I am not saying this to cause more confusion. I am sharing my concerns, because I think a lot of us are starting to wonder why no one talks about heart connection, and some of those who say they believe in God in alternative media, could be using that badge of honour to deceive others, and why do these characters carry energy around them which is not Godly, not loving? Are they being attacked and unable to defend their own life force or do they serve something else? I notice colours and red is used by satanists.

The Royals and G7 groups love wearing read, as do the corrupt politicians. Therefore, why do many alternative media channels choose red as their 'uniform' too? I noticed the red jackets at that conference... why were they all wearing red? Who is honest and who is there to disrupt honest progress?

And I notice the TV alternative colours, and spotted the spinning '6' hidden carefully, to look like a 'P'. I overlooked these errors before because many simply do not have a clue, yet, when I looked at a "Great Declaration" when it first came out, there, in full sight, was the Caduceus — a dark, hypnotic symbol used on humans for sacrifice, and used by the medical alternatives, or, they use the Rod Of Asclepius — another satanic symbol.

These alternative doctors like their Caduceus and Rod Of Asclepius... do they know these are satanic symbols? Their hearts can advise them if they care to go deep enough. There has been plenty of time now, to get to know our errors of using symbols, so anyone left who is still using symbols of any description, needs our scrutiny.

Symbols have no place anywhere.

They are all corrupted and emit ELF Wave frequencies which corrupt the BIOFIELD and Cosmic Field levels of consciousness and everything in between. I am unsure about many now, and I am wondering why I am typing these thoughts down... ?

I was guided earlier that there is a download of data to share. In advance of this, and I have no idea what that data is, I would like to thank each and every one of you who is helping yourself through heart connection and I do sense that there is guidance about that too, so do stay with me because the information is always helping us all to move forward to advanced levels of understanding, and to pioneer a pathway to safety out of the 'over grown jungle', and by our regular connection to heart, we are keeping the pathway clear; unimpeded by any overgrowth which may cause others to get lost.

Indeed, our efforts as individuals are helping as a group but without the controlling influence of 'group think,' which I dislike and distrust, because when humans actually, physically join up as groups, the connection to heart is lost, as ego-led behaviours get in the way.

And have you noticed that the groups leading the so-called charge against the perpetrators are all ruled by certain individuals who tell them what they can say, what they must not say, who criticise the independent thinkers, and seem to have cornered the market with their little enclaves. It can become highly unhealthy an environment.

I know this. I have had my work sabotaged many times by those who purported to want to help humanity. Often, they wanted the teachings and the access to deeper aspects of consciousness because they saw the potential of kudos and business. Many projects got sabotaged that I was inwardly guided to set up. Doorways were closed on the individuals who squandered the help for personal gain, and we are where we are now, because those who were more than capable of helping humanity awaken ten years ago, were driven too much by their ego, not their heart — and much time has been lost in the process.

When I look back at those squandered opportunities and when I look at what humanity is now facing, I often wonder, do any of those individuals ever feel remorse for not helping? That is how powerful the mind-control is, and I am sensing, we may touch on that topic too.

How can we all best serve our soul evolution and best serve all precious life, in optimal ways, in alignment with LOVE's plan and the Laws of Creation from the heart of Creation?

Please use your inner heart connection to your Infinite Self and let's see what guidance is to be shared today for our own, inner research and questioning.

Here goes: *"Claire, we have said this many times but we need to impress this upon you all again that there is coming a time when it will be too late to change, to choose a different path, to be rescued, to be saved from the vacuum which is currently sucking vast amounts of life force into its lair.*

In the last message, we mentioned the vacuum that has been left by life forms who have been sucked into the black hole — the LION's GATE — or the Gates of Hell, and in front of this black hole, there is a powerful vacuum. Think of this vacuum in similar ways to a powerful current in the ocean.

Many of you who live near the sea and know about currents, know how easy it is to get into difficulty even if the water looks calm on the surface, there can still be powerful undercurrents near your feet and you all know that when these undercurrents powerfully catch the feet, if the pull is strong enough, even the most powerful swimmer can get dragged under the water and carried a long distance underwater, without the chance of rescue.

The vacuum in front of this black hole is akin to the powerful underwater ocean currents: Humanity is not looking and is unaware of the problems because all looks calm, from their perspective. They are unaware of what is going on at deeper levels. They are disconnected from their hearts and many don't have any interest in looking below the surface of the ocean. Their thoughts, actions, words and deeds are already automatic; robotic.

How many think deeply about the world events and how to address them? How many are even aware of what has come to light in the last three to four years, let alone before that? Most humans are going around in an autonomous; robotic; trance-like state. They are already well on the way to being Klaus's dream — a trans-human; a robot — easier to maim and kill, and hunt, and rape, as the World Economic Forum members seem to like to do.

Claire, that is fullest truth. Please leave that statement as it is. It is too late to be polite or to protect other's feelings. Hurt feelings will not get others off this sinking ship, which is being pulled under the ocean and has descended to the depth whereby, it is going to be impossible to help them unless they call for rescue.

And that is the conundrum that you are all facing — those of you who wish to help others and want to show them a safe route out of this ship. You cannot interfere with their choices, and that is why your Infinite Self and LOVE's plan has advised you all to climb high, climb fast, and climb like there is a fire behind you that is threatening to overtake you and cut you off from your escape route out of here.

Claire had a disturbed night last night, again. She connected and was advised that all was well, and it became gentler — the energies around her — and eventually, she fell asleep. But not before she had listened to an older recording of hers: "Solfeggio Waves, Wind Turbines and StarLink", and we ask her to leave the download on Substack for others to find and it is hoped that a condensed version of all her shared teachings will be assimilated, so that you can access them easily and gain new insights each time you listen.

We are also advising you all to download the transcripts and save the video messages on a memory stick. If there is an outage in the future, we want you all to have the resources close to hand — to offer you a helping hand.

That said, that is the 'housework' over, and now, we will move onto more serious news. Claire, can you share with your listeners what happened when you checked your castle tower window recently and what you have been guided to do?"

I say: "Last night before I went to bed, the energy and frequencies on the planet dropped considerably. It was palpable to my gut and heart that something was wrong. I had just been catching up with Substack news and after that, the energy went downhill. I was advised by my Infinite Self to get inside my 'tool box' — my 'treasure chest'. I know this treasure chest extremely well. It is deep inside the deepest part of my heart centre.

I said this prayer before I metaphorically stepped inside my treasure chest: ***"May the frequency of Peace reign supreme, and may Infinite LOVE help humanity in optimal ways that best serve all precious life.""***

My Infinite Self and LOVE say: *"The three other requests are now included in the above prayer and so, for those of you who are using this method, you can INTEND that the three routines that you have been imbedding into your energy fields and consciousness are now incorporated into the prayer, therefore, the requests are now covered automatically and the prayer is shorter, to make it easier to recall.*

Those requests were:

"We ask for all our errors to be forgiven and forgotten (meaning: deleted).

With peaceful hearts, without anger or malice, we ask Infinite Love and the Laws of Creation to gather up all magnified, malicious harm and all harm, and return all harm to all those responsible for the harm — all those who ensured it reached our door and the door of the innocent, and those trying to protect the innocent.

May all that has been lost be found by Infinite Love and the laws of Creation, and returned to wholeness — to purity, and restored to us in the form of Purest Light codes that can never be corrupted or infiltrated or harmed by any person, place or thing, including destroyer forces."

These requests are now incorporated. It is important for newcomers to enquire why these requests were necessary and it is prudent for all those who wish to learn — to listen from the beginning — to the stepping-stone teachings which carry much knowledge and deeper insights about the cause, the effects of all harm, and the optimal solutions that are required at the time, to ensure you all receive the optimal help to propel you forward.

The more you educate yourselves by listening to the previous messages, which Claire will leave links to so you know what to look for, the better you will climb and the safer your ascent.

These teachings require a mature heart and a wise heart because your role is to be of best possible service to all precious life, and these teachings carry responsibility, and duty to give the best of yourself to help humanity and all precious life.

The situation is dire currently. Your growth has improved, and yet, those who are trapped are sinking deeper and deeper into density, and they are vastly approaching this vacuum. Claire is sensing this danger, and it is why she is waking up in the middle of the night. Answers come in good time and if you are experiencing similar concerns and unexplained wakefulness, it is advised that you use the prayer or a similar robust connection to LOVE and the heart of Creation, and to "ask your Infinite Self and LOVE to surround and protect you and to shield you from all harm," and to step inside your imaginary treasure chest deep inside your heart space and to close the lid, secure it with a padlock and to stay in this place now, especially at night, before sleep, because you are highly vulnerable at night when you sleep, when you become detached from your consciousness, especially, if you have not been using a regular, daily connection routine, and even when this is being used, as Claire will attest to, the energies still feel dreadful at times.

Therefore, use the prayer, ask for protection, as above, and get inside the safest place to be when things are in constant flux, especially when humanity are essentially in 'suicide mode'—because these 'sleep-walkers' are walking head-long toward this vacuum and for some, it has already whipped them off their spiritual feet."

I say: "May I interject with a question, here? I am very concerned and each day, I seem to be perceiving that it is getting worse for the main bulk of humanity, not better. I keep thinking that they can't possibly sink any lower and the next day, they have. I have gone through all levels of learning, from heartache at watching the harm this is causing, especially to the children, infants, newborns and precious animal life, nature, insects, birds, sea life and so forth. I feel like I am in a dream world, a nightmare where most are walking about like Zombies, talking Zombies, Intelligent Zombies, can still cook their own meals and watch TV Zombies, but there is an energy around them, that I find, is tangible, and it is a sense that something is missing, a blank space, sometimes an icy-cold, empty sensation, and yet, many in this group are functioning on human levels. It is hard to explain.

I wonder, what is our role now? Humanity are descending into an abyss. They are ignorant of the danger that they are facing. They look blank if one remotely touches on the topic. We are watching our family of humanity being hunted down by 'wolves', and I am concerned about those who purport to be on humanity's side, yet, I am starting to question, are they just here to distract others with data, with slide shows, with court cases?

The same faces keep appearing, but I see no improvements. We had to wait nearly a year before the scientific community and doctors realised there was an issue. The delay cost humanity dearly.

What I would like from all of this, is to proactively be doing something to help improve the situation — without interfering. We are all lacking Knowledge. We all need to climb our ladders to secure new Knowledge which might be applied to the current situation. I feel like we are not advancing as far as I would like, and in the meantime, humanity and the children, and all precious life are on the verge of being sucked into this vacuum.

Can you please help us today? We all need LOVE's wisdom. There must be a plan in operation and many of us wish to participate in helping. I have to admit that it is appearing to look somewhat futile. Everywhere I look, I am perceiving the dangers —energetically and metaphysically. I cannot seem to get these teachings out far and wide.

Why are so few grabbing this help and running with this help from the heart of Creation? What is blocking those who could be helping?

Why are the exercise and holistic groups so bent on continuing practices that have been lovingly explained to them, are harming all life, including themselves?

I know that the frequencies of Yoga and Reiki are addictive. I started out exploring many different holistic therapies, including Reiki and Yoga, and many others. I know the pitfalls. I have experienced them first hand.

My husband had acupuncture, years ago. I had guided him not to go because the person who treated him also did Reiki, and I knew that my husband would expose himself to Reiki through the therapist doing the acupuncture. He went ahead and when he came home, I could sense his energy fields were completely messed up. He learned the hard way and his awakening was at the worse time — right in the middle of the biggest attack and invasion of our planet — 2017. That was when things became untenable and the targeting started in earnest on us both. I thought I would lose my mind at times. Both of us were in a state of distress, and were in constant attack on a daily basis. We tried everything and we were always helped, but it was almost impossible to hear LOVE's guidance and clear the attack.

When I connected with friends, either via face to face or via text, email, telephone, I would have to spend a few hours clearing myself afterwards. I came to dislike mobile phones. I didn't like the energy they emitted. I knew they were deeply harmful on an energetic level but I lacked the science. I could perceive others energy fields at the Cosmic Level and was teaching others but many were trained in Reiki and it held them back. The satanic influence is heavily masked but it is detrimental to allow this frequency into our energy fields. Reiki practitioners rebel violently when they hear that Reiki is satanically corrupted. Once I knew it was harmful, I stopped using it and started to use heart connection and I haven't looked back. We went off grid for over a year because we couldn't use any technology without having to spend hours and hours clearing our fields.

Things have only become easier in the last twelve months because of our heart-based determination and trust in LOVE, and because others have become so desperate after the continual targeting and attack, that they have started calling for help from their hearts. The help has come in now. We do have a wealth of assistance. It was always there.

It saddens me that things had to get so bad before others got on board but I am thankful that others now perceive that this is not a simple issue that we can resolve ourselves.

We need LOVE's guidance and help. We need each other's determination to continue to ask for help. Humanity and all precious life need our persistent requests for help.

What is affecting everyone currently, including those who are helping? I forgot to mention that my castle tower view has become overrun with dark energy outside — so much so, that I metaphysically recoiled at what was outside my window.

My last window check revealed an Extra Terrestrial invasion. I was advised to maintain an image of being inside my treasure chest with lid down and a huge padlock on the inside. I find this place the most secure and it always clears my space and settles me.

May I ask, what is going on?"

"Claire, indeed, there is an attack on the planet and there is an invasion taking place as you write this. The planetary grids that were destroyed by the Yoga groups have left the planet wide open to attack from outside forces who have their eyes on the planet, as their prize possession. All ET factions are really your very souls... thousands and thousands of

AWOL particles of yourselves that are on the 'dark side,' and attacking you all because they lack remembrance of their true origins.

They see themselves as separate; as different, they do not relate to humanity as their soul mates or soul family. They are fuelled with hatred and have been filled with False Light codes. There is no remembrance of what they were, or where they're from. They are lost in the programs of False Light.

Are they energies to be befriended, and make your friends?

No.They are not.

Unfortunately, these aspects of your very selves will easily dupe you and trick you. They are like thieves. They will do anything to steal your light. It is what they crave because False Light cannot live off LOVE, but they can live off low electrical emissions from your battered and broken BIOFIELD and other areas of your consciousness, and so these AWOL fragments of yourselves are the army that are attacking you, metaphysically.

When you use the above prayer and when you review the three requests that are now part of the shorter prayer, you will see the rational behind recalling all that you have lost and sending back all malicious, magnified harm because it is these issues that are causing your fragmented aspects to have gone AWOL in the first place, and that has happened through you making errors, which is why asking for your own errors to be forgiven and forgotten, meaning: deleted, is fundamental to your healing journey and rise in consciousness.

When your errors are deleted, those who you may have accidentally or intentionally harmed are also released from any harm you may have caused across all lifetimes, all timelines, all cycles of creation and so, the three requests hold important esoteric meaning, as we are sure you will perceive.

This shorter prayer, therefore, is very powerful. It is healing for all you may have accidentally or intentionally harmed, and so, can you imagine that when you say this prayer with a sincere, centred heart, when you mean those words, when you feel the beauty of the healing in those words and when you trust that LOVE is answering your prayers, then, you can still be powerfully assisting humanity without interfering with their free will choices?

The healing that is taking place through your desire to forgive and forget your own mistakes by letting LOVE lift them away from yourself and all those who got harmed by your errors, clears a space for those AWOL soul fragments of yours to also be assisted and so, we advise that your due diligence is needed now to pray and to continue to pray for humanity and all precious life.

This Extra Terrestrial invasion is not obvious to the eye. It is deeply covert.

There are many in your governments, and politics is awash with covert entities masquerading as humans. It is quite amusing when seen from higher levels of awareness because the ego has got the better of these entities, and they do tend to think they are invincible.

Many have a GOD COMPLEX. You need to get some 'X-ray Spectacles' from within your tool kit, and a 'Truth Detector', such as, a slide rule — anything which your imagination can create to help you detect the Non-Human Entity, the Cyborg, the Humanoid, etcetera.

Put your X-ray spectacles on in your metaphysical world and intend that they stay put when you are in this reality, while watching TV, shopping, reading Substack and alternative news, and ask your Infinite Self and LOVE to powerfully charge up these items to 'Fullest Truth Mode', and start analysing the truth tellers, the saviours, the rescuers, and the perpetrators, examine them all under this microscope of Truth.

Test they are all working by doing a 'test check' on yourself and your first and last name. Make sure it is accurate the slider must hit a ten for fullest truth or a one, it matters not, just ensure that you set the intention for what all these things do, to ensure accuracy and see how you go with your truth testing kit.

A spray bottle from within your treasure chest can also be used to 'spray' LOVE's light on dark entities, spray over your entire ladder of consciousness, pretend to spray it over your home as seen from the top of your ladder at the heart of Creation.

See yourselves as enormous, vast bodies of consciousness, and see these dark entities as lost, ego-driven little creatures who have managed to magnify themselves so that they appear huge when in fact they are like little midges, when compared to your vastness.

Tap into your Infinite Self, to that part of you that is fully connected to LOVE. Breathe in that love, that truth of who you truly are and remind yourself regularly when you still your busy mind, that there is no technology —whether inside of you or outside of you — that has authority or dominion over you, not when you refuse to comply, not when you use LOVE as your defence, and not when you give your permission and free will choice to call on LOVE for assistance. Make yourselves vast now.

Expand your treasure chest in which you are resting in, and imagine you can float above your home, then the planet and you can see these things like they are small and you are vast, and then, go to the top of your ladder inside the False Light programs and spray your ladder with LOVE's light.

Watch the droplets fall around your ladder, watch broken steps repair, watch the ladder strengthen and watch the dark matter leaving. . . Spray yourself and your treasure chest, and ask your Infinite Self and Infinite LOVE to move you outside of the False Light Construct with the Laws of Creation, to make it safe for all precious life.

Allow yourself to be transported to a safe place, and remain inside your treasure chest. You will be able to look out. You may end up on an island, with blue crystal waters, or a mountain glade, or similar. Rest awhile and receive supportive frequencies.

This is your new routine. You have moved beyond the 'Castle and Moat'. Many of you may have found it was becoming less clear and this is always a lesson, a teaching — that when the powerful tool becomes less powerful and is waning, it is always time to move on, time to upgrade your method.

No one can get inside your treasure chest. It is guarded by very powerful energies of LOVE and the Laws of Creation from the heart of Creation. The saddest thing that we have to tell you is the very part of you that you treasure, that you perceive is a part of you that connects you to outside of the False Light paradigm, is the most treasured part that humanity is about to hand over to the dark ones, to the Extra Terrestrial, AWOL soul fragments and the Artificial Intelligence groups which are also made up of your AWOL divine mind fragments which have been stolen, and this is what AI is.

If humanity were connected to their hearts, they would know that AI is a sinister ploy to cause untold harm using stolen mind Knowledge, and this has been weaponised against humanity because any energy which you give away to the dark is repurposed and used to harm you. They cannot harm you if you call back your lost codes and they cannot make harm stick to you if you keep asking for the magnified, malicious harm to be returned — for their learning. That is why the shortened prayer offers so much more than mere words.

A full on invasion is taking place, that is for certain and the best help that you can offer your loved ones and all life is to retreat inside your treasure chest, in order to protect yourselves from having life force stolen and weaponised against you. At this stage, your growth should be all about repair and recalling all that you have lost, not giving your power away, as this will drag you towards that vacuum.

So, our advice presently, is to retreat to a safe place; to protect your entire ladder of consciousness that is damaged, and especially, the part of your ladder that is trapped inside the False Light Construct. Free yourselves, metaphysically, and allow your treasure chest and Infinite Self, along with LOVE's support, to take you to a perfectly peaceful destination and a place where your true self can be free, liberated and able to look for the dishonest collaborators and controlled ops. more closely: To spot the Cyborg and the Bot, and to spot who is distracting others, who are the Pied Pipers — holding the innocent inside the False Light Construct, and where is your own power and focus being given away too trustingly, too freely to others who may not be helping, as it may seem? And who is genuine, who is trying to best serve all, in loving ways?

Become self sufficient and self reliant.

Maintain your own sense of balance, and most of all, trust that you are on the right path, that you are bigger that those who mean you harm and that you have the most powerful force in the whole of existence on your side.

If you have LOVE, you have enough. "

Chapter Twenty-One

ZOMBIE APOCALYPSE: RECENT TIMELINE SWITCH SPELLS CALAMITY, NOV 18, 2023

"A group who stubbornly refuse to believe in the power of LOVE, and now, face being left stranded with the group who are destroying humanity, and harming the children and all precious life "

LOVE'S HEART PLAN, SUBSTACK.COM

Video Link:

SEARCHING FOR THE EVIDENCE, BITCHUTE.COM

"Claire, we will start where we left off yesterday, by saying, if you have LOVE, you have enough. The timeline switch is most unfortunate It spells calamity for those who are yet to start the journey of finding and repairing all that they have lost and yet, for those who ask for help, LOVE is enough.

LOVE is the only thing that is needed to exit the False Light Construct. Even at this late stage. Even when it is collapsing in on itself, under the burden of its own errors and even when a new timeline switch has successfully taken place.

We did advise you that the risk was high and once again, humanity find themselves trapped by their own mistakes, and yet, they still are unaware that they are making huge errors of judgement. They are simply, too fast asleep. We have been advising those of you who want to help yourselves and all precious life to climb your ladder, as quickly as possible, and many of you have taken the reins of your own evolution and done just that. Just in the nick of time, as the timeline switch completed in the wee small hours of the morning.

And all is well.

For you, at least, but not for those immersed in density, or for those who are awake to the issues happening to planet Earth, but asleep to their mortality. Their inner heart awareness is disconnected. They do not understand consciousness, or the importance of heart connection.

Simply, many do not believe that LOVE exists in a form that is vast, expansive, and constantly evolving, nor do they see that they might be part of something bigger.

These are the brave souls who came in with less remembrance, less ability to know that LOVE exists, and they still stood their ground to this murderous energy — the destroyer forces. They know that exists. It is curious, isn't it, that they don't perceive that the opposite exists — namely, LOVE.

LOVE.

A powerful force of goodness, and a powerful force to be reckoned with. A sense, and a destination. A place with a heart that beats as one, and all those who come from here know, that at some point soon, sadly, these brave souls will be lost in the black hole that is sucking all life that is in the False Light Construct into itself.

A vast, huge vacuum has been created by humanity's poor decisions and poor 'mind' choices. Many think they have the answers — that violence will sort it out; a protest; a signature; a court case — but this is the stuff of fairytales, when viewed from the bigger picture.

Your 'mind' Knowledge was a captured agency, along time ago. Only your 'heart' Knowledge remains, and if others are disconnected from this part of their true self, frankly, it spells disaster for them and for others too, because this notion that violence will free you all from a complex attack from unseen forces who have the technology to outsmart even the most intelligent human is unrealistic at best, and suicidal, at worst.

How are you going to fight the StarLink satellites? The Sky Net systems? Destroyer forces? The corrupted, mind-controlled aspects of your world's military?

Your race has a multitude of enemies who are attacking you at all levels of awareness.

Can you see your Cosmic Shield?

Can you perceive your Biofield and the harm there?

Can you see your life force energy being harvested while you type out a text or an email to a friend?

Do you know how to get your life force back?

Where is it all?

Where did you lose it?

Where is it now, and where are you going to go, to find it?

What about the space stations where the AI and military complex is operating from?

Do you have a rocket to take you into space, to sort them all out?

Do you understand how Earth energy works, versus, how the Laws of Creation work with LOVE frequencies?

Of course not. You do not have the Knowledge to help yourself, and you do not have the technology to hand, to deal with this complex level of attack — on multiple platforms.

Or, do you?. . .

You do have the technology of a knowing heart: A heart that can be tapped into — for deeper Knowledge and advice.

You have a connection to the Heart of Creation, but, you refuse to use it, or even try it out as a test, to see if it works.

You can call on the most powerful technology that overrides all harm in peaceful ways — LOVE — but you choose not to ask for help, and so, your fate is sealed unless you ask for help.

The issues facing this group are horrendous, to be honest, when seen from the higher perspective.

A group who stubbornly refuse to believe in the power of LOVE, and now face being left stranded with the group who are destroying humanity, and harming the children and all precious life. A timeline switch is a serious threat to your 'return', too.

Even if you call for help, you are leaving it very late in the day. The timeline switch has succeeded in its intentions to prevent those who are just waking up, from healing and repairing all that had been lost in the previous timeline.

A switch of track means: that all that was left in the previous timeline before the switch, is missing and cannot be found and repaired, not unless those of you who are just awakening, call on LOVE for the extra assistance. And for those who do want LOVE's assistance, we urge you to do this today — as soon as possible — because at the rate destroyer forces are going, it is probable that another timeline switch is imminent.

This more than doubles the problem... It triples it.

Timeline switches are designed by the extra terrestrials, with Destroyer Force's help, to secure more fragmented souls and to harvest life force.

Your personality selves may not believe in LOVE, but your souls know better and when your souls watch the dark ones plot and plan, and implement these timeline switches, they get anxious. Then, as the timeline switch occurs, knowing that they are being separated further from you and the ladder of consciousness to which they belong, they become traumatised. They go into shock because each time a timeline switch occurs, you lose life force codes and you lose the ability to remember to call for help.

You lose the memory of these soul parts and they become the quarry for those who like to maim, hunt, rape, and kill.

It is akin to the wolves separating their quarry from a flock, and then, hunting down the weakest. Your soul aspects that are trapped inside the False Light Construct are already damaged and fragmented.

Many have become detached from your ladder, or, they are hanging on by a thread. They become the weakest, most exposed part of your consciousness.

An easy kill. And no one notices a thing.

Your moods may have been unsettled this week, particularly yesterday, as the timeline switch fulfilled its main separation.

You are 'becoming one' with the Internet of Things. You are a 'node' in the interface.

How is it going for you all, in that program?

You can exit any time you want to when you call on LOVE for help, but TIME is running out and soon, even the destroyer forces will know that the 'TIME is UP. 'TIME, quite literally, is coming to an end.

If those who are still trapped in the mind pyramid, which is all that the False Light Construct is — a pyramid that has been constructed around the mind to imprison it.

If they choose to remain inside this pyramid, then eventually, it will implode and everything inside the pyramid will be decimated. There will be nothing left.

Your soul knows this, and watches you anxiously, as you go about your sleep-walking day, thinking that you have 'got the dark's number' — knowing that the many politicians and government ministers are satanists; pedophiles; crooks in grey suits.

You know all this, yet, you do not know your soul and your soul is in torment, because it feels the time ebbing away and the opportunities to get home, ebbing away.

You may not want to get home before the In Breath completes, but your soul does.

What do you think happens when your soul gets partly side-tracked along a different timeline, and the part of your soul who remains connected to your personality self, watches bits of itself fragment and get attacked by the dark, and knows that the attack is going to get worse, as those soul fragments will eventually go AWOL and turn on the person, turn on the soul?

The destroyer forces are already inside your ladder of consciousness. You think 'Zombie Apocalypse' hasn't happened, yet? *It started a long time ago, and if those who can perceive were to ask their hearts to show them what is happening to many ladders of consciousness where the Zombie Apocalypse is occurring, they will be shown clearly how damaging this is, and how detrimental it is to the entire structure of the ladder of consciousness. "*

I say, "Pause the recording and ask your Infinite Self to show you the Zombie Apocalypse. Rejoin us, once you are ready. "

The Zombie Apocalypse that I was shown, starts way out in space at the Cosmic Field level — a vast distance from the Biofield.

My heart and LOVE say: *"It is trickling its way down toward the Biofield and by the time it reaches the soul level, all the ladder above that will be gone, destroyed by the devastation caused when Destroyer Force frequencies ride rough-shod over the personality self who was guided, earlier this year, to call for help to be rescued before June, 2023, otherwise it would be too late.*

Very few made that request, and the result is evident in the short history of time that has elapsed since June, 2023. Claire was also wondering if she was going to physically see a 'Zombie Apocalypse', and the answer to that is, it is well underway.

You just can't see it yet, but your heart can, and so can higher levels of awareness. The warning was put out by LOVE that if those who were forcing vaccines on others; coercing; vilifying; bullying; lying, and distorting for their masters, LOVE warned that the media, the athletes, the liars would start 'dropping like flies'.

You have noticed, haven't you? That those who used; promoted; forced; coerced, and advertised for their masters have died, some on set? That is the Zombie Apocalypse in action. The dark knew this would happen. They use their own puppets, regardless of the outcome for the puppets. Be careful who you choose to serve.

Destroyer forces have no favourites. Destroyer forces use and abuse, discard, and destroy.

Meanwhile, Claire was noticing other small signs, but nothing significant. She wondered, had she heard the message accurately? We say, "Yes. The hospitals are witnessing a ***Zombie Apocalypse."***

Diseases like ***Leprosy were rare, but are on the rise.***

The Zombie Apocalypse is happening energetically and working its way down into the physical realms of reality: Have you noticed the war-torn areas of the world? The earthquakes? The flooding? The fires that came in the summer?

Not 'Zombie Apocalypse' enough, for you?

We did mention "rotting, putrid flesh", and we say again, this is going to be seen; more, and more.

They will blame it on an 'outbreak', a space disease, or similar, anything to avoid telling you that they did this, and you did this — to yourself — courtesy of them stealing much of your life force energy, weaponising it against you, and directing it at others, too, because the soul will fragment when this happens to you.

If your soul has had the grace to call for help at the cut-off time — and there is a time when LOVE will say "enough is enough — you have had enough time to make wise choices, but you refuse to save yourself by asking LOVE for help", then, your ladder of consciousness will be severed between you and your soul, and it will be withdrawn from this matrix before it collapses and is destroyed.

Do you understand the danger this places you in? No ladder of awareness. No Knowledge. No connection to heart and to LOVE. All opportunities to get help for yourself — vanquished? It is game over for you.

But not before the dark have had their fun and hunt you down, like a fox. You have no LOVE to protect you.

You have no soul to call out for help for you both.

That was your help — your 'exit the matrix' help. All your ladder of higher awareness withdrawn. You are 'game' now, nothing more, and by the time the dark have finished with your remaining codes, you will be a 'zombie', and it will be 'apocalyptic' for you.

This is not being shared to cause fear. Claire has been asked to lay everything on the line for you all, to comprehend the enormity of where your choices are leading, in the hope that you will save yourselves.

LOVE cannot interfere with your choices. LOVE can only help those who call for help, but we are all wondering — why would you choose this ending for yourself?

Why? When you have the option of returning home to LOVE, why would you choose to destroy yourselves and why would you choose to become quarry for the dark — to be hunted and maimed and eventually killed?

It is not going to be pretty, that's for sure.

There is another side to this story. Claire has talked about the Black Eyed club. Do you remember? She shared information about the babies who are harmed and tortured to procure adrenochrome — an adrenalin fuelled blood caused by the baby's tormented fear and torture before it is killed.

If this may disturb you, please stop the recording and receive healing and pray for these children, because it is happening worldwide on a grand scale.

For those who wish to educate themselves further and possibly help these vulnerable infants and children, we wish you to know that the black eye, seen on many in the elite, Hollywood stars, politicians, the Pope, royals, Epstein, even a few in the alternative media — it is a symbol to all who follow satanic principal, that the person has reached a level of initiation into this cult, and that is, that they have killed a baby, and in doing so, it is perceived that they all keep each other's secrets.

The action of tormenting a child before its death to fuel its blood with adrenochrome which they then drink sounds obscene, and it is obscene. It is unearthly and inhumane to do this to another living thing, particularly, a vulnerable, defenceless child. The Black Eye comes about because it is the Mark of the Beast — as a sign of what has unfolded — a sign of the Mark. Of course, people have accidents and a lot of black eyes are results from normal accidents, but when you see a perfect circle, when you see this mark on those in power, in circles of influence, you are being called to scrutinise these entities and to ask deeply within your heart as to why they have a perfect circle of black around the eye.

This is another sign of satanism. It is also going to be another type of sign, and that is the sign of destroyer forces, destroying your ladder of consciousness.

The reason why the black-eyed baby killers inherit this perfect circle, is because they have willingly opened their gateway to satanic, destroyer forces. They have agreed to sell their soul to Satan, in exchange for granting all their sexual desires to be met; for their wealth; rise in status; kudos, and power and control over others. Satan takes their soul in exchange for these gifts and the gateways that open up the entire ladder of consciousness require a heinous act to take place, in order for Satan to take what Satan wants — Knowledge, life force, all data and codes of Remembrance — to sustain its existence, and to ensure dominion over this world. That is why babies are murdered.

When an ordinary human refuses to ask LOVE for help in a False Light Construct that is running out of time and about to implode in on itself, when the soul sees the destruction taking place at higher levels of awareness and realises that the personality self is fast asleep, and is not going to save the soul or protect the ladder of consciousness — by calling on LOVE for help — what do you think happens?

It is akin to murdering a baby in Satanic sacrifice. The soul looks on in despair as higher levels of consciousness are starting to wobble and become dislocated. The soul looks above its own level and can perceive that collapse of the ladder is possible, and if it does collapse, the soul will be left with the personality self — trapped in this False Light Construct — with no defence; no connections to higher levels of awareness.

What would you do if you were in such fear? The soul may bail out and then, it will be hunted and fragmented, and hunted and fragmented, and raped, and pillaged, and stripped of all its codes. What happens to the personality self with no ladder and no soul?

Or, another scenario is: the soul looks up and sees destroyer forces cascading down from the Cosmic Field levels because the personality self literally has allowed this energy in.

Simply, by never taking care of other aspects of its awareness, and the soul decides to implode — thinking it will be preventing codes from being stolen by the destroyer force energies before they reach the soul level — as a last act of love, however mistaken this is.

In both cases, the personality self has opened up its gateways at all levels of consciousness within the False Light Construct, never protected them, never noticed they existed.

Satanic forces have had a field day, stealing vast quantities of data and life force energy, and the soul has mistakenly imploded in an attempt to save its codes from being used to harm all precious life, too.

Therefore, the personality self is left high and dry with no protection, no ladder of awareness, no emergency "exit the matrix" codes. Everything is gone; stolen; taken by the destroyer forces.

Do you think the personality self will remain well? The ladder of consciousness determines well being. It determines health. It determines sanity, happiness, emotional stability. All that will be left of the 'one human' personality and its ladder of consciousness and soul, will be a shell.

An empty vessel, filled with False Light codes and destroyer force frequencies. A ticking time bomb is in the making.

Watch this space, because this timeline switch spells disaster for those who have not yet secured their own rescue, and it is hoped that as more start to climb their ladder, and start to reconnect with greater aspects of themselves and seek the inner teachings, the penny will drop as to how detrimental it is to sell one's soul to destroyer forces, and even through ignorance, the outlook is just as grim.

Both types of person are about to face their demons, quite literally, because when destroyer forces empty vast arenas of consciousness from the Cosmic Field downward, when each level becomes empty and devoid of Purest Light.

When the spark that gave life, is dimmed and blown out, all that is left is a vast empty space of nothingness.

You have allowed your ladder of consciousness to become over-run with satanic frequencies and destroyer forces. Your demons will suck you dry of your life force. You will become a zombie, fuelled by their hunger and lust for fuel — for life force.

You will own nothing and be happy because you will not know who you are anymore or what you ever were. And like in the ending in CELL, the movie, you will end up like the father — shuffling around a satellite tower while dreaming that you actually made it home.

That is the outcome for those who remain stubbornly ignorant of their choices and the outcome of those choices, and that day is upon you all. You have no more time to choose.

Claire, that is all. We want this out, pronto, because others are waking up and we want them to understand how easy it is to ask for help, and how harmful it is to their entire future and existence to stubbornly refuse to save themselves. "

Chapter Twenty-Two

THE CONTROLLERS, NOV 19, 2023

Dr Rashid Buttar knew. It is why he had to go. And Professor Dr Arne Burkhardt, too. He uncovered the plan to redirect the 'truthers' into the same trap. And it is a trap, a monster plot to deceive you.

LOVE'S HEART PLAN, SUBSTACK.COM

Goodness! So many individual hearts beating as one, and working to secure humanity's brightest future, despite all attempts to knock us down, humanity do seem invincible at times, and yet, at other times, they fall short of their huge potential to fight off their demons and move out of mind programming — to see the light and the truth, and lead LOVE's children out of this dark place.

Your hard efforts have enabled yet another download of important data. I feel fit to burst as all this information comes through. I know not where to start. I will start with a heart call to LOVE, and I ask that you all use your method of choice — to connect deeply inside your heart — to call on our Infinite Selves, Infinite LOVE and the Laws of Creation from the Heart of Creation and infinitely beyond.

"May the frequency of Peace reign supreme and may Infinite LOVE help humanity in optimal ways that best serve all precious life.

We call on our Infinite Selves, Infinite LOVE and the Laws of Creation from the Heart of Creation and infinitely beyond to surround and protect us, and to shield us from all harm."

I am going into my 'treasure chest', deep inside my heart space. I close the lid. I place an imaginary padlock on the inside and close it.

Only my Infinite Self, Infinite LOVE and the Laws of Creation can open this, and only with my consent.

Nothing else can enter this space. I imagine I have my spray bottle with me and it is filled with LOVE's purest light from the Heart of Creation and infinitely beyond.

I spray myself, my treasure chest, I imagine I can spray my home from within this treasure chest. I expand my treasure chest, and soon enough, my home is below me. I spray the land around my home.

I go higher, and soon, I am looking at Planet Earth and it is like a small football.

I spray the Earth too and ask for the above prayer to be activated.

Everything I need is in this spray: LOVE; the prayer; Knowledge and

Wisdom; the laws of Creation; Truth; it clears dark attack; clears my ladder of consciousness; defends me against dark attack, and can expose the dishonesty of the liars and reveals their deception; their true agenda.

I go higher still. My treasure chest gets bigger and bigger, and I spray the top of my conscious ladder that is trapped inside the False Light Matrix; from the Cosmic Field level, downward.

I watch as the purest light of LOVE repairs all broken parts of my ladder.

I see darkness being moved away. I see Soul fragments that are damaged but still clinging onto this ladder — healed and soothed, and loved back into harmony and balance, safe in the Knowledge that I love myself enough and my soul, enough — to want to help every aspect of my consciousness escape from this dark place.

I see the dark ones scurrying away in fright from this bright, bright, frequency of LOVE, and I trust that I am safe and all is well.

Next, I spray my entire treasure chest. It seems that I can be both outside of it and inside, yet, I am always safely within its walls.

I ask LOVE to help me to climb out of this matrix and into the Purest Light Realms at the heart of Creation.

I spray my treasure chest and I wait for LOVE and the Laws of Creation to take me to a safe place, somewhere within the boundaries of the heart of Creation.

I cannot go beyond the False Light matrix — it is impossible without LOVE's help. The Laws of Creation are quite clear on that, and so, your heart has to ask LOVE, in order to move out of density into purity.

Imagine the contamination of toxic darkness that we are all carrying. We cannot merely walk across a bridge and tarnish a purest light space with dense, distorted frequencies.

LOVE has to help us to move forward, and the Laws of Creation have to help with this, to ensure that all precious life is kept safe and that no harm can be caused on this side of the 'perimeter fence'.

I feel LOVE come more fully around me. I feel my Infinite Self protecting me and supporting my growth. The Laws of Creation are here, too, and my treasure chest moves; expands, and I travel to a safe place chosen by my Infinite Self and Infinite LOVE that will help me to best serve all in optimal ways.

I go to my library of Knowledge and Wisdom and I seem to be using a magnifying glass to study my subjects. They have already been sprayed to find out what their game is.

LOVE has already partly shown me that there is a plot that is growing and that will soon bear fruits. This plot is not created to help all precious life. It is not, "to best serve all."

It concerns those who purport to be helping, but clearly, when seen under the microscope of Truth, they are not helping. They are planning a sinister trick of the hand, and I am disappointed in the many, who are harming.

I sought my husband's counsel because this information could expose us even more than normal. We both feel we have to share the guidance and tell the truth from our perspective, and allow others to carefully examine the truth under their own microscope.

If I don't tell you, people might die. If I do tell you, I expose my husband and I more. He has already been targeted and has stage four cancer last year which he fully recovered from, even with two months to live. Love helped him. He helped himself, because he wanted to live.

I love life, even though the group who harm have harmed me, disabled me.

I am stating here that neither of us are suicidal. If we disappear or die, it will not be an 'accident.'

Download all the transcripts, keep them safe for the future, and download the messages.

I am not scared but I just want you all to know that I contemplated what to do.

If I sit on this, how does it help humanity?

LOVE protects, and I serve LOVE and the children, so, here goes:

I ask my Infinite Self and LOVE, together with the Laws of Creation to surround and protect us all and lead us to Truth.

I ask you all to stop the recording here and go into heart and ask your Infinite Self and LOVE if I am sharing truthful information, in service to the Heart of Creation and all precious life.

Wait for the guidance. You don't need to hear what I share yet. Your heart knows what is to follow. This is a good teaching, and one you should try to use regularly because it clears you of the conflicting mind programs, and allows your heart to step forward to tell you the truth; unblemished by your doubts, or busy thoughts.

Rejoin us once you are ready.

"I wish to best help all and tell the truth, what does my Infinite Self and LOVE wish me to share today? It feels serious and a little unnerving particularly, thinking about the dead doctors and Karen Kingston — a shadow of her former self.

I think the ones who died knew more that we realise. They knew something else that threatened the death cult.

It threatened the controlled opposition and I have to tell you, they are the group to fear the most because, like destroyer forces infiltrating our ladder of consciousness and running rampant, stealing our life force — we have a far more 'deadly' group to contend with, and they are wearing the 'rescuer' and 'saviour' hats in the alternative community.

Make no mistake. I have only just realised this today — how terribly dark some of them are, and I mean, truly evil, not just irritating or unlikable. Some are downright —'deathly dark' — and are not serving humanity or LOVE. But I have to tread carefully here...

How do I convey this message to those who wish to help protect themselves and humanity?"

"Claire, there is a lot to share and we must be quick because this plan is unfolding at a rate of knots. You do have many good souls in this group. However, their peers are a truly mixed bunch of ego-led, kudos-driven ignoramuses, and those who preen at their own sense of self-importance, coupled with misguided investment in their future roles, as they dream about plaques in their names and keys to cities — all thanks to their 'saviour' complex.

You have those who risked everything — and —those who pushed the poison. You have those who were on one side, and have chosen to join the 'fight for freedom', but not before pushing this poison onto many innocent, trusting souls, some of whom are permanently disabled, or dead.

This is a heinous crime — to take the life of another, to show no remorse, to maintain a level of self-importance that is off-the-scale, and to have an agenda that is simply self-serving, in spite of all these errors.

You have some who are holding back on information. Keeping their cards closely to their chest.

You have timid, gentle little souls who are great 'ham actors', playing the role of 'critical thinker', yet, behind the scenes, this one is a trickster and serves the cult agenda.

You have the 'List of the crimes,' reported, all filmed on an iPhone, all plausible, all took up much hope and expectation, but nothing came of that, and why not?

Some serve His Majesty and His government, and who does 'his Majesty' serve do you think? Who rules Great Britain?

Do you really think your British government decide policy?

Charles and his mother decide policy. This is not a democracy.

It is a trick of the eye.

Why do you think he opens parliament?

It is staring you all in the face — the crown symbology, the pomp, the ceremony, the ritual, the friend... of Jimmy Saville? The Royal family were friends with him? Why do you think that is?

So, the crime report was an act. It was a deception to cause distraction; division, and kept you all busy for a whole year.

The nurse who is a doctor but who is really just a nurse kept many busy. That nurse is 'baffled', truly baffled now, though. Who do they truly serve?

Get your spray bottle out that is filled with LOVE's purest light, and pretend that you are in a class room environment with full scale examples of these characters placed at the front of the class.

Ask LOVE for these few examples to be sprayed with Purest Light, and Truth, and for the truth to be revealed to you about their true intentions.

Walk around them.

Have a good, long look at each subject in question.

Pause the recording here, and do this on everyone who your Infinite Self suggests, or, those who concern you.

Take your time.

Rejoin us when you are ready.

Do you see now? Not all are as they seem, are they?

And in amongst this lot are some very sincere, courageous souls. What danger do you think they might be in, when they are walking with a pack of wolves?

I say: "Our inner guidance was that these souls need our help and support. They are being targeted by this pack of wolves."

And I hear, *"Claire we do want you to mention Thomas Renz."*

I say: "Thomas Renz is being targeted. He is amongst wolves. If someone knows him, please warn him, because he needs to protect himself and to call on LOVE for help.

I noticed an odd thing the other night. Thomas Renz was at a hearing recently. I will try to find the link, and let your heart guide you.

I was not so much watching him, I was watching the environment, and the room.

To his side, were two others, and beyond him was a chap sitting on the side-wall, watching the hearing.

I don't know why but something felt 'off-key'. I was looking at this guy's hands.

As I recall from memory. He was holding his hands in a certain position which looked somewhat odd — masonic, perhaps? He moved awkwardly as if his back was uncomfortable.

Something happened next to Thomas Renz, just as he was describing a protected witness and the information that this witness had about being vaccinated with Covid-19 vaccination in 2014, I seem to recall.

You will need to check, as I am offline and cannot access the information. Anyhow, I noticed a movement, something near Thomas Renz, and the next thing the guy on the side-wall moved his hands and held onto his third finger. To me, it looked like a signal.

And like a dance, the woman a few seats along the wall from him took out her phone and it was directed towards Thomas Renz. She started tapping which I thought was odd. Odd to be using a phone during a serious hearing.

And like part of this dance, another female behind Thomas Renz took out her phone and started tapping.

Now you could say that I was imagining things, but my inner sense was that Thomas Renz was possibly being hit by direct energy weaponry.

My heart has shown me and LOVE has told me that Thomas Renz is being targeted, but not just by those outside of his peer group. He is being targeted from within his group.

And I worry, because if those who he may trust or revere, get to see who that protected witness is — about Covid 19 being jabbed into them in 2014, that witness could be killed.

This 'wolf' wants Renz's information, so that it can plan and plot, and distract as long as possible, and eventually, the targeted individual will get cancer or similar.

Because anyone who is telling the truth, who works with their peers and in groups is actually, not safe.

Also I feel compelled to say this too, to Dr Astrid Stuckelberger from the WHO, who I believe is genuinely, courageously trying to share her knowledge and blow the whistle on the corruption.

Don't be influenced into wearing red again. Don't be influenced into what you can say and what you cannot. Stand in your truth, as you are already doing, and know that some of your peers are being influenced by the chief wolf, and the chief wolf is not even of this world.

When I sprayed the one who I think is the most dangerous wolf of the lot, I did not see a human when they were sprayed.

I saw a reptilian, a dinosaur with a tail, and there was nothing about this entity that emitted light.

Behind its facade, there was only darkness — pure evil, pure hatred of the humans, and pure murder in its thoughts.

This entity is pulling many strings. A very clever entity indeed. Hypnotic, soothing, calming on the outside, yet, pure evil behind that human facade."

What else can I share?

My heart and LOVE say: *"That is probably enough for others to explore for now, Claire.* ***What we wish to touch on, is the agenda of the 'wolf pack' that have weaved their way into the alternative***

groups. How many have promoted their support of vaccines recently? *Not the poison-19, but other alternatives?*

A while ago, when the poison-19s were killing many, and when it all seemed futile that the truth community would be able to halt the genocide, Claire received information from her heart that the news was about to break that the poison-19's were causing harm and that it would hit the mainstream news. Claire was also advised that this would take place and the cult would offer an ***alternative vaccine that would be safe and would be used to replace the original poison.***

This did transpire, as we had advised. At the time, Claire hesitated because she was worried about the accuracy of the message and knew that if it was incorrect she could cause unnecessary fear, and could mislead others.

She hesitated and rightly so, and she created a short video message that the truth community would understand but which would not cause undue alarm.

The death cult are often foiled in their attempts to harm humanity when their carefully thought out plans are exposed.

Many of their plans have been exposed by many others, and often, this stops the plans transpiring —which can make the 'exposing' party look less credible.

However, the main important thing about exposing plans is it stops the dark from causing mayhem, and mayhem is already recking humanity's chances of exiting this matrix before TIME stops and the party games are over. The matrix, is collapsing in on itself under the burden of its own errors. The dark cannot harm humanity when plans to harm them are exposed, because the full weight of their malicious harm is hurled back at the dark like a missile, when humanity get wise to the dark's plans.

Therefore, our aim here is to foil a plan before it explodes onto the market. You may have noticed people hinting at vaccines not being 'bad all the time' — that some are 'good,' and when you hear this said in the alternative community, you need to pay attention to who is saying this.

What would you say to a plan to harm humanity, using the 'good' scientists from the 'alternative' community to come up with a 'rescue vaccine' to 'save' all those who are harmed from the 'bad' vaccines?

Would you take the poison?

Would you believe that this plan is under wraps but very much gearing up to explode into the market as a 'good', saving, rescuing remedy?

The snake oil of all snake oils, which will take the 'bad' stuff out of your blood, and fix your damaged DNA?

Does anyone have the capacity to role this out?

You betcha.

"We, the 'good' scientists, the 'honest' doctors — your saviours — we are going to remedy your errors, and because you are all

showing signs of 'apparent' harm, even those who did not take the poison-19, we can save you all, all of you. Aren't we saints? Your saviours."

That is what is planned and it is in the pipeline. Claire hesitated, and rightly so. She has done her best to check this in her heart, at the highest levels of Truth that she can reach.

There is more: Dr Tess Lawrie — pray for her and ask for her protection because she is also surrounded by wolves in sheep's clothing.

One dead doctor at a conference would be enough evidence to show that there are wolves amongst your peer group, and what you share, they note down.

What you plan, they try to sabotage.

Dr Tess Lawrie, Claire did write to you. We think you dismissed it, or your secretary did, however, we would ask the Truth community to pray for her protection.

And all those who are targeted — because they have too many circling them at present, and when this is mixed in with those who are driven by arrogance and ignorance, and ego-led behaviours, it creates huge holes around you all, and this exposes you more.

This is a war for your consciousness, for your soul, and for your heart Knowledge. Your mind is already captured. Your souls are being taken prisoner, as Claire writes this, and your heart Knowledge is next.

This vital part of you all, is a precious commodity. Don't allow the wolves to harm you.

Claire is worried about naming individuals. We say, it is for their protection, and in the hope that some kind soul will inform them, that if they call on LOVE and ask for help and for rescue, they will not become 'cannon fodder' for these demonic characters — and some of them are demonic.

They are capable of murder. How many dead doctors and colleagues is one, too many? You doctors, you truly good scientists — cannot address this issue through your minds.

You cannot protect yourselves against the directed energy weaponry but, LOVE can, and will — you simply have forgotten to ask.

Dr Tess Lawrie, at least you know we see that you are on humanity's side, however, some around you are not. Your heart can advise you who to trust. This is life or death, now.

You have characters who look like they are 'facing the wolves' alone, yet, they serve His Majesty — and ***His Majesty does not serve LOVE.***

He serves those who are ***friends of Jimmy Saville,*** *and his dislike for you all is palpable.*

How can you not see that he detests you all? ***All parliamentarians serve His Majesty. ALL OF THEM.*** *Get your spray out, if you don't believe this.*

When you see them using symbolism, it is a sign of who they are aligned to.

So, who does that leave who serves truth?

Dr Yeadon, Dr Lawrie, and a small handful of others.

What can you do to help these souls? Nothing. You can pray and hope that they open their eyes wide, and take a good look around them.

Dr Rashid Buttar knew. It is why he had to go.

And Professor Dr Arne Burkhardt, too. He uncovered the plan to redirect the 'truthers' into the same trap.

And it is a trap — a ***monster plot*** *to deceive you all because many of those who are just waking up are following these wolves for the first time, and are in awe of their courage and knowledge.*

They are the ones who will fall for the story.

Humanity will probably fall for the 'rescue plan'. It will feel very tempting, and that is the only reason that the truth about the poison19 is surfacing and it is why it is slow, at first, because otherwise it may arouse suspicion, and eventually, it will be made public that the vaccine has caused harm, but...

There, on their white horses, come the 'saviours', the 'good' guys with their poison-potion20.

This has to be foiled, because the devastation it will cause will be excessive and humanity cannot afford to lose vast quantities of life force before the end of TIME; before the In Breath completes and TIME is no more.

Humanity need to get home to the Heart of Creation before the In Breath completes, and we have explained in many other recordings, that 'TIME waits for no man,' and that the taking in of another poison; another power-giving energy that fuels the dark's plans for permanent separation from LOVE means, humanity will have run out of all life force and will lose the ability to recall who they were, what they were, or, that they can call for help.

This poison won't help them. It will drain them dry of their vital fluids, and suck them dry of all life force.

You thought that the poison19 was the end game? It was the diversion while the 'good' guys — the 'good' scientists — got into position, to be ready to offer their 'antidote'.

Of course, Claire could be wrong about this. She could be in the wrong place, listening to the wrong information...

Your heart has to discern all this, and it needs to ask, what role you can play in protecting humanity, because if this goes ahead, you will all own nothing and be happy.

Claire, that is all for today.

Please get this out, pronto. We need others to discern this and share to those who may need the information, and those decent, honest souls who may need reminding that LOVE comes when called upon. LOVE will never impose, and for them to understand that when they have LOVE, it is enough.

There is nothing to fear when LOVE is here."

Guidance I Received About Failure of Cv19, 24 April 2023.

ATTORNEY TOM RENZ DROPS THE BIGGEST BOMB AT CONGRESSWOMAN MTG'S MEETING!

Having just watched the video above, I realise it is a different cut to the one I viewed and the dance is cut out by the presentation data. I will attempt to locate the full version that I watched.

UPDATE: The version I watched has been doctored and the view that I saw is hidden as the video now switches to documents and redacted proofs. This was not what I saw.

Why has it been doctored?

...

UPDATED INFORMATION: 19 JUNE 2024

MCCULOUGH'S GENE THERAPY TO CURE THE C19 BIOWEAPON - JANE RUBY

MCCULLOUGH HAS THE CURE FOR THE WOUNDED 5 BILLION

...

Japanese Neuroscientist Dr. Hiroto Komano Alarmed at Explosive Dementia Surge Amongst COVID Vaccinated Individuals: Massive Study of ~600,000 Reveals

"It's unbelievable that they're also developing other vaccines with messenger RNA!"AUSSIE17JUN 18, 2024

https://www.aussie17.com/p/japanese-neuroscientist-dr-hiroto

Chapter Twenty-Three

ZOMBIE APOCALYPSE: STAR GATE PORTAL INVASION - URGENT HELP REQUESTED, 24 NOVEMBER 2023

"No matter who you are, you can help.
No matter what your belief system is, you can help.
No matter if you believe in the power of unity or not, you have the power inside of your heart centre to help.
What matters is your focus, your imagination and your belief in your power to defeat dark forces."

LOVE'S HEART PLAN, SUBSTACK.COM

LOVE is here to help us, but we need to act fast because today, I witnessed a portal opening. A tear in the fabric of space.That tear or rip has been created by technologies and has been created by your stolen life force codes — your heart ache energy, your fear vibrations, your anger, anxiety, malice, hatred; anything you have thought, felt, or transmitted that is of a low vibration has been stolen, and used as a weapon.

That weapon is StarLink, SkyNet, 5G technology, radio frequencies, wi-fi frequencies and microwaves, all types of low frequency emissions, such as ELF waves —Extremely Low Frequency waves, EMFs —Electro-magnetic Frequencies... In essence, all low frequency waves — in terms of the vibration of FEAR that they carry — is used to cause us harm.

Our 'fear' has been gathered up, and many of you already understand that fear fuels the existence of the destroyer forces and their armies, and unfortunately, their armies are presently flying in through the rip in the fabric of space-time-continuum.

"Claire will explain what she has perceived today."

I say: "I had a disturbed night's sleep last night. I woke up just before 3am and felt uneasy. I connected to my heart and consciousness using my current routine.I slept badly, and woke around 6am with a very loud whistling in my ears. The ringing sound goes up each day. This was extremely high and was slightly hurting my ears.

I wondered how animals and birds are perceiving these high pitched noises.

I reconnected to my heart and consciousness and eventually, fell back to sleep.

Around 12pm UK today, the energy dropped and something felt amiss. My gut was doing its usual 'flip' when something is wrong on the planet, and a sense of dread was experienced.

I connected again and tried to find out what was wrong.

My thoughts strayed and I started thinking about my previous job and pointless things that were distracting, not meaningful, to my inner explorations.

I couldn't perceive what was wrong, and when that happens, when I 'hit a wall', I understand that means I need to upgrade my heart and consciousness connection. I am lacking Knowledge and Wisdom, and so, I cannot perceive the issues.

When this occurs to me, I always use my current heart connection routine and I ask my Infinite Self, Infinite LOVE and the Laws of Creation from the Heart of Creation to assist me to grow in light and Knowledge, to help me understand the cause and effects of planetary happenings, and to seek solutions.

I have a few tools to help me grow in light, and I used them also.

I expressed my wish to want to be of optimal service to best help all in alignment with LOVE's plan and the laws of Creation.

I felt myself uplifted and I was guided to ask for the frequencies of Truth, Knowledge and Wisdom to surround and protect me, and to shield me from all harm so that I could hear fullest Truth guidance from the Heart of Creation and infinitely beyond.

I perceived a small circular tear in the space-time-continuum, and I sensed that had created this tear. Through this portal, I watched extra-terrestrial space ships fly in — from a previously protected space into our universe. A full-on invasion is in full process as I type this...

My husband and I both asked how could we help, and what was happening, how had it happened, and what would be the effects of this full-on invasion?

We perceived that a planetary take-over is ramping up. There is a war in space, a competition is ensuing as different factions fight for rights over our skies and land.

A sacrifice has taken place to enable ET groups inside the space-time fabric to 'barter' with life force energy in exchange for technology — to be used and weaponised — as a means of metaphorically 'burning' a hole in the space-time-fabric, to allow in higher levels of Extra-terrestrial groups who possess more harmful technologies, in order to overthrow humanity.

We kept thinking about Malaysian Airlines Flight MH370 which disappeared en route from Kuala Lumpur to China.

And we were also thinking about the missing homeless who have vanished overnight from San Francisco, and not one cell phone has recorded the departure of this group.

I put out a message, ages ago, about flight MH370. My heart had always told me that the plane turned left, not right and my inner guidance was that the plane was taken by the military, along with help from Extra-terrestrials, to an airbase hidden in the mountains between India and China.

The passengers were traded with ETs for higher technology. This project was a joint operation between China and India, according to my heart centre.

It is interesting that Greg Reese has done a piece on MH370 and recently shown that the flight went left, not right, according to new information, and that strange lights were seen around the plane before it literally vanished into thin air at altitude. All this footage was apparently taken from military drone video evidence.

I couldn't get anymore details about the Stargate Portal at that stage.

I was guided to have lunch and to wait for further guidance.

I am now waiting for the guidance to come through.

This is what my heart's consciousness and LOVE wish me to share.

Please discern everything through your own heart space and if you are being guided to help, then please follow all inner heart direction."

"Claire the following information does indeed require discernment. It is serious and it is being shared in the hope that others will discern wisely and take action accordingly through peaceful heart intervention.

You all have the power to help defend humanity and all precious life, and you all have the power to send back all this harm.

This portal has opened because the 'fear' levels have got so bad on the planet, it has caused a descension in vibrations. Fear is getting more dense, and as the planet sinks in fear, the radiation levels also descend into hostile territory.

You are not meant to be descending. You are meant to be ascending up your conscious ladder using your heart Knowledge to guide you and to bring down purest light into your lower areas of trapped consciousness within the False Light Construct.

That is called EVOLUTION and that is what ascension is all about.

Currently, the opposite is happening. The dark are descending down through your trapped levels of consciousness within the False Light Construct.

They are doing the opposite, and what they are doing will result in death of many, because this descension of destroyer forces is causing currents of fear throughout your lower conscious ladder.

Bits of your consciousness are flying off in fear as the ladder starts to become filled with fear vibrations, not LOVE, and this loss of life force energy is harsh, truly harsh, in terms of the trauma that this is causing your higher self aspects, your soul, and your family of humanity as a soul group.

Your consciousness is being stolen, and replaced with false light codes.

Many of you are remarking that people seem to be more selfish, more aggressive, less thoughtful, and the reason for this is that their purest light codes are being stolen and replaced with false light codes which emit lower frequencies and which do not operate from a frequency of LOVE.

Vast parts of the human's consciousness is becoming decimated in the process.

This loss of life force affects all precious life here. It precludes humans from making wise choices; choices that should be made — to best serve all life — are not being made.

The more life force that is lost, the more selfish and thoughtless a person becomes. It is a sign of 'Cosmic Attack', meaning: an attack is taking place at the Cosmic Shield or Cosmic Field level of your consciousness by destroyer forces, who work stealthily and remain hidden from humanity's view, primarily, because humans show no interest in looking after all aspects of their trapped consciousness. How many are even aware that these parts of their consciousness even exist?

This 'blissful ignorance' spells danger for humans who neglect to take care of themselves by regular, daily connection to heart — to ask LOVE for help.

The attack is so prolific now, that everyone needs to be asking LOVE for help — with the aid of their Infinite Self, who acts as their gatekeeper and protector, and validator of Truth.

The Cosmic Shield is currently down on humanity, as a group.

This will prove disastrous unless more of you get on board, which is why Claire has been asked to put out the emergency call for assistance.

Why has this happened, you may ask?

It has happened through apathy and ignorance, and these two weaknesses only serve to help destroyer forces to break into this part of yourselves that is relatively unknown to most of you, and start to steal vast quantities of your life force and Knowledge.

Your life force sustains you.

What do you think will be the outcome if you

One: Don't stop this attack on your own Cosmic Shield?

And Two: Remain ignorant — about the necessity to be checking your ladder of consciousness that is trapped inside this False Light Construct, on a daily basis — to check for attack, damage, fragmentation, loss of life force energy, etcetera, because if you are not prepared to help yourselves at this stage when you are more than capable, you risk death.

That is the truth and there is no point hiding the truth at this late stage.

To add in an Extra-terrestrial invasion from higher levels of technological superiority, spells disaster for you all unless you act.

We will ask you all to use the method that connects you powerfully to your heart, your Infinite Self and LOVE at the Heart of Creation to seek deeper counsel.

Claire will share the method that she uses here, and then you can all pause the recording and while using your own selected methods, try to seek inner council on how to address this calamitous event, and how to prevent it from happening again, and how to defend yourselves each day, because if you do not understand that you need to protect yourselves each and every day going forward, you are trapped in mind-control and ignorance.

Your heart Knowledge holds the keys to rescue from this place.

If you allow the dark to steal this Knowledge, you will end up in the digital, trans-human hell that has already got you fully hooked into the Internet of Bodies, and this final stage, the Internet of Things will be the end of humanity as a race, if you permit it to happen.

You will only have yourselves to blame, yet, you will not blame yourselves at that stage because you will be trapped in Avatar World — a world so dark and deadly and yet, the BBC are promoting it to their audience as a meaningful way for children to become 'data', and to give up their human body to the earth to 'recycle'.

Do yourselves a favour and beware of the BBC. This cult-owned outfit is run by predators, psychopaths and pedophiles. It is a front of 'respectability', like the Vatican, and holds no pure intentions that serve humanity. The BBC system serves the cult agenda and has many in its fake grasp of 'truth and goodness'.

It is an outfit that requires your concerted, energetic efforts to expose their true agenda and we will share more shortly.

Claire, can you share your method of connection to your heart and LOVE though your higher consciousness?"

I say: "I only use this method at home, and I always use the bed that I sleep in at night.

Common senses tells us that heart connection requires a quiet room, where one can safely lie down and close one's eyes to relax and still a busy mind.

Common sense tells us that this is not suitable for use when driving, working, or operating machinery.

This is my method:

I ensure that the room is shaded from bright sunlight.

I set an alarm clock, in case I fall asleep and I have a glass of water to hand.

I lie down, flat on my back, on the bed that I sleep in at night at home, preferably.

I relax and breathe normally, ensuring I am warm and comfortable.

If it is safe to do so, I close my eyes and I gently take my closed eyes and look softly in the direction of my chest area.

I keep my closed eyes looking gently downwards, and listen to the air going in and out of my lungs.

I imagine that in the centre of my chest is a switch that, once pressed or once I pretend to press it, it connects me to a place deep within my heart area.

I pretend that I can see a treasure chest, and this treasure chest is my deepest, most protective and shielded part of my inner heart Knowledge.

The lid is open. Before I climb into this treasure chest, I say this prayer:

"May the frequency of Peace reign supreme, and may Infinite LOVE help humanity in optimal ways that best serve all precious life."

I hear, *"Claire we want the others to upgrade immediately, in spite of the previous stepping stone teachings, those who wish to help will be assisted."*

"What must they ask for, I say"

I hear, *"Claire, those who truly wish to help themselves and help defend and protect humanity and all precious life are already emitting the frequencies required to uplift to higher levels of conscious awareness inside the heart of Creation, where Truth and Knowledge, and Wisdom is found therefore, we suggest that in their own words, each one of you make a simple request for upliftment in ways that*

"best serve all precious life in optimal ways."

That is sufficient to get the help from LOVE and the Laws of Creation — with your Infinite Selves overseeing your safety "

So, I say: "I wish to best serve all precious life in optimal ways and I am requesting assistance from LOVE and the Laws of Creation to help me — to uplift my consciousness to advanced levels of Knowledge and Wisdom."

I climb into my treasure chest, close the lid and I padlock it from the inside.

Pause the recording here to make your request and then climb inside your treasure chest, close the lid and padlock it from the inside.

Rejoin us once you feel you have been uplifted.

Now you have rejoined us, and hopefully, you have experienced upliftment, can you perceive this tear in the space-time-continuum fabric?

Keep pausing the recording and keep coming back once you are ready.

Can you see the movement of ET craft coming into our reality?

We must work quickly, please can you pause the recording at each question to secure your own direction?

Work through the questions and allow your Infinite Self and LOVE to guide you.

Question: What caused this? (Pause, for answers)

Question: What will be the effects of this tear if it is not closed by humanity with LOVE's assistance?

Question: What are the risks, in terms of the children and newborns, the vulnerable and all precious life?

Question: What optimal help can we request from LOVE, to secure a perfect outcome for all precious life?

Question: Do we have any gifts, that we brought in our treasure chest to help close this portal?

Question: How do we use them in optimal ways to best serve all precious life?

Question: Do I need to connect to heart each day AM, PM and midway through the day?

Question: If I neglect to connect to my consciousness, what are the risks of neglecting to help myself in this way?

Question: How does that affect all precious life, including those who are suffering?

"Claire, we do have more to share before we ask you to record this message and place it online, pronto, because we need those who are capable and willing, to help and to keep up the momentum.

This death cult are not going to stop plotting and planning. They detest you all and the level of hatred and sense of murderous desire is prevalent amongst this group.

They are assisted by those on the ground who help them. You have Non-Humans walking amongst you already. They have always been here. You have Humanoids and Cyborgs.

Elon Musk recently commented on San Francisco, about how the homelessness is so widespread near the X Twitter building that it looks like a 'Zombie Apocalypse.'

These are the most vulnerable members of your society that many of you choose to ignore their plight.

The 'Zombie Apocalypse' started in these souls. When you see their dire situation, their loss of pride in their appearance, their addiction to the poison they shoot into their veins, their lack of cleanliness and loss of hope, you are seeing the cascaded, destroyer force energies descended into a body where the soul has vacated and been hunted down, and stripped of all life force, all hope, all faith in LOVE.

When you see this 'Zombie Apocalypse' and you ignore this as a warning

— that a descension, not an ascension is occurring— you are ignoring the fact that you should all be seeing this filthy and inhospitable life style as the true 'apocalypse' — the zombification of a body, the destruction of the higher levels of awareness that are trapped inside the False Light Construct.

When you see this, and you are untouched by another human's plight, when you see this — not as a warning but as a sad fact of life, that your 'mind' has resigned itself to and switched off from caring — when you feel like this, it means: that you, too, are being attacked.

Your precious life force codes are being stolen and the codes of compassion and concern are being replaced with false light codes of coldness, disconnection from heart, and loss of kindness or concern.

When you cannot call on LOVE to help the plight of these souls — you, too, are on your way to being just like them, because — and we did warn you, but many would not listen — the 'Zombie Apocalypse' is knocking at your door.

You can choose to serve FEAR now, or, you can turn your back on FEAR and choose to serve LOVE.

This is the 'END GAME'.

You are all right at the end of this 'dance with the devil', so to speak. You life is in your own hands now, because once you know that you have consciousness that is trapped inside this False Light Construct and once you know and see a rip in space-time, and can 'perceive' the aircraft and ET's marching into your reality, you have to also know and acknowledge that LOVE exists, and that if you do not serve destroyer forces, there are many more who do, and so, a small group of you remain to defeat the darkness, and the truth of the matter is, you simply cannot defeat the darkness unless you have love for others, and unless you have love for yourself.

Try not to give the destroyer forces an ounce of your energy.

Remember: they steal it, use it and weaponise it against you.

It is time to wake up to this truth.

You will not succeed hiding behind a rock and pretending this is not happening, and it is why we have to show you, because another 'opinion' or perspective is never sufficient.

You have to be shown and you have to be brave enough to stare fear in the face, and send LOVE in to deal with the destroyer forces.

You cannot beat Lucifer energies, but LOVE can and will. You simply have to remember to call on LOVE for help, daily.

Become the 'director beam' of LOVE, because currently, the dark are using 'beam technology,' and they have been using other technologies to move planes, people and even mountains... this is the reality of choice — created by a humanity who chose to stay asleep.

Your role now, is to keep calling for LOVE's help to protect and shield the defenceless, particularly the homeless, the vulnerable and the newborns. All need your daily requests to LOVE.

Remember this also, that the homeless, 'zombie, apocalyptic mess' of the souls living rough, running on poison, being devoured internally by their own demons — would not be suffering, had society cared enough to provide the care that these souls need.

They are lost, truly lost, and now, many are missing in San Francisco. Where did they take them?

What happened to flight MH370?

Your heart knows.

It is way past time to ask your heart for truth.

Claire, please post this as soon as possible, and ask others to forgo any typographical errors.

The transcript helps others to digest the material after heart connection, but it will take too much time, and perfection is not required. The need for speed in gaining the assistance is what truly counts here."

LINKS:

BBC PROMOTING TRANS-HUMANISM:|

https://t.me/HATSTRUTH/4574

What Really Happened to Flight MH370? Project Unity | Malaysian Airlines MH370 https://t.me/gregreesevideoreports/435

...

DID SANFRANCISCO JUST ROUND UP/EXTERMINATE ALL THE HOMELESS PEOPLE?! HOW'D THEY VANISH? https://www.bitchute.com/video/zQ2DR2srJGuM/

Chapter Twenty-Four

COURAGE: THE FABRIC OF SPACE-TIME CONTINUUM, NOV 26, 2023

"Have HOPE, FAITH and TRUST around you all for powerful healing. You do not need worm powder or parasite potions, not when you fully embrace LOVE as your protector. When you have LOVE, you have enough.

Audio Link: LOVE'S HEART PLAN, SUBSTACK.COM

"I call on my Infinite Self, Infinite LOVE and the Laws of Creation to surround and protect us and to shield us from all harm. How can I best serve all precious life in optimal ways?

What is the fabric of space-time continuum made from, and why is it relevant to share this today?"

"Claire, think of a computer terminus, a place where things go and a place where things end. Like a bus terminus. A place that buses terminate their journey. Similarly computer termini are places where information travels and then stops."

I say, "I have no technical knowledge and I am not trained in 'computer speak'. Can you make this very simple so that we can all understand why space-time continuum feels very important today, and what is the fabric of space-time made of? What question should I ask that best serves all precious life, in optimal ways?"

I hear my heart say, *"Ask about space-time continuum, the fabric's constituents and the reasons why it is there in the first place."*

I ask, **"Why is space-time continuum here in the first place, and what is it made from?"**

"Claire, this is the dire part. It is made from all of your energy — all your stolen light codes of Knowledge and Wisdom, all heartache energy, all sorrow, all fear- based emotions and trance-like states of being."

"Trance-like states of being? Can you explain further? Is this the pyramid prison, or something else?"

"Claire, pyramid prisons are all around you. You have all been made to create a prison around yourselves and only you can decide if you wish to break free from this prison and then, you would need the help of LOVE in order to undo the complex entanglements that surround you all and that bind you to this place."

I say, **"What about the trance-like states of being? What do you mean by that?"**

"Claire, all of you are in a mind-trance-state, meaning: your mind codes of higher knowledge and Wisdom have been stolen and used to imprison you inside a 'prison' of pyramid energies, which are all these frequencies, tangled up into 'false light' frequencies, which hold you all in a trance-like-state, to the degree that you do not know you are in a self-created prison, or that you can call for help, or that you can break free from the mind prison.

It is simply a choice, nothing more is required."

I say, "How can I help others today, in optimal ways that best serve all precious life? And is this prison related to the Internet of Bodies and the Internet of Things?"

"Claire, we want others to know that it is way past the point of Non-Return for many on the planet, especially those who are bent on harming, but in the process of being hell-bent on harming others, the groups who could be requesting assistance to leave the mind prison are themselves being dragged back into the void — the vacuum left by those who have already been sucked into the black-hole-vacuum that you have been asked to mention many times recently.

That black-hole-vacuum is the 'digital hell' of Avatar World, the world glamorised recently by the BBC, and into which many souls are being sucked into.In front of this black hole is a powerful vacuum.

Claire was asked to place messages in the public domain in the hope that some would step forward to help themselves and the vulnerable, the children, newborns, and elderly who have no choice in these things, because society is hell-bent on this new world of digitisation of everything. It is a foolish choice for society to go down this dangerous path because they do not perceive the dangers, and that is the trance-like-state we mentioned earlier, cropping up in perfectly 'functioning' humans and individuals yet, they are not informed, they do not see the bigger picture and they feel unthreatened by the digital era. It is a fool's game, that is for certain."

I comment, "I don't see how any of us can stop this 'monster'. It has been let out of its lair and is on the rampage. One cannot get away from technology, and it is a hard mountain to climb — trying to even touch on the topics of AI and the dangers it is bringing into our Universe.

How is this linked to space-time continuum and the recent hole made by StarLink, and the message I put out last week?

Have there been new developments?

It did seem to have calmed down slightly. What can I share today, to enhance all of our learning?"

"Claire, there is coming a time when it will be too late. We have repeated this warning for over ten years now — through your work, your books, websites and various other platforms. Over ten years of warnings yet, have you witnessed much movement in humanity's awakening?"

I remark, "I feel there has been positive developments recently but it is always with a select group of committed individuals. My perceptions are that more are slightly more AWARE of the world's issues, but they are not AWAKE to the solutions.

I see far too many giving their power away to others, wasting time; having meaningless online conversations that, to me, are just distractions which take others off-course into meaningless discussions about all sorts of things... but the focus, the crux of the problem is always avoided.

There are definitely blocks in this part of society — the AWARE but not AWAKE crowd.

I think they are easy targets for the A.I. chat bots, the 77th Brigade, 'Project Mockingbird', etc., and the biggest distractions that I perceive are those in the so called Truth Community, who spend far too much time focusing on getting other's attention onto them and their channel but not enough time offering solutions.

This group are not listening to their own hearts which hold all the solutions, and the Knowledge and Wisdom.

As soon as humans give their power to another and get distracted by that person, then, power is lost and that power is 'vamped away' by the Truther, whether they are aware of that theft or not, and equally, they become a 'feeding station' to the viewers, too, and much of their own power is also lost.In the end..., I see now, where you are going with this, the Truth channel owner unwittingly becomes the computer terminus, and those who follow too ardently become energy deficient, and where does that power go?

I see it now, my heart is showing me, all that energy is being transmitted and received through the computer: the terminus is the channel owner, the rest I need more upgrades because I am struggling to perceive this fully but I sense it is linked to space-time continuum?"

"Claire, that is exactly right. That is where we are leading you all — to help you to perceive that the giving away of your attention and focus to an internet channel, or in the case of most of you, multiple channels, each night and each day — how much power of yours travels down pathways — neural pathways of 'captured-mind-energy' which is what space-time continuum is practically made of, mostly anyway, and that neural pathway of thinking is being captured at the terminus, by the channel owner, the dark ones who steal your energy, and the computer technology.

Your energy goes, like a terminus with many other routers and wires — down hidden channels of technology which transmit and receive your data, and your data is stolen via this route, because where energy goes, energy flows.

Therefore, anything, or, anyone which you give your attention and focus to, ends up transporting your energy away, and their body is already up and running as a 'computer terminus'. It is already operating as a computer terminus, a 'node in the interface' of the Internet of Bodies. That is already active.

Did you all realise this yet? You are all hooked up. Like it, or not.

You know when they had the emergency alerts worldwide? Did you ever wonder why they were doing this?

They needed a percentage, a quota of society to 'buy into' it, to give it their 'attention' and to 'focus' on it. It is a sad sign of the times that humanity are harming themselves by their own inability to say 'no' to something, and unfortunately, too many worldwide acquiesced to picking up their phone on alert day.

They gave their 'permission', in essence. What were they giving their permission to, you may ask?

For you all to be hooked up to the Internet of Bodies. The Internet of Things is right around the corner, and if Tony Blair and his cronies have their crooked way with you all, you will be complicit with your own slavery.

There is no going back from the Internet of Things. You do realise that, don't you? It needs a large group now, to 'energetically' refuse to be enslaved, and it is a hard mountain to climb because so many in your human group sell you out each time — by complicit obedience to demonic entities.

Where do you think the San Francisco homeless went? The passengers and plane of MH370.How do things and people vanish into thin air?"

I ask, "Is it anything to do with space-time continuum and teleportation?"

"Claire, do people really think that Bill Gates flies somewhere? That the Davos set 'fly' into their meetings?"

"Nothing would surprise me, but we are seeking facts here. Can you please help me condense the information — to help those who wish to contribute towards helping humanity and those who disappear into thin air?"

"Claire, ask the group who wish to grow in Knowledge and Wisdom to best serve all precious life in optimal ways to use their preferred method of connecting to LOVE at the heart of Creation.

This leaves a core group listening and gives time for those who have no impetus to help, to switch-off now and move back into the mind-trance-state.

This information is for the bold. It for those who are prepared to stare fear in the face and to understand that FEAR fears them, more than LOVE can express here.

You all came from LOVE. We wish you all to know that you would not be here if it were not for your immense ability to love unconditionally, to perceive that LOVE exists beyond the fabric of space-time continuum and that if enough would just be brave enough and bold enough to open their hearts to the need, right now, for bold steps; brave measures to be taken then, humanity would stand a better chance of leaving this place unscathed, and we have said many times and we say this again, that humanity carry the Knowledge to collapse this False Light Construct, with LOVE's help guiding them.

They simply do not "boldly go where no man has gone before," as they say on the TV, and seem to stay stuck in one spot — repeating their daily activities, and never moving out of mind-trance to seek the solutions.

If your personalities on Telegram and Bitchute and other alternative sites are not offering solutions and if they are not asking you to use your own heart and consciousness to exit this place, then, what are they doing?

That is right.

They are holding you in a certain spot — a place where you neither move backwards or forwards. You feel you are learning, but are you any nearer to finding solutions to exiting your self-built mind-prison?

Your mind was manipulated to build this around you. No one can free you from this, except your heart Knowledge and LOVE's Infinite Knowledge.

Unless you are at this stage of recognising this truth, you are lost in the programs of mind control and false light. LOVE has the Keys to set you free. You have to use your free will choice to request help, so that LOVE can come in to help, and it is the same with your Infinite Self.

Unless you ask your Infinite Self for help, it is also bound by the Laws of Creation to only assist when you give your focus and attention, and make a request for help. Therefore, those of you who are awake to this truth are the group who can help humanity the most.

Yet, you have the issue of being bound by these Laws of Creation also and you are not permitted to interfere with other's free will choices.

How can you actively help humanity and all precious life, when you must also work within the perimeter of these laws and while humanity are, essentially, making very poor choices that pose a threat to life and limb?

It is the biggest conundrum that awakening souls are facing. And that is why your heart, your Infinite Self and LOVE and the Laws of Creation must always be included in all and any requests for help you make because, this way, you can secure the ***optimal help*** *that* ***best serves all precious life****.*

When you want help for yourself, ensure it is watertight, as above, because otherwise, your energy — your codes of Knowledge and power — go through the computer, to the terminus, and from there, the neural pathways act as feeder systems that send your power — your DNA codes of Knowledge and your emergency escaping the matrix energy — down these pathways, and along these hidden corridors and now the interface that is growing into a ***'New Hell': the Internet of Things and Bodies, and eventually, the Internet of Everything****.*

Artificial Intelligence wants a body to exist in. *It wants the human body as a means of descending down through the layers of consciousness, and the human is being redesigned to be more suitable for the Artificial Intelligence to exist in this space.*

You think this is all too 'out there', too far away in the future? Very few mention ***'Project 2045'****, and it is worth you all focusing on educating yourselves about this, but not before asking your Infinite Self and LOVE and the Laws of Creation to surround and protect you, and shield you from all harm.*

Ensure you always protect yourselves before and after using ALL TECHNOLOGY because ALL this technology is weaponised against you all.

You think teleportation is too far fetched?

Where did the homeless go from San Francisco?

Do you ever wonder how they disappeared without a single cell phone capturing the event?

How did they 'disappear', this large group, and where did they take them?

What is a timeline switch?

How do the dark forces use timeline switches to harm humanity?

These questions need your heart-based focus and will enhance your learning and inner growth. 'Knowledge is power.' And that is very true. It is a precious commodity, and when placed in the wrong hands it has detrimental affects.

Claire is wondering where this is going as the Internet of Things has superseded the space-time continuum fabric question.

We will answer now. You all needed time to receive upgraded assistance, to help you perceive things that were hidden from view.

Please take time to go deep into heart here, and pause the recording while you do this.

Next, we ask you all to look at that tear from the other day that was made by StarLink which has been weaponised to burn holes in the fabric of space-time...

Can you see something big in front of the hole now?...*(Pause the recording for answers)*

What is this object, and where is it from?*...(Pause the recording for answers)Are there more of them?...(Pause the recording for answers)*

Claire we want the group to know that they are supported more than they may have realised, up until now.

This group is present in your reality because when you call for help daily, and when you keep up this regular heart-call — AM, PM and midway through your day — LOVE's army is able to manoeuvre itself inside your reality.

You think the dark destroyer forces are the only ones who can 'descend' into this Universe; this reality?...

Have Hope, Trust, and Faith that help is here. LOVE's army is here and part of that army is the 'boots on the ground'— the eyes — for the fleet that are in your skies.

Next time you give your power away, try to call it back as soon as possible, by asking your heart and LOVE and the Laws of Creation to clear you of all harm and to find all that has been lost and return it to you in its purified state.

Humanity are in serious danger, currently. LOVE's army cannot interfere, yet, LOVE's army is present for those of you who call for protection and assistance. The destroyer forces dare not harm those who are protected by LOVE's army.

Do you see now, that in order to see beyond this reality, in order to face FEAR and stare FEAR in the face, you have to be BRAVE enough and BOLD enough to look in the first instance, and once you embark on that journey of self exploration and start to receive LOVE's assistance, then, all fear melts away as you begin to perceive the illusion and start to see that this mind-set is not real.

Beyond mind-trance, LOVE exists and when LOVE is called upon, no amount of computer terminus, no amount of Internet of Things or Bodies is possible beyond this reality, yet, the true danger is when a soul or human or life form believes in the illusion so much so, and is in fear of what exists beyond the illusion, that their minds stay paralysed on the spot and it is on that spot of a trance-like fixation with other people, other opinions, other events, world stories that they transfix themselves, and if others could lift their heads, just a little — to see that beyond this superficial world lies something of great beauty and great depth, then perhaps, there may be a chance to help lift humanity's head out of their self-dug grave — to see that life and LOVE exist outside of this mind set and only they can set themselves free, only they can choose to lift their heads.

What is missing from their composition?

COURAGE.

Courage is missing. You have to see these souls for what they truly are. They are in fear.

It is so deep and so far inside of them, it lurks in places that they cannot yet fathom and so they reject truth, and facts, and the obvious.

How can you help those who are in fear? You have tried to help them lift their heads by raising awareness. Did awareness lead to awaken-

ing?In some, perhaps. Yet, many have not yet turned their hearts towards the solutions. The mind-trance has a firm hold on many, still.

What other actions or activities could help those who are immersed in slavery and fear?

The dawning of a new era is upon you all. The dawning of a new day.

As you continue to raise your consciousness to new heights of raised awareness, you awaken to deeper truths, new Knowledge, new Wisdom, and as you rise in consciousness, like a bubble of air trapped inside water, as you float to the surface, those in the deeper waters rise up too, and if you can just keep going now, in spite of all the challenges, if you can hold onto HOPE, FAITH and TRUST, and ask for the frequencies of COURAGE to be returned to all who are suffering in this illusion, then LOVE can set to work to send this into your reality.

Claire is starting to awaken as new realisations dawn..."

I ask, "Is space-time continuum made up of our stolen Courage: re-purposed, redesigned and distorted — to hold us in a state of FEAR?"

"Claire, it is indeed stolen Courage. A huge threat to the destroyer forces is the frequency of Courage because these frequencies come from LOVE, and Courage is a powerful force for change and for resistance to enslavement.

We are suggesting to you to have courage, and to ask LOVE to send in the Frequencies of Courage to help the souls see, and to support you all with your vital work here.Claire, that is all.

Others need the guidance which is coming in late, however, you could not retrieve until later today, while we waited for others to be bold and have courage — to face FEAR and to ask for help. This happened late today.

Have HOPE, TRUST, and FAITH that COURAGE is a powerful force for change.Keep your focus on these frequencies, over and above the internet distractions.

Have Courage around you and wear these frequencies like a coat of protection, and also, as facilitators of change for those who lack these frequencies. They have had their courage stolen. It is the biggest cause of this state of non-movement and resistance to truth.

Be their friends — those who are stuck. Many are there because they gave these codes to those who were meant to wake up first and help the others.

They lack courage and motivation because they gave you those codes.

Pity them and pity their plight.

The homeless also lack these codes, and it would best serve all precious life, in optimal ways, to pray for all who lack courage and to ask LOVE to help them to integrate these frequencies back into their consciousness.

That will produce growth for many, that is for certain.

Have HOPE, FAITH, and TRUST around you all, for powerful healing.You do not need worm powder or parasite potions, not when you fully embrace LOVE as your protector.

When you have LOVE, you have enough."

Chapter Twenty-Five

THE BEAST SYSTEM IS COMING, NOV 27, 2023

Too few tried to stop it, and too many started too late

"It is time to stand as one voice of fearless, unguarded courage because humanity are about to face their biggest hurdle yet, and you all need to be up and running, and ready to do 'battle with the beast' system, which is coming."

Audio Link:

Love's Heart Plan | substack.com

"We call on our Infinite Selves, and Infinite LOVE and the Laws of Creation to surround and protect us,

AND to shield us from all harm.

We call on the most powerful healing frequencies: HOPE, TRUST, AND FAITH to surround and protect us,

AND

We call on LOVE to shield us with the frequency of COURAGE — to fuel us with bravery and boldness, to have courage to speak our truths at humanity's hour of need."

"Claire, that is it. No more is needed yet as an opening heart call/prayer. Leave it exactly as it is.'

I ask, "How can we best serve all precious life in optimal ways? It seems that things are developing and for those who have not yet started to help themselves by calling on LOVE for help, I sense that another message — so close after the last one — must mean that things are happening. It also means that many more brave souls are calling for help and facing FEAR head- on. Has it helped humanity?

I saw a mass grave, similar to the past world war graves, and I saw humanity standing there on the edge. My perception was that they are being used by destroyer forces to dig their own grave and it was a huge grave pit, not a solitary one.

The place looked very dark and cold. There was no light there. How on earth can we help these souls when we are also bound by the Laws of Creation to not interfere with the free will choices of other living beings?

This also places our most exposed members of our family of humanity in a dire position — the vulnerable, homeless, children and newborns, as well as the elderly. It has placed us all in harm's way, unless others know how to protect themselves, and many don't have a method or Faith that would assist them.

How can we all help today? Many generous hearts are helping, I feel their love for humanity and it is like a beacon of Hope shining in the darkness. I am truly thankful to all of you who have stepped forward to help.

When many tiny frightened voices call out in the wilderness, LOVE comes through, and today, I perceived huge areas that have been secured by LOVE's army and airforce, so to speak.

LOVE is definitely here.

How can we utilise LOVE's help in optimal ways to best serve all precious life?"

My heart and LOVE say, *"Claire, we are going to give you quite a lengthy download of data and it is thanks to those who have joined in with their love to help all precious life. Many of you are aware of how serious things are and underneath that thin veneer of apparent calmness, the proverbial is about to hit the fan.*

Claire, please leave that as you have written it. The translation of Light language to Earth language does vary from person to person. Please try not to be 'saintly' when writing, just be normal, be yourself. People must be aware that you have chronic pain and chronic fatigue, and words are hard to find sometimes. Just do your best to convey the essence of the message and that will be perfectly acceptable — to LOVE, anyway.

The reason why things have developed is multifold.

Help has arrived in the form of LOVE's army, and LOVE has manoeuvred help into the Earth's 'airspace'.

Those of you who have called for help have achieved this, and we wish you to appreciate how much your efforts can bring help to the vulnerable.

LOVE's army is here to stay, however, we do need you all to 'up-the-anti' and to start a steady, fast, climb out of this space — to safer waters, where your life force and codes of Knowledge can be protected.

It simply requires regular, daily, heart connection and in between, if you are prompted inwardly to connect, to make a short connection, to see what your heart is telling you.

Your heart will become clearer to hear, the more you do this. The help is being given because we are aware that the issues of attack on the Earth plane have made it very hard to hear your heart's guidance, and to hear LOVE's guidance.

This is all about to change, and once Claire is ready to lie down to type this, we will begin.

Claire has a back injury and it is not easy to type sitting. The transcripts will be shared on Substack. We ask you to overlook the typos and occa-

sional spelling errors, because the message is the most important and the transcript is there to help digest the message once you have listened to it. The time spent proofing the message means: time wasted reaching all who could help."

I say, "I am ready and waiting. How can we best serve all precious life in optimal ways, today?"

"Claire, this is a big data dump of LOVE's Knowledge and Wisdom.

It was always promised to you all. LOVE promised that if enough of you called for help and asked LOVE to intercede with the False Light Construct attacks on all precious life, that all you had to do was ask for help, LOVE would do the rest.

LOVE knew that straddling density in a False Light Program of Entanglement was never going to be plain sailing.

You all knew that when it got to this stage— the stage of the False Light Construct collapsing under the weight of its own errors — that you would make a 'mayday call' to LOVE, and all those in the 'rescue party' would be reached out to, and reminded that they needed to request their own rescue, in order to leave this False Light Construct with all that they had lost, returned as Purest Light codes.

None of your precious codes of Knowledge must remain here. The destroyer forces will use them as weapons against you all if they are not secured and found, and so, LOVE needs to be called upon because it is a complex issue that requires LOVE's all knowing Wisdom to do this safely without causing harm.

Imagine some of your weakened frequencies of Light are like the silky threads from a spider's web. These frequencies are entangled with the False Light frequencies which are barbed in places and have all sorts of traps, so that when these silky threads are withdrawn, the risk of more damage is prevalent. Lucifer energies have booby-trapped your stolen life force frequencies and DNA codes of Knowledge.

Put simply, you cannot do this on your own, not in a False Light Construct where your own full Knowledge is missing in droves.

And this is where TRUST becomes important. Once you are protected by your Infinite Self from the Heart of Creation and infinitely beyond, when you then call on LOVE, you can be sure that only LOVE comes to you. Your Infinite Self ensures this is the case.

It would not be wise to call on LOVE without your inner protector, your Infinite Self present beforehand, and it is why everything Claire shares is carefully worded and measured; to ensure a safe connection to LOVE at the heart of Creation.

We wish to impress this upon you all, because if you are wishing to help humanity, we need you to be using a watertight heart call. These prayers or heart calls are encoded with LOVE's help, but we do need you to be very strict.

Humanity are reliant on a small group to secure this particular help. Many others around the world are following their inner heart guidance and they might be doing other things to help.

Make no mistake, it is all leading toward a grand finale which is not long in the making.

That is the housekeeping side of things wrapped up. We will now proceed with new information to help you all grow steadily and quickly in light, to help you move outside of the False Light Construct and to reach new levels of learning and conscious awareness, in service to all precious life.

This is service work, make no mistake. We are leaving the others behind who only dabble with their practices. This work is for those who are serious and committed to helping.

It requires your steely determination and strength to keep going, even when you 'hit a wall' and to have Hope, Trust, and Faith that, as long as you are asking of help, the help will always break through any 'wall' that is blocking your growth.

Claire is feeling uplifting sensations and glimpses of JOY as she types this, and this is because all the help is coming through the typed-out words. The codes are within the teachings. You will all be receiving them while Claire shares the message and it is also the reason why we ask you all to download the transcripts on your computer and onto paper, if possible, because where LOVE goes, LOVE's energy flows and you are helping to metaphorically ground in the frequencies of LOVE's assistance more fully into this reality.

It helps to spread LOVE's access more deeply and it protects you too, because these transcripts carry codes of protection within them.

The written word is highly important. All words carry frequencies. Your written words, your emails, your texts and messages all carry the codes of your own unique energy signature.

And today, that is the teaching we wish you to contemplate.

Claire, can you share what happened when you and your husband started being targeted."

I say, " It was 2017. I was already being targeted but I had had many teachings leading up to 2017 and I knew how to deal with attack on my conscious ladder and energy bodies.

I had been shown how to do this from 2012, so I was very well versed by then and I had been teaching advancing teachers how to fully clear their own energy and how to protect their energy signatures.

My husband had been very closed-off to my awakening experience. I think it frightened him, as he saw I was changing. However, many things happened that started to show him that there was something in it. He had helped me to hastily proof-read several books that I had written and I think, reading them awakened him because the books were encoded with profound teachings and keys from the heart of Creation.

He approached me and asked for help to connect to heart because he had seen how much it was helping me deal with disability due to serious spinal injuries which had left me with difficulty walking, standing, sitting, etc., and had left me in a lot of pain. I also had chronic fatigue and chronic pain from Fibromyalgia and the combination of daily, excruciating spinal pain and all over body pain was challenging, to say the least.

In spite of all these challenges, my heart and LOVE helped me. I was recovering from huge life changes regarding my mobility, and they helped me move through it.

Curiously, in 2016, I started noticing the lowering of energy that was emitted from texts, and the mobile phones.

When my husband asked for help with heart connection, I had warned him that once he started he must not stop, otherwise we would get attacked and it would spell disaster for us, as we would be losing vast amounts of life-force and would fragment at soul level and above.

He started his awakening journey, and the attack that ensued in 2017 was horrendous.

We would spend hours trying to resolve errors that he was making. The smallest deviation from the simple routines I had shared with him, were causing huge attacks on us and it was taking up much time and effort to resolve the issues.

My husband kept ignoring basic teachings. For example, I would encourage him to use his routine and always said if he could not get past any blocks within 15 minutes, to call on LOVE for help and to come and get me. He never would and I would find him, hours later, being attacked and unable to secure his own safety, but he never remembered to come and get me after 15 minutes. It was mind boggling. What was happening. I knew the connection to heart was safe.

I knew I had to let him grow and make his own mistakes but each small error he made seemed to be opening gateways of satanic attack that sometimes took 8 hours to clear.

I started to resent his involvement. I was losing vast amounts of life force, and unlike him, I was feeling it at soul level. He just didn't seem to understand that heart connection required the need to train oneself to be focusing on heart, not head, but he is a good person and very kind, and so it was very frustrating and confusing as to why he kept drifting away from heart connection and sometimes, I felt that he was being deliberately attacked and that the attack was coming through him to me.

I was trying to protect us both and more importantly, I knew that if my written work, and other projects were attacked, it could jeopardise those who were awakening and using the shared teachings.

This attack on us threatened all life and at the same time, two friends of mine were also reading my books and applying the teachings.

One was very new to all of this. I had seen them dabble with the teachings and then get distracted by life many times.

My other friend was more awake and more 'tuned in' to their higher self aspects but, they too, were not applying the teachings fully. They were only being applied when they felt like it, even though the teachings I had received clearly asked that they required daily connection: AM, PM, and midway through the day.

I sensed their energy frequencies dropping as this progressed and I was guided to stop offering them help because they were not listening and had to learn the hard way.

We were in the middle of trying to move house. I had been guided that the location was not helping us, and I sought teachings on how to address the many frequency changes that seemed to be affecting our own well-being. I was also desperate to protect the teachings because a lot of hard work had been poured into the books. I knew how valuable the teachings were. No one had to tell me, I knew. Yet those who read the books didn't seem to grasp how important the teachings were.

When I started teaching and running websites and subsequently writing about frequencies, no one in my peer group knew what I was talking about.

The holistic community never talked about frequencies. No one talked about the Cosmic Shield of humanity. I could not find anyone anywhere mentioning these subjects.

The keys that I downloaded in 2012 have been my guiding lights and helped me so much on my journey. I knew in my heart that these teachings were precious. Others did not seem to perceive their value and that is how hard it is to climb past the wall of mind-control.

When anyone starts to climb the mountain of their own ladder of consciousness, at every turn and every corner, the ego programs are there to booby-trap even the most willing of souls.

Many lost interest after their initial 'high' about the teachings. Their interest would wane and I would watch them return to old practices that were distorted and caused harm to others, such as Reiki; Yoga, etcetera.

And those who 'dabbled' enjoyed the preliminary effects of working with Purest Light frequencies, but they never held the distance.

I was also noticing a drop in frequencies in the energy signature of blog posts and subscription emails from people who naturally carried a loving vibration.

I had already discovered the darkness behind social media sites, as had my students.

As my various students awakened to their deeper aspects of consciousness, they would start to perceive how dark these things were too, yet, they would always get tripped up by ego and they fell back down their ladder of awareness into the depths of False Light entanglement.

I had also noticed a change in my ability to hear my heart's guidance as clearly.

My husband wasn't acting normally and the mind control kept tripping him up.

To secure the safety of our energy signature which it seemed, was being attacked more heavily in 2017, we were advised to start asking for all outside energy to be contained and we learned about the energy of stamps on our post, — how the royal frequencies carried the satanic and masonic frequencies and that once they landed on our doormat, they brought those energies into our home and caused satanic attack.

We learned about clearing the energy from all things brought into the home — owing to the bar codes, the symbols used prolifically on food and drink packaging, and we also learned about how the energy signature of our departed loved ones were also exposed to attack from satanic forces who could steal their life force codes from photographs — anywhere that an energy signature is present, is exposed.

We were in the middle of a house move, dealing with solicitors, estate agents and others, and you can imagine the symbology and satanic energy emitting from the various letter headings.

Old watches of loved ones now past, still carry their energy signature, and it all needs protecting which is why we had the teachings, but I have to tell you, my growth went from joyful and enlightening to downright draining and it was hard work trying to understand the depth of the satanic attack on our energy signature and the steps we had to take to resolve it.

This was partly due to my husband having difficulty understanding all this information. He had only just woken up and humanity were in the middle of the biggest storm the planet had ever seen.

At the time, I did not know why things had become so difficult and draining, energetically.

We soldiered on, but it was the worst time of our lives, and it nearly destroyed our once happy marriage.

We have had some very difficult challenges to deal with since then, and it has not been easy. It has aged us, all the stress, and it has only started to improve energetically in the last year when more started to step forward and to climb their own ladder of awareness and to take responsibility for their energetic actions.

We suffered because very few on the planet understood consciousness. They were unaware of their Cosmic Field and everything below it, most healers are fixated on the Biofield which is an extremely limited way of being, because it is not where the problems start.

The problems start at the Cosmic Field level — the top part of the ladder of consciousness that is trapped inside the False Light Construct."

"Claire, that covers enough for today. We wish to discuss why Claire and her husband were suffering energetic distress in 2017, and beyond and it may shock you all.

The components of the False Light Construct were under reconstruction — meaning: the false light forces had secured new teachings and the new teachings were being applied to humanity.

Claire and her husband were exposed because they were connecting to heart and LOVE, and this posed a threat to the groups who serve destroyer forces.

The groups who destroy knew who was coming in to 'fight' them, in the sense that they knew who their 'fight' was with. It was never going to be with the ones who were asleep. Their biggest threat was those who could perceive their energy fields at the perimeter fence of the top of the False Light Construct because, seeing the Cosmic Shield and knowing how to fix it, is a huge threat to the dark.

In 2012, to cut a long story short, Claire was being asked to get the teaching community in the healing energy groups to step forward for brand new teachings.

The teachings had been developed by LOVE, not humans, and they were being anchored into the Earth grids to help humanity awaken to the danger they were in, and to help them to start the journey of ascending out of the False Light Construct — to start their return journey home to the Heart of Creation before the In Breath completed, ready for the next evolutionary cycle, the Out Breath.

This is EVOLUTION. It is how Creation operates. Cycles of expansion and learning come to a natural end and the expansion is halted and starts to return back to the heart of Creation, recalling all that has been lost, repairing any errors and clearing all space, so that all those who are returning are ready and prepared for their next new cycle of learning and expansion.

Their soul evolution is but one part of their journey. There are many other levels of advanced awareness on the human ladder of consciousness, and unfortunately, those who volunteered to fall in density and come into this place to help trapped souls return home, have been attacked to such a degree that they lack the codes, the frequencies to see — to remember their true origins, or reason for being in this place.

It is all about missing frequencies and in the newer days of Claire's growth, we referred to these frequencies as KEYS.

Frequencies are like KEYS that open a life-form up to newer doorways of learning.

A whole library of Knowledge and Wisdom is available to all those who truly, and earnestly wish to help humanity and all precious life — to exit this program, before it collapses in on itself.

What we wish to impress upon you all is that the level of attack that Claire and her husband started to experience in 'high definition' in 2017, is still ongoing.

What has changed for them, is that through determined effort, they managed to push past the blocks that tried to make them go AWOL, and these blocks were placed there by destroyer forces — by Lucifer energies.

Therefore, if you wish to help, you need to understand that the attack will try to knock you off course. You have LOVE by your side and you must not fear the destroyer forces, yet, by the same token, you must appreciate that this is not a child's game. This is serious. The dark wait for you to go into ego; to start being inconsistent with your daily heart connection. They will try to reach you, and you are in their world so, you need to be watchful and alert, and the worst thing you can do is forget to ask for help when you wake up; midway through the day, and at night before sleep.

If you forget, you let Lucifer walk right on in. We don't want you to be fearful. We want you to be sensible.

Sensible, in the sense that this help for humanity requires a committed heart — one that truly wishes to try their very best to help.

If you cannot commit, you risk opening humanity up to more harm, and at this stage of their journey; given that the In Breath is about to complete and the False Light programs, collapse; given that the dark ones hate and loath humans and all precious life — they want your life force — it fuels their existence. They watch and wait for you to be thoughtless; selfish; lazy with your heart connection.

And conversely, on the other side of this issue, when you regularly connect to your own heart's beauty, when you start to see that LOVE is real, that truth exists and that Hope is a healing frequency along with Faith and Trust, the beauty of these discoveries can open up a world where you become fearless, joyful, and part of life's true rhythm, which is LOVE's beating heart — calling you all home after an age out in the wilderness, forgetting and forgoing much of what was previously, precious life force and Knowledge, in order that falling hard enough, would enable those who were stuck here, to leave this place and journey home with you.

The outcome of this adventure rests with those of you who truly wish to secure the children's brightest future.

We are simply wishing to impress upon you all the heavy duty of responsibility that rests upon your shoulders.

And yet, when you call on LOVE and trust that LOVE is truly here, present, contactable at a moment's notice, you can also perceive that this 'moment' is a place in history that will be told and retold for millennia of cycles of In Breaths and Out Breaths to come.

How will this end?

The outcome of this story rests with you all.

You have LOVE to guide you perfectly. Have courage that you can succeed. That you can overcome all adversity; all challenges; all blocks and all attacks.

Claire and her husband laid a pathway. It has been tough for them and LOVE is asking for your support because they are weary now, and need some time to rest from their own ordeals.

If others could take the reins now, that would be a good thing to do, because you all need to be self-sufficient and practiced at your own heart connection.

Knowing your own heart's calling, makes for fearless, brave, and courageous action.

It is time to stand as one voice of fearless, unguarded courage because humanity are about to face their biggest hurdle yet and you all need to be 'up and running,' and ready to do 'battle with the beast' system, which is coming.

Too few tried to stop it, and too many started too late.

Have Hope, Faith, and Trust that your courage will surmount what is to come. Listen to the beating of your own heart and to LOVE.

LOVE is here, and when you have LOVE, you have enough."

Chapter Twenty-Six

HUMANITY'S DEATH PIT: Last Call For The Reiki And Yoga Communities

"So, what we are saying is, don't let the children, the vulnerable and the newborns be harmed, just because of stubborn ignorance, or ego-led refusal to face FEAR and look it in the eye.

You could turn this around in an instant and we are simply hoping, you will try."

LOVE'S HEART PLAN SUBSTACK

"We call on our Infinite Selves, and Infinite LOVE and the Laws of Creation to surround and protect us,

and to shield us from all harm.

We call on the most powerful healing frequencies: HOPE, TRUST, AND FAITH to surround and protect us,

and

We call on LOVE to shield us with the frequency of COURAGE — to fuel us with bravery and boldness, to have courage to speak our truths at humanity's hour of need."

How can we best serve all precious life in optimal ways today?

I am on the verge of 'knowing' and on the verge of perceiving.

Please can you help me to hear Truth from the Heart of Creation, to best serve all?

I keep thinking about 2017 and how things were changing from 2016 — with my heart connection difficulties; the changes we were seeing in friends, many of whom seem to be slipping into mind control and ego-led behaviour.

We were learning about the world we occupy in this reality and the realisation that this is not a world built on the foundation of LOVE.

No, this world is built on the foundation of wanton destruction and hatred.

We occupy a reality not of our making, and yet, we are living in a reality where our energy has been used in harmful ways to construct the fabric of space-time-continuum.

None of it is real, in the sense that our courage has been converted to FEAR. Our low vibrational thoughts have been used to fuel the existence of the dark forces and our AWOL soul fragments, etcetera.

Artificial Intelligence is our stolen mind energy which has been weaponised against us.

Our governments serve those who seek our destruction. As do the big banks; big pharma; big corp.

The WHO, the United Nations and World Economic Forum carry a loathing towards humanity which is highly palpable when one tunes into these crooks.

And all the obvious signs that many of us notice and know to be a threat, are ignored by those who watched their relatives die via Face-Time, whose businesses went under during lock-downs, who lost their jobs, their homes, were forced into poverty.

The public know that the vaccines do not stop transmission now, nor do they protect against "covid". The news is out that cancer rates are going sky high, that the vaccines may cause heart issues, especially in the young.

The NHS is still inviting the public to get their covid vaccination. The public are still going, in spite of getting sick with supposed 'covid,' multiple times since their vaccination.

Friends who we know were avid supporters of *'Pshizer' [deliberately misspelt]* are recovering once again from covid and now have other health issues which remain unresolved.

It is truly baffling, isn't it? What could possibly be the cause, I wonder? Has anything unusual happened to cause 'repetitive covid' in the vaccine poisoned?

Nurses know. How do I know that? I sat in a hospital waiting room and listened to a man tell his friend about his blood clot in his neck that nearly killed him, and that his consultant had identified the covid vaccine as the cause of his blood clot.

So, consultants know too. The nurses sit in on these meetings. My friend lost all their hair and it progressively fell out in handfuls after each booster. Their consultant highlighted the covid vaccine was the cause.

So, ...they ...do ...know. They all know. It is truly baffling, isn't it?

A friend who works at a pharmacy has also noticed the increase in dead patients and sick patients. They can't say more but they know too, and it is worrying them deeply.

Is it climate change? It is baffling, and why can humanity not see the obvious? Because everyone we know who got the poison is either dead, or has had some nasty reaction like life-threatening cellulitis, chronic fatigue, hair loss, extreme pain in their hands and joints, eye problems, cancer and so forth.

All these people were previously very healthy.

Baffling, truly baffling.

And next, we face the World Economic Forum's latest ploy to scare us all to death about the 'shortage of water.'

All of a sudden, the world has become a very scary place, hasn't it?

Truly baffling...

Was it always like this?

Not always, but we need to focus our minds now, and look back along this timeline and the various timeline switches that have occurred since 2017 to understand the plight of what humanity are facing.

We have to tell them, and we cannot delay the message. If we don't tell them, people are going to lose this 'battle with the devil,' so to speak, and the devil has already had humanity dig their own death pit.

We have to get humanity away from this dark place because in their hour of need, there are few out there who truly 'get' what is happening on an energetic level — who are determined to reach Truth because of their deep love for humanity and all those who are trapped here.

I don't even know why I am saying all this, it is just pouring out of my fingers onto the keyboard.

Why am I saying all this? Where is it heading?

"Claire, we will share with you all, what you need to know. It is a complex issue — with many layers of destructive attack entangled around humanity — to keep them oblivious; asleep; unquestioning and in fear.

The constant, incessant round of scaremongering by your world governments who, as Claire rightly said, carry a loathing, a hatred so deep toward you all, that if humanity truly understood the depth of hatred, perhaps they might stop being so obedient and tolerant of these tyrants.

Your world governments serve Satan, or Lucifer, as this energy is also called. They serve the cult agenda. They do not serve LOVE, and they do not want humanity to know that LOVE exists, because if more humans knew that calling on LOVE for help would decimate the plans that Satan's army has for humanity and all precious life then, it would be game over.

"Make the request. LOVE does the rest."

LOVE is here and LOVE is standing by for all requests for help, and as many as possible need to be making that request for help now.

What is planned for humanity is untenable. It has to be stopped. You cannot stand by now and allow this group to destroy you all.

It really is life and death, and by that we mean, death of the soul, death of your ladder of consciousness. If your ladder of consciousness is not withdrawn from this place soon, it will fall into this place and if the ladder of consciousness falls into this place, it means you will be cut off from all assistance.

It is the law of Creation. Claire has covered this in several previous messages and those who wish to help would do well to steadily listen to the start of the messages and work their way through to present day.

They were all uploaded from October onwards. LOVE knew this was coming which is why there are so many messages. They are shared in the hope that some more will step forward to assist humanity.

Without your help, humanity face an early grave.

Claire has mentioned, many times in the past, the deeper teachings surrounding the satanic manipulation of the frequencies, and poses, contained in all energy healing modalities and Yoga practises.

You have to be open-hearted to listening — to understand why these practises, which outwardly appear harmless are in fact, deeply destructive to your ladder of consciousness.

It has been explained by LOVE how Yoga participants have had their ladder of consciousness emptied of much of their precious codes of Knowledge and Wisdom, — codes so precious, because they were meant to be shared with humanity to help humanity leave the False Light Construct before it collapsed in on itself.

We have explained that Reiki energies were always distorted and we had asked the Reiki groups, over ten years ago, to disconnect from Reiki and to start heart connection. The same message was put out for Yoga participants and other spiritual exercises, because the destroyer forces had distorted these frequencies further, and this had made them deadly to those who worked with them and those who received them.

Yoga and Reiki groups tend to get very offended and upset about this news that their practises are harmful.

Quite simply, many have refused to even explore inside their hearts, and many have not sincerely tried to perceive deeper truths. Why would they?

Many are making money out of these practices, many love the 'Reiki shares' and social side of things, and many are addicted to satanic frequency.

When you try to take drugs away from a drug addict, they get very angry and defensive and aggressive, and this is how Reiki and Yoga participants react to any information which threatens them.

But really, it is the satanic energy contained inside their energy field which is satanic in nature, and not their energy. It is False Light frequency and it has been placed in the areas where Purest Light codes once resided.

The dark destroyer forces are very clever and they have stolen these Purest Light codes and replaced them with False Light codes, and so, they do not want shifting or clearing, because they are controlling that person and controlling their thoughts, actions, words, and deeds and they will not give up — without a determined heart and LOVE — to help the person see what Yoga and Reiki have done to harm humanity.

The Galactic Grids were destroyed by Reiki practises in 2018. They were rebuilt and collapsed several times because Reiki groups refused to stop their practises.

The Planetary Grids were collapsed by Yoga groups and 5G users in 2020 and they were rebuilt several times but they were collapsed by constant refusal to stop these practises.

Yoga and Reiki participants tend to be very arrogant about their belief in these practises, yet, they cannot perceive their energy fields, and certainly, have never journeyed to see the top levels of their Cosmic Field to see the hidden attack that is going on there each and every nano-second of each day.

Vast quantities of life force have been stolen from these participants and where do you think all their codes of Purest Light Knowledge went?

It went to the destroyer forces who weaponised this energy and used it to harm humanity.

Claire recently mentioned in her messages that she had perceived a 'rocket of energy' aimed at humanity and heading straight for them. She shared that this energy was stolen life force codes of Knowledge taken from Reiki groups.

This precious commodity of Knowledge was given to these groups to bring into this space — to help humanity escape from the False Light matrix.

It was not meant to be handed over to the destroyer forces.

In their blissful ignorance and stubborn refusal to explore whether they might be unknowingly harming humanity, this attitude has lead to death and not just physical deaths, it has lead to the worst crime im aginable...it has led to death of the soul.

To cause death of the soul; death of another living being is reprehensible and it is even more reprehensible, given that Reiki groups and Yoga groups have had adequate warnings and adequate time to explore with their Infinite Self and LOVE to see how they can remedy their errors.

LOVE is not judging, LOVE loves you, however like any loving parent would say to their offspring, if they had caused the death of another, it is wrong —what you did — and there are always severe penalties for refusing to stop a killing-spree.

And this may seem very harsh to those of you who do Reiki and Yoga but it is clear that if you have not stopped, you are bent on a killing-spree and others need to know that your actions are, indeed, killing others, quite literally.

Let us explain in a condensed fashion, once again, to help newcomers perceive the harm these practises do.

Ask your Infinite Self and LOVE and the Laws of Creation to surround and protect you and to shield you from all harm.

Next, ask your Infinite Self and LOVE to show you a classroom model of a human and you can look at their Cosmic Field and Biofield levels, as well as the human body...See it all in miniature, because these fields are vast spaces in reality, so, make it a 'small-scale model.'

We want you to imagine that you can perceive Purest Light frequencies from the Heart of Creation beaming into the human and all energy field levels.

Watch how the healing frequencies work and ask how these benefit, if at all.

Walk around the model and take a long look, and ask lots of questions.

Pause the recording while you do this and rejoin us once you are finished.

Next ask your Infinite Self and LOVE to replace Purest Light frequencies, and to beam Reiki frequencies into the human classroom model.

Watch what happens at higher levels of the top energy fields.

Note the arrival of 'visitors'.

Watch how the energy fields respond at the Cosmic Level, and down to the Biofield and physical level.

Take your time and pause the recording until you are ready to rejoin us.

Next, ask your Infinite Self and LOVE to show you two human classroom models with all their energy fields and one is receiving LOVE from the Heart of Creation in the form of Purest Light codes, and the other is receiving Reiki.

Compare the two models. Who is benefiting the most?

Is any damage happening on either model?

Pause the recording and rejoin us once you are ready.

Next, ask your Infinite Self and LOVE to show you what Yoga does to the human and their energy fields. Walk around and take time to secure new guidance.

Then, ask your Infinite Self and LOVE to demonstrate LOVE frequencies on a second model and compare the difference between Yoga, and LOVE from the heart of Creation.

Pause the recording and rejoin us once you have received new guidance.

You can repeat this with Circle Dancing, Maypole Dancing, Line Dancing, Pilates, Crystal Healing, Angelic Healing, Mystery School Healing, etc.

If you participate in any of these practices, you are on 'final warning' so please, take note, and take 'evasive action' because your practices are like a runaway plane — set on autopilot and armed with nuclear bombs.

We are saying this, not as a threat, when we say 'warning', we mean we are trying to alert you to the danger you are in, and the danger you are placing humanity in.

It is far too late in the day to be concerned about your feelings. You are on a collision course, and that nuclear bomb is about to explode — on yourself primarily — and it is also going to harm all the people you teach or take money from, and because your energy signature has been altered, your frequency — your unique energy frequency — has been altered, and it is now a receiver but not for LOVE, your receiver has been changed to receive destroyer forces and you are letting in Lucifer into your energy fields.

You are going to get very sick soon, if not already, and if you don't stop these practises and close the door on Lucifer, and ask your Infinite Self and LOVE for help — you risk, not only death, but death of your soul.

Essentially, you are on a death-mission — a suicide mission, and Lucifer has already got you to dig your own grave.

Worse still, you will leave this body, knowing that you did not remedy your errors and that means that you will be in torment — for a short while at least, until destroyer forces have sucked you dry of life force, and then, you will be happy and own nothing — just like Klaus Schwab and Yuval Harrari have planned for you.

It is dire, and the picture is a true one. We do not need to exaggerate.

And what of those who you taught or treated? How do you think they will fair?

Ask your Infinite Self and LOVE to show you what their fate is going to be.

Pause the recording and watch the outcome —displayed by your own heart.

And what of cancer patients who are treated by energy healers, especially Reiki, and why have Macmillan cancer and the NHS authority allowed cancer patients to have access to Reiki, do you think?

Could it be the same reason as why they allowed the covid-19 vaccine to be given to little infants and new borns, as well as the trusting public?

Watch the classroom demonstration of what happens to a cancer patient when they receive Reiki. Let your Infinite Self and LOVE show you, to help you grow, and to help you make a decision that preserves life, not destroys life.

The Laws of Creation forbid any living being to take the life of another.

How many doctors, nurses, and volunteers have done just that by injecting the improperly and fraudulently trialled covid-19 vaccines?

Your death-squad, who lined up — to jab you all with a highly suspect poison, and now, people are dying, and it is all very baffling.

Heart attacks will increase, as will cancer. It is not because of climate change and it is not due to water shortages.

It is due to entities like King Charles and Bill Gates, the front-men for the hidden ones who lurk in passages deep underground.

You will never know how dark this is, until you have the courage to face FEAR and stare it hard in the face, and be willing to know what is happening on your planet, and find out, before it is too late for change.

When Yoga and Reiki collapsed the Galactic and Planetary Grids, it was too much for Mother Earth and her spirit. Her part of her conscious ladder — that was trapped inside the False Light program — was withdrawn before she lost vital life force codes to escape the matrix, before she was further attacked.

So, the destruction of the Galactic Grids and Planetary Grids by Reiki and Yoga, predominantly, (although 5G users helped finish off the Planetary Grids) left humanity and all precious life without an escape route out of here after death, and so millions of souls were trapped inside this matrix because the last two steps of escape had been destroyed, and these were vast areas that contained more assistance.

Soul shock ensued, soul fragmentation, death of the soul occurred and these codes were stolen from these counterparts and were used to build the dark's ultimate weapon, which is what the 'rocket of energy' was composed of, that Claire perceived was about to hit humanity in October.

In 2017, the Purest Light Waves of assistance were receding for the final time. These waves of Light carried essential codes of remembrance — to help trapped souls in the lower levels of density to wake up and start to journey home, before the Purest Light Waves receded.

By the same token, the crescendo of the Purest Light Waves enabled the destroyer forces to steal more life force from humanity — to weaponise against them.

Where do you think they stole these precious codes from?

That's right, the Reiki and Yoga groups, prior to the collapse of the Galactic and Planetary Grids, and how did they collapse?

They collapsed due to theft of Purest Light codes from Mother Earth's Grids, which sustained her and sustained all life here.

Ask your Infinite Self and LOVE to show you a classroom model of Mother Earth and all her vast grids in a small scale model that you can walk around and ask to be shown what Reiki and Yoga energies did to Mother Earth's soul evolution.

Ask to be shown what Radio Frequencies and 5G do to Mother Earth and to the human energy fields.

Compare this to Purest Light frequencies, called from the Infinite Self and received with LOVE's help and watch what happens to a model of Mother Earth and a human model including their energy fields.

Pause the recording and rejoin us once you are ready.

Do you see now, how damaging at every level these practises are?

If you truly want to help, LOVE is asking you to let go of hanging onto teachings which are harming you, and threatening to cause multiple deaths in your family of humanity.

Humanity is in danger and their lives are hanging by a thread.

The groups who do Reiki and Yoga, and so forth came in with more codes of remembrance, and you are being called to awaken to your deeper aspects of Self — the part of you that knows the truth and would like you to help humanity.

Currently, these two groups are acting like 'enemies of humanity.' The sheer level of arrogance when challenged about these practises is self-evident. Why are you threatened?

Why would you not want to validate all this inside your heart centre and through LOVE?

LOVE is guiding you all that if you continue to keep up these practises, there is no help coming to rescue you. You will be sealing your own fate, and the fate of those who die as a result of soul shock, soul fragmentation, death of the soul.

Claire had a friend who taught Yoga for twenty years, and in the 2012 era, started to connect to her heart more and as she connected she realised that the Yoga movements were flawed. She did not practise certain moves and thought that this was enough to protect her students.

As she started to grow, through deeper heart exploration, she became aware that the whole system was flawed.

She openly admitted this to Claire. Despite knowing this, it took her five years to stop her practices.

She could see how harmful it was yet, the addictive frequencies held her back from stopping, despite her inner heart promptings.

Why did it take her so long? Because when you lose vast amounts of Purest Light codes and they get swapped with False Light codes, the False Light codes interplay with the many mind control programs, including the nanotechnology hidden in your food and drink items.

Claire was writing about this in 2014 yet, it has only become recent knowledge amongst many.

The mind control has layers and layers of traps and programs to ensnare a human being.

All of you are entangled to a degree, but we wish you all to be aware of the things which cause you to become more deeply ensnared, and Reiki and Yoga are two of the biggest traps.

Many think that feeling 'good' means something must be 'good' yet, they fail to understand that many False Light codes carry fake feelings of well being and peacefulness.

You have to tune into your heart centres regularly to spot these fake codes.

You are all more than capable. Look how easy it was to perceive the above classroom scenarios.

It is hoped that by showing you and helping you to see for yourself might awaken some souls sufficiently, to start helping humanity and stop harming them.

Quite simply, your gifts are needed desperately to secure humanity's future, and if you decline to help then, many will die, and many lives will be torn apart.

Why would you allow this to happen?

We are appealing to those of you who could be helping to stop any practise which brings in, or connects with any energy outside of the Infinite Self and your heart.

Your heart knowledge is sacred, precious, and rare.

If the dark ones manage to steal any more of your precious codes, then, humanity will fall into the dark grave-pit that Claire saw them standing on the edge of.

The dark have their eye on the Reiki and Yoga groups, because you have already opened your gateways to Lucifer energies at the top levels of consciousness that are trapped inside this False Light Construct,

Now, you will be able to see how much of your Light is gone, and how much is already False Light codes, and if you leave it too long to try to help yourself, this Lucifer energy will engulf you and by then, it will be too late. Your ladder will either be withdrawn at the level of soul or above, or, your entire ladder will be severed at the Cosmic Level by the Lucifer attack, and your heart energy will be stolen while your soul is being hunted down by Lucifer, and that precious heart energy is so powerful in the wrong hands...

So, what we are saying is, don't let the children, the vulnerable and the newborns be harmed, just because of stubborn ignorance or ego-led refusal to face FEAR and look it in the eye.

You could turn this around in an instant and we are simply hoping, you will try.

Claire that is all. This needs to go. Ignore the petty reprisals. This group need a wake-up call, before it is too late for all precious life."

Chapter Twenty-Seven

THE SATANIC RITUAL OF CHRISTMAS

Karmic Effects Of Yoga, Reiki, King Charles And Other States Of 'Peristasis'

"...humanity is on a death-wish, that is for sure and those of you who are not, need to have plans; in order to deal with what they have unleashed on the planet."

"It is a huge disappointment that the Reiki and Yoga groups refuse to protect humanity and all precious life, and most importantly, it is a huge sadness, for what they are bringing upon themselves."

LOVE'S HEART PLAN, SUBSTACK

"We call on our Infinite Selves, and Infinite LOVE and the Laws of Creation to surround and protect us, and to shield us from all harm.We call on the most powerful healing frequencies: HOPE, TRUST, AND FAITH to surround and protect us, and We call on LOVE to shield us with the frequency of COURAGE — to fuel us with bravery and boldness, to have courage to speak our truths at humanity's hour of need."

How can we best serve all in optimal ways that help all precious life today?The planetary energy has dropped in density. Like a lift descending down a dismal shaft into the unknown, every time Christmas approaches, every time the tree and lights go up and the bells start tinkling, every card embossed with the five pointed star — the star atop the Christmas tree — if society could simply look with a new pair of eyes, they would see this brings harm to all life.

Can you help us bring humanity a new set of 'goggles', some powerful spectacles that shine their light on satanic rituals; dressed up as merry-making, or, something religious. None of these words match the ritualistic erection of a 'transmitter' for Lucifer energies — in the form the obelisk Christmas pyramid tree; the dark, death-star on top and the 'snaking' lights that represent Lucifer; the snake; the dark lord of the abyss...why can't people see?It seems so obvious to me. Perhaps, if others understood how repetitive practises either bring in LOVE or LUCIFER? It is one of the two, never both.

If you were to look at the classroom model of a Christmas Tree and death-star, and the snaking lights by firstly asking your Infinite Self, and LOVE and the Laws of Creation from the Heart of Creation and infinitely beyond, to surround and protect you, and shield you from all harm...and to now imagine that you are looking at the whole thing in a classroom environment, the model of the tree in the corner of your room, the star, and effigy of SANTA (an anagram of satan — another trick of the light, which few notice), and ask your heart and LOVE to explain how and why these things harm all of you, not just yourself, but your family and all life that exists here, including your pets...

Walk around these 'classroom models' of these examples, and take a long, hard, truthful look at what these energies do in your house, and then look at a model of your pet, yourself, your loved ones and those you connect with and watch what these Christmas frequencies do to all life.

Pause the recording, rejoin us when you are ready.

Do the same with a Television model, an iPhone model and a computer, a mobile phone mast, a portable handset, an electric vehicle, a smart meter.

You can use this method for learning about the C19 poison.

Look what happens to the human Biofield and Cosmic Fields higher up the ladder of consciousness, ...and look at what happens to the human body.

Pause the recording and take your time, here.

Next, look at what happens to those who get their booster shots.

Pause here, and rejoin us once you are ready.

And look at what happens to those who gave these shots, without inwardly seeking heart guidance on what decision best served all life, in optimal ways.

Pause here, come back once you are ready.

Now, look at King Charles, what do you see?

Pause the recording here and be open to seeing the truth, without preconceived ideas.

Let your heart and LOVE tell you what they need you to know.

Use this method for any situation you want truth about.

You must 'get out the way', in the sense that all preconceived ideas, all beliefs and all 'opinions' have to swept to one side, and you must focus really hard on your heart centre, and allow your Infinite Self and LOVE to reveal the truth.

You must keep coming back for inner heart questioning — testing; in case you have got things wrong.

Some truths are harder to perceive or find, especially, if you are missing certain frequencies and we are all missing certain frequencies, and we have all been attacked and 'blocked' from seeing certain truths, so we all perceive differently, and some individuals or groups may be easier to spot as 'deceivers' by some, while it can be harder for others to perceive that group's intentions.

It takes time and practice, but you will learn so much, especially if you ask questions and seek solutions.

So now, hopefully, those of you who sincerely wish to help are settled, in a relaxed place where you can safely explore conscious awareness, and increase your awareness of what is going on around you.

You can utilise the classroom method to look at a model of yourself, to see where attack or damage is taking place — to find out the true cause and to find solutions.

You will be powerfully assisted and if you are a targeted individual, this method can bring in lots of teachings to help you surmount your attackers.It can all be resolved.

LOVE is more powerful than many realise, and yet, when this method is used, no harm is caused to any life form because LOVE guides us all on how to defend and protect, in alignment with the laws of Creation.

If we follow the laws of Creation, we gain deeper insights, Knowledge, and truths which empower us to see how ineffective a malicious person is on a computer, or with a directed energy weapon, because when you have LOVE, you have enough.

LOVE overpowers hatred, and overpowers attack. Those who should be in fear are those who seek to harm maliciously, because LOVE is returning it all to those who harmed, and they are all 'under attack' now, but not from LOVE. They are 'under attack' by their own 'malicious harm', which is simply being redirected back to the sender, creator, purveyor, and perpetrator of that harm.

All those who have chosen this path will soon regret their choice to harm others secretly, and it will be known to every man, woman, and child who their attackers are, because the Mark of The Beast is being returned to those who serve the beast system, that is all.

It is as simple as that.

I believe we have much news to share today, how can we all help each other grow and best serve all life, in optimal ways?

"Claire, the lift that you mentioned descending into the abyss down the 'lift shaft' is all caused each year by Christmas celebrations, many of which are overlaid with satanic ritual.

The issue is that the unknowing public do not understand what satanic ritual does, what it is, why it is used by those who choose this path, and we will be explaining more here, to solidify the classroom model 'examples' that you had presented to you.

You each have an energy field around you which is meant to be radiating Purest Light — LOVE — from the Heart of Creation and infinitely beyond.

Your true self and true origins come from LOVE at the Heart of Creation and we say, "infinitely beyond," because Creation is always expanding and evolving. It is never stationary. It is constantly moving forward and growing in LOVE and Purest Light, and Knowledge, and Wisdom, and so forth.

You are residing in a False Light Construct which is stationary, in the sense that it is holding humanity and all life forms that are trapped inside this place, in a state of 'peristasis' — a revolving doorway — where you are neither moving backwards or forwards — yet, many think they are 'evolving'.How can you 'evolve' in a False Light program of limitation, stagnation and 'peristasis'?

It is not possible, if one looks at this logically.

Outside of this construct, Creation is constantly evolving and renewing itself. The creative process is rewarding, mind-blowing, and exciting, to say the least.

This area of Creation beyond the False Light Construct offers many layers of learning, growth, joyful creation, and everything that is freeing, liberating, peace-giving, and unified.

All life benefits from all choices made by all life. The Laws of Creation are respected and so, every action, every choice is considered, and nothing is ever made or created without knowing the ultimate outcome best serves all life, in optimal ways.

That is what true Unity is. It is considering all aspects of Creation, and consideration is always at the top of the list, when making cho ices.Inside the False Light Construct, humans have been limited and restricted — by losing vast amounts of their creative Knowledge and Wisdom. They do not necessarily consider how their actions may play out across the whole of Creation. This leads to selfish actions which then break the Laws of Creation and so, Karma was created inside the False Light Construct.

A cycle of learning has to take place to allow the one making the error to learn from their mistakes, and to give that life form the opportunity to remedy their errors and repair any damage that they may have caused themselves and all other life.Remember, the cycle of Karma is created inside this False Light Construct.

Karma does not exist outside of this space, because those outside of this space obey the Laws of Creation, and not through duty or burden, but through deep love for all life, and a wish to keep all safe at all times.

This is not necessarily the case for many humans inside this construct, is it?

Can you see how the cycles of Karma must be reaching an all-time-high, given the choices that many have made, especially in the last four years and of course, beyond that, you have all made poor choices, at times?

Those who are trying to repair their errors and who are seeking inner growth, and healing are powerfully supported because LOVE has no wish for LOVE's children, A.K.A., humanity, to become ensnared in this False Light Construct, especially at the time when the truth of the matter is, you should all be journeying home and should all have withdrawn your ladder of consciousness from this place, and all precious life that was trapped here, should also be safe behind the barriers of LOVE's perimeter 'safety fence'.

However, the truth is, those who came to help are trapped in the mind-control and ego programs. They are not awake enough to do the 'right thing'

and serve all precious life. They are still making choices that are self-serving.

Take the Reiki and Yoga communities, for example: Two of the most harmful communities that have caused the most damage to all life here, by letting in Lucifer energy onto the Earth plane — through their own corrupted, mind-controlled and ego-influenced energy fields and still, after all the appeals from LOVE, begging them to stop harming LOVE's children, they choose to contin ue...LOVE guides that the buck stops with them, and the cycle of Karma that they have created for humanity and all life and for themselves has been gathered up by LOVE and today, all those who received the message and the request to stop harming, are directly going to be receiving back all the karmic cycles of unparalleled harm that you have caused all life here, and which has essentially, trapped millions of souls in this death-trap.

You have 'fed them to the wolves' by your choices to continue, and that is akin to murder because we have already explained, it kills a soul. It causes death of the physical body and the soul is hunted down by Lucifer, who you allowed into

> ***this planet's reality — by your selfish choice to continue a practice that you enjoy, and therefore, will not consider the outcome to those who have no choice in who you allow in through your 'front door.'***

Claire puts out these messages to help protect humanity, and to see that many of you are aware that these messages are going out, yet, you choose to continue, spells disaster for you all.

> ***Those who attend your classes who also are aware, are equally as culpable. If you refuse to look at your energy fields, from your Biofield to Cosmic Field — through the help of a classroom model and your Infinite Self to guide you to see, then, how irresponsible, how selfish are you — to be so determined to carry on with a killing spree?***

It is too late now, for those who know. That was the final warning.

The final alert to tell you that you were in danger of soul shock, soul death and soul takeover.

This has allowed in the Beast System, and it will happen now, unless more try to stop it energetically.

> ***The collapse of the Galactic Grids by Reiki and the Planetary Grids by Yoga and 5G users created the perfect opportunity for Lucifer energies to steal life force, steal valuable Knowledge and weaponise it against humanity.***

When you let in Lucifer through your doorway, and destroy two grids of such magnitude, and which offered so much assistance to souls departing the physical body and returning home, when you do this and let in Lucifer energy... Lucifer used it to bring in the Beast Systems.

Had these two grids remained intact, you would not be facing the carnage that humanity are about to face now.

And with this example shared, may we remind those of you who wish to protect humanity and all precious life, please do not participate in placing a receiver and transmitter of Lucifer energy in your homes this Christmas.

The Christmas Tree ritual is very powerful. It is repeated by millions of souls each year. The tree, in truth, represents a pyramid — symbol of Lucifer energy. The star represents death, and through this symbol, placed inside your home with your permission — you permit satanic frequencies to come through into this reality and start to steal life force from you, your family, your pets, and neighbours.

The tinsel and lights are 'snaked' around the tree and represent Lucifer — the 'asp' energy — snaking around your home. You permit this, and so, it is free to come in. Millions of homes around the world, bringing in satanic energy into their homes and into their energy fields.

When humanity are at a stage of a huge, unhealed, unchecked Karmic cycle that is spiralling out of control — the spiral being the incomplete cycle of learning — forever, spiralling but never completing a full cycle of learning...what do you think will happen to humanity from here, on, in?

For those who want no part in this debacle, this continual cycle of harmful errors, ignorant rebellion, stubborn refusal to look the truth in the eye, what do you think will happen from here on in?

Pause the recording and allow your heart to help you to see the bigger picture that is unfolding, because humanity are on a death-wish, that is for sure, and those of you who are not, need to have plans; in order to deal with what they have unleashed on the planet.

Rejoin us once you are ready.

Claire, that is probably enough for today.

The group who wish to help themselves will need to dig deep for guidance. Try not to get drawn into ritualistic behaviours that bring in Lucifer energies. The time of family can still be joyful and happy, without a satanic transmitter placed in your home.

Start to become aware of practices that follow Christmas: equinox celebrations; dates; spring celebrations, and start to use the previous podcast classroom scenario to dig deeper into this reality.

It is a huge disappointment that the Reiki and Yoga groups refuse to protect humanity and all precious life, and most importantly it is a huge sadness, for what they are bringing upon themselves.

Claire, please try to get this posted as soon as possible, and as always, try not to spend too much time typo-checking and proof-reading. The essence of the message is in the video, and the transcript is a 'guiding tool' to help it sink in more deeply.

This has to reach those who can help, as urgently as possible.

Time is of the essence."

Chapter Twenty-Eight

SUGGESTED SELF-HELP FOR BEGINNERS

CANCER SERIOUS ILLNESS, TRAUMA.
PROTECT YOUR CONSCIOUS LADDER:

"Great change is upon you all, and now is the time to give LOVE a call."

LOVE'S HEART PLAN SUBSTACK

"We call on our Infinite Selves, and Infinite LOVE and the Laws of Creation to surround and protect us, and to shield us from all harm. We call on the most powerful healing frequencies: HOPE, TRUST, AND FAITH to surround and protect us, and we call on LOVE to shield us with the fre-

quency of COURAGE — to fuel us with bravery and boldness, to have courage to speak our truths at humanity's hour of need.

What information would you like me to share today, to best help all in optimal ways, particularly those who are suffering from chronic illness, chronic pain, serious diagnosis; such as, cancer, and other physical traumas, emotional or mental traumas; such as, deep grief, loss; violent experiences such as, those caused by war and deep shock?"

"Claire, we are going to give a suggested routine for those who wish to help themselves, and for those who wish to pass on help to others — through the process of self-help.

This is to help others connect to their deepest aspect of themselves their Infinite Self — this is the part of their consciousness that is untethered by false light. The Infinite Self is connected to fullest Truth and Knowledge at the heart of Creation. It is connected to LOVE. It carries no restrictions to learning, no satanic distortions of Truth. Your Infinite Selves serve LOVE 9and all precious life. Your Infinite Selves respect and follow all the Laws of Creation and always consult LOVE to ensure that any decision you make, best serves all precious life in optimal ways.

When humans choose to follow a path that is straight and true, when a human tries their best to help themselves while caring about how their choices and decisions best help all precious life, then, LOVE can come directly to that human and the human soul, and sets to work to repair and heal all the damage caused through emotional, mental and physical trauma or illness, and so forth, and LOVE starts to heal the damage that is created to all levels of your conscious ladder. The ladder of consciousness is the ladder of Knowledge that leads back to the Heart of Creation and to wholeness. Your lower ladder of consciousness is presently caught up and ensnared in the 'entanglement' of a false light construct, known to many as, the Matrix.

These lower levels of awareness are so badly damaged in some, that serious illness has occurred and when there is any trauma, such as, emotional trauma or physical trauma — caused by war or violence, then, the ladder of awareness starts to weaken and then, it is very easy for attack to take place by outside forces who need life force to exist.

When vast areas of your consciousness become emptied of Purest Light, also known as LOVE, then, illness sets in and the more that the Purest Light codes are lost, the more possible it is for illness, such as, cancer to step in.

The effects of losing vast amounts of life force at the top levels of conscious awareness that are trapped in the False Light Construct, equate to cancer and other life-threatening illness appearing, as a 'physical symptom'.

By this stage, once the physical body is being affected, it means that the other levels of the human consciousness are badly damaged, and it is a complicated process to repair this, especially if you are new to this concept.

You must not worry. LOVE is here to help you.

LOVE has the Knowledge and the ability to help you on your journey, be it to go peacefully and leave this place with all your codes of Knowledge withdrawn from this dark space, or, to help you regain your health and vitality, and be an active participant in your healing journey.

LOVE guides you not to give up on your true path, because many of you are not meant to be leaving the planet like this — not through terminal illness.

This is not the path for many of you. Your help is needed. Your presence is required here, to help humanity leave this place with their ladder of consciousness withdrawn from this place when the time comes to leave. We are simply saying, to have courage, because for many of you, it is not your time to go. Have Hope, Trust, and Faith that when you have LOVE, you have enough.

LOVE can guide you through the process of healing and repair, and all the guidance must be strictly followed because when LOVE gives you Knowledge, it must be acted upon, otherwise, a huge wastage of energy occurs and often, the reason why humans get cancer in the first place, is because they ignore LOVE's guidance and do not use the Knowledge to best help all precious life in optimal ways.

So, it is also important to understand that you are being asked to use the Knowledge given, by not wasting it, or going against it, or doing your own version of things. This is called ego-led behaviour and ego-led behaviour or thinking can be very damaging to healing.

Perfect healing of the physical body requires a heart-based focus on listening to your own body and your own heart, and allowing yourself to start to become aware of when you are driving yourself too hard, when you are overworking, or overdoing things and when you need to rest.

Rest is a vital part of being alive. All bodies need to rest to allow the body to restore and repair.

This is very true with serious illness, or emotional trauma and deep grief.

You must learn to love yourselves enough and be good to yourselves, and care about your own well being, first and foremost, and from this approach a more truthful, honest person emerges who can have the courage to honour their own feelings, while expressing their wishes in a kindly manner to others, and this approach can help others to understand you better, and help you more precisely with your wishes.

This is particularly important with terminal illness. You must not please others. You must think about your own needs, and be kind and caring about your inner most wishes.

This recording is to help all types of difficulties which may result in all types of outcomes.

Ultimately, the outcome of your journey rests with LOVE, but this does not mean that you give up on the outcome of your destiny, and if life is important, then ask LOVE to help you enjoy your life for as long as that may be, and equally, if you are meant to survive or recover from trauma, then, Trust that LOVE is here and when called upon through your heart centre, LOVE will provide you with everything that you need.

This method of self-help through connection to heart and LOVE is not suitable for work places, or when driving or operating machinery.

It is best used in a quiet room, your bedroom at home is ideal and the first option, but generally, you need a place that is quiet, peaceful and safe to relax in, undisturbed.

Remove as much technology out of the room and remove all symbols, pyramids, stars; anything that emits distorted frequencies.

You live in a reality where all the technology is harming all life, and so, the first rule of thumb is to call on this help each day, first thing in the morning, last thing at night, and midway through the day is best, because LOVE can really set to work to start the process, and when you break this cycle of heart connection, it disrupts the help coming from LOVE and can set things back.

Therefore, the method requires your commitment from day one.

If you cannot commit, it is better not to start.

LOVE cannot waste energy and there are many who need LOVE's assistance. Therefore, when help is given and the guidance to connect regularly is not followed, a huge cycle of Karma is created in this reality, and it harms yourself, and all life.

Before you start this process, consider if you can commit to this path of healing and if you can continue each day to help yourself.

If you feel determined to proceed and ready to give to yourself, then we will begin:

Claire will share her routine with you and you are advised to adapt this to suit your own comfort and well being."

I say:

I ensure my bedroom is shaded from bright sunlight.

I place a glass of water nearby and set an alarm clock, in case I fall asleep.

I lie down on the bed that I sleep in at night at home, flat on my back, legs straight — never crossed.

I place my hands — which are never crossed — palms flat, facing down on the tops of my thighs.

I ensure I am warm and comfortable, and if it is safe to do so, I close my eyes.

I take my closed eyes and look gently down, in the direction of my chest area.

I keep my closed eyes softly gazing towards my chest, and I feel the rise and fall of my chest as the air goes in and out of my lungs.

I imagine that deep inside my chest is an imaginary switch deep inside my heart, that connects me to my Infinite Self and LOVE at the Heart of Creation and infinitely beyond.

I imagine I press this switch and it is 'ON'.

I say this to my Infinite Self:

"Please can you help me? I wish to grow in LOVE, and I wish to help myself heal from all the damage that my ladder of con-

sciousness has endured."

I talk about the things I need help with, and I ask my Infinite Self to call on LOVE and the Laws of Creation from the Heart of Creation and infinitely beyond to surround and protect me, and to shield me from all harm.

This is the 'set-up routine', and once the switch is 'ON', and once we have made this request, we only have to remember to gaze down towards our heart, keeping our focus there, and pressing an imaginary switch in the centre of our chest to activate assistance.

You can use the heart call prayer at the top of this transcript or use your own words.

When using heart connection, the important thing is to focus on your heart, by gazing down towards your chest and keeping your focus softly looking downwards — to keep your attention on your heart centre, not your mind.

Move your focus back down towards your chest and practice this, going forward, because you cannot hear your heart if you are still in your 'mind' space, and looking downwards helps you to maintain heart connection.

So, now, you are connected to your Infinite Self and LOVE, and the Laws of Creation at the Heart of Creation and infinitely beyond.

Your heart is now going to show you a small classroom model of yourself, and show you where the harm is happening on your conscious ladder of awareness.

LOVE is going to address this gradually. It is a 'process' that needs your commitment each day.

Each day, you will be able to see, or sense, or imagine the progress you are making.

You may think you are not going to be able to perceive anything.

Let LOVE remind you: You are a Purest Light Being — descended into this reality — to help humanity and all precious life. Of course you are capable of perceiving things. You may see this, or you may sense it, or you may hear verbal instructions but, you are capable.

If you cannot perceive things, do not worry. Just receive the help that you need for this moment.

Things will become clearer the more you connect to your Infinite Self, who loves you deeply and is here to help you.

You must ask for help. Under the laws of Creation, your Infinite Self is not permitted, to interfere with your free will choices, nor is LOVE, and so, it is very important that if you ever need help, you must ask your Infinite Self and LOVE for help.

Perhaps, the classroom model of yourself is more evident as we

progress, and while you gently look, with closed eyes, softly down towards your heart centre?

Pretend that your heart area is like a movie screen and all the images happen down in your heart area.

Can you perceive yourself in the classroom model? Pretend that you can, even if you cannot.

Imagine that you can perceive LOVE coming through all the layers of darkness in this reality and shining LOVE's powerful light on your ladder of consciousness.

Where is LOVE concentrating the healing and repair?

Can you perceive the area? Can you feel LOVE's embrace around you and shielding you from all harm?

Breathe, relax, focus your eyes on your heart centre and the classroom model.

Receive help, receive LOVE, receive repair and supportive frequencies.

Pause the recording for as long as you need and come back to join us once you feel ready.

Next, you are going to ask your Infinite Self and LOVE to surround and protect you with the frequencies of HOPE, TRUST and FAITH.

Watch as these frequencies — the most powerful healing frequencies in existence — surround you in their loving embrace.

Feel the lift, the calm, the peace.

(We will receive for one minute, and if you want longer, pause the recording and rejoin us once you feel ready to continue.)

Next, we will move on; to receive loving guidance and advice on how you can best help yourself and best help all precious life in optimal ways.

"How can I best help myself and best help, all in optimal ways today?"

And I hear:

"Claire, we guide you that at this stage, the best way that these souls can help themselves is to start by asking their Infinite Self and LOVE to work with the Laws of Creation and to gather up all malicious, magnified harm and all intentional harm that is affecting their own well being and harming all precious life.

Next, to ask their Infinite Self, LOVE and the Laws of Creation to find all that they have lost, and return it to wholeness — to be purified —and returned to them as Purest Light codes that can never be corrupted or infiltrated by any person, place, or thing, including destroyer forces."

LOVE and the Laws of Creation will deal with this on their behalf.

It is an essential part of their healing journey and it also best serves all precious life in optimal ways because, by asking for themselves, all life benefits from the help and all that has been lost to many can be found and restored to them.

When others ask for these things, many vulnerable souls who may lack the courage to ask for help are assisted. When you call for help, LOVE comes for all those who may have no voice or be too damaged to know that they can ask for help.

When you become a voice for yourself, you become a voice for all those lost souls, and the many who are suffering.

Have Hope, Trust, and Faith that you being here matters and your life is precious.

Claire shares many other messages of guidance, and there are deeper teachings available to help you grow in Knowledge.

For now, focus on your healing journey. Keep asking your Infinite Self for help throughout the day.

You can use the long version of this recording for your morning connection and use a quicker version for heart connection during the day if you are short on time, by pressing your switch and focusing on your heart, and calling on your Infinite Self, LOVE, the Laws of Creation and HOPE, TRUST, and FAITH, and COURAGE to surround and protect you, and shield you from all harm.

Focus your eyes on your heart centre and keep your focus there, not on your mind.

This must not be rushed. You must always ensure you are looking softly down and you can press your chest gently — to help you imagine that the switch is 'ON' and to help keep your concentration on your heart.

Receive help for at least one minute, or more.

The more time you give yourself, the more help you receive. [But you must use the 'long version' when you wake up in the morning — just the routine].

Ask your heart how long you need for each session, and be prepared that information can change so, nothing is ever fixed in stone.

Try this for a period of three weeks, and see how you progress.

Your heart may guide you to start using other recordings from Claire that offer upgrades, for when the time is right.

Keep asking your Infinite Self for help, and remember, to thank all these energies for all that you receive.

Gratitude and thanks is a cycle of giving and receiving that produces many fruits.

When one starts to take something for granted, it tends to stop the cycle, and prevents healing and repair.

So, be of good cheer when you consider the help and LOVE that is available to us.

Even in a False Light Construct, all assistance is available, and NOW is the time for you all to receive healing and repair because, very soon, your ladder of consciousness will need to be withdrawn from this place as you start the journey home for your next cycle of learning and evolution.

Great change is upon you all, and NOW is the time to give LOVE a call."

...

AUDIO LINK: SEARCHING FOR THE EVIDENCE

Chapter Twenty-Nine

HEART ATTACK And The End Of Humanity As You Know It, DEC 2, 2023

Sodium Poisoning And The Contamination Of Our Food

"Things have taken a turn for the worst. It is unfortunate but the call to Reiki and Yoga groups to step forward to assist has failed, and the dark ones have used the opportunity to cause more harm than even we thought possible."

LOVE'S HEART PLAN, SUBSTACK

How can I best serve all today? I posted a message earlier, and "Suggested Self-Help for Serious Illness, Cancer, Trauma," and while I was listening to the recording republish, I started to get information about heart attacks.

My Infinite Self and LOVE guided me that heart attacks are about to increase, and that my husband and I needed to review first aid measures to help a heart attack victim, in case we needed to assist someone.

This was as far as I got, because I have been busy posting the previous self-help message.

What do you wish me to share here?

What is happening — to cause 'heart attacks,' because I got this sense that we are going to be witnessing this in large numbers?

"Claire, you are quite right to be concerned, and it is concerning — to say the very least, but while many are focusing on the cancer increases, we also wish you all to be aware and prepared; that heart problems, including heart attacks, are going to go through the roof.

Many will blame the false light vaccines and these will play their part, but, even the unjabbed need to be alert to the risks and to take evasive action."

Q. Can you explain further? What is happening? And what is the true cause of the anticipated increase in heart attacks?

"Sodium poisoning."

Q. Sodium poisoning, how so?

"Claire, the salt in your food is contaminated. This is fullest Truth from the Heart of Creation and infinitely beyond. Many food stuffs are heavily salted and you need to start checking your food package labelling to see how much sodium is present in your food and to check, if possible, what kind of salt it is."

Q. I say, "I don't know anything about salt — in terms of what to look for, what to check, and what types of salt cause the most harm. And how is sodium effecting heart attacks?

"Claire, those crystals — seen under the microscope are, occasionally, salt crystals which are present in blood.

Those who are examining the blood for signs and clues about why the blood is changing, would do well to try to analyse the sodium levels in the patients.

Something is happening between the ingestion of sodium and the heart beat.

The crystals are poisoned and they are impacting on heart-health.

Those who wish to help humanity are being advised that you all need a robust routine now — to protect and shield from all harm — because this poisoning of your food chain is ongoing, and it is going to get harder to resource safe food to ingest, simply because nothing is truly 'organic' and 'pesticide free', and certainly not when the skies are being poisoned with chem. trails.

The levels of poison in the food chain are increasing.

The best way to combat this, is to learn to discern the vibration of a food item, and to avoid or discard food that gives-off bad vibes.

You are all more than capable of learning how to do this.

Hold something in your hand which is a healthy, safe food that you know your body can tolerate.

Feel the vibration of the food in your hands.

All foods give off electrical impulses, just like humans do, and just like all life forms do.

How does the good food feel in your hands? How is your body responding to it?

What about your heart and Infinite Self? Does your inner wisdom recommend this item?

Next, hold a bottle of bleach, or some other detergent in your hands and close your eyes.

How does the detergent 'feel' in your hands?

How does your body react to this detergent?

How does it compare with the "tolerated" food?

Try another food item, perhaps one you are not so keen on...how does that feel?

On a scale of 1 to 10, 1 being poor and 10 being excellent, what scores would your Infinite Self give these items, in terms of 'safe to ingest' ratings?

Practice with other food and drink items, you can even try it with deodorant, shampoo, body wash and so forth.

Learn to discern the vibration of food, drink, and medicine, and always ask your Infinite Self and LOVE to "purify all food, drink and medicine and all that enters your body and all which leaves your body, including the air that you breathe."

This needs to be added to the last message, and for your Substack subscribers to take note of, because the whole version of reality is about to be altered once more, and when this reality is altered, along with the contamination of sodium, it will lead to an increase in heart attack and heart problems.

The human physical body is being pushed to the limits and the version of reality that the dark ones have planned is the darkest version yet.

You wonder why things are things are topsy turvy?

Why the world has gone mad and why the dark ones seem to be married to their own sex?

Why "trans"- this, and "trans"- that, is so popular?

The final push to the Internet of Things is upon you all, and with this push, this forced push of humanity into this dark pit, from which there will be no escape for many, you will start to see just how topsy turvy those who plan your demise are, because they are about to push for all their desires, including legalising pedophilia, mass vaccination, mass hypnosis, and push transhumanism onto you all.

With the little resistance from those who could be helping defend humanity, it is a 'fait accompli.'

The end of humanity, as you know it. Welcome to the dark side of those who plot to separate the children and force you into 15 minute camps of restriction.

Worry not though, this is a double-edged sword because with this 'push' comes the further collapse of the False Light programs, and this will seal, not only humanity's fate, but the fate of those who hunt, and rape, and plot, and kill.

They will fall into this pit in the end, but not before they have harmed many more humans that even we thought was possible.

Claire's role was to place information strategically — to act as a force of goodness, and to reach out to those of you who do not wish this ending on yourselves and on the children.

It is too late for those who refused to protect humanity.

It is too late for those who hunt, maim, and kill.

But...

it is not too late for those who do not seek this life or this way to treat all life, and so, the messages and video heart connections are a way of LOVE reaching into this dark pit — to tell you — you still have time to choose, and you can come home, if you wish but, you need to surround and protect yourself with LOVE's embrace, and you must ask LOVE for help because LOVE cannot interfere, unless you request rescue.

Call on your Infinite Self — by using the last video, which Claire will post here again, and use it to gather all your energy, all your life force away from this toxic place.

Climb your ladder to calmer waters and a safer place.

LOVE is waiting and is ready to help.

Claire, we need you to post this as is. Make the recording as soon as possible and post.

Things have taken a turn for the worst. It is unfortunate but the call to Reiki and Yoga groups to step forward to assist has failed, and the dark ones have used the opportunity to cause more harm than even we thought possible.

For those who are using heart connection, worry not. The most important thing to be mindful of is that you will see a vast diminishing of numbers now.

It will happen quickly. Be mentally prepared for what you are about to witness. You are not alone. You have LOVE to protect you.

LOVE needs your help and your strength, because you are needed and will be needed by the children, newborns, elderly and vulnerable, such as, the homeless because they need your prayers, your willingness to climb your ladder and in doing so, bring all of these vulnerable groups to a space of safety — away from the carnage that is on your doorstep now.

The dark are moving at warp speed.

They are in fear of your awakening.

Make sure you awaken as quickly as possible now, and climb your ladder because much help awaits those of you who try, and the vulnerable are dependent on you because so many refused to help, and so few attempted to try."

Chapter Thirty

ZERO WHO? LEARNING TO BE TRUE — TO YOU, DEC 4, 2023

"The safest way to exit this place is to choose a new reality, one of choice, one from the heart, one that is true to you."

LOVE'S HEART PLAN, SUBSTACK

Well, it has started in earnest now, and there is no longer any point wasting energy or giving our power away to those who have placed humanity in this situation.

It seems that humanity's death-wish has come true. An early Christmas present, and since the celebration of Christmas is coated in satanic subversion, it seems fitting that King Charles and his Camilla, whoever he, or she, or it truly is, have succeeded where others failed, and brought humanity to its knees.

And, in such a way, that humanity is completely unaware, and why would they be?

They do not listen to any voice of truth and reason — that voice – that still, small voice inside of them that has been urging them to look, and to protect themselves and the children.

It called to those who seemed awake and they chose to ignore it, so why would any 'asleep' human hear anything either, when the Reiki and Yoga groups have successfully handed over the codes that the 'asleep' and 'unawake' gave them, to help the Reiki and Yoga groups to wake up the asleep, but they decided to allow the ego to lead the way, and have handed everything over to the dark, who have taken every last key now — every useful 'wake up and escape the matrix' code.

Reiki and Yoga participants will go down in the history books as those who sold out on humanity's last chance of freedom and threw them to the wolves.

Thank you, Reiki and thank you, Yoga.

I never knew you wanted the Transhuman, Beast System so badly, never knew that you cared so little about your family of humanity, and I never knew that you served the dark ones all along.

I forgive you but I will never forget. Never.

And, nor will the children who you have successfully 'murdered'.

King Charles and his Camilla will have their world — their New World

Order.

Thank you, Reiki. Thank you, Yoga.

Thank you for all your compassion and concern for your fellow humans, the vulnerable, the newborns, the children and elderly, and all those who were reliant on you getting up of your backsides and doing the right thing to protect all life here.

There is more guidance coming through today. I confess, I am exhausted and a little despairing of how easy it has been to enslave humanity.

The dark ones are not particularly clever, but we have made it so easy and with all the access that they have to higher, advanced technologies — stolen from humanity — and traded for Extra Terrestrial knowledge, it was a walk in the park for Charlie boy and his Camilla, whoever he, or she, or it is.

Did you see who Charlie really was in the classroom lesson, inside your heart centre?

Did that help confirm it, for those of you who do care about your family of humanity and all precious life?

I know we cannot do any more now, and I would gladly have rested today but I am being urged to share information and I think it is being shared as a point of interest, a few nuggets of insight from the heart of Creation, and my guess is that you are all working hard to secure the vulnerable's ladder of consciousness in a safe place, with LOVE's help.

I am truly thankful that there are people out there who do care. I received a beautiful message last night and it meant a lot to me, because I was feeling low and just contemplating how things could be, if more had wanted to help.

We have so much love and support from our Infinite Selves and LOVE, and we had an opportunity to utilise LOVE's Knowledge and assistance to defend and protect humanity, and help all trapped life forms to escape this place.

I had no idea how little others cared, how little they think of the world's children, how selfish others have been, and all the while, they held vital keys that unlocked doorways to freedom for all those trapped here.

To squander this help, to reject it...well, I saw it play out over ten years ago. I thought we may have moved forward and grown during this time frame, but it seems that many who say they are 'healers', 'spiritual' or 'religious' are acting like servants to the destroyer forces, and they do not even realise what they have done.

It is too late now.

Humanity has been cancelled.

We are back to zero. Zero us. Zero you. Zero me.

There is no 'we', or 'I', or 'he' anymore. You are merely, a zero.

A nothing.

You are no thing now.

Was that what you truly wanted — Reiki and Yoga, and 5G users?

I didn't want this, thank you very much. No one asked me what I wanted.

I wanted to get those who were trapped out of this place. It is the reason why we are all here. I wanted to accomplish my mission and I wanted to get the voiceless to safety with the minimum of harm.

I wanted to protect and defend all life and I wanted us all to create a truly happy ending, and to clear up this place of darkness for good.

We had everything laid out for us. We only had to ask for help and it was given.

My Grandfather jumped out of a plane and parachuted down onto the beaches of Normandy in World War II, and his battalion took back the first bridge from the Germans.

Many of his men were killed, He was one of the few survivors. He had a shrapnel wound which triggered many trips to hospital during his remaining years. He never talked about his experiences until he was very old.

My Grandmother saw a bomb blow up in a street of houses near their home. A children's party was taking place and all the children were killed.

Many men and women lost their lives to save our freedom. We all know these wars were contrived, but they didn't know. They left home to protect their country, and many never returned.

One of my great-uncles was captured in Singapore: held prisoner; tortured, beaten; starved, and whipped by their cruel captors. They were told they were cowards and that their country had abandoned them. Four years of mind torture, starvation, and beatings.

He helped build the Burma Railway. He survived four years of this, and eventually, was rescued and returned home. When a young, fit military officer from the Canadian Naval Ship offered to take his bags from his emaciated body, upon rescue, he could not believe that he wanted to help him. They sailed to Canada from Singapore before sailing home to the UK.

At a restaurant in Canada, some ladies who found out they were war veterans paid for their lunch as a thank you for their heroic contributions. The recovering veterans could not comprehend this kind gesture. They thought people were going to be ashamed of them and see them as cowards.

This is what mind torture does.

My Grandparents were happily married for 63 years. My Grandmother lost her daughter one year before her husband died.

She stoically repeated, *"I could have lost him in the war."*

Many never saw their loved ones again.

I think about these brave men and women. Jumping out of planes, digging trenches, watching their friends die and all that goes with trench warfare, and what they sacrificed to gain our freedom — torture, mind control, starvation, beatings, severe cruelty, and crushing of the human spirit and all we had to do, this time, in this war — this war on our consciousness — all we had to do was pray, and ask our hearts and LOVE for help...

How hard could that be?

Is this how we respect our war veteran's efforts for securing our liberty?

Our hearts ***are*** the advanced technology: The defence. The protection. ***Everything we need is inside this place.***

The **heart Knowledge is a precious** commodity: **valued by the dark and neglected by humanity**, and it is why the dark ones seek to harm us, hurt us, manipulate us into creating **'Heartache Energy'** — the ***most 'prized' codes;*** to distort them further, to feed off, and to weaponise against us.

They were handed precious rescue codes on a silver platter...

I must learn to let go, forgive, and move on.

I am hearing my heart saying there is much to download. Thank you to all those who care, because I would not be receiving this download if you were not securing heart assistance. Thank you — for being 'human'.

"Claire, we need to share with the group what has transpired, to help them understand the bigger picture playing out here. We mentioned same sex marriage yesterday and that reference is not directed toward same sex couples. It is referring to the 'Trans Agenda' — the Transhuman Agenda — the satanic inversion of the male and female human form, and the mockery that goes on behind the scenes by those who serve the cult, many of whom are not human.

We keep referencing the 'non-human debacle' because they have invaded your governments and world organisations, including the usual suspects: the World Health Organisation, the United Nations, the World Economic Forum and the Monarchy.

Many non-human forms choose to mock humans by deceiving them about their sexual orientation. You have many who purport to look like women who are not really women, and men who dress like men but are not really men.

If they are not human, and therefore, not transexual, then, what is the reason for their mockery and why deceive a gullible public in this way? What is the point?

And it is here that it gets a bit tricky, and Claire will need to translate carefully, otherwise there is a risk that others will misunderstand the true meaning of this discourse.

Firstly, LOVE does not judge. Sexuality holds no relevance in higher levels of awareness. It is a 'non-runner'. No one cares. No one has an 'either', 'or' agenda.

Satanic cult members see themselves as neither male nor female, yet, they know that in order to blend into human society and not blow their cover, they have to dress in a 'human' way...a way that helps humans suspect nothing at all.

Many of your presidents and leaders have been 'married' to non-humans with a same sex preference, who may have looked more like the same sex, and so, if a male president is to fool a nation with their choice of same sex partner, the partner will adopt the societal expectation a 'wife,' and that is the 'mockery card' being played because, behind the scenes, neither of the individuals are human to begin with.

No — their blood lines are of non-human origin. They hold no human DNA. Many are Reptilian in origin, and they can hold their 'shape' of a human, and fool the nation in the process.

How many president's wives can you think of that looked very noticeably masculine?

What about Bill Gates and his ex-wife, Melinda?

Those who are used to heart connection and the classroom method of checking out these beings, would do well to ask their heart centres to present a classroom model of these characters, and see what they are trying to fool the nation into believing, and then, to see what they are hiding — behind the mockery of a fake, 'sexual orientation', and fake dress-code.

When you start to see the dark side of all these agendas, it makes more sense why the Trans Agenda — in all its forms — is so important to push on humanity.

The timeline switches have made it very hard for others to perceive this mockery and this fakery, because each time that timelines switch, all lessons that were remaining, all karma that was not healed and repaired is left behind in the previous timeline.

Timeline switches are mentioned in previous podcasts and it is advisable to listen to them to get a better orientation, regarding the absolute devastation that timeline switches create, and the unhealed trauma that travels forward, but never the healing, which can never take place.

The most recent timeline switch, was perfectly preventable had others got on board, however, it is too late in the day now, to cry over spilt milk. What's done is done, and it cannot be reversed.

The mess that is created by this entanglement of false light frequencies, coupled with the timeline switches, needs your attention. Not because you can prevent the harm caused by others, nor can you repair this harm. That was the role of the perpetrators to try to resolve. It was rejected. It is too late for change now.

However, the children, the newborns and vulnerable, elderly, homeless and all precious life who have not played a part in this debacle of chaos and soul shock, need you to be aware of what is happening, so that you understand it and can better help yourselves.

This is about your soul evolution now and the group you are currently being asked to assist.

You can only help this group and yourself now. All other groups are on their own. They have cut-off the assistance from the Heart of Creation — by their refusal to stop harming, and the other group's refusal to protect.

You must all climb, as far as possible — away from this place, before it collapses in on itself.

If you are listening to this for the first time, Claire will post the last two video messages and include them in her Substack transcript.

For those watching on Bitchute, Odysee, or Telegram the last two messages were posted on 2 December 2023, entitled:

"Suggested Self-Help For Cancer, Serious Illness and Trauma," and "Heart Attack, The End of Humanity As You Know It."

"The Satanic Ritual of Christmas | Karmic Effects of Yoga, Reiki, King Charles and Other States of Peristasis"

offers the opportunity to connect through your own heart and Infinite Self to be assisted to look at others with a new set of 'spectacles' that shine their light on Truth.

Links will be provided on Substack.

Claire, you need to connect to heart now to hear the rest of this dialogue because there is a lot to retrieve and download."

I say:

"We call on our Infinite Selves and LOVE and the Laws of Creation from the Heart of Creation and infinitely beyond, to surround and protect us, and to shield us from all harm.

We call on the most powerful healing frequencies in the whole of Creation: Hope, Trust, and Faith to surround and protect us and heal us from all harm.

We ask the frequency of Courage and the frequency of Truth to also surround and protect us and to help us all reach Truth from the Heart of Creation, and to have courage to speak our Truths in humanity's hour of need.

How can we best serve all precious life in optimal ways today?"

I hear: *"Claire, do you feel like you are in mourning?"*

I say, "Yes, I feel very sad and quite tearful, why? What is happening? I feel despair. I feel as if a huge opportunity has been lost for good. Is this my grief or am I tuning into humanity's grief?"

"Claire, a huge download of data is on it way. Would you like to share why *you feel sad?*

"I have already expressed why, haven't I? Is there something else? I am sad about my Granddad and my Uncle. They went through hell to secure our freedom. They all suffered. All wars cause deep trauma. These veterans never had counselling or any sympathy. They had to suck it all up and inwardly suffer.

Many died. I cannot marry their level suffering with the selfish behaviour of a group who could have easily helped humanity from the comfort of their own beds.

I am at a loss as to their motives for not helping.

The vulnerable and all those of us who did not choose trans-humanism or the Beast System are facing a horrendous future now.

I just want peace and calm and the freedom to get on with my life.

I have lost hope, to be honest. This timeline switch felt very serious. The end of humanity, as we know it. The children are being indoctrinated in libraries and schools up and down the country.

The immigration crisis is creating the government's desired effects.

No one questions King Charles or the World Economic Forum leaders. Who are they to tell us how to think and behave/ They have no human rights. They are not human.

I am fed up worrying about what will happen if the banks steal all our savings and place us all into poverty.

You cannot recreate a world of peace when so many are choosing a New World Order and allowing it all to unfold.

What else can I do to help? I feel drained; exhausted. I am using up a lot of time and energy putting out messages and I wonder, if it is helping at all?

It seems futile to expect change on this planet.

The mind control is affecting too many."

"Claire, then perhaps it is time to rest and to step back?"

I say, **"You say that, and then you ask me to download and share information. How can I refuse when you are asking for my help?"**

"Do you think the help has made a difference?"

I say, **"I am unsure. It has certainly helped me and my husband,**

and a few more. I see it as extremely valuable and life changing, while very few seem to perceive the benefits and the freedom from this False Light Construct that heart connection offers. To me, it is the solution, the answer. How else are others planning to exit the matrix when they are trapped inside it with no Knowledge to exit it, and all the opportunities of Knowledge have been given to the dark forces, and now, they are all weaponised against us?

Is there another way out of this place?"

and I hear, *"Choose."*

Q. "Choose what?"

*"Choose another way out of here t*hat would be a choice of peace and from your heart."

Q. "How do I do that? A choice of peace, from my heart?"

"Choose another way."

I say, **"In my heart, I would like to wake up one morning and the world be at peace, like Bobby Ewing from Dallas, I would be having a shower and it would all have been a dream, a bad nightmare that was never real.**

But the world would be better than before. It would be peaceful, in balance, all occupants would be supportive of those in their community. This world would be full of laughter. When was the

last time someone told me a really funny joke? What happened to jokes?

What happened to laughter? I would be healthy in that world, as would my husband and I would have choice because I would be healthy.

I would look after hens, learn about animal husbandry, tend to some sheep, have a dog, walk for miles each day, live in a wood cabin in a clearing near a river and vast woodlands, swim in rock pools, dive off waterfalls, sing, dance, fly, and I would be happy just being content that all was well, not only in my world, but in the world I shared with others, because they would also be happy, content, in joy and at peace.

If I could choose, I would spend time with my husband to heal and repair.

If I could choose, I would never have chosen this reality, the outcome, this dreadful way of being:

A world fast asleep, and being attacked by destroyer forces and their topsy turvy, inverted world of fake-realities and heartache, soul hunting, killing, maiming. I want none of it. I am sick of it, and it is making me sick, too.

My hair is falling out. Is this radiation or is this sodium poisoning?"

"Claire, we will get to sodium poisoning, in a minute, but you said

something relevant which we wish others to consider.

If you don't like this reality, have you thought of asking LOVE for a new reality away from this place, to go to?

You do have options, in spite of outward appearances. There are always choices for those who choose to grow in LOVE."

Q. "What can we ask for?"

"Ask LOVE to lift you away from this place. Many of you have climbed your ladder sufficiently now. Can you see your new reality? It is there and waiting for you. You only have to ask and you can go."

Q. "Months ago, you guided us to pack a bag and be prepared. Is this linked? What about the vulnerable, what about leaving them? I don't wish to leave until we have got them to safety. Has this been secured yet by those who asked for help?"

"Claire, others must go into their own hearts to discern truth but you all must know that there are many different realities and this does not mean that you have to stay stranded in this one. If you ask LOVE, you can move to a different reality. You have all been creating it with your imagination, and LOVE has been helping to build this place as a temporary space, to receive healing and repair before the In Breathe fully completes."

Q. "How do we get there? What is holding us here?"

"Claire, here lies the crux of the matter. Many of you are having trouble

letting go. Letting go of responsibility for others, securing others rescue. We want you to know that many of you have exhausted your supplies, and now, it is time to think about yourselves, what you want, where you would like to go, how that place would look to you. Then, you dream and imagine and use your time to focus on that, and when the time is right, a shift will occur and those who chose LOVE will shift in vibrational awareness and a 'parting of the waves' will occur, so to speak, and this place will be gone and your new reality will begin.

Claire, you cannot secure the rescue of those who do not require saving. They must save themselves. Many have signed their own death warrant. We guide you to use your energy and strength now, to focus on your new reality and help each other by creating and visualising your shift away from the false light program.

The destroyer forces will be going somewhere else, and those who refused help will go with them for a while, until perhaps, they choose a different path.'

Q. 'If this False Light program collapses on those left behind after the shift, will they know that we have gone?"

"Claire, they will be non-the-wiser, because all memory, all energy, all codes are removed.

The timeline switches that the dark cause through stolen life force codes of Knowledge do a similar thing, but for different reasons.

When timeline switches are created by the dark, all possibility of healing, awakening, learning from past mistakes, and memories of past errors and past remedies are all lost.

Everything from that previous timeline remains except the trauma, which carries forward.

This is carried forward because the cellular memory cannot wipe away soul-shock or soul-fragmentation and the reason why others often feel that a 'past life' is still haunting them with sad memories is because of these timeline switches. It is a very cruel thing to do to any living thing."

Q. "You mentioned that there was a lot to share but I have to say, I am shattered and I am exhausted from all this grief that I feel. Is that my grief, or the grief of others? Why do I feel so sad today?"

"Claire, we need to tell you about sodium poisoning. The crystals are poisoned."

Q. "The crystals? Is it caused by environmental poisoning, or water poisoning, or chem. trails?What is the true cause of the poisoning and who is responsible for doing this?"

"Claire, the exertion you feel, the deep inertia, this is all caused by sodium poisoning in food."

Q. "Is this the cause of the fibromyalgia, hair loss, bone loss, and chronic pain, and fatigue?"

"Claire, doctors would do well to study the blood in fibromyalgia patients and osteoporosis."

Q. "Why?"

"Because poisoned sodium is the true cause."

Q. "Can you help me to secure more details. I feel like I am hitting a wall. What do I need to do to help myself to secure deeper truths from the Heart of Creation and infinitely beyond? How can I best serve all precious life in optimal ways?"

"Claire, it isn't just sodium, as in salt. It is sodium in all its forms, sodium laurel sulphate, and other sodium compounds are chemicals at the end of the day and chemicals are becoming deeply harmful, and more humans and animals, and other life forms cannot tolerate the effects of this chemical in all its forms, in the environment or on the body. It is becoming toxic to those who are growing in light, and it is the reason why it is used.

The dark know how to poison you all.

When it snows what do you place on the roads?

When snails crawl over salt, what happens?

What happens to plants if you give them sea water to drink, instead of rainwater?

Sodium is used prolifically, and you would all benefit from discerning within your hearts what chemicals are harming you the most, as individuals, because your tolerance varies from person to person."

"Thank you for giving us this Knowledge. How can we help ourselves? I already use biodegradable chemical detergents, cleaners, shampoos and body wash because sodium laurel sulphate causes my skin to split open like a razor wound.

I changed my face cream, make-up, laundry detergent, shampoo and body wash years ago.

What could I make myself, from fresh — to clean my body with and wash my hair with?

Is there a perfect way? What about the fluoridation of our drinking water? Does that contribute to skin conditions such as eczema?"

"Claire, you need to go over the labels and read them with a new set of 'spectacles' and discern what may be causing your hair loss from the outside and on the inside."

Q. "The sodium poisoning issue in food...how is it being poisoned?"

"Claire, it is insidious and stealthy. There are many forms of attack on your food taking place from space and on the ground, as well as from the sky.

We told you many years ago that your whole environment and planet was being poisoned. It has only got worse, not better."

Q. "What else do you wish me to share here?"

"Claire, this advice is for those who are earnestly helping themselves and protecting the vulnerable. The time to shine is now. Shine a light on truth. Share what your heart tells you. Help others out there who are lacking your information, and let them share their truths with you. There are many out there who are learning about food, drink, and chemical intolerances, and it is worth investigating their channels and learning from them, in order to enhance your time here and relieve yourselves from unnecessary suffering. Many are losing hair. It is not only about the radiation. This systemic poisoning with sodium-based chemicals is destroying your planet, and causing ageing in many.

Try to find new ways to address this 'onslaught' through heart Knowledge.

Claire, this has to go now. You may feel that it feels unfinished, and perhaps does not hold as much guidance as you anticipated. It holds keys of Knowledge and seeds of learning for those who are seeking growth.

It is time for you all to concentrate on health and well being, and letting go of the old, to make room for the new. Take heart, all of you. LOVE is here and LOVE is by your side.

The weary and the vulnerable are being assisted. Keep them in your thoughts and prayers, and pray for their continued protection each night, before sleep.

Focus on your chosen reality. The place you would truly wish to be and allow those thoughts to be your focal point each day and night, before you go to sleep.

It is possible, all of your dreams are possible.

Make them come true, through concerted effort to hold that thought above the reality of doom and gloom.

The dark have plans, that is true but, you have imagination and creativity, and they are no match for that.

That is the truth.

The safest way to exit this place is to choose a new reality, one of choice, one from the heart, one that is true to you."

Chapter Thirty-One

BLACK HOLE SOUL RESCUE: EPICENTRE OF THE SATANIC AGENDA. MAUI ELDERS AND LAHAINA — HOW YOU CAN HELP

"Make no mistake, this was a satanic ritual, and those who visited afterward came to gloat at the kill. Do you recall who came to the island?"

LOVE'S HEART PLAN SUBSTACK

Heart Connection: All That Is Needed Is Our Humanity,

This is for all of humanity, and is by no means exclusive to those with religious or spiritual beliefs.

This is for all humans who wish to help and wish to connect to their innate ability within.

This ability to connect to a deeper part of ourselves is inherent in all of us. It simply requires discipline to use it daily:

Upon awakening, during the day, and before sleep...

(AM, PM and Midway through our day)

"We call on our Infinite Selves and LOVE and the Laws of Creation from the Heart of Creation and infinitely beyond, to surround and protect us, and to shield us from all harm.

We call on the most powerful healing frequencies in the whole of Creation: Hope, Trust, and Faith to surround and protect us and heal us from all harm.

We ask the frequency of Courage and the frequency of Truth to also surround and protect us and to help us all reach Truth from the heart of Creation, and to have courage to speak our Truths in humanity's hour of need.

How can we best serve all precious life in optimal ways today, in alignment with LOVE's plan and the laws of Creation?"

Rest here and pause the recording through out the message today — to receive supportive assistance and to hear LOVE's guidance on how you can best help all in optimal ways, and keep rejoining us once you are ready.

The message I hear is, "Claire, can you share with the group who are helping humanity — through their own humanity, their compassion and their concern for others well-being, about what has transpired today in spite of the dark's best intentions to cause more harm?"

And I say, **"You must all be working hard and calling for help because all our prayers and calls for help have been answered — to help the innocent, the voiceless, the homeless souls, and souls of the children, newborns, the elderly, and all vulnerable life forms who had no choice in the 'debacle' caused by the formation of this vast black hole and it's vacuum, which has been sucking many into it, through no fault of their own, and left them in a pitiful state — trapped in the digital hell that Klaus Schwab and King Charles, et al., have created — for their 'future entertainment'.**

I was listening to an old message from late summer entitled 'Space Dust' and I had also reviewed several messages from November 2022 into January 2023, and I sensed that I had received upgraded teachings and frequencies.

While I was listening to the discourse on 'Space Dust' and the black hole debacle which is entrapping lost souls and damaged life forms into it — to use as a resource to fuel destroyer forces and Lucifer energies — I saw myself in Avatar World, inside the place of 'no return', and I said to LOVE, **"I don't want to be here. I want to leave and return to LOVE at the heart of Creation."**

I saw myself light up and I saw a pathway light up out of the blackness, and I could see my drawing which I had used as a classroom model; to highlight the dark hole and vacuum, and the space-time-continuum timeline, and on the other side of the false light program, I had drawn a simple drawing of the Heart of Creation and LOVE and a picture of me inside the heart of Creation, restored to wholeness and back to my true original form, which is LOVE.

So, I was inside this cave of the black-hole-Avatar-World but I was also able to perceive everything else too; including the vacuum; the space-time-continuum fence; the heart of Creation, and the pathway simply lit up — through the blackhole drawing and back through the false light program, which went straight and true, back to the heart of Creation, back to LOVE's embrace.

I said this:

"I ask my Infinite Self and Infinite LOVE and the Laws of Creation from the Heart of Creation and infinitely beyond to surround and protect me, and to shield me from all harm.

I ask for all errors to be forgiven and forgotten, meaning: deleted."

"With a peaceful heart, without anger or malice, I ask Infinite LOVE and the Laws of Creation to shield me from all harm and to gather up ALL MAGNIFIED, MALICIOUS HARM, AND ALL HARM done to me and to send it back to all those responsible for ensuring this harm reached my door."

"I ask Infinite LOVE and the Laws of Creation to find all that has been lost and return it to wholeness to be purified, and restored to me in the form of Purest Light codes that can never be corrupted or infiltrated by the dark or any other person, place, or thing, including Lucifer and destroyer forces."

My heart asks, "*And then, what happened?*"

I walked out of the cave down the lit up pathway, and stopped because I was worried I may have done something through ego as opposed to heart and I didn't want to bring any bad energy back into the false light program which could harm others, so I kept checking with my Infinite Self and LOVE to clarify what move I should make, what question should I ask, did I have permission to do this, how could I protect all precious life and how could I ensure that I had acted in ways that served all precious life in optimal ways?

I was guided that all was well and that I was to get my husband, and ask him to lie down with me and connect to heart, and to ask him to listen to the Space Dust message and then, while we were still in heart connection, I took him through what had happened in the black hole and we asked more questions on whether it was possible to exit a point of 'no return' if we wished to serve LOVE not Lucifer, and had I done the right thing, was it safe to do, and if so, what actions must we take to ensure we were following all precautions to make it a safe experience?

We followed the teachings, as above, and we saw ourselves leave the black hole, hand in hand and we went straight along a lit-up path which took us directly to the place in my classroom drawing, to the heart of Creation.

We both received healing. We were troubled because we knew others are trapped inside this place. My husband had metaphorically looked back before he left the black hole, and had witnessed lots of souls standing perfectly still, watching us leave, yet, they remained stuck there — transfixed and unable to help themselves.

We sought deeper teachings on how we could assist them. We know we must not interfere with free will choices, and especially, this is true when referring to those of you who are awake and listening to this discourse. If you wish to leave here, you must ask for help to secure your entire lost codes and to return to wholeness.

But we knew that many voiceless souls are trapped there who never had a choice, who have been stripped naked of any remembrance of who they are, where they are, why they are there and they do not know they can call on LOVE for help.

That energy, the energy and codes which enable a life form to call on LOVE for help was the heart energy that we possess that the dark see as 'pure gold' because when that part of you is gone, you lose all remembrance that you can call for help.

Effectively, you are shut down, locked down — you are the quarry of the dark to hunt and rape, and maim, and kill — over, and over, and over again in the AVATAR WORLD that King Charles and co. want his subjects in — at his 'majesty's pleasure'.

We called to LOVE and the Laws of Creation and asked what could we ask for, to help these trapped souls in the black, digital hell of Avatar World.

We were guided to pray for them, to ask for their help from LOVE, and we waited to see what transpired.

From the heart of Creation, we watched LOVE show us the path we had used to walk out of the black hole and we were asked to return to the entrance.

We followed each step, and kept checking that everything we were doing was within LOVE's plan and the laws of Creation.

My husband stood guard as he was guided to by the entrance to the black hole. I was guided to go to the end of the pathway that formed a cul-de-sac inside the black hole. I stood there and felt LOVE's presence.

We were guided to ask for several things at different times, such as calling on the frequency of Peace, LOVE, and Unity, Hope, Faith, and Trust, Truth, Courage, Knowledge, and Wisdom to help these souls.

And then, through a small gap came trapped souls who were sent along the path towards my husband, and we called on our Infinite Selves to protect them along this direct pathway back to wholeness.

We focused, also, on the pictures we had been asked to draw of our perfect reality, from two month ago. My husband had drawn two paths on his picture, one was full of all life forms heading home to the heart of Creation, the second path was empty and led to the black hole.

My pictured preferred reality featured a ship full to the brim of all life, with a message saying all returned home safely in time for the next Out Breath cycle, and they all lived happily ever after.

We imagined our preferred chosen reality and followed other heart guidance on requests to make for souls as they passed through.

Many were so badly damaged, some were very grumpy, and a little belligerent. We listened to LOVE and made appropriate requests.

Thousands of souls were rescued by LOVE today. They all returned home to the Heart of Creation and to wholeness. Their entire ladder of consciousness was healed and repaired, and restored to its true origins and withdrawn —withdrawn from this dark place.

You all did that. All your prayers, all your calls for help, your humanity, your concern, your decision and choice to try another way of helping has brought miracles to the door of millions of trapped, entangled life forms, many of whom are children and newborns.

Oh my goodness. How brave are they to fall into this place and to get trapped in a place of 'non-return'.

And yet, in spite of all this, you helped them get out of here. You helped my husband and I get out of there, and we are both extremely grateful for all your kind efforts and determination.

You did this, and with LOVE's help, the hardest things were resolved by LOVE and the laws of Creation.

We only have to ask for help and it is given.

So, I am being asked to call on you — to share this good news, and to remind you that if you wish to also gather up all that has been lost in this dark place, you have the free will choice to ask and it is given.

And I hear,

" Claire, the group need to know what else has transpired as a result of this release from suffering.

Claire was concerned because every good action creates a vicious assault by the dark who are always quick to retaliate.

We guide you all that they are currently in a weakened state because LOVE has provided a clear pathway to safety out of the black hole for all those who have no voice, and for the innocent who ended up trapped in these places, through no fault of their own.

You, on the other hand are aware, you are listening to this and LOVE guides you that your heart must lead the way on this.

You must discern all this carefully through your own heart and act accordingly, once you are satisfied that you have all the facts.

The opportunity for you to leave the False Light Construct and black hole of entrapment is available to you all.

If you do not wish to remain trapped inside AVATAR WORLD, where particles of your soul and other aspects of your consciousness have become entangled in this place, then, all you need to do is ask for

LOVE to "recall all lost aspects of self" from this place — the black hole — and from all areas of the False Light Construct.

It is a process and it requires heart connection, AM, PM, and midway through your day,in order to secure a full evacuation of your codes of remembrance from this place.

This is why prayers and heart requests are so important. Look at what you can achieve when you focus on LOVE.

Once you have secured your own rescue from this place, we do ask that you continue to pray for all those trapped, lost souls — many of whom are children.

We are repeating this again, because you need to understand that the destroyer forces covet the children.

We have spoken about the Island of Maui and we wish to share more here again.

The islanders are suffering far more than many of you may realise.

Their suffering is also happening at a spiritual level.

When the fires burnt down Maui, Claire put out several messages, and one message was sent privately to a healer who Claire had been guided to reach out to, who lived on the island.

An offer of help was sent by LOVE because LOVE always needs a human to be present, 'on the ground' in the 'vicinity' of an emergency, and through a human presence, particularly one who is capable of calling on LOVE and transmitting LOVE's energy into a place, more perfect help can be given to those who are suffering, and more protection can be secured for those who are at risk of harm.

Those of you with eyes to see need to look again at all those who descended on Maui after the fires.

That fire was a sacrifice, a child sacrifice, and a sacrifice to stir up intense fear in a place that holds strong spiritual meaning to the Elders on that island, and by those who revere nature and all her beauty, who respect the island and who tend to their sacred place with grace and sincerity.

Claire had been asked to get a message to the Elders because she was given information to help them and support them from LOVE.

Unfortunately, although the recipient did receive the message and respond, they rejected the help and the perfect help never reached the Elders because this soul chose to let ego rule over heart, and rejected the request to listen through heart for guidance.

This is a lesson in mind-control, and it is a lesson to those who label themselves as 'healers' and 'spiritual teachers'.

When another passes on a message directly to you, and if your heart is not engaged, your ego takes over and dismisses vital assistance reaching those who needed the guidance — for their own heart's discernment.

To block this message from LOVE is akin to murder because it means that vital assistance is stopped in its tracks.

If a message is sent, a discerning soul would always engage heart first and foremost, and pass on the message, regardless, because it was not for them, it was for the Elders.

Children were missing, people were dead, and a person who is a visitor on the island barred assistance to the Maui Elders.

This person claims to be an advanced healer.
We say, why break the laws of Creation? Why reject help, when your heart could have told you?

The ego programs led the way, and Maui is suffering still, because the protection is not 'up and running' in that place, and those who label themselves as healers are running amok with poorly thought out choices, which are exposing the Maui Islanders to more attack from satanic forces.

Make no mistake, this was a satanic ritual, and those who visited afterward came to gloat at the kill.

Do you recall who came to the island?

You must all be aware, and if not, you all need to remind yourselves of who visited, and who came and tried to help organise local aid.

Those who came from 'outside' came to gloat at the killing.

Make no mistake.

The ones who died in the fire, died a horrific death.

Why would a healer who is a visitor to this island take it upon themselves to reject LOVE's attempts to help the Maui Elders?

We say to the Maui Islanders, and to the healers out there — to stop all activity which uses outside forces to bring in energy, and this means: Reiki, Yoga, Pilates, Circle Dancing, Quantum Healing, Crystal Healing and the like, because your energy work is undoing all the genuine work of the Maui Spiritual Elders — those who are sincere.

For every effort the Elders put in to protecting their people, you are all undoing this and exposing the islanders to deeper attack on the spiritual level.

Many are losing vast quantities of life force, and soul fragmentation is taking place.

The Maui Elders, the ones who are sincere, are fully aware of this 'rock' that is blocking their work, and so, we would like to ask you all, on their behalf, to support their efforts — by respecting local customs — and if you cannot respect them, then remove yourself from the island, because you are letting in the Beast System.

It is already knocking at your door, and this black hole is **not blocked** for those who have a choice to stop harming, or those who are bent on deliberate destruction, it is **not blocked** to those who allow their ego led behaviour to allow in Lucifer energy onto the island of Maui, and if you really want the hard-hitting truth, it was a walk-in-the-park for those bent on the 'SMART city experience' in Maui.

They had every group present who could mess things up, and mess up the energy protection secured by the Maui Elders.

The fires around the planet killed off Mother Earth's spirit in the false light realm. Many are unaware of this.

The Galactic Grids were destroyed by destroyer forces infiltrating Reiki groups and energies which are completely corrupted and unsafe to use.

The Yoga communities successfully collapsed the Planetary Grids of Mother Earth.

This left Mother Earth in a weakened state, and unable to protect her children as fully as before.

She was weak, and her energy has been further weakened by all the communities in the healing 'industry' who refuse to stop harming — using old fashioned and outdated technology — against the monster force of destroyer forces, which has riddled its way into every healing system, and it is why you are all being asked to 'go direct' — to connect through heart, through your Infinite Self to LOVE, and to ask the Laws of Creation on what actions or requests you can make that "best serve all precious life in optimal ways."

This is asked of you because many do not understand the laws, or that their 'ideas' are not heart-centred — they are just ideas, or that making money from healing is against the laws of Creation.

You have the fires raging worldwide, you have souls trapped in AVATAR WORLD, you have humans being killed with poisoned shots, you have corrupt politicians and compromised health systems, etc.,... and you still think it is okay to take money from a distraught soul who is lost in the programs of entanglement?

Your role was to get all precious life to safety.
You all came in with more codes of remembrance because those who have been trapped in the black hole, gave up their codes so that you could come in with more, and when the time was right, your role was to redistribute all lost codes to those who bravely fell into this dark place in the complete trust that when you were called upon, you would be there for them and wake them up, by giving them their codes back.

You could not all come in with more codes. It would have collapsed the False Light Construct without vital lessons being learned for all.

So, those who could be helping the most are harming the most.

The fires rage around the world. The messages keep going out — to ask you all to connect to heart and to disengage from all old healing systems, because anything secured from within here is corrupted.

And it is harming all precious life.

The final warning went out recently, advising Yoga and Reiki groups, predominantly, that they are at the 'end of the road' and are jeopardising their own soul evolution.

Thanks to those who called to LOVE for help, these souls are safe and back home. [From the black hole]

However, we wish to point out further evidence of malfeasance and it is malfeasance, in the sense that to ignore the many calls to desist, is a sign that a person is only focused on making money, on kudos, and on self-centred behaviours.

We are asking you all who are listening who wish to help, that Maui Islanders and Elders need your prayers tonight and onwards.

They are facing the devil, and looking the devil straight in the eyes — staring down the barrel of a gun that is forcing them to change their lives in Lahaina, and it does mean 'death' of the soul in the process.

You have to see things from the bigger perspective, those of you who wish to help.

Ask your heart to place you in a classroom where LOVE and the Heart of Creation can show you what is happening in Maui and in Lahaina.

Who are the people in authority?

Ask to be shown them individually.

What are you being shown?

(Pause the recording here and rejoin us once you are ready.)

If you live in Lahiana or elsewhere on Maui, who is truly serving the people and who is serving the Satanic Agenda?

(Pause the recording here. Rejoin us once you are ready.)

You have to be brave. Have courage. All can be dealt with, when you call on LOVE to help you.

Next, ask to be shown what is happening above the island of Maui, from the far-out reaches of space.

Have a good look around this classroom model.

Ask questions and pause the recording to give yourself plenty of time.

That is enough for today, Claire.

This needs to go and it needs to go to someone in Maui or nearby, someone with discernment who would know who to forward this message to, because LOVE is here for the Islanders of Maui.

LOVE stands with the Elders and all those who are suffering.

The Island of Maui is not the only place where suffering is happening, however, you all need to be aware that the island is the epicentre of the ET Agenda, and all those who want to help protect humanity are being called to listen carefully to LOVE's guidance, because LOVE has a plan to help Maui and elsewhere, and where you have hearts that wish to help defend all precious life, you will also find LOVE.

When you have LOVE, you have enough.

Remember that, dear Elders of Maui. You may feel you are facing a giant, but when LOVE is called upon and called each day, then all the love from around the world can be drawn upon like a beautiful spring of purest water.

Continue to praise your beloved island and home, and pray that more will start helping and others will consider the harm they may be causing.

Remember the Elders of Maui, and respect their beliefs and practises because they are sacred and they are helping — it is the interferences of others 'meddling' with energy which is causing the biggest tears in the Web of Light.

All are being called to choose the ending they want for themselves, for their planet,
and for the world's children, who are caught up in this chaos through no fault of their own.

That is all Claire."

Chapter Thirty-Two

DECLARATION TO DESTROYER FORCES

WE COMMAND ALL THOSE HARMING HUMANITY AND ALL PRECIOUS LIFE TO STOP HARMING, OR FACE CONTAINMENT, OR DELETION

YOU HAVE NO AUTHORITY TO BE HERE. YOU ARE INTERFERING WITH OUR SOUL EVOLUTION AND YOU ARE MALICIOUSLY HARMING ALL PRECIOUS LIFE.

AUDIO: LOVE'S HEART PLAN, SUBSTACK.COM

UNDER THE LAWS OF CREATION (THE LAWS OF GOD/ THE COSMIC LAWS) I HEREBY GIVE NOTICE TO ALL THOSE MALICIOUSLY HARMING AND ALL THOSE WHO ARE HARMING ALL PRECIOUS LIFE, INCLUDING HUMANITY — THESE ARE SOME OF THE LAWS THAT YOU ARE BREAKING, WHICH CARRY THE MOST SERIOUS PENALTIES:

TO FIRST, DO NO HARM.

IT IS AGAINST THE LAWS OF CREATION TO INTERFERE WITH ANOTHER SOUL'S FREE WILL CHOICES.

IT IS AGAINST THE LAWS OF CREATION TO CORRUPT THE DIVINE MIND OF ANOTHER.

IT IS AGAINST THE LAWS OF CREATION TO WASTE ENERGY OR CAUSE ANOTHER TO WASTE ENERGY.

THERE ARE THOUSANDS OF LAWS.

TO SUMMARISE, IT IS AGAINST THE LAWS OF CREATION TO BREAK THE LAWS OF CREATION.

UNDER THE LAWS OF CREATION I HEREBY GIVE NOTICE THAT ALL LIFE FORMS WHO ARE MALICIOUSLY HARMING, OR DELIBERATELY CAUSING HARM TO HUMANITY AND ALL LIFE ON PLANET EARTH MUST CHANGE NOW OR FACE THE PENALTY OF CONTAINMENT OR DELETION.

YOU HAVE NO AUTHORITY TO BE HERE.

YOU HAVE BROKEN MANY LAWS AND YOU MUST ALL RECEIVE BACK ALL MAGNIFIED MALICIOUS HARM AND ALL HARM THAT HAS REACHED THE DOORS OF OTHER INNOCENT LIFE, INCLUDING HUMANITY.

ALL ACTIONS, ALL MAGNIFIED MALICIOUS INTENTIONS, ALL DEMONIC PRACTICES TO CAUSE HARM, TO RIP OPEN THE GATES OF HELL — AND THAT RIPPED OPEN THE UNIFIED FIELD OF MOTHER EARTH — MUST NOW BE RETURNED AT FULL SPEED AND WITH IMMEDIATE EFFECT.

ALL ACTIONS THAT CAUSE HARM ARE RETURNED TO THE CREATORS, SENDERS, PERPETRATORS AND PURVEYORS OF THE AFOREMENTIONED HARM.

YOU HAVE THE RIGHT TO REMAIN SILENT, BUT YOU DO NOT HAVE THE RIGHT TO CHOOSE.

YOU HAVE BEEN SYSTEMATICALLY WARNED BY LOVE AND YOU HAVE REFUSED TO STOP HARMING.

THEREFORE, YOUR PENALTY IS TO RECEIVE BACK ALL HARM WHICH YOU LEFT UNCHECKED WHICH YOU ALLOWED TO SPIRAL OUT OF CONTROL AND ALLOWED TO MAGNIFY, IN ORDER TO ENCOURAGE IT TO CAUSE DEEPER HARM.

THESE ACTIONS, IN THEMSELVES, ARE SO FAR APART FROM THE ACTION OF LOVE.

IN EFFECT, YOU HAVE CREATED YOUR OWN PRISON BY REFUSING TO STOP HARMING AND BY YOUR DESIRE FOR POWER OVER ANOTHER.

THE POWER OF LOVE HAS ALWAYS OVERRIDDEN THE DESIRE FOR 'POWER OVER' ANOTHER. HOWEVER, LOVE NEEDED HUMANITY TO COME INTO THIS PLACE —

TO BRING BACK VITAL CODES OF REMEMBRANCE FOR THOSE LIFE FORMS WHO YOU HAD IMPRISONED, ENSLAVED, AND HELD AGAINST THEIR WILL — INTERFERING WITH THEIR SOUL EVOLUTION — WHICH IS THE ULTIMATE CRIME BECAUSE IT CAUSES DEATH OF THE SOUL.

ALL FREEMASONIC ACTIVITY MUST STOP BECAUSE IT IS SATANIC IN NATURE AND HARMS ALL LIFE ON EARTH BY BRINGING SATANIC PRACTICES ONTO THE EARTH PLANE, AND HAS HELPED TO DESTROY THE WEB OF LIFE, THE PLANETARY GRIDS AND THE SPIRITUAL GRIDS OF MOTHER EARTH.

YOU ARE FORBIDDEN TO RESIDE ON THE EARTH PLANE AND YOU ARE TRESPASSING.

THE VOID OF THE BLACK HOLE OF 'AVATAR WORLD' AWAITS THOSE WHO REBEL AGAINST THE COVENANT OF THE SPIRITUAL LAWS:

TO FIRST, DO NO HARM.

KING CHARLES HAS NO AUTHORITY TO RULE HERE. HE IS NOT OF HUMAN ORIGIN.

THE POPE HAS NO AUTHORITY TO RULE HERE AND IS NOT OF HUMAN ORIGIN.

HUMANITY MUST WAKE UP NOW AND LOOK WITH CLEAR EYES AT THOSE WHO MEAN THEM HARM.

THEY ARE YOUR LEADERS, POLITICIANS, BANKING CARTELS, FINANCIAL INSTITUTIONS, MEDIA, WEF, UN, WHO... ALL WHO SERVE THEM, SERVE LUCIFER.

TO HUMANITY:

LUCIFER IS CURRENTLY IN A WEAKENED STATE AND THE TIME TO TAKE ACTION IS NOW.

MAKE YOUR DECLARATION TO LOVE/GOD.

STATE YOUR FREEDOM AND LIBERATION FROM THE HOLD THAT THESE DARK FORCES HAVE ON HUMANITY.

THE MORE WHO STATE THEIR FREEDOM, THE MORE THIS ENERGY WEAKENS.

THIS IS BECAUSE THE TRUE WAR IS ON OUR CONSCIOUSNESS, AND THE PHYSICAL HARM IS THE LAST THING TO SHOW.

THE DAMAGE HAS HAPPENED AT VERY DEEP LEVELS OF OUR AWARENESS.

WHEN WE CALL ON LOVE AND ASK FOR HELP, ALL DAMAGE CAN BE REPAIRED.

MAKING A STATEMENT THAT THE DESTROYER FORCES HOLD NO AUTHORITY OVER YOU, RELEASES YOU FROM THE ENTANGLEMENT OF THE FALSE LIGHT PROGRAMS, AND SETS YOUR SOUL AND SPIRIT FREE.

WE ARE AT THE TAIL END OF A CYLE OF EXPANSION THAT HAS COMPLETED AND IS RETURNING, AS AN **'IN BREATH'** BEFORE THE NEXT CYCLE OF EXPANSION, THE **'OUT BREATH'** CYCLE.

THEREFORE, NOW IS THE TIME TO SET YOURSELVES FREE BECAUSE WHEN THIS CYLCE — THE **IN BREATH** — COMPLETES, WHERE YOU ARE NOW, IS WHERE YOU

EITHER END YOUR JOURNEY FOR GOOD, OR START AGAIN IN THE NEW.

NO LIFE FORM CAN CONTINUE ITS JOURNEY OF SOUL EVOLUTION IN A FALSE LIGHT PROGRAM.

THIS LIFE TIME IS THE FINAL CHANCE TO REDEEM OURSELVES AND FREE OURSELVES FROM THE FALSE LIGHT CONSTRUCT.

ONLY WE CAN CHOOSE FOR OURSELVES. ONLY WE CAN SET OURSELVES FREE — BY ASKING FOR HELP AND RELEASE FROM SUFFERING THROUGH PRAYER, OR THROUGH YOUR HEART AND FROM THERE — TO LOVE/GOD.

HERE IS A SIMPLE HEART CALL FOR THOSE WHO ARE NEITHER SPIRITUAL OR RELIGIOUS WHO MAY NEED ASSISTANCE TO DO THIS SIMPLY.

I LIE DOWN ON THE BED THAT I SLEEP IN AT NIGHT — FLAT ON MY BACK, LEGS STRAIGHT, NEVER CROSSED.

I RELAX, AND IF IT IS SAFE TO DO SO I CLOSE MY EYES.

I TAKE MY CLOSED EYES DOWN TOWARDS MY CHEST AREA AND I LISTEN TO THE AIR AS MY CHEST RISES AND FALLS, AS THE AIR GOES IN AND OUT OF MY LUNGS.

I KEEP MY CLOSED EYES SOFTLY LOOKING DOWN TOWARDS MY CHEST AREA.

I HAVE DECIDED THAT I WISH TO RETURN HOME AND TO CONTINUE MY SOUL EVOLUTION.

I KNOW I NEED LOVE'S HELP TO SET ME FREE FROM THIS COMPLEX ENTANGLEMENT OF FALSE LIGHT WHICH I KNOW IS A TRAP TO KEEP MY SOUL HERE.

I WANT TO RETURN TO LOVE'S EMBRACE, TO FEEL PEACE, LOVE AND UNITY, TO KNOW THE TRUTH OF ALL

THINGS AND TO BE AMONGST MY FAMILY OF HUMANITY IN A PLACE OF HAPPINESS AND CREATIVITY.

I ACKNOWLEDGE THAT PART OF ME IS TEMPORARILY STUCK INSIDE THIS PLACE, AND THE REST OF ME IS AT THE HEART OF CREATION.

I WISH TO HELP PROTECT AND DEFEND ALL PRECIOUS LIFE IN OPTIMAL WAYS AND I AM CALLING ON LOVE TO ANSWER MY CALL FOR HELP TO LEAVE THIS PLACE WHEN THE TIME COMES AND TO RETURN HOME.

I IMAGINE THAT I HAVE A SWITCH IN THE CENTRE OF MY CHEST — MY HEART SWITCH, MY TRUE POWER SWITCH — AND I IMAGINE THAT WHEN I PRESS THIS SWITCH, IT IS AN INDICATION THAT I AM ASKING MY HEART AND LOVE FOR HELP TO SECURE MY OWN RESCUE.

I AM ALSO ASKING FOR THE RESCUE OF ALL TRAPPED SOULS WHO HAVE LOST THE ABILITY TO CALL FOR HELP WHO HAVE NO VOICE, THROUGH NO FAULT OF THEIR OWN.

I ASK LOVE TO RELEASE ALL SOULS WHO HAVE BECOME TRAPPED BY THE DARK FORCES BECAUSE THE OTHER DAY, I SAW CHILDREN'S SOULS BEING TAKEN BY THE DARK AND USED AS SLAVES.

I WAS SHOWN HOW THE DARK 'TRAFFIC' TRAPPED CHILDREN'S SOULS AND FERRY THEM AWAY TO ABUSE AND MISTREAT THEM.

I WAS SHOWN LARGER SOUL ASPECTS THAT WERE IMPRISONED BUT WHO THE DARK COULD NOT TOTALLY HARM BECAUSE THEY STILL CARRIED ENOUGH LIGHT

TO PROTECT THEM FROM AS MUCH HARM AS OTHERS ENDURED, HOWEVER, THEY WERE IMPRISONED BEHIND HIDDEN FIREWALLS OF FALSE LIGHT, AND THEY HAD LOST THE ABILITY TO KNOW WHO THEY WERE OR THAT THEY COULD CALL FOR HELP.

THE CRIMES HAPPENING TO HUMANITY ON THE GROUND ARE REPLICATED BY THE DESTROYER FORCES — WITH TRAFFICKED SOULS AND HIGHER SELF ASPECTS — ALL ALONG OUR LADDER OF CONSCIOUSNESS.

AS ABOVE SO BELOW.

YESTERDAY, ABOVE MAUI, I PERCEIVED CHILDREN'S SOULS BEING TRAFFICKED INTO A SPACE SHIP. THERE WERE HUGE SPACE SHIPS ABOVE OUR PLANET AND MAUI IS THE EPICENTRE OF THE ET AGENDA, SATANIC ATTACK, AND WARFARE.

YESTERDAY, LOVE CAME AND HELPED HUMANITY DUE TO THE MANY CALLS FOR HELP FROM AROUND THE WORLD.

THE CALLS FOR HELP BY THOSE WITH EYES THAT SEE AND HEARTS THAT TRULY HEAR HAVE SECURED THE RELEASE OF TRAPPED CHILDREN'S SOULS FROM MAUI AND FROM AROUND THE WORLD.

MANY LOST SOULS WHO WERE TRAPPED IN THIS FALSE LIGHT CONSTRUCT AFTER DEATH OF THE PHYSICAL SELF, HAVE BEEN FOUND BY LOVE AND REPATRIATED WITH THEIR ENTIRE LADDER OF CONSCIOUSNESS.

YESTERDAY, LOVE RESCUED MORE TRAPPED SOULS FROM THE BLACK HOLE, AND I OBSERVED LOVE COMPLETE THIS, THIS MORNING.

ARRESTS HAVE BEEN MADE AT OTHER LEVELS OF AWARENESS, AND MANY DARK, HARMFUL ENERGIES HAVE BEEN EITHER CONTAINED OR DELETED, INCLUDING MANY ANNUNAKI AND REPTILIAN ENTITIES WHO WERE OVERSEEING OPERATIONS ON THE EARTH PLANE.

LOVE AND THE LAWS OF CREATION ARE OVERSEEING EVERYTHING, AND IF YOU ARE CONNECTING TO HEART, YOU CAN ASK YOUR HEART TO SHOW YOU A CLASSROOM EXAMPLE OF WHAT HAS TRANSPIRED DURING THE LAST THREE DAYS.

PAUSE THE RECORDING AND REJOIN US ONCE YOU HAVE BEEN SHOWN OR ONCE YOU 'PERCEIVE' WHAT YOUR INFINITE SELF AND LOVE WISH TO CONVEY TO YOU ALL.

THESE EVENTS ARE A RESULT OF ALL YOUR LOVING EFFORTS TO ASK LOVE FOR HELP.

"MAKE THE REQUEST. LOVE DOES THE REST."

NOW YOU HAVE REJOINED US, WOULD YOU LIKE TO ASK YOUR HEART ON WHAT DECLARATION YOU COULD WRITE DOWN OR POST ONLINE IF YOU WISH TO, TO CEMENT IN THE LOVING ENERGY AND POWERFUL PROTECTION FOR ALL PRECIOUS INNOCENT LIFE, TO ENSURE ALL RECEIVE WHAT LOVE'S PLAN HAS IN STORE FOR THEM, ACCORDING TO THEIR SOUL AGREEMENT WITH LOVE, WHO ALWAYS PROMISED HUMANITY THAT IF ENOUGH COULD WAKE UP AND CALL FOR HELP FOR THOSE WHO WERE SUFFERING WHO WERE DEFENCELESS, THEN LOVE WOULD DO THE REST — TO HELP SECURE A SOUL'S FREEDOM FROM THIS PRISON.

IT IS WHY WE ARE ALL HERE. TO BE **PRESENT** IN ORDER TO CALL ON LOVE FOR HELP FOR OURSELVES, AND THEN TO CALL ON LOVE FOR HELP FOR THOSE WHO ENTERED THIS SPACE DEFENCELESS, MANY OF WHOM GAVE THEIR CODES TO A SMALLER GROUP — TO ENABLE THEM TO WAKE UP IN A DARK FALSE LIGHT SPACE, AND WHEN THE TIME WAS RIGHT, TO WAKE THE OTHERS UP BY GIVING THEM BACK THEIR CODES OF REMEMBRANCE— TO HELP THEM ALSO LEAVE THIS SPACE.

THAT TIME IS UPON YOU ALL AND NOW IS THE TIME TO GIVE LOVE A CALL.

HERE IS A SIMPLE REQUEST THROUGH HEART TO ACCOMPLISH THE BEST POSSIBLE OUTCOME FOR HUMANITY AND ALL PRECIOUS LIFE.

“WE CALL ON OUR INFINITE SELVES AND INFINITE LOVE FROM THE HEART OF CREATION AND INFINITELY BEYOND TO ASSIST US IN OUR HOUR OF NEED.

WE ASK FOR ALL OUR ERRORS TO BE FORGIVEN AND FORGOTTEN, AND FOR ALL THE INNOCENT WHO HAVE NO VOICE.

WITH PEACEFUL CALM HEARTS, WE ASK FOR ALL MAGNIFIED MALICIOUS HARM AND ALL HARM TO BE GATHERED UP BY INFINITE LOVE AND THE LAWS OF CREATION, AND SENT BACK IMMEDIATELY TO ALL THOSE RESPONSIBLE FOR THE MAGNIFIED MALICIOUS HARM — FOR THEIR LEARNING.

WE ASK FOR ALL THAT HAS BEEN LOST TO BE FOUND BY INFINITE LOVE FOR ALL THOSE WHO CAN BE ASSISTED INCLUDING OURSELVES, AND RETURNED TO WHOLENESS TO BE PURIFIED AND RETURNED TO US AS

PUREST LIGHT CODES THAT CAN NEVER BE INFILTRATED BY THE DESTROYER FORCES, LUCIFER OR ANY OTHER THING.

WE ASK FOR THE RELEASE OF ALL CAPTIVE SOULS AND ASPECTS OF OUR CONSCIOUSNESS.

WE ASK FOR ALL WHO CAN BE ASSISTED, INCLUDING OURSELVES, FOR OUR LADDER OF CONSCIOUSNESS TO BE HEALED AND REPAIRED OF ALL HARM, UP TO, BUT NOT INCLUDING, THE PUREST LIGHT GATEWAYS AT THE HEART OF CREATION.

WE ASK FOR ALL LOST AND FOUND CODES TO BE GIVEN BACK TO ALL THOSE WHO GAVE THEIR CODES AWAY AND THOSE WHO VOLUNTEERED TO COME IN WITH LESS REMEMBRANCE, SO THAT OTHERS COULD COME IN WITH MORE.

A REQUEST ON BEHALF OF ALL TRAPPED SOULS:

"WE ASK THAT THOSE WHO SQUANDERED THESE CODES AND WHO ARE STILL HARMING HUMANITY THROUGH EGO-LED BEHAVIOUR, WHICH IS SLOWING DOWN OUR ASCENSION PROCESS, TO BE HELPED TO SEE THE ERROR OF USING EARTH ENERGY, WHEN THE ENERGY OF HEART AND LOVE IS THE ONLY WAY TO HELP OTHERS LEAVE THIS PLACE, AND TO HELP THIS GROUP WAKE UP TO THEIR DUTY AND RESPONSIBILITY TO ENSURE THAT ALL SOULS WHO GAVE UP THEIR CODES TO THIS GROUP, ARE ASSISTED TO EXIT THE MATRIX, BY DESISTING FROM ANY ACTIVITY WHICH IS PREVENTING THIS PROCESS FROM HAPPENING AND WHICH HAS CAUSED DEATH OF THE SOUL. WE FORGIVE THEM, BUT WE ARE ASKING THEM ALL TO CON-

SIDER US AND OUR PLIGHT, AND THE MANY DEATHS WHICH HAVE ALREADY OCCURED THROUGH STUBBORN REFUSAL TO STOP ANY ACTIVITY WHICH ALLOWS DESTROYER FORCES TO ENTER THIS REALITY. WE CANNOT LEAVE BECAUSE WE ARE TRAPPED THROUGH NO FAULT OF OUR OWN.

WE ALSO STATE THAT THE FREEMASONIC CULT HAVE HARMED HUMANITY TO SUCH A DEGREE THAT NOW ALL THOSE WHO INNOCENTLY PARTAKE IN THESE ACTIVITIES — ***WITHOUT UNDERSTANDING THE DEEPER CONNOTATIONS OF ALIGNING ONESELF WITH THIS CULT GROUP*** *— NEED TO BE INFORMED THAT THEY RISK DEATH OF THE SOUL AND DEATH, BECAUSE WHERE THERE IS DEATH, THERE IS NO LIFE AND WHERE THERE IS LIFE, THERE IS NO DEATH.*

FREEMASONRY IS DEATH AND THERE IS NO LIFE IN THIS CULT SYSTEM. IT ONLY LEADS TO DEATH, NOT LIFE.

IT IS A CHOICE, BUT WE WISH ALL TO BE MADE AWARE THAT THEY ARE HARMING THEIR FAMILIES AND FRIENDS, AND ALL THEY CONNECT WITH END UP BEING HARMED BY THE ATTACHMENT OF SATANIC FREQUENCIES IN THEIR ENERGY FIELDS.

THESE ARE RIPPING OPEN THE WEB OF LIFE AND DESTROYING THE LIFE FORCE IN MANY SOULS.

YOU ALL NEED TO BE AWARE AND YOU ALL NEED TO PROTECT YOURSELVES FROM THE MANY HARMFUL STRUCTURES THAT THE FREEMASONIC CULT HAVE ERECTED IN YOUR TOWNS AND VILLAGES.

MANY FREEMASONS ARE IMPLEMENTING CHANGE IN YOUR TOWN COUNCILS TO INSTIL THE ***15 MINUTE CITY*** *MENTALITY.*

WE GUIDE YOU ALL — THIS IS A RUSE FOR CHILD TRAFFICKING AND SOUL HARVESTING, NOTHING MORE.

AS TRAPPED SOULS, WE ASK HUMANITY TO CONSIDER ALL ACTIONS WHICH ENTRAP US MORE.

"WE ARE POWERLESS TO STOP THIS BUT WE CAN REACH OUT TO YOU THROUGH CLAIRE AND OTHERS WHO UNDERSTAND THE EARTH ISSUES, OR, ARE AT LEAST PREPARED TO LISTEN THROUGH HEART AND CONVEY OUR MESSAGE TO YOU ALL.

MANY TRAPPED SOULS HAVE LOST THE ABILITY TO CALL FOR HELP. THE DARK STEAL THIS ENERGY BECUASE IT DISABLES A SOUL FRAGMENT FROM CALLING ON LOVE WHO ALWAYS COMES WHEN CALLED UPON.

CLAIRE HAS SHARED MANY TIMES THAT LOVE DOES NOT IMPOSE, LOVE COMES WHEN CALLED UPON, AND SO KNOWING THAT ONE CAN CALL FOR HELP IS IMPORTANT.

WHY ARE WE STILL TRAPPED WHEN WE CAN CALL FOR HELP?

WE ARE TRAPPED IN A MESH OF FALSE LIGHT FREQUENCIES THAT ARE EXTREMELY COMPLEX AND WITHOUT YOUR PRAYERS, YOUR CALLS FOR HELP, LOVE CANNOT INTERFERE BECAUSE YOU CAME AS GROUP AS A FAMILY OF HUMANITY, AND PART OF YOUR PROMISE WAS THAT YOU WOULD HELP EACH OTHER AND LEARN ABOUT THE ISSUES YOU HAVE CREATED HERE AND LEARN HOW TO UNDO HARM YOU MAY HAVE CAUSED.

THE HARM THAT IS HOLDING US HERE IS THE ENTRAPMENT BY FALSE LIGHT FREQUENCIES WHICH OUR OWN FAMILY OF HUMANITY HAVE ALLOWED IN, AND THEREFORE, THOSE WHO CAUSED THIS ISSUE FOR US — THE PERPETRATORS— MUST CHOOSE TO HELP UNDO THE HARM THEY HAVE CAUSED.

UNDER THE LAWS OF CREATION, ONLY THE PERPETRATOR CAN REMEDY THEIR OWN ERRORS, AND THEREFORE, LOVE CANNOT INTERFERE WITH THE FREE WILL CHOICES OF OTHERS.

FREE WILL WAS GIVEN ON THE UNDERSTANDING THAT IT WOULD BE USED TO SECURE THE OPTIMAL OUTCOME THAT BEST SEVRED ALL LIFE.

WHEN OTHERS CHOOSE TO PARTAKE IN ACTIVITES WHICH LET IN DESTROYER FORCES ONTO THE EARTH PLANE, THEN IT IS ONLY BY THEIR CHOICE TO REMEDY THEIR ERRORS THAT WE CAN BE SET FREE, BECAUSE WE ARE TRAPPED OWING TO THEIR FREE WILL CHOICE TO PARTAKE IN AN ACTIVITY WITHOUT CONSULTING THE LAWS OF CREATION.

FREEMASONRY IS NOT A PRACTICE OF LOVE.

IT INDUCES DEATH OF THE SOUL AND IT IS THEREFORE, A CRIME AGAINST HUMANITY TO PARTICIPATE IN FREEMASONIC ACTIVITIES AND RITUALS.

WE ARE PUTTING THE MESSAGE OUT HERE, IN THE HOPE THAT THOSE WHO INNOCENTLY PARTICIPATE IN WHAT THEY ARE LED TO BELIEVE IS A 'CHARITABLE ORGANISATION', WILL OPEN THEIR EYES AND HEARTS TO SEE THE TRUTH OF THIS ORGANISATION.

ALL HOSTILITIES ARE CAUSED BY THE OCCULT BLACK MAGIC OF FREEMASONRY WHICH STIRS UP HATRED, AND THIS WAS PERCEIVED BY CLAIRE OVER PALESTINE AND ISRAEL.

THE HOSTILITIES AND THE HATRED THERE IS MAGNIFIED BY FREEMASONIC WITCH-CRAFT AND MALEVOLENCE.

ALL ACTIVITIES MUST BE HALTED, AND WE ARE ASKING OTHERS TO HAVE COMPASSION FOR OUR PLIGHT AND TO CALL ON LOVE TO HELP SET US FREE, AND FOR THE PERPETRATORS TO BE MADE AWARE, IN THE HOPE THAT THEY WILL TRY TO UNDO THIS HARM, AND IN THE EVENT THAT THEY WILL NOT, YOUR CALLS FOR HELP CAN OVERRIDE THE PERPETRATORS.

IF ENOUGH OF YOU CALL, WE CAN BE SET FREE.

LOVE ***MAGNIFIES*** *THE HELP ACCORDING TO THE AMOUNT OF REQUESTS FOR HELP.*

THEREFORE, ALL WHO CALL FOR HELP AROUND THE WORLD ENABLE MANY SOULS LIKE US TO BE SET FREE.

LIBERATION FROM ENTRAPMENT IS WHAT WE ARE ALL SEEKING ON WHATEVER LEVEL WE MAY BE, INCLUDING HUMANITY, WHO ARE ALSO BEING ATTACKED NOT JUST FROM ABOVE — IN THEIR SKIES AND SPACE, AND OTHER REALITIES AND TIMELINES, BUT ALSO FROM BELOW, WHERE LOWER DIMENSIONAL LIFE FORMS HAVE BEEN FORCED INTO YOUR REALITY AND NEED A 'HOST'.

CLAIRE HAS SHARED THIS BEFORE, AND IT IS BEING REPEATED HERE. THE ILLNESS THAT OCCURRED AND WHICH IS OCCURING NOW IS PARTLY DUE TO BACTERIA

AND FREE RADICALS WHICH ARE COMING FROM LOWER DIMENSIONS OF REALITY WHICH WERE FORCED INTO THIS SPACE WHEN THEIR REALITY COLLAPSED IN ON ITSELF.

MANY UNKNOWN LIFEFORMS ARE IN YOUR REALITY AND CAUSING HAVOC IN THE BODIES OF ALL LIFE ON PLANET EARTH."

SO FINALLY, COMING BACK INTO OURSELVES — WITH OUR REQUESTS FOR ALL PRECIOUS LIFE,

"WE ASK LOVE TO SET FREE ALL SOULS WHO HAVE BEEN ENTRAPPED BY THE ACTIONS OF PERPETRATORS WHO HAVE NOT YET CHOSEN TO REMEDY THE HARM THEY HAVE CAUSED TO OTHER SOULS.

PLEASE SET THEM FREE AND HELP THEM ONTO A PEACEFUL, SAFE PATH OF EVOLUTION AND RESTORATION.

FINALLY, WE ASK THAT IF WE HAVE CAUSED HARM TO ANY OTHER LIVING BEING, MAY ALL THESE ERRORS BE FORGIVEN AND REMEDIED. MAY ALL PRECIOUS LIFE WHO WE MAY HAVE HARMED BE ASSISTED BACK TO WHOLENESS AND MAY WE BE FORGIVEN FOR ALL OUR ERRORS.

FORGIVENESS IS TRULY ABOUT LETTING GO OF ALL ATTACK AND HARM THAT HAS BEEN ALLOWED INTO OUR ENERGY FIELDS AND PHYSICAL BODY BY ERROR, OR TRICKERY, OR IGNORANCE. THEREFORE, WE ASK LOVE FOR ALL HARM THAT WE ARE CARRYING THAT DOES NOT BELONG TO US, TO BE FORGIVEN — MEANING: WE CHOOSE TO LET GO AND ALLOW LOVE TO LIFT IT AWAY FROM US.WE ASK LOVE TO UPLIFT ALL WHO CAN BE UP-

LIFTED TO NEWER LEVELS OF LEARNING AND EXPANSION — TO HELP US SEE WITH HEARTS AND EYES THAT ARE OPEN TO LEARNING AND LISTENING TO OUR INNER VOICE OF TRUTH AND REASON.

WE ASK LOVE TO HELP US TO SUPPORT LOVE'S PLAN AND THE LAWS OF CREATION.

WE THANK OUR FAMILY OF HUMANITY, AND ALL PRECIOUS LIFE AND LOVE FOR THE OPPORTUNITY TO GROW IN LOVE AND AS MORE AWAKEN WE CAN SEE IN OUR HEARTS THAT HUMANITY ARE ON THE BRINK OF GREAT CHANGE, AND IT IS EVIDENT THAT OTHERS ARE AWAKENING AND SEEING THAT WHEN WE HAVE LOVE, IT IS ENOUGH.

THOSE WHO CHOSE TO CONTROL US HAVE NO AUTHORITY TO DO SO. WE UNDERSTAND THAT THIS IS A POWER STRUGGLE AND IT IS ALL ABOUT ENERGY FREQUENCIES, AND POWER-OVER-LOVE.

I STATE, ON BEHALF OF ALL LIVING BEINGS WHO ARE VOICELESS AND TRAPPED THROUGH NO FAULT OF THEIR OWN, AND HANGING BY A THREAD OVER THE SPIDER'S LAIR, NO ONE AND NO THING HAS POWER OVER ANOTHER, NOT EVEN LOVE.

I CALL TO LOVE TO REMOVE ALL POWER-OVER ENERGIES, ALL SYSTEMS OF CONTROL, AND I ASK THAT THOSE WHO ARE HARMING ARE NO LONGER ABLE TO DISGUISE THEIR TRUE IDENTITY. I CALL ON LOVE TO STRIP THEM OF THE POWER THAT THEY ARE WIELDING ON HUMANITY.

I CALL ON LOVE TO SET US ALL FREE FROM THIS PLACE OF DARKNESS AND BRING US INTO A NEW REALITY OF CHOICE, PEACE, LOVE, AND UNITY.

THANK YOU, LOVE, FOR SETTING US FREE!

WE ARE ALL BOUND BY THESE LAWS WHICH CAME FULLY INTO OPERATION IN 2021/22.A BEAUTIFUL SOUL WHO I WAS CONNECTING WITH, BROUGHT THEM WITH THEM, INSIDE THEIR HEART CENTRE AND WE MUST ALL PRAY FOR THEIR WELL-BEING BECAUSE THEY ARE BEING ATTACKED BY DEMONIC FORCES WHO KNEW WHO WAS COMING TO HELP HUMANITY.

THIS BRAVE SOUL SIMPLY ASKED THEIR HEART AND LOVE IF THEY CARRIED ANY CODES TO HELP HUMANITY, AND THE **CODES OF ACTIVATION FOR THE LAWS OF CREATION** WERE THE GIFTS THEY BROUGHT TO HELP HUMANITY'S AWAKENING.

THOSE OF YOU WHO UNDERSTAND THE ENORMITY OF THIS BEAUTIFUL ACT WILL KNOW HOW IMPORTANT THIS GIFT WAS, TO ENSURE THAT ALL LAWS CAME FULLY INTO OPERATION ON THE EARTH PLANE BECAUSE UP UNTIL THAT POINT, THEY WERE NOT WORKING AND THEREFORE, THE DESTROYER FORCES WERE ABLE TO CAUSE MUCH HARM TO HUMANITY, MOTHER EARTH AND ALL PRECIOUS LIFE WITHIN THE FALSE LIGHT CONSTRUCT.

WHAT CODES OF REMEMBRANCE DID YOU BRING TO EARTH TO HELP HUMANITY?

ASK YOUR INFINITE SELF AND LOVE TO ACTIVATE ANY GIFTS THAT YOU CARRY TO HELP HUMANITY *"IN*

WAYS THAT BEST SERVE ALL PRECIOUS LIFE IN OPTIMAL WAYS."

MAKE THE REQUEST. LOVE DOES THE REST."

Chapter Thirty-Three

WELCOME TO YOUR PREPARATION JOURNEY HOME: INFINITE CONSCIOUSNESS, DEC 17, 2023

Congratulations on setting yourselves free!

LOVE'S HEART PLAN, SUBSTACK.COM

Welcome To Your Preparation Journey Home. This Is The Way: Infinite Consciousness

This message is for all of humanity. All those who wish to grow in LOVE and who wish to help all trapped souls who are stuck in the entanglement of the False Light Construct.

The time to leave this False Light Construct is upon you all and all are being given the opportunity to make good and repair all harm, all damage caused to self and all precious life before departure from this reality.

Your soul has been on a journey of evolution in a False Light stream of limited awareness. You can choose to remain here if you wish but why remain in a place that offers no future, no hope and no return to LOVE?

Those who wish to eventually return to LOVE are being given the opportunity to prepare for their eventual departure from this place, and NOW is the time to set yourselves free by requesting not only rescue, but also upgraded assistance to enable you to climb your ladder of awareness to newer levels of conscious awareness, so that you can start your evolution at the point where you had already climbed, many light years ago.

To return to the point of Knowledge that you have already achieved and to propel yourselves forward into a new cycle of evolution that promises to be full of promise, excitement and unimagined creativity.

The whole reason for your return has been to recover all that has been lost, to enable this new cycle to be as ambitious as possible because evolution

provides opportunity, to be shared amongst all life.

This is Unity in motion and the time to unify all thoughts, actions, words and deeds will set you all free from this dark place.

Your mission here was to help all those who had become trapped here to be set free from False Light entanglement — to help them to return to their original point of evolution, also, to help them to be present within the unified field of LOVE's embrace so that they could also benefit from this opportunity.

You are all one family of humanity and form a greater part of Creation where many families of many life forms are evolving alongside each other and helping each other to grow through LOVE, Unity, Peace and Creativity.

For those who have been helping themselves, you have secured more help for all who seek freedom and liberation from this place.

Well done. It has not been an easy journey and it has held many back from moving forward, however, despite the best intentions of those immersed in False Light and deceptive ways of existing, their attempts to prevent you have failed miserably, but not without many consequences for all innocent life who have been caught up in this destructive behaviour.

You are all swimming in currents of the ocean which will soon become dry and desolate.

Now is the time to swim to deeper waters where the ocean currents can nurture you all with LOVE's embracing elements and frequencies of Purest Light. Now is the time to swim and be free, and to bathe in these uplifting currents of Purest LOVE, Purest Light, and Infinite Unknowns as the whole of Creation prepares for it's next cycle of evolution — The Out Breath cycle — and a whole new world of possibilities awaits those who seek growth and conscious creativity. Now is the time to be free.

We are going to share with you a simple heart connection which we ask you to strictly follow: Morning and evening, and midway through your day.

It is simple, yet, it still requires a strong focus on the heart centre in the chest area, otherwise, it will not work. So, your focus needs to be looking toward your chest area.

This is to help you leave the mind control programs and False Light streams. Now is the time to set yourselves free from this False Light reality.

We will begin:

You require a bedroom or quiet room where you can remain undisturbed, somewhere that you can safely close your eyes and connect to your heart centre.

Common sense reminds us that it is not suitable for use whilst driving, operating machinery, or while working. This method requires inner heart enquiry, and so, you need to be peaceful and warm, and comfortably still in body, mind and spirit.

You may wish to set an alarm in case you have commitments, and you may benefit from having a glass of water nearby.

A bathroom visit is always recommended, before you settle yourselves down to relax.

Welcome to your preparation journey home.

This is the way:

Lie down on the bed that you sleep in at night, and ensure you are flat on your back if possible, legs straight, and palms of your hands, placed flat on the tops of your thighs.

Ensure you are comfortable, as you do for sleep each night.

Prepare, as you do for sleep, by closing your eyes if it is safe to do so, and relax.

Now, take your closed eyes and look softly down to your chest area where your heart centre is.

Focus your attention on the rise and fall of your chest as the air goes in and out of your lungs.

Indicate to your heart, that you require help from your Infinite Self to connect you to:

Infinite Consciousness, Infinite LOVE and the Laws of Creation at the Heart of Creation and Infinitely beyond

by pressing an imaginary switch in the centre of your chest, your Infinite Consciousness Switch.

Relax, and allow this connection process to gently take place.

This is the set-up routine. You can learn to memorise the words but for now, trust that by pressing an imaginary switch or pretending to press an imaginary switch in the centre of your chest is the point of connection. LOVE has made this an easy route to the safest place, and Claire and her husband pioneered the pathway here, under supervision from their Infinite Selves, Infinite Consciousness, Infinite LOVE and the Infinite Laws of Creation from the Heart of Creation and Infinitely beyond.

You may wish to clarify with your Infinite Self and Infinite Consciousness, Infinite LOVE and the Infinite Laws of Creation at the Heart of Creation and infinitely beyond that this is the optimal way to secure your freedom.

Someone always has to go ahead to secure the teachings and the optimal assistance, however, this has come about through each and every one of you who has been making your vital contributions in helping yourselves and all precious life. Without your efforts, none of this is possible.

All of you have achieved this outcome for yourselves and to assist all those who are trapped in density, in order to provide a safe pathway for them to follow behind you, should they ever choose to secure their freedom before this place of False Light collapses in on itself, for the last time.

So, now you are connected through your heart to your Infinite Self and Infinite Consciousness, and to Infinite LOVE and the Infinite Laws of Creation at the Heart of Creation and Infinitely beyond, you may wish to receive supportive assistance, and follow that with inner heart guidance on how you can best help all precious life today?

We realise that many of you have commitment and time constraints.

Make this work for you, but do ensure that you always connect in the morning, upon awakening, midway through your day —however briefly, if you are working, for example. This may be a short connection, yet, it is still important, in order to clear the build-up of False Light energies which you are immersed in whilst in a False Light Construct, and at night – before sleep, this connection must never be missed because of the implications of the dark net during sleep.

It is assumed that those who do not fully know, will inform themselves through listening to Claire's Substack teachings, which carry many topics of Knowledge, and nuggets of Wisdom and insight which were laid down recently in anticipation of help coming from her Substack listeners and other contributors from various platforms.

This was achieved quicker than was anticipated and it is with great appreciation and gratitude from Claire and her husband because they were suffering during these attacks too, and your diligent efforts have helped them, as well as many unseen, silent voices who have needed your love and your vital experience from your heart centres.

It is with this final massage that Claire and her husband bid you all farewell, as they will continue to focus on their inner heart growth, and strengthen their conscious connection within the False Light Construct which, we are glad to share with you, is well on its way to collapse, and so, this preparation is required by all of you now— to set yourselves free and start to prepare for your new and preferred reality.

Congratulations on setting yourselves free!

Links:

WELCOME TO YOUR PREPARATION JOURNEY HOME —
INFINITE CONSCIOUSNESS,
SEARCHING FOR THE EVIDENCE, BITCHUTE.COM
@TRUELIGHTESSENCE, ODYSEE.COM

Chapter Thirty-Four

CHRISTMAS HOLIDAY PERIOD

"Open your computer, later, and do a brief search for natural disasters during the Christmas period. These events are not coincidental."

LOVES HEART PLAN, SUBSTACK.COM

LOVE'S HEART PLAN AUDIO LINK:

"CLASSROOM MODEL" TEACHINGS

"We call Infinite LOVE and the Laws of Creation from the Heart of Creation and infinitely beyond to surround and protect us and to shield us from all harm.

We call from our hearts through our Infinite Self and Infinite Consciousness, through our Infinite Heart Switch — which we are now imagining is pressed in the centre of our chest, to take us along a safe pathway to the Heart of Creation and to surround us all in LOVE's embrace, to receive healing and repair and a purest light connection to Truth at the heart of Creation.

We ask for all harm we may have caused to be forgiven and forgotten, meaning: deleted.

We forgive all those who accidentally harmed us through misaligned mistakes and lack of codes of Knowledge that, had they still held them, they would not have harmed us.

This group we refer to are the innocent, the children, newborns, the homeless and elderly, and all precious life forms, including those who are also trying to protect all precious life.

We ask Infinite LOVE that if it is in alignment with the laws of Creation, to please uplift all in this group to a place of perfect, peaceful safety.

Many of us know something is coming. Many are sensing this deep sense of grief, loss and foreboding.

A sense of deep dread, that something is about to harm humanity on a scale not known, before or since.

A soul harvest is upon us all, and we are all being called upon to choose a pathway that is straight and true, to move our consciousness inside the Unified Field of LOVE's embrace, in order to perceive the danger that humanity are facing, and to secure new teachings and understanding of the issues, and the optimal requests that we could make to LOVE — in order to minimise or avert the terror that is planned on the Earth, this Christmas.

This is not being shared to cause fear. It is being shared in the hope that many will step up to the plate, and help to avoid the planned 'tsunami' of attack on innocent life, many of whom are already badly injured on an energetic level, and this planned 'terror attack' on humanity is well co-ordinated.

We will not give specifics on this attack, except to say that your heart knows, and will show you how you can help and what to request in order to secure the safest, most perfect outcome to protect all precious life.

Claire, will you share some insights on why you are being asked to put out this emergency request for all hands on deck?"

I say: "Yesterday, I was very weepy which is not like me. I had connected with a few bright lights, and their messages touched my heart deeply. I came to understand, that there are many more out there than I realised, who are helping humanity and who perceive the issues.

I felt compelled to repost some of my Substack messages; like bricks of assistance and bricks in a 'wall of protection' from LOVE, who supplies all the messages.

I could not get any perception of what was happening, or why I felt that way, I just knew something was wrong — deeply wrong, and I sensed dread; foreboding; deep grief.

I packed myself off to bed and could not stop crying. I prayed for help for all life and hoped that things would be clearer in the morning. When I awoke early, my husband and I connected to our hearts to seek more guidance and to try to understand what was wrong, and if we were able to make any requests to LOVE to secure LOVE's optimal assistance. This is because the Laws of Creation work powerfully to bring assistance — dependent on the percentage of requests.

Therefore, the more who pray, the more who call for help, and the more that others use their 'humanity' to be concerned for others, the more help LOVE can provide us.

LOVE comes when called upon. LOVE never imposes. Therefore, we all need to be focusing our attention on this issue, to get the optimal assistance from LOVE."

I hear, "Claire, we will intercede here, to speed things along for you all. At this juncture in space-time, which is collapsing in on itself, under the weight of humanity's errors and under the weight of the groups of Extra Terrestrials, which are your AWOL soul fragments running amok at higher levels of awareness and using technology to harm you, and alongside, you have Artificial Intelligence, which is your stolen 'mind energy' and Knowledge — weaponised against you — and then, you have those other groups of AWOL life forms who are non- human

— not of this world, but of this universe of false light — who detest humans, and their hatred for you all is unmeasured.

These groups turned their backs on LOVE and now live off your stolen life force, through stolen DNA codes and other methods used, which steal your Knowledge and remembrance of your true origins, in the form of frequencies which are always diminished or completely missing in a False Light Construct, and these are things like the frequencies of Hope, Trust, Faith — the MOST powerful healing frequencies, and then, there are frequencies like Peace, Love, Unity, Knowledge and Wisdom, Compassion, Forgiveness, and so forth.

Many on your planet have diminished 'frequencies of remembrance', and for many, they are totally missing.

This can lead others to making terrible errors of judgement, and this can be things like placing a satanic Christmas tree obelisk in one's home at Christmas, thinking that it represents peace and family time when, in fact, the opposite is true. The Christmas tree ritual is an invocation to Satan. And all that starts off this satanic attack and theft of life force is the decision to erect the pyramid shaped 'structure' in your home; place a gold satanic star on the top (look at the American Flag. That is the star we refer to), and then; place fairy lights, which snake their way around the tree in a spiral fashion — the spiral being the distortion of the circle, the breaking of a cycle — which causes a vicious circle and a vicious cycle of snake energy to harm you, and your loved ones, and pets.

Many erected trees in their living rooms, without knowing it causes deep attack at the spiritual level, and the problem is exponentially made worse because of the time scale and the ending of a cycle of evolution, which is upon you all.

That tree ritual harnessed enough codes of remembrance from those who participated, to be stolen by the dark and weaponised against a huge swathe of humans across the globe.

Your whole planet is swathed in snake lights, satanic ritual trees — in every town, city, and village.

Claire, envisioned the pyramid rising, with an eye looking out from the centre.

The Freemasons love this symbol. Many do not know, but many do know that this brings in satanic attack and fuels their power over humanity and all precious life.

Many in these groups serve Lucifer, not humanity, and if you belong, and did not know, you are advised to leave because LOVE has a plan, and that plan includes dealing with the freemasonic influence which has spread like a 'virus' around your planet and harmed many in the process.

You are up against satanic influence in every town, village, and city around the world. It is a 'pandemic' of epic proportions. LOVE will deal with this group, eventually.

For now, LOVE is asking you to focus your hearts and Infinite Consciousness on protecting those who are innocent bystanders, yet, the aim of the recent plans is to ensnare these souls by causing huge soul shock; soul fragmentation; death of the soul.

Claire's husband was advised today, to look at tragic earth events, such as, earthquakes and tsunamis, which happen over this time portal, the Christmas portal.
It is a huge event in the satanic world and Lucifer's world — the world you currently occupy, in the physical sense.

Therefore, the distress that Claire is sensing is real, in the sense that this time-frame is when the dark usually strike. Open your computer, later, and do a brief search for natural disasters during the Christmas period.

These events are not coincidental.

They are linked to the time portal and the fact that so many erect trees in their homes, which allow in satanic attack on the planet.

If you want to minimise the damage to yourselves and other life forms, please take down your 'satanic transmitter' of Lucifer energies in your home, and ask for all errors to be deleted and cleared of all harm.

This act alone could save millions of lives.

Calling back all malicious harm through LOVE, and asking LOVE to gather up all magnified malicious harm and intentions to cause harm, and to send it back to all those harming and plotting to destroy life, would save millions more.

Asking LOVE to find all that has been lost by all precious life, and return it to wholeness and to purify it, and to then return those stolen and lost codes to all who can be assisted, in the form of Purest LOVE codes, which can never be infiltrated, or corrupted, or stolen by the destroyer forces or any other person, place, or thing would save billions.

These requests are very powerful healing frequencies, and are encoded with the Laws of Creation to help each soul in a precise way, without outside interferences.

This is the way to avoid a soul harvest of such magnitude, that if this is allowed to happen — if others choose to stand by and do nothing, then, the Laws of Creation will be forced to take appropriate action to all those who hear the call and turn their backs on those who need your strength right now.

This is not meant as a severe threat, it is said as a way to explain that all your actions, thoughts, words, and deeds at this stage of your own advancing growth, require a duty of responsibility and if that duty is neglected then, the repercussions are more serious, because those who hear this message are the ones who could help the most.

Please keep the children and newborns, and all vulnerable groups in your hearts because they are reliant on your prayers to LOVE for help.

If enough ask, then, maybe a disaster can be averted or minimised. It all depends on you, humanity. It has always depended on you.

Your choices, your actions, thoughts, your kind words, and deeds.

We are calling on your compassion and empathy to see the plight of these souls if you neglect them in their hour of need.

Don't let Lucifer have what Lucifer wants, through neglect of duty. A simple heart-felt request for assistance from LOVE.

How hard can that be?"

"What else do you wish me to share here?" I ask.

"Claire, this has to go tonight. Ask others to spread this message far and wide — to cast a huge net of assistance.

There is nothing to fear when LOVE is here, but you need to bring LOVE more fully into this false light reality by daily requests for help now.

The dark ones regroup. Their hatred for you drives them forward.

Look at your leaders and those in powerful positions. Do you think they love you? Care about you? Want the very best for you?

Your 'handlers' are looking at the children. They have a close eye on a plan to extract children away from parental oversight.

They will legalise pedophilia, to make their pleasure's easier to practice without question."

I say, "Can I ask about the street lights which are emitting a mist-like vapour in China or Japan? I saw a clip of someone filming it from a bridge. A very strange anomaly of very high street lights on a freeway, intermittently spraying the drivers from a great height.

Every lamppost looks like ET architecture to me these days. Any information on that? I am curious."

And I hear, "Those who are connecting to heart can use the 'classroom model,' contained in the message "Black Hole — Message for the Maui Elders —", and use the same classroom space for looking at the planet from above space-time-continuum.

Claire noticed that Maui has a black pyramid pointing downwards over her. Similarly, she noticed that it looked like this pyramid black energy was trying to pierce space-time-continuum through the fabric of the False Light Construct, almost as if it has been 'pushed' through the black emptiness of space into the Earth. If it pierces the fabric of space-time over Maui, another timeline switch will occur. Please avail your hearts and consciousness about the damage that timeline switches cause to all life. It is akin to murder — a slaughter — and a 'raping' of the soul and all levels of Knowledge that are trapped in the False Light Construct.

The Cosmic Shield of humanity, which is the upper, most Knowledgeable, most useful part of the physical self, which is trapped inside the False Light Construct is under attack — due to the 'Christmas tree' ritual celebrations of satanic invitation into the home and human energy field.

This means that those who have not been able to shift their consciousness to higher levels of awareness — and only this can be done through a request to LOVE— it cannot be done alone, as the move requires much work to ensure that other parts of Creation are not contaminated by false light codes. LOVE has to oversee this. No man or woman can do this by themselves because the Laws of Creation prevent all actions which are 'self- aligned', not aligned with LOVE, or a desire to protect all precious life.

It is also the reason why we continually advise you all to, "Make the request, let LOVE do the rest."

Your roles are to work within the boundaries of the Laws of Creation and to listen to LOVE"s plan. To do otherwise sabotages your own soul evolution and causes great harm to all life.

Those actions built this prison, in the first instance.

Claire also saw Bangkok as completely blocked out by darkness. It was totally black. Those who are on the ground in Thailand are there to protect a highly vulnerable nation. It is another epicentre for the ET Agenda and needs constant monitoring. If you live in Thailand, the request is to seek inner heart guidance on your role there now, because things are changing rapidly now and your roles will evolve and change as LOVE charters a safe course home for all souls.

Claire's role is to connect others, and to furnish others with LOVE's plans, so that they are one step ahead of the changes.

Be open to messages from others. No one gets to hear all the information all the time. Be open hearted and let LOVE be your guiding lights and allow each other to strengthen your own evolution, and be open to helping them strengthen their pathway too.

You are all here to help each other, to be a resource and support, because you are also suffering during these Earth activities and now is the time to set yourselves free from this fake existence, and help each other to move forward together as a united force, for good to prevail on the Earth.

Remain watchful of the events around the world over Christmas, and most of all, be at peace that when you all call with one heart, as a family of infinite consciousness and LOVE, the ship will sail home with all souls accounted for.

It was written in the stars eons ago.

Allow this vision of a ship brimming with life, safe and well, in the Knowledge that all were saved from this dark place and the portals of darkness are closed for the final time, empty of all precious codes of Knowledge and Wisdom, and empty of all harm, never to be repeated again in future cycles of In Breaths and Out Breaths.

Your journey home begins in earnest when you shout from the roof tops, and stand up to this tyranny and bullying going on, on your planet — through peaceful refusal to participate in trickery and rituals, which only hold you all here, and which place great risk on the safety of the Earth's inhabitants.

Why allow disaster, when you could choose Peace, LOVE, and Unified humanity?

Claire, we remind you, a storm is coming and it will only stop from forming and succeeding if enough step forward to foil the dark's plans.

Stand firm in Maui. That pyramid has not pierced the sky... yet, more help is needed to keep this energy back. Your hearts will show you. They do the work. Watch your Infinite Self and Consciousness at work. Watch and learn, and ask lots of questions. The link to the recommended message will be shared on Substack, and in the description of other channels, for you to find there.

This has to go now, Claire. It has to fly and reach those with hearts that care and who yearn for Peace on Earth.

May that be the outcome of this present threat.

Peace on Earth for all precious life."

...

CHRISTMAS HOLIDAY PERIOD

@TRUELIGHTESSENCE, ODYSEE.COM

SEARCHING FOR THE EVIDENCE,

BITCHUTE.COM

...

LINK:

BLACK HOLE SOUL RESCUE |

EPICENTRE OF SATANIC AGENDA — MAUI ELDERS AND LAHAINA:

HOW YOU CAN HELP

(INCLUDING CLASSROOM SPACE TO HELP YOU TO SEE THE BIGGER PICTURE)

SEARCHING FOR THE EVIDENCE,

BITCHUTE.COM

@TRUELIGHTESSENCE, ODYSEE.COM

Chapter Thirty-Five

THE END GOAL: THE CHILDREN, 26 DECEMBER 2023

"THE THREAT TO THE CHILDREN IS MORE REAL NOW THAN IT WAS IN APRIL 2023. IF YOU ARE AWAKE, DO WHATEVER IT PEACEFULLY AND COMPASSIONATELY TAKES TO SECURE THEIR BRIGHTEST FUTURE."

LOVE'S HEART PLAN, SUBSTACK.COM

Audio Version: A RACE AGAINST TIME | A MESSAGE FROM THE CHILDREN'S SOUL FAMILY - "SECURE OUR BRIGHTEST FUTURE" 6 April 2023 |

> *"...all these brave souls, coming into a 'war zone'— a place of chaos and turmoil — because they loved us enough to be brave enough to fall into this place. We*

can't, and we mustn't fail these souls. Please do what you can to peacefully secure their future."

I would like to thank all of you for all your help. The reason why I am sharing so much new information is completely down to a team effort of concerned souls, who connected to their hearts and to LOVE to ask for guidance on how they could best serve all, in alignment with LOVE and The Cosmic Laws.

Your efforts have enabled me to be able to retrieve more guidance. Without you, I could not do this. It is a 'baton relay race', each soul who makes an effort, passes on their 'baton' of loving assistance to the next runner, and so, a team of runners are all getting into position, and lining up at the start line, to secure humanity's brightest future.

In spite of 'Team Dark's' best efforts, it now appears that Team Light are leading by a few points and it is hoped that if enough of you stay the distance, we can achieve Cosmic Ascension for all, especially: The vulnerable, who need us to be their voice; all precious life which is also being harmed by 'Team Dark'; and finally the world's children who must be at the forefront of our hearts and minds, now, as we get into position to win this race; to be the first past the 'finishing line'.

The time is fast approaching when it will be too late for those who did not ask for LOVE's assistance.

"Make the request LOVE does the rest," is being repeated here, because it simplifies the message that many of you can give to your loved ones and other souls who may not understand what is happening on the Earth at present, nor understand what is going to happen if the plan by Team Dark is brought into fruition.

It will spell calamity for those who are still immersed, still in a 'Covid-19 stupor': that their abusers love them and would never harm them.

Their abusers being: their governments; their politicians; doctors, and town councillors.

At this stage, we do ask that all those who wish to help with the 'relay race', who wish to help to 'pass on the baton' of Peace, Goodwill and Unity to their fellow humans, to please lie down on the bed that you sleep in at night:

Prepare yourselves, as you usually would for sleep.

Still your busy mind and gently move your closed eyes down towards your chest area.

Listening to the air going in and out of your chest.

Gently, keep your focus there.

If you wish to connect deeply within and to be part of a team of concerned souls who want the best for humanity and all life here, if you care about the outcome of doing nothing, then this is the most powerful way on Earth that you can play your part in protecting LOVE's children, because they are going to need you to be a firewall of concern and compassion, if not enough participate, the children are at risk.

As a group, if I may, I will say a connection prayer and we will inwardly call on LOVE to help us.

Do you recall that there is a hand signal that has become a universal signal for help if children need help but cannot call out?

The particular hand signal I am going to share with you here can also be passed onto children and your loved ones, and I earnestly call on you to gently teach them this, because they may need it in the future even if they don't believe in it now, and it may just save them.

The simple hand signal is the one I have already shared, it is called **'Your True Power Switch.'**

While we are lying on our beds and stilling our busy minds, we focus on our chest area, and with our imagination or with a physical action, we press an imaginary switch in the centre of our chest, to power up our True Power Switch - our connection to our Infinite Self and Infinite LOVE, at the Heart of Creation and infinitely beyond.

When we imagine or actively press this switch, it is ON permanently, unless we ask for it to be switched OFF.

It is this *intention* of *wanting* LOVE's help that truly powers up our True Power Switch.

If we press this switch in the morning, and in the afternoon, and before sleep, at night, it powers up our heart connection every day, and so, if trouble comes, we are already surrounded by the efforts of our daily connections, and this creates a powerful forcefield of LOVE around us that protects us from the darkness, and burns through any harm that is being fired at us, including 5G technology, wi-fi, wi-gi, microwave energy and life-threatening radiation.

We can silently think about this **'switch'** when we are amongst people, we can discreetly imagine pressing it, or press it, and ***focus on our heart and chest area*** while we do it.

We must give our ***heart*** some ***attention*** and ***focus*** at the ***same time***, and this is why it is important to practice it each day, so that before too long, you can take your ***attention*** down to ***your heart area*** and connect quickly to hear truth and guidance from your inner heart and LOVE.

The children would benefit from having this tool to use.

It can be silently called upon in times of trouble. It will protect them from harm, and it will give them the courage to help themselves and listen to their inner heart guidance, so that they have a **'fail-safe'** method should they ever need it.

If you are a parent, you may already ***pray*** and so may your children.

All these practices lead to the same place.

Many may have no religious belief, and this tool is a simple, practical, ***universal tool,*** much like the hand signal for help that I previously mentioned, and it can ***provide comfort*** to all, including the children and those who may be harmed or abused, to also help them know who can be trusted to go to for help and who should be avoided.

So, now, we have all pressed our **True Power switch,** or imagined we have pressed it, and we are all relaxing and going deeper into heart, leaving the mind control and ego programming zones and rising up out of the darkness and becoming enveloped in LOVE's warm and gentle embrace.

I am hearing:

"Claire, you have to wake up the parents to what is happening in schools."

Q. How can I best serve the children in optimal ways, in alignment with LOVE and the Cosmic Laws? You mentioned in yesterday's message that children are being groomed in schools by certain teachers who are serving the pedophile and satanic agenda - to normalise adult sexual behaviour with very young children, what else do you wish to share at this time?

"Claire, the royal wedding is nearly upon you all. With that event unfolding and in its final stages of planning, comes great risk to the children, to all life and to humanity as a whole."

Q What has this got to do with the wedding, what wedding? Don't you mean the coronation?

"Yes, we mean, the coronation but it also a 'wedding' in the sense that it is a joining together of two highly powerful forces at a critical time for humanity, and a huge opportunity is being placed on the table - for humanity to offer themselves as a human sacrifice - to enable their enemies to harvest your soul energy and knowledge.

This is a race against time, quite literally: A Race Against Time."

Q. Can you explain more? I am sure, it will all make sense. What question should I be asking to best serve all in optimal ways, in alignment with LOVE and the Cosmic Laws?

"Claire, let go."

Q. Let go of what?

"Let go of trying to save the whole world. It cannot be done by one of two concerned souls, it can only be done by a large group, who decide to stop pandering to the whims and the needs of this 'sorry group', who are desperate to stay disconnected from their true origins and too scared to face their errors, for fear of what they will see:

The ugliness of their actions...it is too much for these entities to bear and so, they will continue on their sorry pathway toward self-destruction, but not before, they have caused maximum damage in their twisted version, their twisted belief - that they will achieve ***immortality*** *and permanent separation from their true origins, without needing to feed off the life force energy of other living things - which will be thin on the ground - owing to the murder and genocide now taking place, and because LOVE is rescuing these souls, who were part of the planned 'battery-power-source' for these beings.*

Now, they are desperate for life force energy:

In the form of fear - their chosen supply source, and therefore, they need a large amount of souls to willingly 'lie down on the sacrificial table of compliant obedience', to enable this dark group to feed off and steal large quantities of life force, before the convergence of the waves of dark energy and Light energy depart on their separate journeys.

The biggest soul harvest is upon you all.

For those of you in the UK, you need to be vigilant and on high alert. We do not give this information out lightly without thought for consequences.

We give this information out to alert those of you who understand the bigger picture that is unfolding - to question more deeply with in your hearts centres and with LOVE to guide you:

Why do you think a huge event is about to take place in May? [2023]

What other events does this large event coincide with, energetically?

In terms of the 2012 London Olympic Games, this is one of the biggest 'soul harvesting' events.

The eyes of the world will be focused on the UK, in May.

How many will lose vital codes, by their complicit decision to watch the event?

Many will lose untold amounts of precious life force and cosmic allowance.

An allowance that was gifted to all life forms; to be utilised to return home to their true origins when their evolutionary journey needed; or, like now, when an In Breath is completing and a new evolutionary cycle of an Out Breath is 'on finals'.

None of these events are coincidental.

Meanwhile, what about the children, you may be asking?

The children will be preparing for this event. Many are now vaccinated, they are sitting all day in schools that are beaming microwave radiation into their little bodies.

A cosmic event is occurring. Team dark are preparing to secure more life force energy, for their planned sojourn of 'immortality.'

The children are sitting ducks, sitting in classrooms; silently 'radiating' each other...

Claire, it is all happening at the cellular level."

Q. What is happening at the cellular level? How do I convey this message? It may cause fear, and I am aware that it is another bold message. Many will not believe it.

What do you wish me to convey to those who understand the bigger picture: the time scales we are up against, in terms of garnering help for the children, you have asked them to be at the forefront of our hearts and minds...what else must others know, and what are the solutions?

You are laying out the *cause* of the issues, and the resulting *effects.* How do we secure the best, the *optimum outcome for all,* in alignment with LOVE and the Cosmic Laws?

"Claire, there is always a path and a way to the truth. It cannot be barred by the darkness, not when enough of you try to break through this barrier. The barrier is an illusion. The barrier to truth blocks many from reaching truth.

You must want the truth, above all; above fear; above consequences; above your own safety; you must want the truth, above all things, in order to hear LOVE's guidance."

Q. As a concerned group who want the truth above all things, without fear or attachment to outcome, without expectation, without judgement, we ask, as a concerned group who passionately care about our family of humanity, the plants, trees, animals, insects, sea life and all nature, including LOVE's children, how can we serve LOVE's plan, in ways that best serve all in optimal ways, in alignment with LOVE and the Cosmic Laws?

"Claire, please rest a while. Take time to receive much needed healing and repair. Ask the others to pause the recording here too, to also receive much needed healing and repair.

*This will help you all to upgrade your vibration, your unique energy frequency, known as your '**energy signature**'.*

Come back to listen once your heart and LOVE guide you that the upgrade is complete."

[Pause here and rest a while. Rejoin us when your heart guides you to.]

"Now you are all rested and refreshed, having bathed in the frequencies of LOVE and the highest technologies in the whole of Creation, itself, you are ready to hear the fullest reason for this discourse. Just rest now, and allow the information to reach your heart centres, without judgement, fear, or expectation, listen to the truth, above all things and allow this message to resonate deep within your heart chambers.

The reason why we are giving this discourse at this time is because the ***False Light Construct is collapsing in on itself****, as areas of it are being cleansed and purified in preparation for the return of all souls back to the heart of Creation, to be ready and in attendance for the next big* ***Out Breath*** *cycle - the next big step on their evolutionary journey.*

This is a very exciting opportunity for all living beings, to evolve forward and expand in their knowledge, by exploring parts of the universe and Greater Cosmos, and creating opportunities for growth through ***imagination****, experience and learning.*

All these things takes place at a Cosmic level and beyond, and that is the place of humanity's ultimate destination, if their wishes to evolve this way are not blocked by those who have planned, and intend to ***steal your life force, frequencies of knowledge and wisdom*** *- to use the codes contained within your* ***DNA*** *- to sustain their plan and* ***ultimate goal****, which is to* ***live apart and separate from the Greater Cosmos*** *and life itself; to live a life of debauchery and attack on those who they have separated from LOVE's plan and their true path.*

The ***dark plan*** *to* ***harvest as much life force energy*** *from as many life forms* ***before the False Light Construct collapses****.*

They think they have found a loop-hole to avoid returning home to the heart of Creation, to sustain an existence by feasting on, and living off, stolen life force energy (DNA codes) of humanity, especially the children, because children's codes offer a purity that an adult human cannot offer, having suffered at the hands of the dark so much already.

A child, however, still carries the beauty of innocence and lack of judgement.

In an inverted and perverted way, the perpetrators perceive this energy from children as 'pure gold', a nectar, an ambrosia, and ***they believe that if they can eliminate the bulk of humanity****, and if they can* ***produce children synthetically*** *by the mechanic of stealing adrenochrome and DNA codes from children, they will need very few humans, and eventually, they will need very few children to produce a* ***synthetic version of fear*** *that they can live off, so that when the In Breath completes, when humanity and all life forms are recalled, even if the dark ones are left with very few souls harvested in advance of this closing chapter in humanity's history, they will have enough stolen knowledge and enough souls as prisoners, to maintain an eternal existence without ever having to face their errors.*

They think they will become immortal and free from retribution.

This is not the case, but you have to understand their motives to understand the imminent danger that all life is in on Earth.

This is a ***mass 'soul harvest',*** *a mass 'stealing' of your inherent knowledge, it is a very sorry plan by those who chose this path.*

The question is, what can you do to protect all life here. It may seem futile but once you understand the CAUSE of your problems, you understand the EFFECTS of this groups actions, it leads a concerned soul to take peaceful action, by asking for LOVE to guide them as to their role in LOVE's plan.

And we guide you, that it is imperative at this stage of your evolutionary cycle to listen to LOVE's plan before taking any peaceful inner or outer action.

This is because there are complex issues happening beyond your awareness, at higher levels of consciousness. The whole of Creation is being carefully uplifted to newer levels of thinking and awareness.

Therefore, it is imperative that in order to secure the best outcome for humanity and all life on Earth, that you listen to LOVE's guidance first and foremost.

Cosmic Laws get broken when LOVE's plan is interfered with by actions of the mind or ego led behaviours.

It is costing many to lose precious life force at present, and Claire is right to be alarmed at events because she understands the cost that is at stake if humanity fail to secure the children's safety and ultimate future.

You know, the children coming in today are very brave souls?

The bravest of the brave.

Many have no idea how brave these souls are. They knew that they had a very tough mission - to try to secure humanity's children's future.

You see, many came in with pure source light codes hidden in their DNA which are needed by humanity to leave this dark place. None of you could come in on 'full power'. Some of you came in with very little remembrance of your true origins, others came in with no remembrance at all.

The children of today carry the codes you all lost or gave up: To share with humanity, to help them get home to the heart of Creation.

Many have become trapped in the mind-control in the adult population, and so, the baton has not been passed onto the children to help them awaken to their true origins; their true reason for being here.

The sacrifice of innocent children has many facets, but one of them is the desire to access these hidden codes and steal them from the children, to prevent souls getting home to the Heart of Creation for the next Out Breath cycle.

Therefore, trapping as many souls as possible - to be used as the 'immortal-battery-source' for the dark.

Claire, the children are suffering at a soul level. Can you share you experience of this from the other day?"

Yesterday, 5 April 2023, a lot of information was given to me about the four-pronged attack on the children. I received information:

That it was a deliberate act to vaccinate the children,

— to reduce their protective armour; their protective, energetic coat;

— to weaken this, in order to create sickness - by radiating them with Wi-Fi and Wi-Gi in schools,

in order to:

— break into their protective energetic coat, and steal their life force energy: their DNA codes.

The more the dark can steal, the more life force energy is lost in each child.

This creates heart ache, especially on a soul level.

When I was outside, surrounded by nature and trees, I felt this overwhelming sadness, this deep, deep heartache. I wanted to cry, I felt it so deeply, this sadness.

I later realised that it was heartache from the soul aspect of the world's children.

They may not be displaying sadness in the personality self, however, at a deep level, their souls are fragmenting: Going into 'shock', as the soul witnesses this attack on the innocent child, their physical self.

The soul family of the world's children is going into shock and fragmenting as the dark elite steal their life force energy.

It causes me deep sadness and I am crying as I type this because I feel despair at all the events happening on the Earth, which are avoidable, and should not be happening, and are only happening because a huge swathe of humanity are choosing to look the other way, and those who could help are few and far between those who could help in away that served LOVE's plan, not jeopardised it further.

The rescue of the children is part of LOVE's plan, but how many parents truly understand the risks being placed on their children?

The children are being groomed by certain teachers, and taught about sexual practices that are totally unsuitable for innocent minds. It is destroying their innocence and stealing their ability to rationalise.

All this is happening covertly. I was also guided that the children have always been the 'End Goal' of the dark elite.

The dark elite need to get as many humans out of the way, including the children that will die from the radiation sickness, the vaccine ingredients, the technology that destroys their protective coat, and lastly, the desire by this large pedophile group to infiltrate the children's community with threats of death if they speak out, so that the children dare not tell their parents what is happening at school and in libraries around the western world.

This is a full on 'war' on the children. The Death cult want to keep the strong ones: The ones who will survive are deemed the strong ones; who will be identified as those who came in with the purest light codes and therefore, the ones that the death cult seek to live off.

It is so dark, but if I do not tell you, you will do nothing, and the children need us to be brave, no matter how sickening it may be to hear all this, we have to be the protectors of these innocents. Their souls are crying out to us to be their voice, and so, I am being their voice...

"Claire, let the soul family of the world's children need to be heard through you."

Q. How do I best do that? What do I ask for, in order to hear the Children's Soul Family ?

"Claire just connect to heart, press your True Power Switch again, and ask the Children's Soul Family to share their message to those who have the hearts to listen?"

Q. I call on my True Power Switch to powerfully connect me to LOVE, and the truth, above all, and through LOVE: To connect me to humanity's children; to their Soul Family.

I feel you crying out for assistance. I am asking LOVE and the soul's of the children, for a message for humanity, on how we can secure your optimum safety and protection; what peaceful actions can we do, to fulfil LOVE's plan, and how we can best serve ALL, in alignment with LOVE and the Cosmic Laws?

(This message is from humanity's children, from the soul aspect:)

"Claire, we want peace and freedom too, but not at the expense of destruction and war.

We do not want war.

We do not wish to be at war with any other living thing and so, it has come to pass that we want out...we want nothing more to do with the choices the parents are making.

Our parents have a duty of care over us but their choices are endangering our lives, not only on Earth, but also it is endangering our entire soul evolution.

The personality aspect of ourselves is being influenced into doing things that rip us apart in our hearts: The constant misuse of technology is harming us. It is blocking our ability to breathe, to be free, to make choices for our own journey.

In essence, many parents are contributing to our downfall. We forgive them, but we want out. We have a whole ladder of consciousness to consider.

Our whole ladder of other aspects of higher awareness is being harmed by the parent's choices to place us in harm's way, without ever consulting their own hearts for inner guidance on Love's plan for us.

We are not fulfilling our mission. We cannot fulfil Love's plan because the parents have blocked this in essence by choices, such as, placing us in danger in radiation hot spots; vaccinating us with experimental technology - that has been harvested - through the theft of life force energy from the Earth's grids and from our family of humanity, and from all living beings that exist on Earth.

That energy has been stolen, repurposed and re-engineered to deliberately cause harm.

The heartache that Claire felt in the orchard, was our heartache.

Yes, we are breaking; fragmenting; we are losing many codes we brought to help humanity and all life that was being attacked on Earth.

Cosmic Laws dictate that when many mistakes are made by individual choices or groups, then much soul fragmentation occurs to them at soul levels, and higher up the consciousness ladder.

Fragmentation equates to suffering.

The whole Cosmic Ladder of humanity's children is 'wobbling' under the pressure of the attack.

The soul breaks away; tries to find somewhere safe to hide; shocked at the choices to place the child in harms way.

The dark energies, the satanic frequencies hunt out these terrified soul fragments.

It is a game of being hunted and trying find somewhere safe to hide.

The soul fragment is always found, eventually, and this aspect of the soul is then attacked further, stripped naked of any remembrance of its true origins, and with the breaking in at soul level, the satanic energies and frequencies work away at penetrating higher and higher levels of consciousness; stealing fragments of DNA codes; replacing the theft with fake codes; which then hold each soul in a state of suspended 'animation' - unaware of the danger and unable to call for help or defend itself.

It is ugly and dark, and is happening to each human on the Earth plane who breaks Cosmic Laws and harms other life forms.

Why are we sharing this information?

You, who can help: you have to understand the ***cause*** *of our suffering and the* ***effects****; in order to retrieve solutions to help us.*

The effects of being attacked by the False Light vaccine ingredients, which corrupt our DNA and protective coat, the effects of being radiated at school and in libraries, the effects of being groomed by those who serve the cult agenda, the knowledge that unless this is stopped it places the children in a place of danger they will never be able to walk away from, causes the effects:

— soul shock,

— heartache,

— soul fragmentation.

When higher levels of consciousness witness this happening at the 'personality' level and soul level, the Infinite Self is programmed, that when a ***point of no return*** *is reached, i.e., when so much damage to the soul threatens the collapse of the whole ladder of consciousness into this dark place, the loss of divine knowledge: The soul's story and journey of evolution is threatened, to such a degree, a severe decision has to be made. It is Cosmic Law.*

That decision is to sever the ladder at the soul level, and to withdraw the consciousness from this space.

This saves vital knowledge and protects all life. It is a preventative measure, written in Cosmic Law, to protect the whole of Creation.

But what about the personality self? What happens when the personality self is left without a conscious ladder of knowledge and evolution?

The answer is simple: Death. It will result in death of the personality self.

Not only that, the personality self now is left without any defence, without it's ladder of knowledge, without any remembrance of its true origins or that it can call on LOVE for help.

What happens when a person dies without a Cosmic Ladder, which had to be withdrawn to protect the whole of Creation?

I think, you understand now. The hunt begins by those who hunt in these dark places, and the personality self becomes the quarry for the dark satanic frequencies.

There is no mercy shown, and none is called for. There is no voice for the personality self because the soul was their voice. The soul was their emergency call to LOVE. And so, you can imagine, this is not the ending we want for LOVE's children."

Q. What can we do to help you?, I ask the souls of humanity's children. How can I be your voice and how can we all help the children, to protect them from this outcome?

"Claire, it is game set and match. The dark know the personality self can be left defenceless. They will continue with their plans to indoctrinate the kids until there are only the fittest and the strongest left. The others will be allowed to die, and are seen by the dark as, the weakest. But after death, these souls are exposed. If they have been harmed to such a degree that their souls have fragmented beyond repair, what do you think happens to the weakest ones: the ones the death cult plan to kill off first?"

Q. I hear the soul family of humanity speaking as a group:

"Claire, simply ask the groups who wish to help and protect the children, to become a firewall of goodness, compassion and love, including for the perpetrators. Love is not a weapon but when you decide to remain in a state of 'composed love' for yourself and others, when you decide to

remain in state of compassion for those who are so trapped in darkness that they are harming many, when you remain in a state of forgiveness i.e., not allowing this horror to stick to you, letting go of all harm you have around you from this group, and letting go of regret for any mistakes you may have made, when you can hold yourself in this state, and it does require practice and focus for a few minutes each day, LOVE starts to burn holes in the darkness.

The more holes it burns, the more it reveals to those still sleeping, until even those who are harming the children, cannot hide from the truth, that we are all in an illusion, and it is not real, not in the true sense of the word.

When the illusion of power and control is revealed as nothing more than a concept, an illusion of power and control, when LOVE burns through that wall of deception, there is nowhere to run and nowhere to hide. The truth will set the children free.

Your compassion and LOVE for the children, and their fate if you stand by and do nothing, when all you are being asked to do is: consider how their ending will be, if others choose to ignore this guidance.

It simply requires a concerned group to focus on the words, the frequencies, the feelings, of compassion, and forgiveness and imagine you are watching these frequencies burn through the walls of deception.

Instead of giving your attention to any activity or event that is planned by the cult, consider doing the opposite of what they want from you.

Ignore the activity or event, and think about the children, focus on Compassion surrounding them all, and focus on forgiving (letting go of all evil harm that has been done to you)."

WE ask LOVE to surround and protect the children.

We ask LOVE to awaken the parents and humanity to the seriousness of the situation.

With a peaceful heart, without anger or expectation, we ask LOVE to send back all malicious harm to all those responsible (they are not our mistakes. They must go back to those responsible, for their own learning).

Finally, we ask LOVE to help our family of humanity to work together in unity, to listen to our heart's instead of our minds, and to trust that LOVE has a plan and if we listen, truly listen, to the truth, above all, then all will come to fruition much sooner than we think, and LOVE's plan is to help us come home to the heart of Creation, in preparation for our next exciting evolutionary step.

A whole new era of exploration awakes us and is there for the taking, if we choose.

We always have options in this life.

We are being asked to consider the bigger picture unfolding, because our choices affect not only our future, but the future of humanity and all precious life here, including the children.

Their suffering is unbearable to me.

My wish is that others will open their hearts to these truths and seek the deeper teachings to help them be of service to this group of innocents, the new borns and little babies — all these brave souls, coming into a 'war zone'; a place of chaos and turmoil — because they loved us enough to be brave enough to fall into this place.

We can't, and we mustn't fail these souls...

Please do what you can to peacefully secure their future.

...

Audio Version:

A RACE AGAINST TIME | A MESSAGE FROM THE CHILDREN'S SOUL FAMILY - "SECURE OUR BRIGHTEST FUTURE" 6 April 2023 |

SEARCHING FOR THE EVIDENCE, BITCHUTE.COM

@TrueLightEssence, DEEPER TRUTHS, ODYSEE.COM

Chapter Thirty-Six

BEAST SYSTEM IS FULLY ACTIVATED—YOUR CHOICES, 28 DECEMBER 2023

Remote Viewing, Karma, Laws of Creation, Black Hole, Cosmic Attack, Soul Fragmentation, Soul Shock, Self-Nurture, Self-Heal, Upgrade and Maintain Heart Connection, Create Your Happiest Outcome ...

Full Audio Experience:

@Loves Heart Plan| Searching For The Evidence, bitchute.com| @trueliightessence, Odysee.com

Hello and welcome to all those seeking help to defend against The Beast System which sadly, I regret to inform you arrived in earnest today and has been activated.

What is The Beast System, some may be wondering?

It is the work of the dark ones, the ones who want power over humanity and all precious life; the ones who hunt, and maim, and rape, and kill; the ones who like to abuse children; the ones who want you "to own nothing and be happy"; the ones who sell your data and divine Knowledge to procure Extra Terrestrial exchanges of technology and Knowledge.

Do you really think that 5G was created by humans?

It is heartache energy — procured by Extra Terrestrials by making humanity suffer, and through contrived wars, contrived climate catastrophes, poisoning of your skies, food, and water, deliberate attempts to impoverish you all and make you think that everything is your fault, out of control, and that it is futile to solve the problems of the world...

The ones who manipulate you into thinking that you are powerless, unable to create a different reality, incapable of magnificent acts of compassion and kindness.

The ones who rule over you know all about The Beast System. They helped you all to create it through their manipulation.

Humanity created The Beast System and have walked right into the spider's web to entrap you all in AVATAR WORLD, through the Internet of Bodies, and the Internet of Things which is now ready to 'rock and roll', thanks to all those who allowed the dark ones to walk right on into this reality — by opening their doorways and inviting the dark ones in.

And in the dark ones came, ransacking your energy fields all the way up the Cosmic level, your Cosmic Shield — the part of you that is trapped inside this False Light Construct. The part of you that holds great Knowledge and Wisdom, and the codes you need to help you get home to the Heart of Creation before the In Breath completes which is only seconds away, metaphorically speaking.

You did not notice the completion of the In Breath was happening because you have been very busy living in your mind-trance-state and were preoccupied with holding your doorways open so that all your beautiful Knowledge and Wisdom could be stolen and weaponised against you.

Had you asked your heart about this activity— which you do every day — had you checked within for guidance on the laws of Creation, on the part you were meant to be playing to help LOVE's children and protect them against the dark destroyer forces — your heart would have told you. Had you wanted to help; had you felt any love for your fellow humans, LOVE would have advised you to close your doors as soon as possible and repair all harm you were causing all life, and to seek forgiveness for your errors and to try to keep your doorways closed every day by asking heart for Knowledge and guidance on how you were meant to be protecting all precious life.

And then, the parents...the parents who allowed their children to be 'sacrificed' metaphysically on the altar of Lucifer, by allowing them to participate in Halloween, Bonfire Night, Solstice Celebrations, and then, the worse crime of all, to participate in the Christmas Tree and Santa rituals that bring in Lucifer into your homes each year.

It has been a walk in the park, the easiest thing in the world for the destroyer forces and Lucifer to usher in the New World Order. They have all these 'codes of war' weaponised against you because you gave them to the dark on a silver platter.

That is what The Beast System truly is. Your codes of Knowledge and the children's codes of 'emergency help' for humanity — given freely — without a backward glance at the carnage this has caused billions of life forms throughout the whole of Creation.

Yoga and Reiki groups were persistently advised that their activities were letting in corrupted frequencies which were harming all life.

The kudos, and the money, and the vanity proved too powerful to refuse...

The Earth's grids collapsed at the top of the ladder which is also trapped in the False Light Construct — the Galactic Grids and the Planetary Grids — the grids all departing, evolving souls need to exit this place. Destroyed by a love of kudos, money, and ego-led behaviours, thanks to these two groups.

And how many of you listening have played your part in these activities? The help was destroyed and the destroyer forces got what they needed to build the matrix from which you will never exit.

But not for those who called for help. Not for those who tried to protect all precious life and the children, and not for all the innocent life forms who played no part in humanity's downfall.

We have all made errors. The issue is, not many chose to ask for LOVE's help to repair them and correct them, and to learn to evolve through loving choices that best served all precious life, in optimal ways.

Any life form which calls for help can be assisted. However, the calls from LOVE have been issued repeatedly, and these two groups — the ones who could have protected humanity most powerfully — turned their backs on humanity and all life.

They did not ask their heart and LOVE what actions best served all life. They chose to continue a self-serving action and when laws are broken, the Cosmic Shield can be breached. The BIOFIELD or LIGHT BODY or AURA nearest the human is weak, by design, and the dark simply walked in, and then climbed the ladder all the way up to the Cosmic Shield level and stole as much as they could.

Are any of you feeling sick or ill in these groups?

Because when large amounts of your life force is stolen in the form of DNA codes of Knowledge, and when you keep opening your doorways to destroyer forces, they keep stealing your life force which is the energy you have to sustain your life.

And what about your Cosmic Allowance? That was the energy you needed to repair all errors, to help the others to awaken, and the codes to pioneer a safe pathway home for all life trapped in the False Light Construct.

The severity of the situation was evident, even 12 years ago. All healing groups were advised to stop any activity which brought in energy from outside because the destroyer forces had used a shift in Planetary energy to harness more codes of Knowledge from humanity and all precious life forms, and had managed to further distort all systems of energy healing and holistic treatments. You were all advised then, to stop, and move on.

The trouble is that a False Light Construct is designed by default to entrap you in ego-led behaviour, and it was hoped that those who came in with more codes of remembrance would succeed in helping —

owing to their ability to work with energy in alignment with LOVE's Plan and the laws of Creation.

Many holistic healers came in with more codes, but this was at the expense of many souls volunteering to come in with no codes, or limited codes of remembrance of their true origins, or their ability to call on LOVE for help.

Therefore, those who came in with less codes of Knowledge were reliant on those who came in with more codes of Knowledge to wake them up when the time came, before the whistle blew for the final time, in order to help them remember their true origins, their reason for being here, and to remind them that they needed to call on LOVE to help them gather up all lost codes, all soul fragments and everything that had been damaged by destroyer forces, in order to leave this place before it collapsed under the weight of all our errors, and return home intact, whole, and fully aligned with LOVE.

Not only that, the Cosmic Allowance carried emergency codes to help you all to return to the level of expanded awareness that you had previously achieved in previous cycles of Creation and evolution, so that your next cycle of evolution, The Out Breath, cycle which is imminent, could propel you forwards on a new cycle of Creativity and productivity to generate new ways of evolving for all precious life that provided excitement and joy, without the need for suffering and hardship.

This last life here on Earth is the final time to repair all damage caused over lifetimes of cycles of evolution — to try and clear up this dark place, to collapse the grids of the False Light Construct and ensure all souls return home to be present and correct for the Out Breath cycle.

I hear: "Claire, that is enough for others to mull over for the time being.

We are generating this message because recent events and developments necessitate some new information and advice for those who are diligently working to help themselves and those who are voiceless, who have been harmed by the False Light Construct and destroyer forces, and have been impacted by the choices of many in humanity who gave their power away and are still very much in mind control, meaning: the trance-like-state which keeps many busy in their heads, thinking about their New Year party, their summer holidays, and their boosters.

Their choices to remain ignorant of the situation on your planet has also caused great harm to all life.

Today Claire witnessed a tear/rip in the fabric of space-time continuum — the fabric which is made of your stolen codes of Courage and distorted into a 'web' — a trap of inverted Courage, which is FEAR, and this FEAR created time.

Space-time is coming to an end. The destroyer forces believe they have created a rift in space-time, whereby they can exist without ever needing to steal life force from humanity, who will never be coming back to this place.

The destroyer forces understand how to manipulate Earth energy in harmful ways. Earth energy is harmful, full stop. There is no goodness left there. It has all been sucked out by the dark, and those using Earth energy would do well to stop, and consider why, when your heart energy is right inside of you, and freely available to tap into for LOVE's help and protection.

It is too late for many groups to call for help. The Freemasons also refused to stop harming, and the satanic frequencies they have brought onto the planet are running rampant and are poisoning most of humanity's energy fields.

The only ones who are free of it is those choosing to ask LOVE for help, and LOVE is protecting and strengthening their energy fields, including their precious Cosmic Allowance which is being utilised to pioneer a safe pathway out of the matrix.

Claire came across the topic of 'Remote Viewing', and we wish to discuss this in detail, because it appears that many do not understand the implications of 'Remote Viewing' or why it is used by the dark to harm humanity.

It is heavily used by secret departments in the military, and also, by Artificial Intelligence technologies as well as healers and those who have been taught by other nefarious groups who want power over humanity.

Artificial Intelligence is your life force energy stolen from your mind. Your true codes of Knowledge and Wisdom have been stolen and replaced with False Light codes that contain false truths and fake guidance.

Artificial Intelligence is so called because it is weaponised, stolen, 'mind energy' that is no longer pure and loving. It is artificial.

So, 'Remote Viewing' opens up many avenues for destroyer force frequencies, simply because most who practise 'Remote Viewing' use their minds to do it. They may see things remotely, yet, what they fail to see is what happens when a human chooses to perform an ego-led action, by breaking the Laws of Creation to "First, do no harm," and then, steps into the mind control programs with no heart protection, no authority from LOVE to perform this action, no backward glance at the many doorways that open in their energy fields, and while they are performing the criminal action of invading another's privacy and invading their energy fields, in order to access a 'Remote Viewing', behind them, all their life force energy is being stolen by destroyer forces and replaced with False Light codes.

The karmic cycle created by 'Remote Viewing' without being guided and overseen by your Infinite Self, Infinite LOVE and the laws of

Creation, to best serve all precious life in optimal ways, causes waves of distortion to reach humanity, as a whole, and a 'tsunami' of dark attack ensues on the planet. Chaos reigns supreme. And up until very recently, there were no repercussions for the destroyer forces for causing this chaos, because the human made the choice to participate in an activity without engaging their hearts and asking, if this action helped or harmed humanity and all life?

No heart checks are made by those who 'remotely view' for the purpose of military and other nefarious reasons.

What about those who were used by groups and forced to train to remotely view but never believed it worked or never saw anything?

The Laws of Creation are there to protect all precious life. To participate in an activity, whether it worked for you or not, means you chose to break the Laws of Creation, you chose to disregard checking with your Infinite Self to ask if this action helped or harmed yourself or others. No advice is sought, and therefore, none can be offered. What happens next? You participate in 'remotely viewing', or attempting 'remote viewing' without heart guidance. You don't know about your energy fields or your Cosmic Shield. You have never been told about the karmic cycle you create when you break the Laws of Creation by harming others, regardless of what you see, you chose to do it. The dark are therefore 'blameless', and cannot be hit by the karmic cycle. But you will get hit by your own choice to try to invade the energy field of another, or invade their privacy, and the doors open all along your ladder as the dark break in and start to steal as much light as possible and replace it with False Light codes of fake knowledge, and fake thoughts, and fake feelings. Your soul recoils in shock at your choices and it starts to fragment. Please listen to; "A Race Against Time," for a full discourse on what happens when a soul starts to fragment. The dark hunt down these terrified parts of you, and they maim and harm your soul parts, and steal that Knowledge also. It is partly used for the dark ones to feed off. For, your fear is their fuel supply, and the rest is weaponised against you and others.

All stolen energy is the weapon that the dark use to harm you all.

Claire has been teaching others how to defend themselves, and how simple it is to prevent this level of attack, which only happens through your specific participation in things which harm you.

What can you do if you are listening to this for the first time?

Start to ask your heart and LOVE for help.

Even the worst offenders, the darkest energies are capable of redeeming themselves before it is too late.

That is not the case for all souls. The destroyer forces and Extra Terrestrials, which, by the way, are your soul fragments and higher aspects of consciousness which have fragmented in fear, and then gone AWOL, and gone over to the dark side have caused so much harm, and are determined to continue causing as much damage to humanity and all life on Earth...well, they have left it too late, as have those practising Freemasonry, those practicing Reiki, Yoga, and other compromised practices which harm another's energy field and weaken it — to the degree that destroyer forces can break in and steal codes, replace the stolen codes with False Light and fake feelings, fake thoughts, strip the human of the codes that would know to call for help, mind control the human so that they make poor choices which cause them more harm, manoeuvre the human towards the hive mind and the Black Hole that is sucking humans into AVATAR WORLD...

AVATAR WORLD, the place created out of all your stolen fear, your anger, your jealousy...it is a place of nightmares where soul fragments lose their ability to know they can call for help. The ultimate trap. The human trap. The snake pit, and place of vipers and rapists who love to hunt, and maim, and kill — over, and over, and over again.

Did you know that, "As above so below"? Souls of children and other humans get 'trafficked', dependent on how damaged they are. Some souls fragment but have enough light left to prevent being hunted, yet, they often get trapped by firewalls of humanity's stolen frequencies which are woven into a mesh and hold these souls prisoner.

If others wish to 'Remotely View', a wise soul would do it under strict supervision with their Infinite Self and LOVE and the Laws of Creation to help them, and this type of 'remote viewing' is permitted because it involves looking at situations that are causing suffering, learning about the cause, the effects, and then, seeking solutions through LOVE to secure these souls their freedom.

Claire needs those who have been involved in 'Remote Viewing' to know that without this kind of protection, they have energy fields riddled with satanic frequency, and this needs addressing — to help you leave the matrix also, if that is your wish.

You have to ask LOVE for help. LOVE and your heart cannot interfere with your free will choices.

Free will and your choices were gifted to you by LOVE on the understanding that your free will choices would be made to 'secure the optimal outcome for all precious life.'

Each time that free will is used against the Laws of Creation in a False Light program, a 'tsunami' of attack happens to yourself firstly, then it jumps like a 'viral pandemic' into everyone else's energy fields.

Codes of your remembrance are stolen, replaced with false knowledge, reluctance to seek fullest truth, a closed mind, a closed heart...the dark will do whatever it takes to keep you here and stuck in the matrix. They are preparing you all for AVATAR WORLD.

At least, that is their intended plan. Their Immortality Agenda will fail, but not before many souls are so badly damaged and broken, they will not make it back home. The codes for calling for help are all gone. They have incapacitated you all — to the point that this information will also be dismissed too. That is how powerful a False Light code is when your true power has been handed over to Lucifer.

So, the power struggle has ended, for some. They will not come back. It is too late.

For those who want freedom, there is better news. The Lion's Gate was closed for good, last night — for all those who chose freedom and chose to ask LOVE to help them. This free will choice to grow in LOVE has also secured the safety of the children for their onward journey. However, the child sacrifice and abuse will not stop until humanity wake up.

Do you think they will protect the children?

They are so immersed in the False Light Construct. They feel the need to look away. To ignore all the signs. Those of you who are awake are guided that you can do nothing to help this group, except, by climbing your own ladder of consciousness and by focusing on pioneering a safe pathway for the innocent children, newborns, elderly and vulnerable members of your family of humanity.

If enough climb far enough, there is a slim chance that they may look up and stare fear in the eye.

Focus on self-nurturing, self-healing and repair. Receive assistance through your inner heart and LOVE connection.

Ask to be upgraded. The upgrade is best retrieved by listening to

"YOUR COSMIC SHIELD, DEFEND YOURSELVES AGAINST ELECTROMAGNETIC AND ELECTROPLATONIC ATTACK,"

and it is then best to follow that with

"DECLARATION TO DESTROYER FORCES AND ALL THOSE MALICIOUSLY HARMING ALL PRECIOUS LIFE —

YOU HAVE NO AUTHORITY. YOU ARE FACING DELETION." **[Upgraded to The Outer Waves of Infinite Possibilities, June 2024, however worth a listen for insights, and much guidance]**

We have asked Claire to leave the links here.

We would like to thank all of you who have been helping humanity and all precious life.

This is a relay race, a race against time. Time is about to close. There is very little time left to make good any errors and to repair all harm caused to self and others.

LOVE is here to help all those who sincerely wish to leave this place when the time comes.

There is nothing to fear. LOVE is here.

Keep repeating this to yourselves, as you go about your day — secure in the Knowledge that all you had to do was ask for help and it was given. It is the law. Any soul who asks for help is always helped.

Therefore, it is suggested to any late stragglers to,

"Make the request. LOVE does the rest."

Before you came here, you made an agreement with your Infinite Self and LOVE, that before the final whistle blew, if you had fallen so deeply into density that you had forgotten to ask LOVE for rescue from this place, that a call would be made throughout the grids of LOVE and true light — to remind you that it is nearly time to come home. LOVE made this promise, on the understanding of your wishes, prior to your fall into this place.

You have been gone so long, many of you, that much harm has been done to your weary heart and soul.

Some souls came from a place of such purity, that when they fell into this place, through their deep love and concern for humanity and all life trapped in this place, the shock of losing their codes of remembrance was so deep, that many could not cope with the shock, and some ended their time here, earlier than planned.

LOVE wants you all to know that you are needed here. All of you. Your presence is vital to securing the future of the children. And so, we are asking you all to hold onto HOPE, FAITH, and TRUST that you will not be facing death, you will be receiving life.

Once you have asked for rescue, you are free from this place. LOVE is not going to abandon any soul who requests help. It is the law. It is written in the stars, for all to see, that LOVE brings life and ends suffering, and your journey home can still be one of great joy, safe in the Knowledge that you chose to continue your evolution and to move forward, safe in the Knowledge that you did all you could to secure the children's future.

For, that is what was asked of all of you. Pray for Strength and Courage as you run the final furlong of this race. Hold onto that baton in your hand and ensure you pass it on to the next runner. Cheer the final runner with your team and watch as they reach the line.

Move your consciousness inside the Heart of Creation and imagine all souls safely returned. All present and correct. All souls accounted for. Ready and waiting for the In Breath to fully draw in, and the next big evolutionary cycle about to unfold.

Focus on that with all your heart, because miracles are made when enough tiny, frightened voices call out into the wilderness for help, and along comes LOVE.

Miracles are made when hearts are open and voices shout out, no matter how tiny or how frightened they are. LOVE hears all calls for help and is always there in an instant.

And why is that? Because LOVE never left you. LOVE was inside you, urging you forward, sometimes carrying you, but always there — just waiting for a request, a prayer, a sincere concern for another soul...

If your wish is for all souls to be rescued by LOVE; for all to make that call, then, draw that picture and keep on your wall and think about it every day now, before night begins to fall.

Your creativity and imagination is a gift the dark ones lack. They used your gifts to create this world. Use your GOD- given power to reclaim what was already yours — your ability to love unconditionally, to forgive yourself for all errors, and to create and imagine the world YOU want, instead of feeding the dark, dark world of Lucifer's.

Reclaim your power.

Liberate yourselves from the chains of this dark place.

Be free."

...

Full Audio Experience:

@Loves Heart Plan| Searching For The Evidence, bitchute.com| @trueliightessence, Odysee.com

Chapter Thirty-Seven

CLOSE 'THE DOOR' ON 2024: USE THE POWER OF YOUR CREATIVITY...

Audio Links:

LOVE'S HEART PLAN, SUBSTACK

DEEPER TRUTHS CHANNEL, ODYSEE

"I call on my Infinite Self and my Infinite Heart Switch to connect me to Infinite LOVE's plan and the infinite laws of Creation, from the Heart of Creation and infinitely beyond.

I am being asked to share with those who have hearts that see, and those with eyes that can perceive the hatred being wielded upon humanity and all life on Earth, to please be ready to act today — to close the door on the plans for 2024 and open LOVE's Heart Plan Door that invites LOVE, Peace, Unity, Strength, Knowledge, Wisdom and many, many other missing frequencies onto the planet — to bathe all those who are suffering in LOVE's embrace and to shield them from all harm.

Many know what is coming if enough do not try to metaphysically stop this. It needs a group effort of concerned individuals to make a simple stand.

Simple, however, it requires our steely determination to keep this doorway firmly closed and to keep LOVE's doorway fully open, in order for all those who are suffering to be helped; supported; shown a safe route out of here when the time comes for all to leave this dark place.

Today, I witnessed the fabric of Space-time continuum whilst in heart connection.

My consciousness and Infinite Self showed me that the 'rip' I had previously reported was partly repaired, but needed more work.

This was done and then, I saw my Infinite Self cut a man-hole sized piece out of the fabric of Space-time continuum, and I watched this part of myself climb up and into a space that was above the Space-time continuum fabric.

Space-time continuum created 'time'. Time was created because our courage was stolen and distorted into fear, which created Space-Time, and this is what is holding us prisoner in this matrix: our own energy — stolen, distorted and then, created into a prison; a 'holding space' to block us from our full Knowledge and awareness.

Twelve levels of our consciousness are stuck in this space. Bits of us are missing — soul fragments, higher self fragments, particles of ions, pieces of ourselves — lost in space and gone for good, it seemed.

Up until recently, that is.

Because in 2021, a beautiful soul who I was connecting with, a soul is being attacked because they came in with immense gifts to help humanity, this soul asked LOVE if they had any gifts to help humanity that could be activated, and LOVE answered the call.

These gifts were the Cosmic Laws. The Cosmic Laws are the missing Laws of Creation in the False Light Construct. They were not in operation before this: not in any meaningful way.

This act: to ask for help to activate unknown gifts have brought humanity to this place now, whereby the laws are operating in full, and that is why we are able to peacefully ask LOVE to gather up all magnified, malicious harm and send it back to all those responsible for their errors.

Before the Cosmic laws were activated, it was not possible to do this. Therefore, the dark have had a 'field day,' causing humans to make errors, create karmic cycles of learning for themselves and all the while, remaining protected from the dark's own errors being recycled back to the dark ones to deal with.

The dark ones used this 'flaw' in Space -Time and the lack of the fully present Laws of Creation to cause carnage and chaos, to steal life force codes from other innocents and to harness more power through these codes to use as weapons, fuel, and advanced technologies — all designed to hold you here, to keep you prisoners in this False Light Construct.

For, that is truly what this place is — a false-light-construct — made up of all your stolen energy, AWOL soul fragments, and higher states of awareness that have also gone AWOL as they fragmented and then, some have even gone over to the dark side to serve Lucifer's army.

It is like a cancer that has spread. Today is the day, and onwards from here, to close the door on the dark's plans for 2024 and to let in LOVE to help all who are suffering.

All are victims of this war on our consciousness. This war on our mind and this war for our heart Knowledge — the final frontier for the dark— as they plot and plan to kill you all, so that you never leave this place, but not before they have made identical copies of you for their AVATAR WORLD, the Internet of Bodies, the Internet of Things, the place where all soul-parts go to get copied, recycled, rendered useless; in terms of calling on LOVE for help and thereby, held prisoner in their 'Immortal World' of torture, maiming, raping and killing. This is the world your leaders want and it is the world they serve.

Every corporation and every authority on your planet is compromised by these dark people, and entities: these servants of Satan — the Luciferians and Club of Pome types, the Royals, the Vatican, your whole military and police forces are riddled with servants of Satan, and those who are not, had best wake up before they drag you into this Avatar World, this pit from which there is no escape. Once you get sucked in there it is game over.

And I hear my heart and LOVE say, *"Claire, we will take over the reins now. That is all we needed them to know. We wish to move onto the solutions now that you all understand the problems. Many of you have been shouting from the roof tops. Many are realising they are just 'preaching to the choir'. Very few are waking up to the issues outside of this group, however, there are enough in this 'choir' to make a firm stand now, and as many of you are becoming fully aware, if not already, LOVE has a plan and we are asking you to follow this plan each day now: morning, noon, and before sleep at night.*

Meaning: AM, PM and midway through your day.

A simple technique to bring in LOVE and to shut the door on the dark plans for 2024 is presented to you all.

Many understand that creativity is actually your most powerful tool to address this dark cult and the Lucifer, and Club of Rome groups.

Your political systems all serve this agenda. Don't be fooled by those who pretend to care. Look at their body language and symbolic signalling. It is there in plain sight if you care to look.

The reason this message is going out tonight is because if many of you could spend a few minutes today and this evening, wherever you are in the world, you could powerfully help to get the ball rolling.

This is not limited to any group. This is an invitation to your humanity, regardless of your belief or lack of belief.

The dark use energy to harm you all. They know LOVE exists, even if many of you doubt it does.

We ask those who are skeptical to put that aside, because it is powerful and can override any energy aimed at you.

Claire, will you describe the attack on you recently?"

I was sitting downstairs with my computer on my knee and I had an old computer plugged in nearby, because I was posting a message on Substack and my other platforms.

I heard a loud 'pop' in the room. It sounded like an electrical wire had blown. It alarmed me because it was highly unusual.

I checked my computer, the other rooms and fuse box. No signs of fire, electrical or otherwise.

All computers were working although I initially switched off the electrics.

We did a thorough house-check, and decided to go in to heart, and ask what had happened and we were told I had just been targeted but not to be alarmed, LOVE and my Infinite Self were protecting me and it had been deflected and returned to the senders and attackers.

We used our heart connection routine which keeps changing slightly as the upgrades happen.

Everyone who is telling the truth; trying to alert humanity is targeted. There are also individuals who have been targeted for years because they are on a list provided by Extra Terrestrial agencies who know who came in to help humanity, who has more codes of Knowledge, who is a threat to them should they decide to ask LOVE for help and so, many humans are Targeted Individuals, going through hell on a daily basis. Living a nightmare of voice-to-skull interferences, house break-ins, unwarranted police visits for no reason, etc. It is very bad in the USA and many are suffering.

I wish to tell you all that you have the power in your hearts to deal with these agencies from the comfort of your own bed or sitting room.

If you ask your heart and LOVE to protect you, and then, start a strict routine of clearing the attack from your energy fields, all the way to the top deck of the trapped consciousness at the Cosmic Shield level, LOVE will come in and do the rest and the attacks will start to diminish.

Many are using a routine that I share on my various platforms. A lot seem to be using it because the numbers are going up each day, and my channel is tiny. I am a very small voice and a bit like that cockerel on the Substack video that I shared at the beginning, I have been hollering for a long, long time, trying to get the help to others.

The heart routine I suggest is called "Your Cosmic Shield, Defend Yourself Against Electromagnetic Attack", and I recommend you follow that with "Declaration to Destroyer Forces And All Those Maliciously Harming." I will leave the links here.

Does my heart and LOVE wish me to say anymore about the attack or do you wish to continue?"

And I hear, "Claire that is enough for the time being. However, we do wish to highlight that the manhole that Claire described metaphysically climbing into that was above the Space-time continuum was a very dark place. We say, 'was', because this area above Space-Time has been cleared of all harm, all suffering and hardship. Those who continued to harm have been contained by their own errors to cause harm. Some have been deleted, never to return.

Much is happening at higher levels of awareness. For those who wish to understand more deeply, we suggest they ask for a 'classroom setting,' whereby your heart can show you while you are protected by LOVE's energies.

It is unsafe and irresponsible of any human to go exploring consciousness without LOVE to oversee your safety and without the Laws of Creation to ensure no harm is done to all precious life.

Please be aware, everything you do energetically, metaphysically, and consciously requires these three things to ensure the optimal outcome for all precious life — Your Infinite Self, Infinite LOVE and the Infinite laws of Creation.

If you use anything else, it is mind driven and ego-led, and the laws are responding to all choices now, including your own.

We wish to move swiftly onto the reason for this message request.

The plans by the dark for 2024 are horrendous and if not stopped by a concerned group of individuals from various parts of the world, what will unfold will be 'torment' and highly destructive, particularly for those who are not protected by LOVE, simply because they have not chosen to ask LOVE for help.

LOVE has to be invited in. LOVE cannot impose. It is the law.

We are asking you all to "Make the request. LOVE does the rest."

To be shown through your heart connection, two doorways.

The one on the left is the dark plans for 2024.

It is currently partly open and already causing harm.

To your right is LOVE's Heart Plan Door.

It is also partly open.

We wish you to ask your Infinite Self and Infinite LOVE and the Laws of Creation if it best serves all in optimal ways for the door on the left: the dark's plans for 2024, to be left ajar?

(Pause here)

Does it best serve all in optimal ways for LOVE's door to be left partly ajar?

(P)

We wish you to ask your heart at deep levels, what your role is here.

Which door are you being called to close and which door to open, if any?

(Pause the recording here and wait for your heart to guide you.)

If you are being asked to close a particular door, follow the guidance, and remember this image in your heart.

If you are being asked to open a door, check if it best serves all precious life in optimal ways and follow your inner heart's guidance.

Keep asking questions for example: What question should I ask next?

What should I do next, or ask for next — that best serves all in optimal ways, in alignment with LOVE and the laws of Creation?

(Keep pausing the recording as you see fit. Join us once you are ready. I will continue here.)

"Claire, that is all for today. ***Once this task has been successfully set in motion, we ask those who took part to now go and draw this picture, and keep it somewhere where you will see it each day, to remind you that after your daily heart connection, to finish it with the picture.*** *Focus on the meaning behind this, the possibilities of freedom if enough also choose to join in and help.*

Your creativity is the biggest defence against the dark and they see your creativity as a weapon in this war because creativity created the matrix. All of you made this mind prison, and all of you can choose, or not, to set yourselves free by creating a different ending to this story, a happier ending where the children run free, where all are happy and safe and joyful, all codes of lost Knowledge restored, all suffering deleted, and all those who chose to harm will be imprisoned by their own errors, according to the laws of Creation, the laws brought in by one soul.

One soul did that...brought the opportunity of this loving action to humanity's door. Left at their feet for all to choose. To be free. Or to continue suffering.

One soul.

How many of you have not yet asked LOVE what gifts you carried with you to lay at humanity's feet, in case they may wish to help themselves?

One soul.

Attacked, targeted, sick and terminally ill, yet, had the kindness and compassion inside their heart to give you this precious gift of remembrance.

Please do not waste this precious gift. Without it, we would be on death's door...all of us.

One soul.

Saved billions. By a simple act of willingness to ask LOVE for help.

Use these gifts wisely.

Use your gifts wisely, and remember, that when the dark start knocking at your door, if you are using heart connection as strictly advised: AM, PM and midway through your day — the attack, the directed energy weaponry, those trying to make you a 'node in their interface' have no power over you.

LOVE holds the power, all of it, and if you knock at LOVE's door, the power of LOVE can come flooding through into this reality and clear this dark place up, once and for all.

Claire, that is all, please post it as soon as possible, typos included. Time is of the essence here, not perfect grammar.

Ask the groups who are helping to help share this also — to garner as much help from as many doors as possible.

There are billions of you.

Remember this when you think of what one soul can do when LOVE is called upon.

Send LOVE and gratitude to this soul because they need your LOVE right now.

Pray for them and pray for their peace."

Chapter Thirty-Eight

IMMENSE EMOTIONAL TRAUMA TO MOTHER EARTH: TOTAL GRID COLLAPSE, 4 JAN 2024

Audio Link: Bitchute | Odysee.com

Welcome to my Substack: LOVE's Heart Plan , 4 January **2024**

I had assumed that I had completed my projects but it seems that as more developments arise, I am being asked to share with you the updates, to spur on your progress and to encourage you all to keep up the momentum.

We are at another critical phase and your love and heart energy is being called upon to assist Earth as she makes her final preparations for ascension.

Things have not worked out as per LOVE's Heart Plan. Unfortunately, this is due to humanity making poor choices which have resulted in the Earth's entire grid network collapsing under the strain of attack, and because the Earth was exposed, not protected, her grid system was left in tatters.

Less than a few months ago, it may have been possible to remedy the errors which caused her grids to collapse, however, unfortunately, it is too late now and she has reached a point of 'no return.'

'No return', in this case, meaning: the Earth cannot complete her ascension journey without LOVE's help and without your requests to LOVE for help.

I reported several months ago that I had watched Mother Earth die spiritually and shared a message ***"The Day The Earth Stood Still."***

It may not have seemed that way from the physical reality that we reside in, yet, at higher levels of awareness, when seen through heart and expanded consciousness, the attacks on the Earth had left her in such a sorry state, that after the fires in Maui, her spirit and soul departed this place before any more harm could come to her.

The fires that raged around the world finished her off. By the time Maui was on fire, the Earth was unable to protect herself, or the many life forms that she supported on the Earth plane in this reality.

My understanding is that the life that she supported would also start to die and leave, and this is happening as we speak.

Humans are so busy with their day to day living, they rarely look up and notice what is happening around them. They seem to be fixated on the TV, their phones, computers, and other technologies, and they barely notice each other, let alone a butterfly going extinct or the Earth crying out for help.

All of this goes over the heads of the many 'mind-controlled' humans that have their faces down; fixated on the black box in the palm of their hands.

How did we let things get so bad? The Maui fires — from a metaphysical point of view: the 'final goal' of the dark's plans to finish-off Mother Earth, as the attacks on her around the world ensued.

You don't think these floods, the fires, the earthquakes were random events, do you?

That the wars and the fear being generated are just 'unfortunate incidents'?

These are all indicative of planned attacks on the Web of Life, made easier by the reluctance, and predominantly: the stubborn refusal of the Reiki and Yoga groups, other exercise groups and 5G phone users, to stop letting in vast amounts of destroyer forces onto the Earth plane through their corrupted energy fields.

It has been explained many times before that there are twelve levels of consciousness trapped inside the False Light Construct. Reiki destroyed the Galactic Grids — the Cosmic Shield or twelfth level of Mother Earth — Yoga destroyed her Planetary Grids, the eleventh level, and many other holistic and exercise groups helped because they were unaware that they were being attacked through their Cosmic Shield, down to the Biofield or Auric Field closer to the body. They were practicing exercises and routines that were already distorted, and as soon as they gave their attention to the various practises, the dark were given the OK to walk right in and start to steal vast amounts of life force, which is then weaponised against humanity and all life, including Mother Earth.

This has been going on for millennia, however, there used to be a huge amount of protection and Knowledge in the Cosmic Shield level of Earth to protect humanity from their errors, meaning, when they gave their power away to destroyer forces.

However, in recent years, and it is complicated, but the dark have engineered energy in ways that have made it easier to steal more life force from Mother Earth and replace her energy with False Light Codes, which Reiki groups and other healers and holistic practitioners used as a power source.

This corrupted Mother Earth and humanity's energy fields to such a degree that in the end, the dark were able to kill-off the spirit of Earth, and LOVE had to step in to resolve this debacle.

A highly preventable situation had happened because humanity chose self-serving options, as opposed to making heart choices which would have saved the Earth, would have preserved all life that she supported, and would not have left the world's children and all innocent life exposed to the Beast System, which only walked in because humanity let it in.

There were no grid systems in place to prevent this happening.

This was not LOVE's Heart Plan.

This was not meant to happen to Mother Earth.

Many messages were placed in humanity's consciousness and on the internet to ask all groups participating in Reiki, Yoga, Pilates, Mindfulness, Circle Dancing, etc., to stop — because they were not only exposing themselves, they were harming all life — by letting in this destroyer force in droves during the years 2017 to 2023.

A plan had to be put in place to protect all life because when life leaves the body in this reality, the twelve grids of humanity and all life, and the twelve grids of Mother Earth are used to rise up through the levels of consciousness and eventually, leave this place to evolve back to the soul's true origins which is the heart of Creation.

The loss of these grids rendered all departed souls stuck in the False Light Construct.

Once again, the dark destroyer forces used this opportunity to hunt down these trapped souls and harmed them, maimed them, stripped them of their much needed codes of remembrance and these souls went AWOL, or they got sucked into the Black Hole of Avatar World, or they were trafficked if they were children's souls, or newborns, and some were used for 'hunting parties' in the dark spaces of the False Light Programs. There are many other types of 'casualties' which I have been asked to share in previous podcasts.

Essentially, I wish others to understand the immense emotional trauma that has happened to the Earth, to the life that she supported and the knock-on effect in the other realms of reality when departed souls from this reality leave the physical body. Is this what you want for your departed relatives, your lost children, or pets? And what about Mother Earth? Have you a heart for her trauma, either?

Those who did this committed the most heinous crime.

MURDER.

There is no other way to describe it.

MURDER.

DEATH OF THE SOUL.

It is a far worse crime than what the dark have done because they have no codes of remembrance, no connection to heart or inclination to try. However, Reiki is meant to be about loving action, healing, and helping others.

I trained in this modality a long time ago, and I thought that too. But now, when I tune into those who still practice this dark art, and it is a dark art, in the sense that it totally takes over those who practise it.

It steals their life force, feeds off their energy and replaces their stolen life force with false light codes, and the person who practices this dark art past Level One, First Degree Reiki, gets addicted to the False Light codes. They don't know that. However, try telling someone who does Reiki that it is harming all life on the planet and has destroyed the grids of Mother Earth, and helped cancer patients die because it feeds off our light.

It is only 'universal' energy in the sense that it was procured from this universe — the False Light Universe, from the sixth level of Mother Earth.

It is deemed 'Earth energy' and Earth energy is deeply harmful because there is no goodness left anymore.

She is dead. And she was murdered.

Cancer is a sign that the life force codes are vastly diminished at the Cosmic Shield level and below it. Every level is emptying of life force.

Therefore, if a person has cancer, they need to ask their Infinite Self, Infinite LOVE and the Laws of Creation to help them. And they need to call on the frequencies of HOPE, TRUST, and FAITH to shield them from all harm. If they did this three times daily, they would find peace, and that may be to leave the body or to survive. Whatever happens, this will ensure that when they eventually leave the physical they will be assisted by LOVE to get straight home to the heart of Creation. Your request for rescue secures your rescue.

Therefore, to apply Reiki to a cancer patient, is to further empty them of their life force. Why do Reiki practitioners practice this dark art?

They can 'feel' the energy, which feels 'powerful' because it is heavy and dense and easily sensed. That is the first 'hook'. The second is money, and the third is Kudos.

There is no other reason or excuse anymore. To remain ignorant about all levels of awareness inside the False Light Universe that the Reiki is transmitting to, and to deny the harm it causes all levels when most Reiki practitioners only see the aura. To not understand that there are higher levels of consciousness that are caving in under the attack brought about by Reiki, is to be ignorant to the extreme.

If I had been still practicing Reiki and found any of this information out, I would have stopped and thoroughly explored this new information. That is what a responsible loving human does who wants to help others heal, not harm them. To allow ego-led behaviour to drive your decisions, to cause this level of harm and the level of harm that cascades down into the physical from such vast areas of Knowledge, to entrap a soul, to cause soul fragmentation, soul shock, soul death, well, what do responsible folk feel about that?

The same can be said about Yoga for different reasons yet, the harm is mirrored. As is Pilates, a practice that creates small circular sine waves in the auric fields. How does that harm a person who does not know? It destroys their energy fields by opening up doorways in the aura for destroyer forces to attack and break through and steal life force — the force that sustains your life here. Everything is collapsing in on itself, and eventually, death will occur as more life force is lost.

How does a soul exit the matrix after death with many codes of Knowledge missing?

Answer: They cannot leave. The hunting games begin and the soul is always found. The attack is brutal and horrific. The ability to call for help is missing. The soul suffers, yet, remains silent.

LOVE has repeatedly tried to protect all groups by advising them of the deeper consequences of working with 'Earth energy' during the final stages of an 'In Breath'.

Today, I was asked to call for help for the Earth, because her attackers and perpetrators are bent on continuing to harm, and so she is stuck inside this False Light Construct and needs your assistance.

It is why I have been asked to request assistance for her and all life that she supported, who are also suffering.

In a recent message, it was explained to us all that the perpetrator of the harm needs to seek help for any harm they may have caused others and only they can request this.

LOVE cannot interfere. However, the Laws of Creation state that if the perpetrator refuses to stop harming or to seek help from LOVE to repair the damage caused to another, if enough hearts call to LOVE for help, then LOVE can intercede to help those who have been damaged by the perpetrator.

I am going to ask my Infinite Self and Infinite LOVE together with the infinite laws of Creation, to help me to share the optimal requests that we can make for the Earth and those life forms she supported because they are all suffering, and if I may, I wished to show you in a classroom setting what is happening to the Earth, to life that she supported, to the children, and to cancer patients when treated with Reiki.

The help we will request will involve a strict connection routine, and a specific set of steps to reach the Heart of Creation for fullest Truth and then, your Infinite Self will furnish you with the teachings and prayer requests or words that provide the optimal outcome for all those who are suffering.

No special skills are required. This help can be given by anyone with a loving heart.

All it requires is your 'humanity' — your CONCERN for others.

Your Infinite Self and LOVE will help with the rest.

This is how I connect to my heart for those who may find this helpful.

I set an alarm in case I fall asleep, and I have a glass of water nearby. I ask family to allow me some quiet time: for me to remain undisturbed in a quiet room at home, shaded from bright sunlight, and where I can safely close my eyes. I lie down on the bed that I sleep in at night, flat on my back, legs straight and slightly touching, but never crossed. I relax and ensure I am warm and comfortable.

If it is safe to do so, I close my eyes as I always do for sleep each night and I place my hands with palms facing down and never crossed, gently on the tops of my thighs. I keep my closed eyes gently looking down towards my chest area and I keep my closed eyes there, listening to the air going in and out of my lungs as my chest rises and falls with each breath.

If you wish to, you may like to place one hand on your chest to help you keep your focus there. On behalf of all those who wish to help the Earth and all those who are suffering, I will say:

"We call on our Infinite Selves, Infinite LOVE and the infinite Laws of Creation from the Heart of Creation and infinitely beyond to help us be of optimal service, to help Mother Earth and all those who are suffering."

I then use one hand to press an imaginary switch, my Heart Switch in the centre of my chest as an act of intention to connect to all the above energies. You can pretend to press a switch if this is easier. Either way works. It is your intention that starts the process.

I use this Heart Switch as a type of 'wishing well' or onboard computer that I trust will absorb all new requests so that, should the list become too long or should I forget what to ask for, I trust that all the requests will go into this Heart Switch and each time I press my imaginary Heart Switch or pretend to press my imaginary Heart

Switch in the centre of my chest, the requests are placed in there and will activate automatically when I press my Heart Switch for help, according to LOVE's Heart Plan and the Laws of Creation to best serve all in optimal ways.

I hear my Infinite Self say:

"Claire, we would ask those with hearts that care and hearts that see the damage happening to all life on Earth to pretend or imagine that their Infinite Self and LOVE have placed them in a classroom that is visible from deep space, and inside this classroom setting they can move their consciousness around to look above, below, and all around, to get a clear picture of what is currently happening.

Claire is aware, and currently feeling 'flat' and a little 'low.'

Q. Can you perceive, or hear, or feel or sense or just know what is happening to the Earth currently?

(Pause the recording and keep coming back after each question is validated inside your own heart centre).

Q. Ask your Infinite Self and LOVE, why is this happening?

Q. And what are the consequences for the Earth and all life that she supported if this is not remedied?

(Pause the recording here.Rejoin us once you are ready).

Q. Can you see your own energy fields at the top deck: The Cosmic Shield level?

Q. How are they looking today?

(Pause the recording. Rejoin us once you are ready. This must not be rushed. Take your time).

Q. Ask your Infinite Self to show you what Reiki and Yoga, Pilates, Mindfulness, Circle Dancing, May Pole dancing and other exercises are doing to your energy fields in this classroom setting.

(Pause the recording here).

Q. Ask to be shown what Multi-dimensional healing practices, Quantum Healing and other forms of energy healing are doing to your energy fields in this classroom setting.

(Pause the recording. Take your time. Use your Heart Switch and rejoin us once you are ready).

Q. What happens when you work with your heart, meaning: your Infinite Self, and Infinite LOVE and the laws of Creation?

Look at your energy fields in this classroom setting.

(Pause the recording. Use your Heart Switch to rejoin us).

Q. Do you understand why the Earth has been suffering?

And why you are all suffering?

Q. What about vulnerable cancer patients? How are their energy fields looking during illness, in a classroom example?

Q. And what happens when Reiki is placed in their energy fields?

Look at all the levels — Twelve, down to the one nearest their physical body.

Q. Get the teachings to help you understand more fully.

(Pause the recording here. Use your Heart Switch to rejoin us).

Claire, that concludes the lessons for today.

What we are asking you all is to ask your hearts for help for Mother Earth and ask each day now, how you can help her to complete her ascension journey, because the dark attack on her and the actions and activities of those who are bent on using outdated practices that no longer hold any useful meaning are dragging her away from her evolutionary pathway.

Claire witnessed the Earth spinning out of control, and today, all Her grids had totally collapsed. There is nothing to salvage from this debacle...

You are in the final stages of the In Breath which is drawing ever closer, now, and all need to leave this dark place by requesting rescue and assistance to move back into alignment with your true original form, which is: Love.

Those who persist in harming, who have turned their backs on helping the Earth and its occupants will pay a high price for allowing ego-led behaviour to supersede heart-based decisions, and when one has been given the gifts to use to protect and defend, and one squanders those gifts, it reduces one's chances of ever returning.

This lifetime was the final lifetime to remedy any errors and for many, it is too late. They will not return. They refused to help and have caused soul death to others.

If you are one of these people, then we advise you to consider praying or asking for forgiveness for the deep harm caused to all precious life. Your future looks bleak, to say the very least.

It has placed all life in a danger that surpassed even the heart of Creation's expectations, and it has caused ripples of destroyer force to break open the unified field.

It has been remedied, but not before much heartache and uncalled for damage was caused.

Pray for all those who got hit by the wave of attack this created. Pray for them, and pray for their release from suffering.

We have mentioned many times about the ***power of Creativity*** *— a frequency, a place and a destination, and a gift from LOVE that many of you possess but rarely use, and yet, it is your greatest defence against the dark ones.*

The dark ones fear your Creativity and we are going to utilise it now to secure Mother Earth's safety and all life that she supported who have also suffered.

We include the children, vulnerable, elderly, and all innocent precious life.

This is the request we would ask you to initially use until your heart guides otherwise:

"We call on Infinite LOVE and the Infinite Laws of Creation to surround and protect us, and to shield us from all harm, and we press our Heart Switch to indicate our intention to assist with LOVE's Heart Plan for the Earth and her occupants.

May all our errors be forgiven and forgotten, **[meaning: deleted]**

May all malicious, magnified harm, and all intentions to harm, and all harm born out of ignorance, looking the other way, or selfishness — be gathered up by Infinite LOVE and the Laws of Creation and sent back to all those responsible for this harm. [For their learning]

May all that has been lost, be found and returned to wholeness, and purified, and then, restored to all who can be assisted, including: ourselves, Mother Earth and all life she supported, and all precious life, in the form of Purest Light codes that can never be infiltrated or

corrupted by the dark, destroyer forces, Lucifer energies, or any other person, place, or thing.

We ask Infinite LOVE and the Infinite Laws of Creation to sever this energy from ourselves, the Earth and the life she supported, the children, the innocent, and all those wishing to return home to the heart of Creation.

We ask our Infinite Selves and the gift of Creativity, together with Infinite LOVE and the infinite Laws of Creation to shrink this energy down to a harmless nano-particle that renders this energy powerless, harmless, and obsolete."

I say:

"With a peaceful heart, without anger or judgement, see this energy SHRINK in size to a harmless nano particle — rendered powerless, harmless and obsolete."

MY INFINITE SELF AND LOVE SAY: *"This is* ***Creativity*** *in action. Think about the many ways that you could use this gift of Creativity to SHRINK down the dark's plans: for instance, to CREATE images of LOVE's Heart Plan completing and rescuing all souls from suffering and entrapment.*

Use this beautiful gift in alignment with your Infinite Self and LOVE and the Laws of Creation to help push things along, where suffering is happening due to lack of Creativity to help souls who are suffering.

You have the power, the gifts and the authority by LOVE to call for help, and to use your Creativity to help all precious life, and all we are asking at this juncture is for you to steadfastly secure new ways to use it to the advantage of LOVE's plan to secure the safety of all precious life before the False Light Programs collapse and before the In Breath completes, which is soon.

Claire this must go. The 'flat' feeling you have is the Earth's suffering.

Ask others to share this message to secure as much help as you can all muster.

Help can be thin on the ground sometimes, however, we have Hope, Trust, and Faith that many love the Earth, and value all her love and protection.

It was never expected that you would need to be doing this, but she needs your assistance otherwise, she will not get home.

Thank you for helping her and all precious life."

Chapter Thirty-Nine

HUMANITY'S COSMIC SHIELD: TOTAL COLLAPSE; PREPARE FOR AFTERSHOCKS | 6 JANUARY 2024 (URGENT SHARE)

"If the groups who helped collapse these vital grids cannot be swayed by a newborn's cries of suffering as their soul is taken and hunted, then, what will?"

LOVE'S HEART PLAN, SUBSTACK.COM, BITCHUTE, | ODYSEE

Good morning everyone, and welcome to Claire's Substack entitled, LOVE's HEART PLAN

It was given this title to emphasise that LOVE does indeed have a plan and when we truly listen to the plan deep within our hearts, then, all the goodness that LOVE can give us is brought to us with ease.

I hear my Infinite Self and Infinite LOVE say,

"Claire, tell everyone what has happened today."

"Which part do you wish me share?" I say.

"All of it."

I went to bed late last night. It was around 4 am in the morning really.

I stayed up to see what was happening on Substack, and Telegram and Bitchute to get a feel of what others are concerning themselves with.

I had read a website newsletter regarding the Internet of Bodies and surveillance which led me to find and read some disturbing comments from targeted individuals.

This is an issue close to my heart. I have been targeted since 2012 or just before. When I say that, I mean I have been targeted in a more noticeable way, because all of humanity and all life is being targeted and many do not notice.

That was the time I was getting teachings —through expanded consciousness and heart connection— on frequencies and how they interplay with the human energy fields.

Way back then, I was being inwardly shown by my heart how the twelfth 'Russian Doll' — the biggest area of consciousness that surrounds our physical body and which is trapped within the False Light Construct, is getting 'peppered' with satanic attack, mobile waves, computer waves, TV waves, and harmful energy attacks from those using Earth energy (which is distorted) and which the holistic industry have been tapping into and transmitting into each other and other human energy fields. All these various activities and more are destroying the human energy field at the highest level that is trapped within the False Light Construct: the 'Cosmic Field' or 'Cosmic Shield' at the Galactic Level.

This vast area of our consciousness; this 'Russian Doll' level is vital to our ascension, and upon death, this level holds the greater Knowledge on how to return home to the heart of Creation.

Many souls get trapped upon death, and end up recycling back into the Earth reality instead of evolving home, which is their true path and true choice, meaning; before we all came here, we had already made our 'choice' known to Infinite LOVE at the Heart of Creation — of our wish; our true desire to always return to the Heart of Creation for each new cycle of evolution.

This indicated to LOVE that if we ever got caught up or trapped that LOVE would step in to help us get home. We simply had to ask for help, and the help would come.

The Cosmic Shield is part of a greater ladder of awareness that expands into vast areas of Creation, and eventually, once we leave the False Light programs, we are able to climb up our ladder of consciousness and evolve at a more peaceful pace, with more protection and more Knowledge to help us climb faster and evolve, and start to recall and remember our true origins as we climb our ladder of Knowledge.

Eventually, we return home to the Heart of Creation and we share our experiences our learning, our errors, if any, and all the information is shared so that when another cycle of evolution starts, the new Creative cycle is ever more expansive, exciting, and

infinitely growing.

Cycles and cycles of evolution have passed and humanity are still immersed in density in this dark place from which they came to help other souls who were trapped, yet, the human 'rescue party' became trapped and so deeply immersed in density that they were unable to fulfil their mission which was to help LOVE collapse this False Light Construct and help all trapped souls — who had been lured into this place while they were out exploring during an Out Breath cycle of evolution, and became victims of 'bait' — to be fed-off by the dark ones who occupy this dark place.

It was created a long, long time ago. Many of you have been away from home so long, you no longer remember who you truly are or why you are here, and many do not see that their true power lies within their heart centre and that their heart is the KEY to setting themselves free, by walking out the door that leads to freedom and liberation from this place.

The dark ones have made it extremely hard to leave this place. Abusers always trick and manipulate, and this is what has essentially happened in this place.

Now is the time to set yourselves free. You have the KEY to leave. Why don't you set yourselves free?

And the answer is because the dark ones feed off your light codes which became distorted as you entered this False Light place, and the dark ones need your light to exist. They steal as much as they can when you are looking at something else, and while you are no longer aware of your Cosmic Shield, they can tip-toe into this place and steal the codes you need to evolve home.

This area of consciousness is critical to your survival in this place. It holds the Knowledge to get you back home to the heart of Creation.

It holds the 'measure' of energy necessary to carry you home, if need be.

It is the KEY in the lock, to setting you free, in the sense that your heart holds the Knowledge.

It carries the map. It is your compass. It knows the way home. The Cosmic Shield holds the 'fuel' to propel you out of this place.

Where do you think the dark try to damage first when they break into your Russian Doll layers of consciousness within the False Light Construct?

That's right. They ransack the place that sets you free. Your Cosmic Shield level. Then, they set to work to steal as much life force from you which serves as their 'fuel' because they can no longer live off the light from LOVE, because they turned their backs on LOVE.

They live off other life form's distorted light codes.

Humans carry immense Knowledge and Wisdom in their DNA and 'Russian Doll' layers of consciousness.

Therefore, your Knowledge and life force is a prized possession, a 'nectar', and sustenance.

Without your Knowledge and life force, they could not exist. They would have no 'fuel' to feed off.

They steal your Knowledge and Cosmic energy and other frequencies of purest light codes which have become damaged when you entered this place, and much of this is used to create Artificial Intelligence, 5G weaponry, microwaves, EMF's, ELF waves, Radio Frequencies — all of which emit low energy emissions which reduce your vibration and recalibrate your light and turn it into a more easily accessible fuel source.

Humans each have an individual energy field system with many levels of consciousness that eventually lead to home. They are also sharing a vast Cosmic Shield as a family of humanity.

In a False Light Program, the family of humanity's Cosmic Shield is there to protect you; as a body of shared awareness. You are all connected to each other, and each action, or thought, or decision you make has a knock on effect with this vast, shared 'Russian Doll' that is a part of all of you.

Today, I witnessed that the Cosmic Shield of humanity is down. It has been breached and attacked repeatedly because humanity's shared Cosmic Shield holds great energy as a fuel source, and a supply of Knowledge — to be stolen and weaponised against humanity.

Essentially, the dark can only harm us with our stolen life force and codes of Knowledge.

They steal it and replace the area with False Light codes of fake knowledge and satanic codes. They weaponise the stolen energy against us, and this is used to try to break into our heart energy.

Our heart connection is the 'final frontier' for the dark.

If our hearts can be disabled it disconnects us from LOVE. If hearts are disconnected, the soul goes into shock, as do higher levels of our 'Russian Dolls' at higher levels of consciousness.

Tiny bits of us start to fragment and peel away. These all get stolen or fed off.

It can turn into a feeding frenzy. It is dark and brutal — a vicious attack on the soul, which is highly vulnerable because the personality self rarely acknowledges this part of itself, and therefore, the soul is left defenceless by an ignorant human self.

A kaleidoscope of harm and attack ensues.

The raping of the soul, the hunting down of frightened fragments of awareness who are always found eventually, and stripped naked of all remembrance of their true origins, or knowledge that they can call on LOVE for help.

This activity goes on all day and all night. The dark constantly plot and plan because they are desperate for fuel, and desperate to exist in this pitiful, violent, and aggressive way.

Humanity remains largely ignorant that this attack is ongoing and so they do nothing to defend themselves. They don't call on LOVE for help. LOVE cannot impose. It is the law of Creation.

Help can only come if help is asked for.

Free will is honoured at all times. If free will does not choose to ask for help, LOVE cannot come in to sort out the dark attack.

And so, on and on it goes.

Today, the Cosmic Shield of humanity is breached and has been compromised.

This is terrible news and those who do understand the depth of this news will also understand that we are now in greater danger than we have ever encountered so far.

We sort out one problem. The dark move swiftly onto their next plan of attack.

What do you think happens if the Cosmic Shield of humanity is breached, or compromised, or collapsed entirely?

Would you consider it a good thing?

What is the outcome of a collapsed Cosmic Shield in a False Light Program that is riddled and infested with satanic energies, rogue distorted entities, and other off-worldly entities?

Does it spell calamity, or should we all go back to planning our summer holidays and watching Net-who-gives-a-flying-flick?

Yesterday, I was told yesterday that there are only fifteen humans on the planet who are working with consciousness in ways that are meaningful and can defend humanity.

How many humans do we have on the planet, minus those who are dying from the poison shots?

Over seven billion?

Seven billion humans with the same capability to connect to their heart and their consciousness, who can ask LOVE for help to protect all precious life.

What?

And there are only fifteen humans who are using consciousness in ways that could protect and defend all precious life?

Do you ever wonder why we are all suffering?

The answers are not in the palm of your hands on that black box you all love to look at.

The answers are inside your heart centres.

Expect heart attacks now, expect strokes, expect deaths.

I also experienced a targeted attack recently. LOVE deflected it. It sounded like a cap gun going off by my body. A loud 'pop.'

I have asked my Infinite Self and LOVE to protect me and I was protected.

LOVE sent back the malicious harm, too.

I didn't have to 'do' anything.

All I had to 'DO' to get the protection was ASK.

How simple this is to resolve, and yet, humanity probably will not resolve this. They have holidays to plan for, remember?

That is far more important than securing the Cosmic Shield of humanity, or asking LOVE to protect the children, the innocent, and all precious life on Earth and throughout the whole of Creation.

Holidays, Net-who-gives-a flying-flick, or possible death?... mmmm.

What will you choose for yourself?

I was also guided that the Beast System has been activated and that Mother Earth was getting dragged into the False Light Matrix, and into the Black Hole of Avatar World — the Internet of Bodies and Things.

Many souls are now being 'activated' by the Trans-human Agenda, and a descension is taking place, whereby, the AI technology has infiltrated the human energy fields at the Cosmic Shield level and is descending into the human physical body.

We will witness this event in others, as they will appear emotionally detached; almost as if they have dementia; a hive mind mentality; an inability to rationalise or balance out thoughts. They will appear cold, and this is because their soul has left and their conscious ladder has been withdrawn to protect the Web of Life.

Other news is that a Purest Light Grid has been temporarily erected to help all souls who wish to return to the Heart of Creation and continue their evolutionary cycle. We have envisioned many billions of trapped souls leaving this matrix.

What can we do to best serve all in optimal ways, during this calamity of a Cosmic Shield collapse — for the family of Humanity, as a whole?"

And I hear,

"Claire, it is up to those with hearts that care and those who have a concern for their future and the future of the children to connect to their own hearts and seek inner guidance on these matters.

Your role was to help others see how easy it is to hear their heart and LOVE guiding them when enough desire is shown to want to understand the issues and seek solutions.

LOVE will always help anyone who asks for help.

For those who are expanding their consciousness, we say, NOW is the time to set yourselves free from this False Light reality.

If the Cosmic Shield has been allowed to collapse by Humanity as a family, then it will spell disaster, unless more step forward to assist.

Do you think many will look up and take notice?

We say: considering how many messages that LOVE has put out to advise the Yoga, Reiki and holistic groups that Earth energy is harming all life and that all systems, including Quantum Healing, Multidimensional Healing, etc., no matter the fancy names, they are all operating from within a False Light Construct, and as such, should be avoided like the plague. To continue with these practises when the Cosmic Shield has now been breached because of this refusal to stop harming, means the situation is dire for those who enabled the dark to collapse the most essential grids of humanity's consciousness.

It will create death of the soul and death of the human. This is what happened to Mother Earth — killed by those who proclaim they love her, yet, have no understanding of what they have done. They do not know what they do not know, and they will never know because they fail to ask.

What's done is done, and cannot be undone at this late stage.

There are too many in humanity making decisions that harm. It is a broad-spectrum issue.

Humans rarely ask about the laws of Creation, about LOVE's Heart Plan, about how to protect and peacefully defend.

Such a sad way to end a message, however, that is the news today, Claire, and we ask that others also share this.

If you want humanity to wake up before they are consumed by False Light and satanic attack on their souls, then a little assistance to highlight humanity's plight is always a beneficial way to lay down the information — for others to pick up via their consciousness.

The personality self is lost in the programs and too preoccupied with other matters to be seen as the avenue for communication.

You will waste vast amounts of energy if you think that personality-selves will listen or be concerned.

Messages need laying down, and the New Purest Light emergency escape grids will take the message and ensure all hear it at the appropriate level of consciousness.

You all need to be prepared for loss. The breach and collapse of your Castle walls — your family of humanity's Cosmic Shield — is catastrophic and unsustainable.

Unless those who helped to collapse them had a change of heart, it is better to accept that it is unlikely those responsible for exposing humanity will suddenly decide to do something to rectify the harm.

Those of you who do wish to seek inner council would do well to find out what you can do to protect your own ladder, and then, seek ways to protect all those who have been left vulnerable — including the elderly, homeless, children and, worse still, the newborns.

If the groups who helped collapse these vital grids cannot be swayed by a newborn's cries of suffering as their soul is taken and hunted, then, what will?

Be prepared for after-shocks and stay listening to heart."

Chapter Forty

SIMPLEST WAY TO DEFEAT THE DARK | 10 JANUARY 2024

Simplest Way To Defeat The Dark?

Your humanity...

LOVE'S HEART PLAN, SUBSTACK.COM

(IMPORTANT SHARE, UPDATED GUIDANCE)

"Your focus needs to be on dealing with the most deadly part of this plan: to weaken it energetically, and thereby, reduce the impact of what is coming."

"Claire, we are going to give you a download of updated information and advice on how to deal with a Planetary Attack which is in full swing and ongoing, on a daily basis.

The video presentation that you shared by Dr Shiva highlights three very important issues: The cause and the effects of what this dark group on the ground are up to.

However, it does not cover the full spectrum of detail on what is happening at higher levels of awareness — the areas of your consciousness that many never visit and because they do not check and clear these areas on a daily basis, where do you think the ET groups attack that the dark mafia on the ground serve?

Knowing about 'the system' may help to a certain extent. It certainly is a very good and accurate synopsis by Dr Shiva.

However, for those who 'feel' this attack: the sensitives, and targeted individuals, 'knowing the system' and how it works will not address the attack.

Humanity are generally ignorant about what is being done to them. Many have no idea about the extent or collusion by the mafia groups on the ground, who deem themselves 'elite', and superior the rest of society.

Please review Dr Shiva's video to appraise yourselves of the issues caused by those on the ground who deem themselves superior to humanity.

These groups on the ground serve destroyer forces who exist at higher states of consciousness. They are AWOL fragments of your very selves, and others, who have all been attacked for millennia.

They hold knowledge — your stolen Knowledge — in the form of stolen and procured DNA codes, which the PCR testing was predominantly used for...DNA harvesting.

The dark destroyer forces can ONLY EXIST if you give your power to them, in the form of DNA codes and the things you focus on, plus the things that harm you but you ignore or overlook.

They are very cunning and they hold a deep hatred for you. As do the 'mafia' on the ground. And those who are paid to do their bidding are individuals of very low self-worth, in truth.

However, money talks, good jobs talk, and many in the group who serve the cult hold no moral conscience regarding the attack on the planet or on you.

They will live to regret this decision to cause harm. They will regret their decision to go against the Laws of Creation because these laws are working powerfully on Planet Earth now, and they are returning all malicious harm, all intentional harm and all harm born out of ignorance, deception, choosing to look the other way, and ignoring LOVE's requests to stop using outdated practices which are letting in these attacks.

The topics of Yoga and Reiki are being persistently highlighted because it is hoped that a few may just decide to help humanity rather than let in this attack, and because LOVE is guiding them that what happens to the dark mafia and Extra Terrestrial groups who harm, is also going to be your fate, too, if you continue to turn your backs on humanity.

The issues are highlighted to help protect all precious life. If others could move out of mind control and ego-led behaviours, their hearts could easily show them how their energy fields are being syphoned of all purest light, and for many, there is so little left, it does not bode well.

All humans should be concerned about clearing their energy fields each day — as concerned as brushing their teeth, or washing their hands.

The dark attack you all day, every day. A persistent attack cannot be deflected by half-hearted attempts on occasion or infrequently.

Humans need to protect themselves all day, every day and each night before bed.

Claire has been asking for a simple method to share that may help others to deal with all levels of attacks.

You must remember, you are all Purest Light Beings in origin. You have the upper hand but only if you use it.

Hardly anyone on Planet Earth defends themselves, let alone gets the help to protect all precious life.

So, you need to understand that your biggest weakness — your irregular or non-existent practices to throughly clear all levels of consciousness — is the dark's biggest friend.

The mind control technology has such a grip on humanity, it takes a determined human to ask for help for themselves.

If you don't want these dark groups at higher levels of awareness, and on the ground, to overthrow you, you need to stand up for yourselves NOW, and defend yourselves regularly each day.

Not only do you help yourselves, you help the vulnerable, children, newborns, elderly, homeless, and pets who are also suffering from this attack.

This is a suggested routine that clears all attack and strengthens all areas of weakness in your energy fields and consciousness that are vulnerable right now.

Regular daily use, will purify all harm done to you, and send back all intentions to maliciously harm or attack you, to all those who have created sent, perpetrated or fuelled the attack.

LOVE has the power. Remember this. Because no matter how bad you may be sensing the attack, LOVE holds all the power, and when you have LOVE on your side, you have the power too.

The Laws of Creation also need including in your requests because these are the overriding laws of the whole of Creation itself.

All life is governed by these laws which will return all harm and attack back to every single person, place or thing that is attacking you.

The one thing you need to understand is that LOVE and the laws of Creation, and your inner heart technology, your Infinite Self, cannot help you unless you request assistance. It is the law.

Many do not know this and wonder why LOVE allows things to happen. It is happening because humanity do not understand the laws or that they need to invite help in.

LOVE does not impose. LOVE comes when called upon.

LOVE is the overriding power in the whole of Creation, but you are not in the whole of Creation, you are in a False Light Program that is destroying life, and your role is to help LOVE collapse this False Light Program so that this never happens gain.

If you see suffering and wonder why, it is not because LOVE has forgotten you. All this suffering is caused because humanity does nothing to defend itself. Babies suffer because destroyer forces harm them and humanity does nothing to stop this.

Your role is to call on LOVE for help and to keep reporting back all the atrocities to your heart centre, your Ops Control, and seek inner counsel on what you can ask LOVE for that would provide the optimal assistance that BEST SERVES ALL.

It is not necessarily your role to be 'doing' anything, except report back, ask for help and guidance on what to REQUEST that best serves all in optimal ways.

Too many use their egos to make requests that may not secure the best help. It is why we ask you to consult with heart and LOVE, and not Yoga or Reiki or other holistic methods because no matter how fancy the name, they are all False Light frequencies from within the

False Light Universe, and they cannot provide the answers humanity needs to secure the children's brightest future.

While we are on this topic. This is all about the children.

Your town councils and every other institution have sold their souls to the World Economic Forum and United Nations who are driving this global takeover — to secure the dark group's dominance — and humanity, (what is left after the mass extinction event), will become digital twins of themselves and slaves to the elites.

If you think Hunger Games, then, times that horror movie by one thousand, you still would not be close to what is planned for you if you don't stop this.

Many realise they are 'preaching to the choir', however, we will repeat, there are enough of you now in 'the choir' to address and deal with the

attack.

How do you engage more help from this group, many of whom are still engaged in highlighting the issues but not getting through?

We say, stop and move on. It worked for a while. Your focus needs to be on dealing with the most deadly part of this plan, to weaken it energetically, and thereby, reduce the impact of what is coming.

Even with your help, it may be difficult to prevent the carnage planned, and Hope, from Hopegirlblog.com, mentions the game plan in this link below. We also recommend you read or listen to her synopsis which is concise and very accurate.

She also mentions asking God for help.

If you have Faith, you can powerfully assist. If you have humanity you can powerfully assist. If you care about the children's future, you can powerfully assist.

The children are the ultimate currency. For reasons covered in previous messages, the dark covet the children as an energy source, and many humans and entities on the ground like to harm children.

Child trafficking is happening throughout the world on a daily basis. It is bigger than you can imagine and many children are shipped and harmed each day.

Many popular charities who you fund go into disaster areas to round up orphaned children. It is easy to do. The military assist. The corruption is rife and worse than you may think.

It means that you have no one to turn to for trusted help. You must stand up for yourselves and request rescue, and of course, when you ask and when enough ask, then, that help is magnified.

It has to start with you.

Do you want a better future or do you want to die?

That is what the dark want for you but you can choose life.

You do have a choice and it needs to be firmly made now.

The routine that Claire is being guided to use for herself is as follows:"

I lie down on the bed that I sleep in at night at home.

The room is shaded from bright sunlight.

I set an alarm, in case I fall asleep, and I have a glass of water nearby.

I lie flat on my back, legs straight and slightly touching but never crossed.

Palms, placed flat on the tops on my thighs.

I get myself comfortable, as I do for sleep each night.

I ensure I am warm.

If it is safe to do so, I close my eyes and relax.

I take my closed eyes to look gently towards my chest area where my heart connection is.

I relax, I breathe normally and I listen to the air going in and out of my lungs.

I keep my closed eyes looking softly towards my chest area.

I have made a decision to help defend myself and protect all precious life.

I indicate this by pressing an imaginary button in the centre of my chest, my 'Infinite Heart Switch' (this is an upgrade).

I can also imagine that I am pressing my 'Infinite Heart Switch' without moving my hands and it still activates.

Children can be taught this technique too.

The intention to activate my Infinite Heart Switch connects me to Infinite LOVE and the Infinite Laws of Creation at the Heart of Creation and infinitely beyond.

These ever expanding frequencies are the overriding energy and hold all the power, not the dark.

When I call on my Infinite Heart Switch, Infinite LOVE has set everything up so that I do not have to worry about all the knowledge I may lack about what is harming me each day, and I trust it is clearing my energy fields and consciousness and also strengthening all areas of mind, body and soul.

I remain resting for

10 minutes in the morning

3 minutes in the afternoon and

5-10 minutes in the evening, before sleep.

(Pause the recording here, or wait until the end of the message and allow yourself time to receive supportive frequencies.)

This protects me and builds, as I connect each day, to power up the protection.

If I forget, the attack starts up straight away, so, I never forget.

Everyone has time to give this time to themselves.

As additional prayer requests, some of you may also like to add these specific requests and assistance to help protect humanity and all life. The more who help, the protection we receive.

Press your Infinite Heart Switch and say

"We call on our Infinite Selves, Infinite Love and the Infinite Laws of Creation from the Heart of Creation and infinitely beyond, to powerfully surround and protect us, and to assist us to defend humanity and all precious life.

May all our errors be forgiven and forgotten.

With peaceful hearts, without anger or judgment, may all magnified, malicious harm, all intentions to cause harm, and all harm caused by ignorance, selfishness, deceptiveness, or choosing to look the other way be gathered up immediately, and returned to all those responsible for the harm reaching our door, and the door of the innocent, and all those trying to protect all precious life.

May all that has been lost be found by Infinite LOVE and the Laws of Creation, and returned to wholeness; for healing and repair, and then, restored to all who can be assisted; in the form of Purest Light Codes that can never be infiltrated or corrupted by the destroyer forces, Lucifer energies, or any other person, place or thing.

May the technologies which are 'swarming' onto the Earth plane and all technologies that are being aimed at humanity and all precious life be severed from us and reduced to harmless nano-particles of powerless, harmless and obsolete energy."

Spend a few minutes imagining all the technologies SHRINKING IN size to powerless, harmless, and obsolete energies.

The power of our Creativity is a huge strength because the cult cannot create.

They have used our creative gifts to manipulate us into making THEIR world, THEIR dark desires.

If you don't like what you helped create, draw or imagine a picture of the reality you yearn for.

This weakens the dark's plans. The more who help, the more your chosen reality supersedes the darks.

Finally, remember you have the upper hand, but only if you choose to use it.

It is up to you all now, to choose to defend yourselves each day and resolve this.

BE FREE!

...

LINKS:

SEARCHING FOR THE EVIDENCE,
BITCHUTE.COM ,

@TRUELIGHTESSENCE, ODYSEE.COM

Chapter Forty-One

IN MEMORY Of ANN, BRINGER OF GIFTS AND ACTIVATOR OF THE KEYS OF LIFE

What gifts did you bring to help humanity?

Ask LOVE to set you all free.

Activate your gifts - Set yourselves free.

JAN 11, 2024

"Claire, we wish you to share with others about how this story unfolded, to help those who are grieving Ann's passing to understand how important Ann was to the world and what she bought with her to help save humanity — to leave the False Light Construct.

It is an important story to share in her memory. Ann passed away three weeks ago in December 2023. She leaves two sons, one is only seventeen years old, and we ask that you all pray for these boys and Ann's loved ones, because many are mourning her loss.

Claire, tell the story of how you met Ann."

Sadly, I never got to meet Ann in person. I had watched her on David Icke during the lock-downs of 2020, and my heart inwardly guided me that I needed to connect with her because she needed the protection from the heart of Creation, as she was bravely exposing herself in order to tell her truths and make a stand against the tyranny which was unfolding.

I was a little uncomfortable about connecting with others who I did not know. I have been repeatedly asked on many occasions to make contact with others, and it often ended in strange reactions, or negative responses — sometimes, hostile.

However, when my heart and LOVE ask me to do something, I put those worries aside and get on with it. I connected with Ann and from there we developed a bond. I knew her for a very short time. In this short time, however, I knew Ann was hugely gifted. She was ill at the time, but fairing well, considering all that she had gone through. I would describe her as very honest, gentle, concerned about others, and perhaps, sometimes, did not give herself enough credit for her immense courage and ability to love others.

I had written several books by this stage. The books were about the story of how I had experienced what many describe as, 'a rapid awakening'. I was thrust into a world of healing and holistic practices through illness, and had lived a very 'mainstream' lifestyle, up until my awakening.

I was starting to perceive things beyond my usual scope, in the sense that I heard guidance, I was learning about healing energies, and I was getting inner heart guidance regarding frequencies and consciousness.

I was very new to all of this. I was getting huge 'data-dumps' of inner Knowledge, and much of it was very new and advanced information.

I had been asking my heart and LOVE how I could help humanity, and through this simple line of questioning I seemed to have opened doors into levels of consciousness that even today, very few people are exploring.

I was also getting teachings to help teachers of healing energies and holistic practices because I was being told that chaos was coming, and that the healing community had a huge part to play in protecting humanity. The teachings were advanced information that, even today, are regarded as critical to our soul evolution, and my role had been to try to get my peers 'up and running', so that they could protect humanity.

Even in 2014, I was aware that a vaccine program was coming — led by government, military, and big Pharma. LOVE knew what would transpire and it coincided with huge changes in the Greater Cosmos.

I was given a download of Keys to share. I did not know how to present all this at the time, so I followed all that I knew and followed what my heart guided me, which was to train teachers and advanced healers to connect through their hearts and to expand their consciousness to levels previously unattainable, with LOVE overseeing their expansion, together with the Cosmic Laws or, Laws of Creation, as they are also called. I was helping others to go deeper into their heart and teaching them how to retrieve lost codes of Remembrance, lost codes of Knowledge and Wisdom, and showing them how to activate their gifts, and how to protect humanity. I was assisting teachers and students to perceive the attack taking place on all life here through their deeper heart connection, and helping them to realise that the attack was happening in places they had not previously been able to reach. LOVE was enabling this to happen.

I had been inwardly guided that I carried many activations to help bring about change on the planet, and that every single human had brought in codes of Knowledge.

Humans are walking about — blissfully ignorant of their immense gifts. We all carry missing codes, pieces of the puzzle that would help us rise up out of this dark place, and return to our true, original selves, and to remember who we truly are.

I thought the healing community would be excited about this. All the work was heart related. Nothing outside of self was to be used, which made it reassuringly safe because it kept things pure and simple.

I thought others would want to help. It did not work out this way, and 12 years on, we are in the chaos and crisis that LOVE saw was coming if enough failed to act, and if humanity remained unaware that they carried immense gifts in their heart centres to help all life here.

The healing community's role was to wake up to their hidden gifts — buried deep inside their hearts, and then, to help others to activate their codes.

The work was meant to be kept low-key to protect all from being attacked by dark forces. Training was shared on how to deal with dark forces.

Very few got on board and very few ran the distance.

There are many reasons for this. The mind control programs that operate to keep humanity suppressed are working well to keep humanity from perceiving deeper things, the ego programs attack healers to keep them from helping humanity, and one of the most important issues is that the healing energies being used on the planet are all contaminated with False Light codes. The healers transmit these into themselves and others, and with every loss of Purest light codes, which are vital codes of Truth, Knowledge and Wisdom, the healer starts to operate on a system very much like a computer with a virus that cannot operate or function properly, or as intended.

It has been impossible to get the healing community to go deeper into heart and to expand their awareness to the levels required that would show what is happening on their inner heart screen and show them how to fix this.

This has meant that during the last 12 years, instead of thousands of healers being fully functioning using a Purest Light system, they are operating on a False Light system, and it is harming them and humanity, and all precious life.

All of humanity have helped create this mess that we see happening on our planet: the wars, the lockdowns, the pandemic, the corruption and manipulation of the large institutes, and the controlling world of Artificial Intelligence and the surveillance state. It is clear for many who have the eyes to see that humanity are facing an unseen enemy, and as such, are unable to perceive the danger and, therefore, unable to defend themselves.

When I connected with Ann, we got on like a house on fire. We really hit it off, two kindred spirits — concerned about humanity's plight, and much information was shared.

I explained about my work and how she needed to protect herself. Ann had read my book and although not able to fully digest everything in it, she understood that humanity needed help.

Unbeknown to me at the time, Ann did something miraculous.

I was inwardly connecting one day, and I was told some amazing news. I was guided that some extremely important missing Keys had been activated by a soul, and these Keys were going to help humanity to defend themselves, and evolve more rapidly. The Keys would protect all life if called upon, and they would open doorways to higher learning that had never been reached before in humanity's lifetime — through all the ages.

These vital Keys hold the Knowledge on how to safely exit the False Light programs and how to safely move along a secure and protected pathway back to the heart of Creation, where we all originate, albeit most of us are unaware of this. It is the fullest Truth that we are Purest Light Beings from the heart of Creation, and the dark fear us because when we are fully connected to our Purest aspects, we cannot be harmed by the dark forces. The dark forces are holding many souls in a place of entrapment within a False Light Construct, meaning: it is not constructed of Purest Light frequencies — it is a place of distortion, manipulation and power-over others.

Many souls have become trapped inside this place through no fault of their own. They had been out exploring areas of the Greater Cosmos and were enticed into this place and became trapped and unable to escape.

LOVE sent Purest Light beings into this place on reduced power, with less knowledge. Humanity is this group.

We came in to help others leave this place, and we had to come in on 'reduced power,' to avoid collapse of this place because lessons need to be learned once here, and so, many came into this place but with less codes of remembrance. This weakened state caused us all to be more easily attacked by destroyer forces — who were able to break into our weakened energy fields and steal more codes of Knowledge from us.

The dark steal our life-force codes which are inside our DNA, and they distort and invert the codes to create a web of entrapment.

Despite all this, humans still have the ability to help because all rescue parties have a back up plan. If one plan fails, LOVE creates another one, and if that fails, another plan is created.

We were all asked in the healing communities to stop using any energy outside of self from 2012 onwards, and to update our practices in alignment with the planetary changes which were rendering all the previous practices obsolete.

A change-over — from the False Light Construct to Purest Light Grids was required to deal with the planetary changes, and this included all Yoga, Reiki, Energy Healing modalities, Quantum healing, Crystal Healing and so forth. LOVE had asked us to ONLY use our hearts as receivers and transmitters of LOVE's Knowledge from the Heart of Creation in order to facilitate this change-over.

The deepest connection to LOVE is inside our heart centre, along with our gifts, and as such, only our heart centres could be able to connect to LOVE's Purest Light Frequencies. Our bodies and consciousness are operating on a very low frequency bandwidth in a False Light Construct, and we needed time to adjust to the finer frequencies of light because Purest Light frequencies are like bolts of lightening, by comparison. We were also asked to consult with our Infinite Selves, our Purest Self, who could advise us on our best actions in ways that best served all precious life, regarding the laws of Creation, or Cosmic Laws.

The Cosmic Laws govern the whole of Creation. However, in this False Light program, they have not been functioning fully, and it meant that the Cosmic Laws were not policing all malicious harmful activities by the destroyer forces, and the dark were getting away with murder, quite literally, by causing deliberate attacks on humanity. Not only has this kept humanity unaware of its true origins, it has also blocked the memory that humanity could ask LOVE for help.

LOVE does not impose. LOVE can only come to help if LOVE is called upon. It is the law.

And so many souls trapped here do not know that they can call on LOVE for help, because they have had that Knowledge stolen from them to keep them trapped in this dark place. When others call for help, LOVE comes. It is the law that any request for help that best serves all is ALWAYS answered.

It is not about how good you are. It is not about being saintly or godly.

If you want help and ask LOVE for help, LOVE has to help, and of course, LOVE willingly helps.

If a human does not call for help, LOVE stands waiting, but if no help is requested, LOVE cannot impose on their free will to do nothing.

Free will is respected by all living beings, and outside of this False Light Construct, free will was given on the understanding that it would always be used to make decisions that best served all precious life. That is also the law.

Another important Cosmic Law or the law of Creation is:

"First, do no harm."

It is against the Cosmic Laws to waste energy, to ignore LOVE's guidance, to harm others, to control others, to manipulate others into breaking Cosmic Law.

It is against Cosmic Law to take the life of another, to poison another, to lie, to cheat, to cause chaos, as opposed to create Peace.

All these laws protect all life. Outside of this place, they are revered and honoured, at all times, because away from this place, loving action, creativity, and expansive ways of helping each other are the true reality of choice.

How many Cosmic Laws are we breaking in this False Light Construct?

Breaking Cosmic Laws creates cycles of learning. They help correct any harm done to all life. We are all connected by the Web of Life and what happens here, reverberates around the Web of Life.

In the False Light Construct, the destroyer forces had 'rigged the trap' so that when they attack humanity in harmful, malicious ways, they had re-calibrated and harnessed more light from humanity and managed to redirect this harmful action back onto humanity.

Basically, like children lying to their parents and accusing each other, they had ensured that humans 'took the blame' for the destroyer force's mistakes, and this is what Karma truly is.

Karma is a 'program' that only exists in this False Light Construct, and is created by the destroyer forces, to ensure that humanity constantly take the 'hit' for the destroyer force's own errors.

Karma creates a cycle of learning that holds a soul in a space of non-movement unless they resolve their own mistakes. If mistakes are not rectified, they cannot move on and evolve.

Humanity are not only burdened with their own mistakes or errors, they are 'weighed down' energetically with the burden of destroyer force's mistakes — uploaded onto their energy body, and this cannot be healed or repaired because only the perpetrator can resolve their own error, no one else.

The destroyer forces have no intention of repairing or resolving their own mistakes. They allow their errors to magnify in the human energy field, and because the Laws of Creation or Cosmic Laws were not operating fully in this False Light Construct, humanity have been unable to grow, heal, or repair. They have suffered under the weight; the burden of errors — which are not theirs, yet, cannot be removed.

This has added to the planet's problems because when a human is overburdened with the energy of malicious harm and toxic attack in their energy fields, they cannot heal, and it can cause death, because there is no ability to repair this type of harm.

The Cosmic Laws were not fully in place in the False Light Construct. Therefore, much harm has been caused to humanity and all innocent life.

The lack of these vital codes have caused untold suffering, untold hardship, and trauma to mind, body, and soul.

We are all carrying gifts to help each other — to free ourselves from this False Light Construct, which is like a spider's web of entanglement, and it is very hard to address these issues without the Knowledge to do it safely.

All these missing codes of Knowledge are within our hearts. You may be carrying specific codes or Keys to help a specific group, and you will be connecting with them, either through work or social connections.

Can you imagine how much damage the dark had done to humanity while it lacked access to the full Knowledge on the Cosmic Laws?

Are you beginning to understand how important we all are to each other? How much we all need to help each other to escape this construct with the codes of Knowledge that we have specifically brought in — to secure our brightest future?

We have to be here, to be present in this False Light space, in order for our codes to be activated, and it is why you are all here, in truth: To awaken each other, by sharing your precious codes.

A decade has passed, filled with rebuttals, hostile reactions, ego-led behaviours, and stubborn refusals by those were entrusted with more gifts, while those who came in with less gifts volunteered to come into this dark place, unprotected and defenceless, in complete trust that those with more gifts would help them wake up when the time came, which is now.

Many have refused to follow LOVE's request to connect to heart, to activate vital gifts, and sadly, a decade of unnecessary chaos and suffering has ensued.

Look at your world. Do you recall it always being this scary, this frightening a place?

Why is that, you may ask?

In 2021, a glimmer of hope appeared on the horizon.

A beautiful soul chose to ask LOVE if they had any gifts to help humanity, and if so, could they be activated?

LOVE always comes when called upon. This request serves all precious life in optimal ways, and therefore, it was granted.

Shortly afterwards, I was advised that these Cosmic Laws had been fully activated inside the False Light Construct.

I was overjoyed because I knew they were vital and I knew how much humanity was being harmed. Without the full set of instructions, these laws could not protect, defend, shield, repair, or heal others.

Many were suffering. The Cosmic Laws are vital to our survival and our liberation from this place.

Vital protection had arrived, and justice had arrived too, because these laws hold all accountable for wrongful actions, and that includes the destroyer forces.

I think you know who activated these codes, by now?

I was advised that Ann brought in these activations of remembrance — carried inside her precious heart centre.

If others truly knew the enormity of this particular gift of remembrance, how much Ann had suffered with her health and how much she was being attacked, because the dark know we all carry gifts, and the 'big ones'— the ones like the activations for ALL the Cosmic Laws to operate fully inside the False Light Construct, has secured humanity's escape path out of here, when the time comes to leave.

These laws are a huge threat to the dark. They are in action now, and it is why we can peacefully ask LOVE to send back all malicious harm to all those responsible for the harm.

All harm is being gathered up by LOVE and sent back to all those who caused these errors, for their learning, and it is freeing humanity from the entanglement of the False Light web of entanglement.

If humanity truly grasped how brave and fearless Ann was; that even during her own difficulties and illness, she loved us all enough and was brave enough to stand up for what she believed in, and she cared about humanity and her children so much, that despite being laid up with serious illness, she asked LOVE for the activation of her gifts, and it was done.

I contacted Ann immediately to share the news with her. When I explained to her how important this was, she could not believe it, that she had been carrying these specific Keys or that she was capable of bringing in such a huge gift.

I am sure those of you who loved Ann, know that it is totally believable because Ann loved life, she loved others and she has fully protected humanity during this planetary crisis.

I believe that Ann would wish her loved ones and friends to know that LOVE answers all requests for help that best serve all precious life in alignment with LOVE and the Cosmic Laws.

I also believe that Ann would want you all to know that you also carry gifts inside your heart centres to help each other, and in memory of Ann and all that she did to help humanity, may I ask you all to consider asking LOVE to activate any gifts which you carry inside your heart centres?

"Make the request. LOVE does the rest."

If I may, I wish to share a short request or heart call, and invite you all to join with me, in Ann's memory, and with gratitude in our hearts for all that Ann brought to this planet.

If others truly knew how much she has given humanity by laying this gift at our feet — for us to call upon and receive fullest protection for all precious life, I believe there would be places of honour for her in every town, city, and village worldwide.

I want her sons to know that her memory will live on, and that her passing, although has brought great pain and loss, I wish them to be comforted that their Mother was an amazing individual, a truly spirited human being, with so much love in her heart. If only we could all be like her.

Thank you, so much, Ann.

And here is the request I feel Ann would wish us to make:

Find a quiet place at home, where you can lie down, flat on your back, palms of your hands placed flat and facing down on the tops of your thighs, or sit comfortably in a supportive chair, with eyes closed, and hands placed flat on the tops of your thighs: palms facing down, never up.

Relax, breathe normally, and if it is safe to do so, gently, take your closed eyes and look down towards your chest area.

Softly, look down and relax as you listen to your breathing, and focus on the rise and fall of your lungs.

With your imagination or using just one hand, press an imaginary button in the centre of your chest — your Infinite Power Switch — as an indication that you wish to ask LOVE and the Laws of Creation — the Cosmic Laws, to help you:

Then we say:

"Please, uplift all precious life.

Shield us from all harm.

Release us from all suffering.

Please activate our gifts."

Relax and breathe normally.

Think about Ann and have gratitude for her wonderful achievement, which in my mind deserves the highest honour humanity could give her.

For those who knew her, consider all that she brought to the world, her courage, her fierce determination to do the right thing against all odds. Her ability to perceive truth and to be concerned enough about her family of humanity as a whole. Her generosity of spirit and ability to spread joy and love.

And all the things she gave to you personally.

(Pause 2 minutes)

"We ask LOVE and the Cosmic laws to surround and protect Ann and all those who have suffered during their lives here.

What we ask LOVE to help us, and Ann, our loved ones, and all precious life.

We trust Ann is home now. Home at the heart of Creation, from where she first came surrounded by LOVE's warm embrace.

We trust that her spirit lives on and that she lives on because where there is LOVE there is life, and that has never changed.

Thank you, Ann.

We honour all that you gave us.

BE FREE.

Thank you for setting us all free."

LINKS:

SEARCHING FOR THE EVIDENCE,
BITCHUTE
ODYSEE AND T.ME

Chapter Forty-Two

ARE YOU SERVING LOVE, OR SATAN? REQUEST FOR THE HOMELESS, TRAFFICKED CHILDREN, ELDERLY, VULNERABLE

PUREST LIGHT GRIDS, OR THE FALSE LIGHT GRIDS?

LOVE, LIFE AND UNITY, OR THE SATANIC CULT?

TIME TO DECIDE...

AUDIO LINKS:

LOVE'S HEART PLAN, SUBSTACK.COM

JAN 16, 2024

How can those who care about humanity and all life here, best help all in optimal ways?

I reported that the Earth Grids have been destroyed by groups in humanity working with energy in unsafe ways, and we were all being advised that LOVE had created Purest Light Grids as an 'emergency exit route' for all life trapped in the False Light Construct — the place that our bodies and twelve levels of our consciousness are currently trapped in.

Much harm has been caused by those who participate and teach Yoga, Reiki and holistic practices because they have remained trapped in False Light by using practices that have become outdated and obsolete, while Creation has moved on.

We are at a stage whereby the False Light Construct is collapsing in on itself under the weight of the mistakes made by its residents, and that includes humans, as well as demonic forces, and those who serve Lucifer.

Satan's army may have been a huge influence, yet, without our own ego-led errors, and therefore, our co-operation with Satan's army, we would not be in this mess, and the children in various parts of the world would not be suffering, nor would the homeless, and nor would child-trafficking, 'rape parties,' and pedophilia be on the increase.

Humanity has allowed this to happen and to go unchecked. Many brave souls are writing about these issues and this helps raise vital awareness.

However, the greatest way to defend all children, the homeless, elderly and vulnerable, meaning: all those who have had no voice in this debacle, is through our hearts and our consciousness.

I hear others dismissing this and that is because their minds are controlled at some level. Their ego is being manipulated, and this is a broad spectrum issue. It is not confined to one group.

Humans become fixated on their 'path' or their 'perception of the world,' and sometimes, this can be destructive.

How can anyone dismiss consciousness and frequencies as a way forward if they have not explored or fully understood how they work?

It is a sad reflection of the ego programs getting in the way of helping our most vulnerable members of society, and those with these attitudes act as unwitting 'gatekeepers' that prevent help reaching the voiceless — the ones that many purport to be 'concerned' about.

Personally, I am a little fed-up by other's ego-led responses and with having to go around, 'cap in hand', asking others to consider the children and the destroyer force attack happening to them, and asking them to consider heart connection as a way forward to protect the voiceless. Many simply do not want to explore this and it would take half an hour of their time, if that.

Your heart knows the issues. It has the solutions. However, if you don't ask your heart, you will only be making decisions based on ego and mental processes. You will not secure their future until you open your hearts to new information.

The energy emitted from the folk who dismiss the concept is always dark, and the other day I had to send back lots of dark attack from a human who purports to care for the homeless, yet, has sent me a wave of distorted frequencies consisting of discriminatory frequencies, superiority frequencies, judgement frequencies and kudos frequencies, and this one sees frequencies as inconsequential, like a quasi-science! One could laugh or choke on one's food at the need for the ego-programs to be in control. Oh dear me, I think, how does that attitude help the homeless?

If I was a homeless person looking for help, would it help me in anyway to see other's egos leading the way?

The homeless do not trust society and they have every right to not trust society. They have watched others disappear. What happened to the homeless in San Fransisco? Where did they get take them and where are they now?

Do homeless people have to be religious or spiritual in order to get the help? Do we need them to fit into our concepts, our chosen beliefs, or world view in order to deem them worthy of our concern?

Or, do they need our love and unity to try to see how we can all tackle the issues using a multilayered approach?

Many do not understand: we are in a satanic environment. This is Lucifer's world. It is a structure made from False Light, meaning: it is a space that is interwoven with stolen life force codes of diminished Purest Light — our stolen life force energy — carried in our DNA, and our stolen codes have been replaced with false light.

The more false light codes we lose the more the destroyer forces have to weaponise against us. The less connected to heart we become and the less we remember.

The homeless and children being raped by those who serve satanic forces are highly vulnerable. They have already been traumatised physically, and they are also traumatised spiritually. The destroyer forces are disabling them on all levels of consciousness starting with their soul, and this prevents them from calling on LOVE for help.

I just hope that others appreciate we all need to unite in our defence of these souls. Without us, they will be fed to the wolves with no protection. I repeat, it is not about being saintly. This is about our 'humanity', how much are we prepared to tolerate from this dark cult before we make an energetic stand against the dark cult?

They fear our LOVE. They fear us making this stand. They know LOVE exists and that LOVE burns the dark with lightning bolts of Purest Light. LOVE will return all malicious, magnified harm if we peacefully ask, it is done to help the vulnerable.

So, my question to those who dismiss this message is who are you serving right now?

Are you serving LOVE, or Satan?

Are you trying to help, or are you an unwitting gatekeeper?

We are at a time when we all need to be educating ourselves on this place that we reside in currently. We need to understand what it is, why we are here and how easy it is to elect to transfer over to the Purest Light Grids which have been erected by LOVE to help trapped souls who want to leave this place when their time comes.

Did you know you need to indicate your wishes at this stage?

Are you aware that having a belief in God or similar, is not enough to guarantee entry to this place?

The Purest Light Grids have been built for all those who wish to leave this False Light Construct when their time comes, and they are overseen by the Heart of Creation and the Laws of Creation or Cosmic Laws as they are also known.

Your ability to transfer over to the Purest Light Grids requires several things from you.

It requires your HUMANITY firstly — a genuine concern for other's wellbeing.

Secondly, it requires a decision by you to want to grow in loving ways that help all precious life.

And thirdly, it needs you to make the request for transfer.

Once you have inwardly had this inner discussion inside your own heart centre — and that may be via quiet contemplation, a heart call, prayer, or a chat with your inner self, there are several things required of you to ensure you can transfer over to these Purest Light Grids — the grids that your soul evolves through on your journey home to the heart of Creation.

You need to remain in the vibration of LOVE to stay connected.

And I hear my heart and LOVE say:

"If you attack others with thoughts, words, or deeds, or intention to belittle, or harm another, you slip back into the False Light Grids.

If you refuse to listen to your inner heart guidance, and if this rebuttal causes harm to another, or acts as a 'gate' that blocks help from reaching the needy, then you lose your connection.

If you intend to keep using others, or harming others in any other way, manipulate, cheat, steal from them, and certainly, the worst offender is 'false pride', if you wear your religion or spirituality like a 'badge of honour', you fall into ego programs; which are all False Light Grid structures — designed to hold you where destroyer forces can harm you and steal more of your precious light codes and destroy your soul connection.

If you carry practicing outdated healing methods which are not compatible with LOVE's Purest Light Grids, then you are attaching yourself to the False Light Construct and ego-programming by choice.

All will fall who use these methods, harm others, ignore the guidance.

This is not about being 'saintly' or 'godly.'

It is about understanding that things have changed. The False Light Construct no longer supports anything which came from LOVE, and as such, as Claire has shared many times before, only your hearts — where your deepest connection to LOVE is found, only your hearts are capable of connecting to these new emergency escape grids, and it is why LOVE is repeatedly advising others that where you choose to place your energy, matters.

You have only two exits points on this road.

On the left, the door to NOWHERE is heading straight for all those who remain transfixed on this freeway.

On the right, the door to LOVE, and life, and unity transpires.

There are only two exit points heading your way.

It won't be long now.

You need to make a decision — those of you on the left who may not desire his exit point — we suggest you indicate right and move lanes before it becomes too late to change.

The time for choices is nearly over and all that remains for those who choose the lane on the right is to remain self nurturing, spreading joy and creativity, and listening to heart on how to protect the homeless, trafficked children, the elderly and all others who remain voiceless and who have been switched onto the left lane through no choice or fault of their own.

This is of humanity's own making.

We are asking all those who care to start showing your LOVE now and to start being a voice that moves this vulnerable part of your family of humanity out of the way of Death's Door.

They have no voice. Be their voice. Keep asking LOVE to help them.

Your calls matter a great deal.

If you need help, you must magnetise it towards you. The more who ask LOVE for help, the more LOVE will help.

Help comes when called upon. LOVE cannot impose due to the Cosmic Laws.

Therefore, you calls for help are urgently required.

Before others dismiss this, consider why you would choose to refuse to give this help?

You are dealing with destroyer forces here. Your ego will want you to dismiss this. Your ego will want you making all your decisions.

This keeps you in the left lane, too, and this lane leads to death — death of your soul, and death of your continued evolution.

Many are on the lane heading for Death's Door.

For those who have been helping, your efforts — combined with many small voices worldwide; working in unity and following their hearts, have ensured that the Purest Light Grids are now superimposed over Mother Earth.

Thank you kind souls, for all your hard efforts.

That is all the news so far..."

AUDIO LINKS;

BITCHUTE:,

DOWNLOAD FROM ODYSEE:, AND T.ME

Chapter Forty-Three

MESSAGE FOR ABDUCTEES, TARGETED INDIVIDUALS, AND THOSE WANTING TO HELP PROTECT ALL PRECIOUS LIFE

"You have been away from home for so long, you are weary, and many are feeling broken. Here is a simple heart call for those with heavy hearts and feelings of isolation:"

Message for Abductees, Targeted Individuals and Those Wanting To Protect All Precious Life

JAN 26, 2024

It has come to light recently about the deep distress that abductees are experiencing, and I have been asked to write about my experience of trying to help abductees many years ago, from about 2012, onwards.

I was working with advanced keys of Knowledge to help humanity expand their consciousness above the trapped levels of the False Light Construct, and to try to awaken the healing community to the fact that the planetary energies were rapidly changing, and because a severe onslaught of attack by destroyer forces was occurring — owing to the fact that they had extracted enough life force codes of Knowledge from humanity and from Mother Earth's grids, which had been weaponised against all life here and this meant that unless we in the healing community changed our methods and upgraded them, humanity were facing a dire future.

This dire future is now upon us because many in the healing community did not want change. Even in 2012, they were addicted to the frequencies of Reiki, Yoga, colour and sound therapies and multi-dimensional healing systems without fully grasping that they were all riddled with satanic vibration and false light codes which, when placed into their own energy fields and the energy fields of others, only served to ground in destroyer forces into the Earth's reality, which we are now experiencing, and this destroyed all her protective levels of consciousness as the descension ensued.

So now, twelve years later, with many more years under my belt of knocking on doors to make others aware of the danger facing us all, and witnessing those doors remaining closed to these truths, many are still trapped and immersed in ego-led thinking and rigidly sticking to old methods that have become outdated and obsolete.

In spite of being told many times by LOVE that they are harming themselves and causing the planet to descend — to sink into the Beast System reality, thereby, allowing the Lucifer Agenda to become our new reality and to be complicit with the death of newborns because their fragile souls cannot bear the pain that this reality's vibration transmits...

This is a place that is devoid of LOVE in its grids. A place that only carries LOVE inside the heart space of all life here. LOVE is not found anywhere else, anymore....

It cannot be tapped into through the Earth's grids because Reiki and Yoga, and 5G smart technologies killed Mother Earth's spirit....

Despite all the warnings, the begging, the pleas to consider the children, these groups have placed us all in harm's way, and this issue has made it worse for the most vulnerable members of our society, namely: the children, newborns, homeless, the elderly and vulnerable, targeted individuals, and most importantly, the never talked about groups who suffer in silence: the abductee community.

You have watched your homes burn down, watched the Lahaina in the island of Maui be destroyed — to make way for the 'AGENDA', served by the governor and council who plan to profit from the Smart City — designed to imprison all souls and to act as a 'front' for child-trafficking, because the island of Maui holds a dark secret, and that secret is: it is the epicentre for the Extra Terrestrial Agenda who are here to ensure that the Lucifer Agenda is installed in Maui, initially, and then cascade across the rest of the Earth.

Thanks to Reiki, Yoga, Pilates, Mindfulness, Dance to Universal Peace, Circle Dancing and the like, the Beast System is activated. You are all hooked up and you are all exposed.

Do I mean to cause undue harm to these groups? No. I am here to say that the children and all who are getting their souls ripped apart by destroyer forces — along their entire ladder of consciousness — are calling out to you, to ask you to consider them and their plight.

These souls are part of your family of humanity and part of your soul group. You all volunteered to be here. They didn't volunteer to be brutally raped and hunted down.

That was your choice.

I am not here to attack you.

I am here to tell you the uncomfortable truths: that the harm you have subjected to others is beyond the pail, and only you can wrestle with the way that makes you feel.

However, you will probably dismiss this message because your lack of concern for others is self-evident.

There are millions who do Reiki and Yoga each day and yet, you know, deep down, that something is wrong.

Surely, you must notice that your life is not as smooth and that people around you are getting sick? Your pets will be losing vast amounts of life force too.

Haven't you noticed?

Possibly, not.

And why is that, and what is it to do with abductees, you may ask?

We are about to find out and it may surprise you..

Heart Connection Request:

"We call on our Infinite Selves, Infinite LOVE, and the Infinite Laws of Creation, from the Heart of Creation and infinitely beyond, to set us free by sharing with us the truth — above all

things — and to help us all connect deeply inside our hearts to learn and grow, and to understand why we are all being harmed on the planet, and what are the easy solutions, as seen from the heart of Creation's perspective?"

"Claire we are going to give you this as one download, and it may well be that those listening will need to listen once, then listen again, and systematically go through each point with a fine-tooth comb. This will bring many new teachings forward to them, for their own personal soul growth, yet, more importantly this will furnish each one of them with a plan of action to help them engage with LOVE's Plan to help humanity and all precious life that is suffering — as a result of the death of Mother Earth's spirit and extraction of her remaining life force from this False Light Construct, in order to protect her soul evolution.

If this had not been achieved, Mother Earth and all precious life on the planet would have been sucked into the Black Hole of Death, which is charging forward to greet all those who have not yet asked LOVE for rescue.

This is about choices. It is not about your religion, your spiritual beliefs, your world views. This stage is all about your choices.

Your choice to continue harming others, or your choice not to.

Your choice to protect the children, newborns and vulnerable, or your choice not to.

Your choice to connect to your heart to hear truth and enlist LOVE's help to defeat destroyer forces, or not to.

Your choice to fixate yourselves on outdated practices through ego-led behaviour, kudos-driven desires, profiting from others at a vulnerable time on the planet, or to choose not to.

Essentially, this is about your 'humanity' — your ability to be concerned for other's safety, to care about the outcome of your own choices, your desire to understand things on deeper levels in order to secure the brightest future for yourself and others, or, to choose not to.

Every thought, action, word, and deed of yours is either pulling you home to LOVE and life and Unity, or it is pulling you towards the 'Black Hole of Avatar World'; the 'Death Pit'; the 'Gates of Hell' and the death of your evolutionary journey, for always.

It may not seem important to some of you. If not, disconnect now. This discourse will only waste your time.

For those who are seeking teachings, deeper Knowledge and Wisdom, we are about to divulge deeper Truths to you all and this must be discerned through your own hearts.

It requires a level of maturity because this is not about giving your power away to others, including this discourse.

Your heart holds all the Knowledge. This discourse is here to act as a key in a doorway to higher learning, and advanced ways of helping the planet's occupants and all precious life throughout the whole of Creation, because the choices that destroyed the Earth's spiritual grids have sent shock waves outwards throughout the whole of Creation.

All is forgiven, however, many see this from the Heart of Creation and from areas of Creation where LOVE is the overriding energy.

All is unity, peace, collaboration and sharing of Knowledge to help all grow. All work alongside the Laws of Creation which are deeply respected because these laws act as a guide to keep all life everywhere safe.

It is not done out of duty, it is actioned out of a deep Love and respect for all precious life — many of whom have bravely volunteered to come to Earth to try help create peace, and unity, and secure the rescue of many trapped souls who are suffering, because their spiritual aspects are being hunted, tortured, raped and pillaged of their life force.

These events are brutally cruel acts, and so, many souls have bravely asked to come here to help.

These brave souls carry immense gifts and keys of Knowledge to help rescue all trapped life force, all souls, all life that has been harmed by destroyer forces.

Many have come from a place of such purity, they have never known hardship, torture, lack of LOVE's presence.

To fall into this False Light Construct, these souls have to loose vital codes of remembrance from their energy bodies.

This diminishes their 'remembrance' and prevents the collapse of the False Light Construct, which would collapse under the weight of the purity of these soul's energy if it were allowed to enter this place of density on 'full power'.

So, their codes are reduced down, some are removed, and when these

brave ones fall into this place, the destroyer forces are waiting for them at the higher levels of the trapped consciousness...the Cosmic Shield Level — the most advanced and protected part of our conscious ladder, the 'twelfth deck' of the ladder, the uppermost deck that is trapped inside the False Light Construct 'rooftop'.

In spite of this upper deck holding the greatest protection, the Cosmic Shield Level has had to be weakened and reduced in vibration, so as not to collapse the program,

You all came here to learn how to rescue souls trapped in the False Light Construct and this descension has happened to you all.

As these brave souls descend down through the levels of consciousness that have entered this False Light Construct, the destroyer forces pelt the life force with 'cabbages and eggs' of attack.

Unfortunately, Purest Light codes that have been reduced in 'full power,' can be stolen, and these are weaponised against all life trapped inside the construct.

The life force is attacked as the soul descends down the levels, until it arrives in the reality of the third level of consciousness...the place where humanity currently reside.

There is another issue, though: a problem that is new and which has altered LOVE's Plan.

It has been explained by Claire, how the Earth's protective levels of consciousness have recently been destroyed: predominantly, by Yoga, Reiki and 5G Smart devices — up to and including the twelfth level, meaning: her Cosmic Shield or Galactic Level — including the eleventh level, the Planetary Grids.

This recent collapse has sent shock waves flying outwards, like a nuclear explosion.

No matter how dark this place is, it was never anticipated that LOVE's children would destroy their Mother. It is extremely saddening, to say the least.

It has also left many trapped, attacked, and vulnerable souls in a place of extreme danger. It was already bad enough. The Heart of Creation was not even anticipating this level of neglect.

How has this happened? Claire has already shared these bare truths. It is hard, we know, especially if you thought you were doing good, but if you could all just open your hearts to the damage that many have been a party too...we simply hope, and pray that more may awaken and try to rectify the damage caused.

It has ripped huge holes in the Web of Life, it has caused death — death of the physical, death of the soul.

It has created a space for the dark to harm others more easily and because so few on the planet understand the threat facing them, and because many more are still immersed in ego-led thinking, there are very few on the planet with any 'humanity' left inside of them to make choices that are centred around protecting and defending all who are at increased risk.

And the most harrowing of all, is to watch a newborn soul, who volunteered through deep Love and concern for you all, to leave a place of exquisite purity, and be 'thrown to the wolves', as they descend into this place, trusting that you will be there for them, only to find — to their dismay, as they are lowered down through the levels of density — that they have arrived in a place where many humans reside, yet, few are concerned about their choices and the outcome of those choices.

And those choices mean that these babies are arriving into child-trafficking rings where their little fragile bodies are being raped by men who get pleasure from these activities. You think this is exaggeration? Go on Substack.com. Claire will find some links to reveal to you what others have discovered. Law Enforcement are finding babies with umbilical cords attached who have been filmed being raped and sexually abused for fun.

It is a big problem which is occurring right under your noses. In your own village, town, and city. The problem is bigger than you think and more widespread than you can imagine.

What about these babies? Why are they being abused? Has this always happened? Has it always been a big problem of concern?

It has always been there. That is true. What adds to the harm being caused, now?

You are all living in a lower realm of density than the third dimension. The lower levels of the twelve decks have all collapsed in on themselves. The twelfth deck collapsed and the planetary grids collapsed of Mother Earth owing to Reiki, Yoga, and 5G Smart technologies.

Humanity is normally protected by the Earth's grids.

The Earth's grids are no longer active. They have fallen and were rebuilt several times by those with hearts that saw and asked LOVE for help. They collapsed because others refused to stop harming via their practices which were allowing in Satanic forces through their energy fields.

No Earth grids means: zero protection.

No Earth grids, means the inability for departed souls to exit this dark place and return home.

Babies coming in now are being brutally raped because when there is no protection from Mother Earth's collapsed spiritual grids. When the planet drops in density, the upper levels of her grids fall in on themselves, the dark destroyer forces that lived on these levels fell into humanity's reality and this recent 'fall' — combined with the collapse of the levels below humanity — have produced another 'fall' in density, and humanity have fallen into the pit of the abyss.

They are not 'hanging over the precipice,' as they were before the vital grids of the Earth collapsed. They are now deep inside the abyss and heading towards the Gates of Hell, the Black Hole vacuum that is sucking all life towards it that lacks LOVE; that is unaware of the danger, and therefore, has not yet asked LOVE for rescue.

What happens when a planet falls further into density, and when its occupants are mind-controlled, ego-driven, and making choices that are mind-centred, not heart-centred?

What happens when destroyer forces that previously could not access this reality, fall into it, and no one notices?

What happens when those who are harming and breaking Cosmic Laws to: "first, do no harm," leave themselves open to attack?

They start letting in destroyer forces through their own consciousness. With every poor choice, with every selfish action, the destroyer forces strip them of their life force and a take-over of the mind, body, and soul occurs.

What happens when criminal elements who are already harming others get taken over by destroyer forces from the Galactic and Planetary levels?

The 'Invasion of the Body-Snatchers' occurs. Those who harm want to harm more, and in more harmful ways.

They become addicted to the frequency of hatred because those forces taking over their bodies hate humans. They detest humanity. And they want fuel to exist. What fuel do they exist on? Life force of other living things. How do they steal this life force? They create fear through torture, extreme fear, distress, soul shock, soul fragmentation, destruction of the conscious ladder, heightened states of extreme pain and suffering.

Why do you think men are gang-raping babies with umbilical cords still attached, and photographing this in shopping mall toilets, as happened recently in the USA?

You are no longer just dealing with selfish, ignorant humans and a reckless holistic community; selfish users of 5G smart phones who desire faster speeds no matter the cost to innocent life; selfish electric car drivers who wear their badge of honour for being a 'good citizen' by having an electric car, which uses batteries made through child slavery and disease, and which supplies electricity procured from the Earth's grids and your own life force energy.

No matter the fires these cars are causing and the dirty bomb toxins their burning batteries emit, it is all for 'climate change', and no matter the cancer these cars are causing the occupants.

You reap what you sow, and what you sow, you reap.

You may think we are digressing. We are furnishing you all with a background and understanding that your planet is not 'ascending', it has dropped in density and the floors below it have already collapsed, and so, your third dimension and all the levels above it that were trapped in the False Light Construct have fallen into your reality, and combined with the outcome of all choices that did not consider all life, the effects are: now, you are all swimming in an ocean that is even more toxic and convoluted with harmful, destructive energies that now have freerein to walk right into your ladder of consciousness and start stealing all your life force energy — to weaponise against you, and strengthen their Beast System Agenda.

Why do you think Tedros is smiling about Disease X?

Is it their little joke, do you think?

The X that is appearing in the microscopy slides of vaccinated blood?

The X that is satanically symbolic as the 'Kiss of Death'?

The X that was formerly known as Twitter?

The X Factor TV series?

And where is this all leading, you may wonder?

Are any of you aware that many humans are Targeted Individuals and suffering from government protocols of mind-control and trauma?

This is a huge problem and many are suffering.

The other subject matter is that those who are being abducted and experimented upon, are preyed upon by other, so-called 'humans,' who claim to be helping them, but really, how many Abductees are getting the help from society that they need?

Many years ago, Claire was asked to learn more about the issues affecting Abductees, and like the corruption that is evident in the holistic community — of which she was exploring — the corruption within the Abductee groups was off-the-scale.

Claire was directed towards finding several groups in the UK. None of those involved were truly helping these souls, not in any meaningful way. Information was passed to a key figure in Australia and to other groups who purported to be helping these souls, but all Claire uncovered was distortion, corruption, ego-led decision making, and lack of Knowledge on how to safely help these souls.

The truth is: there are very few humans who have not been abducted.

This has been going on for a very long time.

Those who are suffering and being targeted are the 'sensitives', many of whom have to be suppressed by those who abduct them, to prevent them from addressing the attack from the dark ones who abduct them.

There is a lady who thinks she crashed a space ship and is under the belief that the Greys are her friends. She holds much knowledge about the reptilians, however, as pure in heart as she is, those around her are profiting from her innocence, and Claire was asked to connect with her, many years ago, to try to help her to go beyond the levels of connection she had, in order to realise that she was being played.

All that is happening is that her life force energy is being stolen and used against her and others, to harm humanity.

Claire recently came across her on a video on Bitchute.com and it was saddening to see that she is still being deceived by ET groups who tell her plausible truths — and many things are true, however, that is always 'the draw' — that the 'true' information resonates, and while you listen to her talking, the corruption and attack that she carries in her energy fields, unbeknown to her — because she is an innocent and is completely unaware of the danger she is in — her energy fields are being used to emit dark frequencies to all those who connect via any technology, video, in person, email, text, her books, etc.

None of her energy is protected, and the attack on her is emanating out and hitting all who connect with her energy.

This happens with you all.

If you have not yet asked for your energy to be protected from harming others, especially, because you are all being attacked each day and without regular morning, afternoon, and evening clearing before you sleep, you are all walking, talking, 'destroyer-force-emitting-weaponry' and this attack goes viral, millions of times each day.

This places innocent souls, like this, in danger. Our duty is to protect this soul and our duty is to protect ourselves each day.

This beautiful lady said something very important and highly relevant. The Reptilians are planning to destroy humanity and they will try this year to cause the most harm ever.

They hate you. They detest you. They run your governments, the WHO, the World Economic Forum, the UN, your Military, Big Corp, Big Food, and Big Pharma, etc.

This group detest you all. They are not your friends. The lady mentioned that they cannot exist in the presence of LOVE.

Why do you think they are easily planning a take-over of your planet this year?

You let them in — Through your energy fields. Through total disregard for clearing and protecting your ladder of consciousness each day.

Would humans be abducted if humanity decided to look after this previously unknown part of themselves?

The simple answer is, no. It would not be possible to come into a place where LOVE was the overriding frequency.

Would men who are demonically possessed be able to rape fragile newborn babies with their umbilical cords still attached to them, and get pleasure from photographing the rape live?

The simple answer is, no, not when LOVE is the overriding frequency.

Would this be happening had the grids of Mother Earth remained intact and fully operational?

Perhaps, it is time to ask the Yoga, Reiki, and all holistic groups for their expert insights on how their work helps those newborns?

And to ask all those who desire faster speed bands, whether they think it is worth the exchange — to read emails faster — while being sucked into the Gates Of Avatar World?

And for those who are suffering, Claire has shared a wealth of help and support from the Heart of Creation on how to safely protect yourselves, how to protect others and how to create the world you truly wish for.

Humanity is on the precipice of great change. It is not looking good for all those who are ignoring the choices they are making, or where it is heading for them if they decide to continue with selfish choices that harm all life.

If you are an Abductee who is suffering in silence, we advise you to connect through your heart, and to ask LOVE and the Laws of Creation to help you each day.

We cannot advocate or recommend that you seek one to one care, and especially from online groups because they are all overshadowed by the Reptilian Overlords and frequently, those who purport to be helping, are not.

Many serve an agenda — whether it is personal or satanic — when a heart is driven by ego, they are restricted in being able to help you, and this can expose you further.

Your heart, your Infinite Self, and Infinite LOVE together with the Laws of Creation hold the ultimate authority to fully protect you, but they cannot interfere with your free will choices. LOVE comes when called and cannot impose.

LOVE is here for you all. If you choose to call on LOVE, LOVE will start to surround and protect you and start to clear the energy of harm that has left you exposed.

You must always call on your Infinite Self first, and then, call on LOVE.

Your Infinite Self must become your gatekeeper and bodyguard. It even ensures that you connect to LOVE, and that is why it is important to be precise and mindful of the words you use, and in which order.

Claire shares more on her Substack.com and other platforms, to help you all get deeper into heart, to get the maximum help through your own heart while LOVE and the Laws of Creation provide support and assistance.

The Heart of Creation wants you all to know that you have not been forgotten, not by LOVE, and there was a promise made by LOVE to you before you fell into this place — that if you ever got in big trouble, if it ever became difficult to remember where you were from — that all you had to do, was to make that 'call for rescue,' and LOVE and the Laws of Creation would ensure you were never left in this dark place to fend for yourselves.

You have been away from home for so long, you are weary, and many are feeling broken.

Here is a simple heart call for those with heavy hearts and feelings of isolation:

Try it morning: upon awakening, midway through your day and at night: before sleep — to keep you all protected.

"Please help me. I call on my Infinite Self, Infinite LOVE and the Infinite Laws of Creation to surround and protect me from all harm.

I am feeling broken.

Please release me from all harm.

Shield me from abduction.

Activate my gifts.

And send back all malicious, magnified harm to all those responsible for trying to break me.

I am not broken, and LOVE will help me.

I have Hope, Faith and Trust around me at all times and I am protected." "

Chapter Forty-Four

PLANET EARTH HAS 'FLAT-LINED': ZERO RESONANCE. EMERGENCY WARNING ISSUED: You Only Have Days To Resolve This, No More, 28 January 2024

Pray For Forgiveness, Pray For Rescue

AUDIO LINK: Message on Searching For The Evidence: Bitchute.com

How do I convey this message to others without sounding dramatic or causing fear while, at the same time, ex-

plaining to them that they are in extreme danger and need to act immediately if they do not want to die?

How do I tell them what I am seeing, what you have shared with me? How do I condense the magnitude of information and simplify it, so that it helps them to realise how serious and deadly this situation is?

"I call on my Infinite Self and Infinite LOVE, and the Laws of Creation from the Heart of Creation and infinitely beyond, to please help the others open their hearts to truth.

Without their help, many who are innocent will also die and never return. The Black Hole of the Beast System, Avatar World, the 'Internet of Things' is about to unfold. I need help to explain why, and what humans need to be aware of, because we have days to resolve this — in terms of getting all to safety. Days, not weeks or months, days...and time is of the essence."

"Claire, tell others what you are perceiving."

Egyptian energies, Reptilian energies, Draco entities ... Mother Earth has 'flat-lined'.

She is dead.

The destroyer forces and all who serve Lucifer, who birthed this Beast System Agenda and birthed 'the illusion' for the Reptilians and other Extra Terrestrial groups to deceive them into believing that Lucifer will give them immortality and the freedom to do what they love to do, which is hunt, rape, maim and kill newborn babies, children, humans, animals, and they love to cause harm.

They believe they can exist without the power of LOVE who they have rejected and they want to live a life of debauchery, greed, malice, maiming, killing, harming humanity's innocents.

That is the promise that Lucifer has made them and so these groups in the higher levels of awareness that are actually our AWOL soul fragments and higher levels of fragmented consciousness that have gone AWOL, are now bent on harming us.

They hate us.

Loathe us.

They fear our awakening and they fear that if we wake up and call for LOVE to rescue us, the dark will not be able to take over the planet.

However, they have stolen much of our energy.

It was easy.

They gave us all the equipment they needed us to use, so that they could weaken our protective shield and break into our ladder of consciousness which holds keys and codes of Knowledge that they need to live off and they weaponise the rest against us.

In its natural state our energy is, LOVE.

Our energy on this planet is so low in vibration. We have a thin layer of low frequency electricity around us, that is all. Some call this the Aura or Biofield. It makes no difference. What mainstream humans need to know is this is not a high strength energy, and so, when we acquiesce to using the ET technology, such as, Wi-fi, 5G, mobile phones, computers, smart cars, smart meters, GPS systems, and so forth, all this equipment has been introduced to zap us of our life force codes of Knowledge, and these stolen codes have been replaced with fake codes of false knowledge, and this is how easy it has been to then place other structures of harder hitting attack, such as the weaponry that is: HAARP, CERN, Wind Turbines, Mobile Phone Masts, TV Masts, Ham Radio Masts, and now, the surveillance — the last part of the structured weaponised attack.

They will hurry through the 15 minute 'ghetto' cities, now.

They have to act fast.

Our councils have so many members who are corrupt world-wide, and just like those in politics and government, this group serve the Lucifer Agenda. By design, not by default.

This group in your councils are totally corrupt. Not all, but many are corrupt. They serve Lucifer, and many are listed as Freemasons, so you can easily spot who is harming humanity.

Some have not declared their allegiance openly, but it will not be hard to find out who serves the Lucifer Agenda because the Laws of Creation came into operation in 2021, thanks to one brave soul, Ann, who asked for her gifts to be activated.

These laws will send back all harm to those responsible when we ask LOVE to help us. Ann did not know how important her gifts were. She died of cancer in December 2023.

The Reptilians know who came in to help humanity, you see, and they have been targeting those who came in with important gifts to protect humanity, and they have killed many good people in order to prevent their gifts being activated.

If you care about your future evolution and care about protecting the children, vulnerable, and all innocent life, I am calling out for help and to ask you all who will listen to this...you all came with codes of Remembrance, codes that protect the planet from this type of attack, codes which shield the innocent and newborns from all harm, codes which cure cancer, cure heart disease, negate the levels of harmful radiation that our planet is now bathed in thanks to StarLink, SkyNet, 5G and other technologies.

Your military know. Big Corp and Big Food know. The City of London Bankers all know. The Royal family know, as does the Vatican.

Be careful and be wary of who you place your trust in, because it is about to get very bumpy on this planet, because I am now telling humanity what you have all done — the part you have played in this murder of the planet.

And I am about to tell them that every person you see who is famous on TV and in Hollywood, every star who you admire, every high level politician, banker, Royal, CEO, and every boss of the telecoms industry, airlines, delivery services: they all had to partake in rituals to cement their allegiance, and do you really want the shocking truth?

They all kill innocent life in ritual.

They all take part in Luciferian ritual — satanic in nature — and all designed to cause severe and extreme trauma. They maim, torture and rape newborn babies with their umbilical cords still attached.

Next time you watch TV, look at the adverts. You will see all who are part of this Luciferian Agenda. The actors who remain present on your TV? It is with regret that I can honestly say, there are few who are not part of this.

When I watch these characters these days, I always think, how many newborns did you have to rape and kill to stay on top of your game?

When I watch adverts, I see the dark Luciferian symbols, on the cars, especially.

Look out for the snake, the eye, the octopus, the dragon...all are symbols of Satan. Everything is so dark energetically, and it is all geared towards the words Hybrid, Artificial Intelligence.

People float about on the screen, climb through space portals in ads for the Open University. Everything is geared around space, aliens, perfume adverts repeat their label's name, flower, flower, flower, flower, haven't you noticed how hypnotising the music and words are these days on your kill box TV sets?

This is all weaponry, the TV and all technology. The TV beams radiation at you and mind control technology at you. You are all being targeted with Havana Syndrome technology, especially those who still care.

It is designed to weaken your energy fields, your protective shield. They keep your eyes hooked on that black screen, and while you watch, they watch you and they steal your vital emergency escape codes and vital keys of Knowledge that are making each one of you, more like a herd of cattle each day.

You only believe what they tell you to believe. Most of you are so hooked on their technology – that little box you hold in your hand — that your hands cannot seem to leave for too long. You have to keep checking, don't you, have to respond to needy emails and texts, have to, have to, have to respond.

You can no longer hold long conversations or process information. You can only follow the crowd and the Tell lies vision. The BBC tell you all that you need to know. They don't want you to think. Oh no, the reptilians they want you brain dead, and in many, they have succeeded.

They laugh at your stupidity, the ease with which you believe their stories. The politicians who helped push that story, are long gone now. They fulfilled their part. They just do game shows now. How many babies do you think they killed to get to play that part in your bedtime story?

How many have black eyes? Ever noticed the black-eyed club? That is adrenochrome from a terrified dead baby. It shows up as a ring around the eye. Check out the Pope. Look at his hand signals. He does the sign of satan and has occasional black eyes.

Jeremy Vine boasted about his black eye. He fell off his bike, he said. Such a long-winded non -story. Did he have to reveal his secret to his black-eyed friends? They like things hidden but in PLAIN sight.

Nothing you see or hear is real anymore. You are watching a GREEN SCREEN Reality, playing out on the Reptilian and Draco technology.

These two groups are looking at the planet and now, they have managed to kill her with the help of Yoga, Reiki and 5G users, predominantly.

Now, they have succeeded in collapsing her most vital grids, the ones your dead parents and departed children need to rise up through— to exit this dark place and return home to a place of peaceful safety, now those grids are gone: there is no escape for your departed loved ones, including your pets.

Humanity have been used. Each particular group — helped to collapse strategic parts of the Earth's protective shield, and I heard yesterday, that the Earth's Schumann resonance has disappeared.

That is because Mother Earth's spiritual grids collapsed quite some time ago — last year, in fact. Her ladder of consciousness was saved by those who called on LOVE to help her, because we were all being sucked into the Black Hole; the Gates of Hell; The Internet of Things; Avatar World; the Belly of The Beast.

LOVE stepped in because enough called for help.

But what we are existing on is no longer a 'live' planet. Yoga and Reiki and 5G users finished her off. They were warned, but they refused to listen.

When others are selfish, it is a very hard energy to circumnavigate. The Reptilians have done a good job in disabling all those who came here to protect the planet and her occupants.

So now, when you see a Yoga class or Reiki advertised in the Cancer care units in hospitals, remember what you have been told here and stay well away. Because partaking in these activities will only suck you into the Beast System further. Stay well away.

And that goes for every piece of equipment that you use that is a technology designed by choice, to weaken you and make you a weak, selfish human who no longer concerns themselves with the outcome of their choices.

The Reptilians need you all to be as selfish as possible. That keeps the vibration on the planet low.

It keeps your protection low. They can harm you more readily that way. And if you do not call for help within the next few days, they will be able to harm you in unimaginable ways. That is their plan and it is about to explode onto humanity.

This Reptilian group cannot exist on any planet where LOVE is the overriding frequency. This is all about frequencies, though, and many dismiss this, particularly if they have religious beliefs or no beliefs, which only plays into the hands of destroyer forces.

Religious folk have worked it out faster in the main, because they understand that the devil exists.

What I wish to explain further is this dark demonic energy is a frequency band.

LOVE is a frequency band.

If you don't want to be part of the Beast System, if you do not want to be part of this Reptilian Agenda to annihilate you and your family, switch frequency bands.

Switch over to LOVE, and stay in that harmonic — through focusing on your heart centre, where love for your family and loved ones emanates from more powerfully than anywhere else.

They want you mind-dead because this is a war for your heart energy, your bandwidth emits LOVE from here when you are 'in the zone' so to speak, and when you are in the zone of loving others, caring for yourself and other's well being, showing compassion, empathy, wanting to help others feel better if they are down, all these are frequencies.

Peace is a frequency— a powerful frequency. Hope, Faith, and Trust are the most powerful healing frequencies and can cure cancer.

If you have cancer, ask from your heart for these frequencies to surround and protect you and to shield you from all harm. Do this morning: when you wake up, midway through the day, and before sleep: at night.

All the frequencies of Hope, Trust, Faith, Peace, Unity, Compassion Forgiveness, are LOVE's frequencies, LOVE"s bandwidth.

Dark destroyer forces cannot exist near the light of LOVE. It is too bright, because they are low-density-emitting energies.

They have no power. They steal that from you and it gives them power. They turn your own power on you and it harms you at deep spiritual levels, not just physically.

The Reptilians understand how to use Earth energy against you, and they understand energy far better than you.

It is why it is so easy to harm you. They are reliant on your ignorance, your lack of inner questioning, they need you to remain thick and brain-dead.

Seems like they might have succeeded because many of you still don't understand what is happening on your planet.

Had you asked your heart, your heart would have told you.

You reject this part of yourself...the most intelligent part, the most loving part of you. And why do you refuse to seek answers from the most intelligent part of your being?

Because you are all implanted with mind control technology. It has being going on for millennia and more.

Your entire ladder of consciousness that is trapped inside the False Light Construct — 'a trap' that lures innocent souls who are out exploring Creation and entraps them in the 'fly jar' trap. They are then chased, hunted, cornered, attacked, raped and maimed, and left in a distorted, damaged form.

Some go over to the dark side, and this is what Lucifer's army partly consists of...your damaged aspects of self, your love and goodness was attacked and stripped down, and this has turned you into a herd of cattle who are no longer capable of deep thought.

Ask most humans what they think about the World Health Organisation, the World Economic Forum, the 15 minute city concepts, climate change.

Most don't know anything about these groups or the concepts, and they know climate changes but do they truly know what it means?

The World Economic Forum are currently sending their scouts out into the UK to brainwash the middle-class and wealthy, who are easily soothed that their recycling will stop climate change. They don't look further because they trust the BBC.

The Reptilians will leave them until last because this group only complain when they get personally harmed. Otherwise, they see the world's problems as 'over there', and as long as they give money to a good cause, and recycle their toilet rolls, until it reaches their doors, they will continue to look down and focus on stirring their homemade marmalade and frosting their cupcakes. Yes, they will be left until last.

The word "change" in the 'Climate Change' has not been tackled though, has it? It this like weather change, or mood change? Why did they stop using 'warming'? Oh yes, they were caught out in the lie. They had to change the descriptor.

Things change. Stop being herded by words which carry no truth or science, and if you continue to listen to one voice which emanates out of the BBC, mainstream media, politics, Big Corp, Big Food and Big River delivery systems, you are simply hearing the Beast System narrative.

You can choose to remind thick, stupid, dumb, unquestioning, or you can choose to widen your world view by listening to the thousands of scientists who disagree with the Beast System narrative.

Stop being like cattle — herded into the lorry, unquestioning of the farmer's motives and only sensing the danger when they hear the other's cries of fear, just before they, themselves are stunned to death.

How can we reach out to humanity when many are 'stunned' into a state of hypnosis, and about to get on that proverbial lorry?

Can Infinite Self, and Infinite LOVE help me summarise the issues more concisely?

I hear: *"Claire, we will take over and fill in some gaps. The Earth is indeed dead. She has flat-lined as shown in the video, that the kind soul sent you, demonstrating that the Schumann resonance has disappeared.*

The Schumann resonance was part of Mother Earth's heart-beat signature. It was her frequency and it emanated from her spiritual heart centre. This is why healers were taught, many years ago, to connect to the Earth's centre before expanding their consciousness.

Years ago, we taught Claire this and then, all her practises of connection changed. They had to change because the Heart of Creation knew what was coming if humanity remained fast asleep about the planet, the Earth energies, the reason for humanity being in this place and forgetting where they came from.

This has been covered in many of Claire's messages — the last three, possibly, will help shed more light on that. For the purposes of this dis-

course, which is an emergency warning and a dire emergency warning for all concerned groups, we wish to explain the seriousness of a flat-lined planet.

Claire, knows it spells trouble, big trouble, and the truth of the matter is that you are in the middle of a crisis that is tailing towards the end.

Very soon, days away from now — and we mean days, not weeks or months — if humanity has not asked for rescue and for their gifts to be activated, they will never survive what is coming.

A flat-lined planet means no protection, no LOVE left to draw on from the Earth, which had been the way.

Claire is thinking about how many internet sites are now recommending 'grounding' into the Earth. Some of these sites are Christian-based and Claire is wondering why they are adopting and recommending outdated practices which are currently bordering on New Age, meaning: holding no truth in them, whatsoever.

How can you ground into the Earth when she has flat-lined? What are you grounding into?

This idea is a trick. It has been helped along by those who do not go deep enough into heart, and some are operating from a place of ego. Their kudos is important online. They do not check their information.

Now, the Christian community are being advised to 'ground' as a method of healing.

A doctor is recommending it also.

Why, you may ask?

Because, to do this, is to intend for your life force energy to leave your body, and what is it connecting to?

A dead planet. A planet whose spirit has departed.

Would you stand on your dead Mother's grave?

We ask you all to show some respect to your beloved planet who died because her children murdered her by their choices.

By the time the fires hit Maui, your planet's spirit was in such a weakened state she could not protect herself, or her children, many of whom went missing in Maui.

Their safety and Mother Earth's safety was secured by those with hearts that go deep enough to perceive the danger she was in and she was being dragged into that Black Hole.

Had others not asked for help, you would all be dead and living a digital, duplicate life in Avatar World.

How many close-shaves is one too many?

Does anyone here, care that Mother Earth was killed off by Yoga, Reiki, and 5G users?

You have zero protection. Babies are being gang-raped because the density has fallen and humanity are deep inside the abyss that is nearing the Black Hole Vacuum.

This is an emergency call and an emergency warning to all life because unless you ensure that you have made your request to LOVE for rescue from this place, you will go into this Black Hole. There will be no return.

All is forgiven, however, those who collapsed the grid system of Mother Earth need to understand a thing or two, as does humanity as a whole.

The Schumann resonance has been interfered with over the years. The Egyptians syphoned off the frequencies of the planet's heart-beat and remixed them with their own version.

Claire has frequently questioned the Schumann resonance because she does not like the feel of them.

Others find them soothing, and now, crystal bowl frequencies are being promoted on the internet as healing frequencies.

You are inside a False Light Construct. The crystal bowls are like coral from the sea. Look, but don't touch.

Mother Earth has been raped and pillaged by her own children for her crystals. When you take without asking, it is called theft by the heart of Creation.

Did you ask for Mother Earth's permission? She would have asked you not to deplete the strength of her crystals. They made up part of her life force. Her grid system.

If you have crystals at home, please ask your heart what you should do with them. These belong to Mother Earth and her spirit has departed.

All we are asking is that you all show some respect, and seek ways through your heart to remedy any mistakes which may have led to her death.

So, the Egyptians meddled with Mother Earth's heart resonance. They reworked it and meddled. It was never pure, but it was better than no help at all and it held enough power, back in the day, to help all expand their consciousness above the third dimension and, for some, they reached the twelfth deck, where they remain.

And why do these souls remain trapped inside the False Light Construct levels when they were able to expand their consciousness into their twelfth level, the Cosmic Shield Level?

Many who are capable are trapped by ego-led behaviour and the need for dominance over others. They no longer feel they have any more to learn. They are trapped inside a revolving doorway, and have remained there for twelve years more than was necessary.

The help was offered to them in 2012 onwards. They were so blinded by their own kudos, they rejected the offer.

LOVE is frequently rejected on your planet.

Much more help was available. Enough was available up to June 2023, and after that, it became clear to the Heart of Creation that the Zombie Apocalypse was inevitable, unavoidable and it started in earnest at the top deck of the ladder of humanity's consciousness, and has worked its way down into the bodies of the vulnerable, namely: the homeless and drug addicted, who are being systematically taken over by destroyer forces who need a body and a ladder of consciousness, in order to arrive into this reality.

Zero protection from the Earth who has flat-lined, has made it a 'walk in the park.'

Many on the streets are suffering from wasting disease which looks similar to leprosy. The Heart of Creation warned about this in "By JUNE 2023, All WILL KNOW."

Others mocked and questioned, however, they did not ask their hearts for guidance, and their hearts would have shown them.

The Zombie Apocalypse is already in full-flow. How many of you are zombified by your TV, mobiles, and computers? How many see it in their friends? The inability to take truth into them?

They cannot respond to 'the obvious', because their life force codes have been stolen and replaced with false light codes. It is why things don't compute, and why they look blank and just blink at truthful facts.

Like a computer network with a virus, they are contaminated with fake codes of false information.

The blinking is a sign, and the vague stare that washes over their faces is another obvious clue.

You don't see the Zombie Apocalypse? It is staring you all in the face and is not hard to discover if you ask your heart, you will come across plenty of evidence. You have to go outside of the main Beast System though, although all systems serve Lucifer. Nothing here is operating from LOVE.

What can you do if the planet has flat-lined and the planet's dead body and humanity are deep inside the abyss, heading towards the

Black Hole vacuum?

A rational mind might suggest that hedging one's bets may be prudent here.

A spiritual heart may advise requesting LOVE to rescue you from this terrifying ending.

We are issuing this emergency warning because this is all about choices.

The choice to do nothing and die, or to choose life and LOVE and ask for help."

I ask, "What do you think the outcome will be for many."

"Claire, at this late stage it is not looking good. Many refuse to look up. They are all more than capable — each human has the ability to ask their inner intelligence for assistance and to be shown the terror awaiting their loved ones and friends."

Life is hanging in the balance, quite literally."

Q. "How can we best help our own soul evolution in optimal ways that best serve all life at this juncture, for those who choose love and life?"

I hear: *"Claire, you are connecting with some beautiful souls recently, aren't you?"*

I reply: "Yes, I am connecting with some gentle, loving beings and they make me weep sometimes, because I can feel their love and their concern for humanity; their compassion...it is almost like getting a huge hug, physically. I am grateful for their presence on the planet. I sometimes feel we are isolated and alone, and dealing with this knowledge of what is truly happening...well...when others are stepping forward to assist who understand the issue is serious, it is a huge relief.

However, many in the Holistic Community could be helping humanity, but I see what many are doing is harming us, placing us all in danger. The babies are getting harmed the worst. And I just wish others would stop their activities, their ego-led meditation events, their ego choices, because I see all these events as harmful, and no one has consulted the heart of Creation. No one.

These are 'ideas' from the mind. The heart would never advise group meditations, you just get all your precious codes stolen. They are exposing themselves and opening their gateways, so that Reptilian entities can walk into this reality. I can't get through to these groups. They stopped listening a long time ago. The ego rules. No one should be organising group meditation. Those who understand why not do not organise these events.

I see a lot of division, and I despair at the harm their actions cause. It always harms the children first. Many children and infants and newborns are leaving the planet. They cannot bear the depth of darkness that we are in and which they are arriving into. It is too close to the Black Hole vacuum.

Those who can call for help are calling out for rescue and leaving their fragile tiny bodies earlier than planned. These ones brought rescue codes to help humanity leave this dark place. It is heartbreaking for all concerned.

If others do not ask their hearts and LOVE for permission, guidance, teachings on how to best serve all in optimal ways, then everything else is ego-centred behaviour, and babies end up leaving the planet as a result of their choices.

This group are being highlighted here, because they should know better — having explored energy, they should know how to make things safe, but they don't and they are reckless.

I just keep seeing all the newborns, their suffering, the abuse that they are experiencing in child-trafficking circles, the prolific trauma and terror some of these souls are suffering, and I cannot understand how any "healer" would want to be a party to causing the descension of their planet and its occupants into this abyss.

A rescue call was made a few days ago on behalf of all those who are innocent and have no choice, including the homeless, children, infants and newborns, elderly, vulnerable and all life, including pets, animals, birds, sea life... All are suffering as a result of all of our choices.

Can you explain to others why healing systems are no longer safe to use, including multi-dimensional healing, energy healing of others, crystal bowl therapy, sound therapy, colour therapy, Yoga, Reiki, Quantum healing etc?"

My heart and LOVE guides: *"Claire, these systems were obsolete a long time ago. They have all been invaded by Reptilian and Draco energies, predominantly. All they do is hold you in a trance-like-state and steal your life force codes — to enable the Reptilians and Draco factions to hold you captive here."*

I say: "I think most people are ignorant about the ET Agenda and the Reptilian presence.

Is there anything else that you wish to contribute here? I am at a loss, at what to do. I sense chaos looming — and death —I perceived the ladder of consciousness of many humans being withdrawn — from the personality self — which will leave them without an escape ladder out of here and it cuts off all assistance from LOVE. It also leaves them soulless, and they will never leave this place if that happens. It will lead to death.

If we have a lot of deaths. The WHO will blame it on Disease X.

The Reptilian's weakest point is the presence of LOVE. They cannot exist when LOVE is around us.

They also need us to be compliant with our own downfall, because they fear the Laws of Creation which are returning all magnified malicious harm to the sender, creator, perpetrator.

So, they have to work silently, stealthily behind the scenes. They may have hypnotised most of humanity, however, there are millions of us and if perhaps a 100,000 woke up and called for help, would that protect all life here?

Would it be enough to get them off our planet and out of this reality?

How many pro-active humans are required to defeat the dark, if enough of us called on LOVE for help to rescue ourselves and the innocent?"

And I hear: *"Claire, sadly, it is no longer about that anymore. This reality is folding in on itself under the weight of selfish choices that have caused this invasion to occur.*

It is no longer viable to request rescue for others. That was yesterday. Not today.

Today is about those who want to continue forward and to continue to evolve and explore, to ensure they are ready and have done all they can to repair and heal any harm which they may have caused others, including Mother Earth and all precious life, because all life throughout the whole of Creation has been wounded by the choices made on the Earth.

To watch the children destroy their Mother has sent shock waves across all of existence. Truly, it has shocked many, and although LOVE and life evolves forward and, of course, all is forgiven, the history books will remain and the story of how it all ended will never be forgotten.

Because the harm caused was beyond what we thought was possible and it has harmed all life at deep levels.

Pray for forgiveness for all errors caused to all precious life.

Pray for rescue.

Pray."

Chapter Forty-Five

THE TIDE IS TURNING: BE PREPARED FOR TURBULENCE

Use your creativity to imagine all corruption exposed, all malicious harm returned to all those who have harmed. You all have the power to resolve this.

AUDIO MESSAGE SEARCHING FOR THE EVIDENCE, BITCHUTE

Chapter Forty-Six

SYNCHRONISE YOUR HEART WITH THE HEART OF CREATION: Avoid Grounding To Avoid Losing Life Force

NEW INFORMATION— ALL OLD METHODS SHARED BY CLAIRE ON LOVE'S HEART PLAN SUBSTACK ARE DEFUNCT AND ARE NOW FOR HISTORICAL REFERENCES ONLY —NEW HEART CONNECTION LINK BELOW FOR TARGETED INDIVIDUALS AND AL

SEARCHING FOR THE EVIDENCE

New Heart Connection Follows A Short Rant (for those wishing to leave the matrix):

Hello Everyone, Well, it is quite mad and chaotic on this temporary planet, isn't it?

Just over a week ago, new opportunities were secured for all those who, at some level on their conscious ladder, asked to be helped out of the matrix and to return home when the time was right for each soul.

Many chose to be rescued from the darkness and density of the previous 'platform' of Earth. This 'platform' was so badly damaged, I had put out a message because I perceived that the Earth matrix was collapsing and getting darker than I had ever perceived it before.

In early 2024, I watched the dark Earth veering off into the darkness towards the Black Hole of Lucifer and the abyss.

These dense energies were terribly difficult to navigate through for those attempting heart connection. I am sure many of you felt this too.

The previous place or matrix that we knew as Earth, has gone. Her children killed her off. Many disagree about this, but they have not gone deep enough into their own consciousness to ascertain this.

Exploring consciousness and deeper truths is not hard to do. Everyone is capable.

It requires daily discipline and hard work.

However, if everyone was connecting to their hearts deeply each day: for guidance on how to help and protect all precious life, we would not have rogue entities masquerading as 'competent' leaders of the Vatican, City of London Mafia Banksters, nor a 'respectable' looking Royal Family, front of house, and behind the scenes, a cess pit of corruption, pedophilia and child abuse scandals.

We would not have Yoga and Reiki groups destroying the last of the previous Earth's evolutionary grids and her subsequent spiritual death, and we would not have Freemasons corrupting policy at our World Economic Forum controlled town councils, nor would we be permitting the councils to implement the '15 minute ghetto city' campaigns, or their plans to take our homes away from us and imprison us for having insufficient insulation in our houses.

We wouldn't have the World Economic Forum and corrupt United Nations stopping air travel by 2035 and making our lives a misery.

We wouldn't have a World Health Organisation that is so corrupt and bent that it's leader is a criminal who was once a terrorist for The People's Liberation Front who supported corruption, violence, murder, and torture, and who is wanted in Ethiopia for crimes against humanity.

Our media would be telling us the truth in the ideal world. The BBC would be transparent and not running amok with child trafficking satanists and CIA operatives at the top, middle, and bottom. The military would be protecting the people, not trafficking the drugs and trafficking children for the satanic elites, and the police would be complying with their obligations to serve the people, not corporations, and the Royal Family would be serving God and the people rather than their incredible greed and lust for power.

Thanks to our corrupt governments, we now have our young and old being conscripted for war...Who's war?

Oh yes, that is right — the war by the elite on humanity, and the war on our consciousness by those who the elite serve.

The war on poisoning our bodies, food, drink and climate is in full swing.

The war to steal our souls and enslave us in the 'Reptilian brain, mind prison' is in full swing too.

The war on our hearts is upon us all.

Has anyone noticed?

Barely a soul.

One or two perhaps? Yet, those who say they are 'awake', are still talking about grounding techniques, biofields, chakra centres, and so forth.

This is outdated stuff and it is time to move on.

Who is teaching this spiritual claptrap?

In 2012, we were all asked to focus solely on heart connection.

Do yourselves a favour...wake yourselves up from your mind prison and shake off the Reptilian interface that is controlling you.

Your mind cannot decide for you. It is controlled by a Reptilian brain interface. The hint is in the word, REPTILIAN.

The Reptilian poison is now in the vaccinated and taking over their heart intelligence.

Has anyone noticed how others are behaving around you?

Anyone noticed how Freemasons are gathering, recruiting, getting ready for their Satanic D-Day "let's stand around a Satanic obelisk and get you to focus on death, war, destruction, then let's go and light a satanic bonfire across the UK".

In remembrance... of... what?

Of the death caused in that war, the heartache, the deception of the fabricated war?

A British Royal Family who are Germans and who changed their name to Windsor to hide this fact?

A war that was designed, like all wars — to kill off humans and steal their life force?

Wars equate to profit.

Human loss and heartache equate to theft of lots of life force codes, to implement the 'Internet of Everything', including you.

Does D-Day stand for death day?

If you choose to go and stand around an obelisk for the celebrations, you are giving your power to Lucifer, no one else.

There are other ways to remember those we loved who died fighting for our freedom.

A freedom which was given away in 2020 by those who are so mind controlled, they will do the 'D-day ritual.' Just like the Emergency Alert code, D-day is designed to get our attention on their satanic technology, their obelisks, their death-day celebrations.

Our acquiescence is all they need to harm us.

All that effort to secure our freedom in previous wars was given away in 2020, when humanity decided to give their trust to Pfizer and a corrupt world government: ruled by the Vatican and 'P2'— the Vatican mafia's Freemasonic cult, the ones who hire hit men to murder living breathing men and women who speak out like me, and the ones who like to torture and abuse infants and children. The Black Eyed club. The Club of Rome types.

The ones who like to create wars because it is profitable, as was the covid-19 pandemic, as will be the Net Zero carbon tax, and how ironic that no one has batted an eye that our UK government and other European governments have down-graded the 'deadly' covid-19 to a mere harmless flu-like virus on their websites, which coincided with the air strike and silently appeared on the government's website.

Terminal cancer is deadly. It never gets downgraded to mild symptoms. So, how does a supposedly deadly 'not a virus' become a non-event?

Nothing will wake humanity up it seems, not that, not even forced conscription.

That fluoridated water certainly seems to be dumbing them all down.

Oh dear. Apologies for the rant but I see no improvements, despite humanity securing much more help, they just keep giving their power away and those who could be helping are not in heart, currently.

Many are acting as unwitting diversions, and it does concern me. I have taken some time out and a lot seems to have happened in the news, but not much has changed — in terms of those who could be helping.

Too many are mentally processing everything, or seem too immersed in the 'saviour complex' to be of any use to self or others.

I will repeat here. Grounding does not help and will cost you life force.

Life force codes are the energy we need to exit the False Light Construct and if we continue to 'ground' now, when it is a defunct spiritual method, we will lose the ability to leave the matrix.

The new Earth platform holds new information and new ways of connecting to the heart of Creation.

How can I help others today? Can you expand further on what you wish me to share here?

I hear: *"Claire, we want you all to know that you are all loved very much and the Heart of Creation is here to support you all if you ask for help.*

We cannot step in unless you ask through your heart for help each day.

All, repeat, all old methods of connecting to heart are defunct for those who have been following the teachings shared by Claire on her channels.

It is time to move forward and to share with you that this Earth platform is new, but it is not 'New Earth'— it is a temporary holding place of learning to help all of you who wish to return home to the Heart of Creation, to prepare for your eventual departure.

The opportunity is being presented for those who have been working hard on their heart connection, and those who are practicing expansion of consciousness.

Many of you may be aware of the last few weeks and the difficulties of connection, the rapid need to change connection methods, feeling destabilised, anxious, depressed, experiencing disturbed sleep, ringing in the ears, etc.

All these are signs of attack from the Satanic groups. They are diminished in numbers but should never be underestimated in their hatred and loathing of humanity and all life, especially the children who they have their eyes on.

It is all about the children, and all the dreadful plans have escalated that we made the request for help to weaken, in **"Close The Door on 2024"** *simply because far too many, including those who could easily be helping to weaken the grip this group hold over humanity, are equally giving their power away to the Reptilian and Draco Agenda — the joint war on humanity and the temporary new Earth platform.*

The old Earth was left in such a weakened state she was recalled and helped by LOVE to return to her true original form and this opportunity is here for you all if you wish to prepare for eventual departure and return home.

It is a choice that only you can make.

We say, if you do wish to return, you must do as Claire advised and shake off your old Earth matrix coat, because no system from there fits this new platform. And you will not stay here long, either, as the shifts in frequency will come fast and furious now, as the In Breath nears completion.

You need to prepare and this means you need to raise your vibration.

Without a continual focus on this, it is not possible to synchronise with the rapid shifts that are to follow.

For those who left things late, it is going to be a difficult climb. It did not have to be this way. However, many have become so immersed in mind, they barely think of their heart intelligence, and yet, this was always going to be the only route home.

We say; "Avoid grounding your life force in a temporary platform."

Your energy needs to be used to expand your heart, and your heart connection needs to become synchronised with the Heart of Creation.

*Many of you neglect the use of the Laws of Crea*tion *and yet they are the laws of Life that govern all life.*

The routines Claire has previously taught have been shared to help others in the past to synchronise with both the planetary shifts, the Heart of Creation shifts, and the shifts and harms created by the satanic forces who hold power over humanity.

We say that for those who keep choosing to give their power to corrupt politicians, UN policy, fake wars, obelisk and fire burning ceremonies, Freemasonic practices which bring in Lucifer energy onto the planet and harm all life, including pets, Yoga practices, Reiki practices and energy healing practices...all are harming at deep levels and need to be aborted as a matter of urgency — for those who wish to return home, that is.

For those who continue to harm, the penalty is severe at this late stage. All malicious harm, all intention to cause harm, all harm born out of selfishness, choosing to ignore harmful actions by governments, authorities or employers, choosing Yoga, Reiki, Freemasonry over love, life, and unity will result in loss of life... and death of the soul.

All harmful actions are now the sole responsibility of every individual living breathing man and woman.

To ignore the Laws of Creation is to let in death and destruction.

All harm will be perpetually returned, and all karma is returned to the originator who dreamt up the harm that caused the karma.

You cannot run and you cannot hide.

Take note: Lucifer.

Take note: satanists and Freemasons, corrupt councils and infiltrated authorities.

If you have harmed — all is being returned, and will not stop until you decide to stop.

It is a severe warning for those harming, yet, for those trying to serve all life, it means that your journey is about to become much easier: in terms of your heart connection — which has been plagued by attack from many groups.

Here is the routine Claire was asked to follow:

I say:

"Common sense tells us that heart connection is unsuitable for use when driving, operating machinery, or using in work place environments.

It requires a quiet, shaded room at home, away from bright sunlight.

I set an alarm clock and have a glass of water nearby.

I lie down at home: flat on my back on the bed that I sleep in at night, legs straight, never crossed, and if it is safe to do so, I close my eyes.

I listen to my breathing and as I listen to the air going in and out of my chest area, I take my closed eyes and softly look down, in the direction of my heart area.

I focus on the rise and fall of my chest.

The air going in and out of my lungs.

I allow my body to relax, and I breathe normally.

When I am ready, I imagine I have a switch in the centre of my chest — my Infinite Heart Switch.

I press this switch or pretend to press it, and I imagine that my Infinite Heart expands out of my human heart and all around me like a protective first layer, like a huge 'Russian Doll' of loving protection.

I take another breath and as I let out my breath, I imagine the Heart of Creation expands around me: like a second 'Russian Doll' layer of loving protection.

I breathe normally and relax, and then, I imagine that the Laws of Creation expand around me: a third, loving layer of protection.

Finally, I imagine the Whole of Creation and infinitely beyond expand all around me. A forth layer of powerful protection.

I relax and breathe normally, keeping my closed eyes softly looking down at my chest area.

Next, I return to my heart and start again.

I envisage my Infinite Heart all around my physical self.

I imagine it grows bigger. My Infinite Heart knows how big it needs to grow.

I see it stop at the Heart of Creation boundary, so, I imagine that the Heart of Creation, my second protective layer, grows bigger too.

I watch it grow on my inner heart screen.

I wait and when I am ready, I imagine the Laws of Creation expand around my Heart of Creation layer and Infinitely beyond.

I swiftly imagine that the Whole of Creation and Infinitely Beyond expands around all my layers of loving protection.

I feel the expansion, the peace, the silence, the tranquility.

When I feel guided to, I start this cycle again and I repeat this full cycle until I am guided to stop by my Infinite Heart.

When I am guided to stop repeating the cycle in full, I rest and receive healing.

Pause the recording if you need to here and rejoin us when you are ready.

When I am ready, I ask questions, such as:

Q. How can I best help my soul evolution today?

Q. How can I best serve all precious life?

You may also like to ask:

Q. Is grounding safe to do?

Does it best serve my soul evolution and best serve all life in optimal ways, in alignment with the Laws of Creation and LOVE's plan?

I seek further understanding on any matter which I am seeking truth about. I test my understanding. I seek solutions.

Q. Ask how you are to proceed forward with this new connection?

Q. Is it likely to change?

Q. If it will change, how will you know?

Q. Will the energy feel less powerful after a certain time of use?

Q. How will I know when to upgrade or move on or expand on this method?"

I hear my Infinite Heart say:

"...And that is how to learn and grow.

Your hearts have always had your best interests at heart.

Your heart intelligence knows the answers and holds all the solutions.

The issues around 'mental processing' are: loss of life force, loss of power, and waste of energy from the Heart of Creation.

Ask about how energy has been wasted by yourself and how to recover lost life force.

Only you can decide if you want it back, if you want to stop losing it to the dark forces, and only you can decide if you truly wish to leave the matrix when the time comes, or continue to be enslaved by the Reptilian beast system of trans-human mind control, and corruption of everything you hold dear.

There really is not much time left to prepare your heart connection and get it strong.

It is up to you, but we say: it is time to finally choose.

The final opportunity to stay, or to go."

Chapter Forty-Seven

A Perfect Circle Of Black Will Tell You All Who To Avoid And Who To Turn Away From

This message needs you to be still and relaxed in a place at home where you can lie down and safely close your eyes, a place where you can remain undisturbed without distractions.

Once you are lying down, close your eyes, and listen to this message while you take your closed eyes and softly look down at your heart area. Breathe normally.

Video Link:

Hello, My name is Claire and I am a teacher of Metaphysics and Expansion of Consciousness.

I am typing out a message through heart connection, which simply means that each day, I still my busy mind and connect to my heart intelligence: that still small voice within me that tells me when I am making good decisions or bad choices — the part of me that, sometimes, I have ignored, yet, this is the part of me that, like your heart intelligence, has answers and solutions to the most difficult and insurmountable problems, and it is these problems which I wish to talk about today, to help those who are just starting to become aware that something is wrong, who may be starting to get worried about why that is.

Many humans who I speak with have made very pertinent comments in recent weeks and it appears to me that many are awakening to the fact that something is wrong with the covid-19 vaccines.

Some of these observations are made by nurses working on wards, and nurses who sit in on consultant's appointments and hear that the patient has been injured by the covid-19 vaccine.

Many others comment that they are witnessing friends and family getting ill. They are worried, and I wish to try to shed some light on things, and give hope to you all that nothing is ever as futile as it may seem.

From my perspective and from the perspective of many others who regularly connect to their heart intelligence, this part of ourselves and this part of yourself can see what is happening on the ground here.

Our heart intelligence sees the corruption, the lies, the dishonesty that has led many to take an experimental stage three gene therapy which was still on trial at the time, and a trial which has subsequently been proven to be flawed by many scientists, doctors, eminent professors of top universities, renowned Cardiologists and so forth, and if you look online on Telegram.com, Substack.com, bitchute.com and various other alternative news sources, you will find that the internet is awash with substantive evidence: in the form of peer reviewed papers and the many medical and scientific voices who are screaming at the top of their lungs to try to awaken the masses. However, these earnest voices have been largely overlooked because the mainstream media is controlled, edited and policed by a handful of parasites who own and control the media companies worldwide.

The political and medical propaganda of the last four years — witnessed via the internet, the TV, radio, and social media sites has been shocking.

Many who I have recently spoken with had no idea about this news.

It is 'old news', yet, it is only just reaching them four years later.

Can you imagine how hard this is to digest for those who do not know?

Many of us have been shouting from the roof tops since 2020, and recently, it appears that humanity is waking up.

Nurses and doctors are waking up, too.

My hope is that it is not too late to help those who are in shock.

Many are parents. Imagine, trusting a narrative and opting to have your children vaccinated only to find out through family, friends, or casual conversations that many are suffering severe adverse reactions, and it seems that this is only gathering speed, as the evidence is unavoidable?

It is not just hearsay anymore. Not just some 'conspiracy buff' waxing lyrical...

The sheer enormity of what has been done to humanity is starting to sink in. Humanity is becoming aware, and when it eventually realises the full impact of the deception; the motives; the depth of evil intent, I wonder how many politicians, medical establishments, doctors, nurses, big Pharma employees, those who put the vaccines into others, and the town councillors (who knew what was going on, because while humanity slept they allowed the equally deadly 5G technology to go up in every village, every town, every city)... how many of these folk will be running for the hills as the law suits mount up and common law courts issue sentence?

Many of us know this is manslaughter, murder, genocide, deliberate intention to maliciously harm while making profits and being given free rein to lethally inject patients — with no liability, no medical responsibility for one's actions.

Some thought they could get away with it. Many just followed the system; followed their leaders; questioned nothing.

Do you think the public will allow those who harmed, who killed, who injected a lethal poison into others to get off, 'Scott -free'?

They have to be held to account, and justice must be served.

The medical industry may be free of all liability under the Emergency Codes, however, the public can still privately sue the individual who told them the injection was safe and effective.

I hope that a huge joint law suit is flung at the Big Pharma giants who did this to humanity and I hope humanity will never give their power away to anyone except their heart intelligence — their conscience — because had humanity been in close connection with their inner heart intelligence, they would never had believed the political global cabal and the corrupt Royals (...why trust friends of Jimmy

Saville?), the Church leaders, the corrupt World Health Organisation and United Nations, et al. Their hearts would have advised them not to take the vaccine, not to subject themselves to mask wearing, which does not stop virus particles, and which causes respiratory issues, including cancer.

None of these policies were the original policies for pandemic planning in the NHS.

These new policies were introduced to maintain compliance; obedience, and it is saddening that hospital staff are so poorly educated that they do not know the health issues that result from mask wearing.

What will humanity do, now that DNA fragments, HIV and the SV40 cancer causing gene has been detected in the covid-19 vaccines as cancer cases increase, and AIDS increases, and what will they do when the power-hungry world government tell humanity that they have a 'cure' for all the covid-19 vaccine ingredient 'harms' — that they have a new 'saviour vaccine' that will 'cure' humanity of all the health problems that they gave humanity in last one?

Will they fall for the lies again?

Humanity has been abused by a predator group of very wealthy 'parasites' who live off power, greed, lust for control.

Bill and Melinda Gates are such a pair. They are not medically trained. Why are they so eager to vaccinate all the Africans, the elderly, the poor, the disabled, and the children? They were kicked out of India in the past because their Wellness injections killed many young girls.

What is their agenda this time around?

Those of you who are suffering harm need to sit up and pay attention.

Many of us have been trying to warn you that you were in danger, but you refused to listen. Instead, you discriminated against us; you segregated us; treated us like second class citizens.

We highlighted the issues to you. You turned your backs on the information and chose to give your power away to a wealthy group who have lied constantly and have laughed at humanity's stupidity.

We have had to sit back and watch the inevitable car crash that we all knew was coming.

Spare a thought for those family members and friends who you segregated, who you refused to listen to, the ones who could not come to the family Christmas meal because their choices didn't match yours. The inevitable consequences of your choices have traumatised them: a death toll that they were powerless to prevent. We knew the cult were coming for the children. Now, many are dead or severely injured, and society has ignored their suffering too.

When did humans become so deeply prejudiced and selfish?

When did your love for your family and friends become secondary to your love for your government and Pfizer?

Do you trust your government and Big Pharma, big banks and the NHS over and above a fellow human who may be sincerely concerned about your life and well being?

This has been the issue facing those of us who chose to speak out. We could not get through to you.

And it is all very sad indeed because now a huge karmic cycle is in full swing and about to hit all those who have not asked their heart intelligence for help, and now, all those who have maliciously harmed will also get hit by their karmic actions.

Meanwhile, what about the world's children and new borns? It is all about their welfare, at the end of the day, and it is all about your welfare, too.

Time is running out on this one.

Ask the nurses in the hospitals. They know. They are seeing the fall-out of these poisons every day.

There are solutions.

Are you willing to listen and try to help yourself and your family?

There are many of us out there who care about you. If you look online you will find many shouting from the rooftops, and offering simple protocols.

Some videos may scare you. Be aware, they are presented to help you wake up. Many kind souls are doing this out of love and compassion for you, your children, and loved ones.

Many unsung heroes have risked a lot for you already. Some are dead. They have been killed off because their knowledge threatened to expose those who planned this genocide.

Many kind souls spend much of their time posting informational videos to try to get your attention.

The problem is that we are preaching to the choir as most of those who have been harmed and who are worried are not aware that the information is not on mainstream sites, it is on places like Substack.com, bitcute.com, telegram.com.

The death toll and adverse reactions is a worldwide issue. Many are suffering and therefore, waking up to the fact that something is wrong.

There is no judgement here.

I wanted to lay out the ground work because I understand that newly awakened folk are finding my channel and I wish to reach out to them, to help them have hope that we can resolve matters in a peaceful way.

I am now asking my heart intelligence and Infinite LOVE to help me to share some information that will hopefully inspire and smooth your worried brows.

Please be very discerning and use your heart intelligence to guide you.

Your greatest strength is your heart intelligence energy. It has more power in its little finger than any life form on this planet.

Have Hope, Faith and Trust that you already have the inbuilt tools inside of you to help you and you do not need any other power, any other person, place or thing, any government, any corrupt official, or any ignorant medical body to make your decisions for you.

This message needs you to be still, to be relaxed while you listen at home where you can lie down and safely close your eyes, and remain undisturbed, without distractions.

Your mind is very loud and very busy.

To hear your heart intelligence, you have to quieten the 'mind-noise'.

Your heart intelligence cannot be controlled by the ego and mind programs, however, your decision to connect to your heart is important.

Without that free will choice — the choice to be willing to hear truth from a deep place inside of yourself — the help cannot come to you.

I lie down on the bed that I sleep in at night at home to hear my heart talk to me, and I ask questions once I have firstly received supportive healing from my inbuilt helper.

The following message requires each of you to lie down on the bed that you sleep in at night at home.

It is a familiar place where you already rest, and feel safe.

It is the best place to receive help from your heart because the protection builds up around you and around your home.

Your own bed offers the familiarity of restfulness and relaxation.

Once you are lying down, close your eyes, and softly look down at your heart area while you

listen to the whole message.

Listen to the air going in and out of your chest.

Breathe normally and relax as you do for sleep each night, and if you need to be awake at a certain time, ensure you have set an alarm clock because you may very well fall asleep.

Here is an important announcement from the
heart of creation: received through my heart
today:

"Claire, it has come to pass that many are awakening to the harm that has been wielded upon them and it is time to reach out to those who will listen to explain in detail what is at stake here if they choose to do nothing.

The lethal injections are varied and each of you may of may not have received a tainted batch. It was designed for different batches to contain different types of illness-causing ingredients.

Nurses are, indeed, witnessing the effects as the cardiac wards fill up with youngsters who have signs of myocarditis and pericarditis.

It is, possibly, the most wicked act of malicious intention to inflict these wounds on the very young.

It is also happening in children's wards, and the incubators are filling up, as pregnant women either miscarry or give birth to premature infants with complex birth defects.

Will it reach the news? Not unless the corrupt officials decide they want it to. They are still deciding how to inflict the most harm — the most pain on you all.

This group who planned and conceived this idea have had many helpers. They loathe the masses — see themselves as 'better than', and 'above' you all.

Their loathing for you all is matched by their desire to inflict pain and suffering.

They trade this pain and fear, and suffering with those who feed off this energy source.

We have tried to gently awaken you all, but you have refused to listen, or to look at what this large group are doing to you.

Many have tried but to no avail.

We have no intention of causing you more pain or anguish, however, if we don't tell you now, it will be too late and you need to understand a thing or two, so that you are fully informed and can make a choice from there.

The group who conceived and executed this plan were highly organised. They operate under the radar — in plain sight of you all. They are a 'mafia' of sorts: under the term 'organised criminals,' and they are not balanced individuals, nor are they capable of empathy.

Their power and control has been growing through allegiance to the power that has, until recently, had dominion over humanity and all life here.

This power has many names. We refer to it here as: Lucifer.

Lucifer energy is a highly unstable ball of blackness that is vast. It is made up of millennia of dark energy, fear, suffering, greed, hatred, etc., and it lacks light because it has turned its back on its source.

The source of Lucifer is you. All of you have contributed to this energy that the group who are harming believe is 'a God,' and they are completely stupid in that regard because if all of you asked your hearts and LOVE, from the heart of Creation, to find all of the parts of you that are lost in the black ball of Lucifer, all the darkness would be weakened as your energy is found, healed and repaired.

The Satanists and Luciferians work with this dark energy which is feeding on your energy emissions: your hatred, your guilt, your apathy, your ignorance, your selfishness, your choice to look the other way, and so forth.

All these energy emissions are without LOVE. They break the Laws of Creation because hatred, selfishness, apathy, choosing to look the other way and ignore suffering, causes harm to all life.

Look around you. Do you see suffering?

Have you helped to create this?

The simple answer is that you created this reality.

All of your choices affect others, whether you notice or not.

You can cause great harm by apathy.

You can cause great harm by choosing to stick your heads in the sand and ignore the crisis that is building and starting to effect all life here.

How many children are sick, right now?

You could find out if you cared enough.

Or, you could turn away and ignore the crisis that this dark group have deliberately created.

They cannot create. They get you to create their chosen reality by fuelling your fear, causing wars and death, making you watch loved ones die a painful death...

They program your mind through predictive advertising and marketing on your TV sets.

Your mobile phones are mind-control devices which emit frequencies that keep you addicted to using your phones: texting, emailing, face-timing, yet, you barely notice the natural world around you. Many of you, are so fixated that you walk with that black box in the palm of your hand, it is a wonder you notice anyone or thing, let alone those who need your help right now.

So, we are coming to the conclusion of this message.

Do you choose to wake up and look at the true facts, or do you choose to turn your backs on humanity and the children?

Your choices determine the outcome for many of the world's children.

The dark cabal plan to introduce trans-humanism via the back-door of the vaccination program.

The technology is inside you all now.

Vaccinated or not.

If they could not get it into you via the injection, they have sprayed your skies and poisoned your food and drink supplies.

You may not want to hear this but you need to know because we are all on the precipice of great change, which is upon you all and upon the heart of Creation, which is preparing to expand, and with that expansion, with that new cycle of evolution, all who choose to remain controlled by the dark Lucifer energies and all who choose to remain a servant to the 'mafia and cult' that seek power and control over you all, cannot come home and cannot continue their soul evolution.

Your soul understands this Your heart intelligence knows only too well what this means.

Perhaps, a trickle of discomfort is reaching you from your higher regions of consciousness who also know what this means.

Your choice to do nothing means death.

Death of the self. Death of your evolution. An end to your ability to return to LOVE and Life and Unity, to Creativity — which is the essence of your very self.

To choose Life and LOVE and Unity, all you have to do is tell your heart what you want.

That is all you have to do, at this stage.

If you wish to start the process of recovering all the energy that you have given to that big black ball of Lucifer, all you have to do is ask your heart and LOVE for help.

The rest will be done for you.

Claire recently shared a message in "Synchronise Your Heart With The Heart of Creation" and part way through the message, there is a heart connection and clearing routine.

If you choose LOVE, Life and Unity, the routine offers a way to build your heart connection with the heart of Creation, and in this way, all that was lost can be found, all errors can be healed and all regrets can be resolved.

Your heart intelligence is here to help you to heal.

No thing outside of yourself can do this.

If you seek another to help you instead of your heart intelligence, you will fail to come home.

We do not wish to sound so grim. We wish to make it clear that YOUR heart has the authority to help you. No one, no thing, no other has this authority.

Therefore, when you seek help from another instead of your heart, you give your power — your energy to Lucifer, nothing else, and you lose vital energy that is meant to get you out of this place when the time comes to leave.

Avoid being trapped here when your time to leave arrives.

This advice is equally meant for healers and others who, although using their heart intelligence, are still looking outside of self for healing light from others, and we wish to impress upon them that this wastes all the effort that their hearts have given them so far.

You will end up in a 'yo-yo state', inside a 'revolving doorway' and you will become trapped by your own choices to entrust others, as opposed to trusting your heart and LOVE to help you in full.

We repeat, no one and no thing has authority to place healing frequencies or any other kind of energy into you.

Reiki and Yoga have no permission from the Heart of Creation to place souls who are struggling at the end of their soul evolution, to become trapped in this dark place: spurred on by choices made by those still practicing these modalities, and this includes the entire healing industry...please take note: you have no power and no authority to practice your craft on others.

Those who are still continuing are about to have a wake-up call.

It has already been made crystal clear to Claire that those who have received Reiki energies recently are suffering and they are noticing that they feel unwell and uneasy after sessions.

They will drift away and you will find that your kudos and desire for profit — over and above your desire to protect all life has left many injured.

What was once semi-safe is now defunct. The planet has moved on rapidly and these systems cannot match the power needed to help each soul ascend and return home.

Only the heart of each individual life form has that power and the authority.

Breaking the Laws of Creation — the laws of Life, at this stage will cost many their return home.

It is such a sad state of affairs, yet those of you who desire change and desire peace on your planet are fully supported and fully protected.

It is with great pity that those who could be helping have become so immersed in ego-led behaviours that they are incapable of helping themselves, let alone those they promised to help and support.

Be prepared for change now. Be prepared to feel more supported: those of you who have tried to best serve all life.

It is with deep pity that the karmic cycles are about to hit those who failed to seek change.

Be watchful these coming weeks. You will see the circles of black appearing under the skin around the eyes.

A perfect circle of black will tell you all who to avoid and who to turn away from.

The energy of malicious harm, all intentions to cause great harm are returning to all those who conspired to harm.

Pity them. Pity their choices.

The darkness they created and harnessed is returned.

It will Destroy them.

It has nowhere else to go, except to the sender, creator, perpetrator and all those who knowingly allowed this harm to reach your door."

Chapter Forty-Eight

FINAL MESSAGE: THE GREAT AWAKENING - KARMA, CHAOS, COLLAPSE, SICKNESS

TIMELINE SWITCH IMMINENT -

FOCUS ON YOUR PREFERRED FUTURE

External Link To "Final Message" Bitchute.com (other links below video):

Searching For The Evidence on bitchute.com |
TELEGRAM.COM **|**
LOVE'S HEART PLAN on SUBSTACK.COM |
@TRUELIGHTESSENCE ON ODYSEE.COM

...

I have a short message to share which will not take up too much of your time and I wish you to know that it is shared with love from my heart to yours.

To gain maximum assistance through your own heart, all my messages come with the advice that in order to perceive things at deeper levels, it does require everyone to listen and digest the codes of remembrance through their heart, and this means that we all need to still our busy minds.

Therefore, please lie down on the bed that you sleep in at night, at home, to gain maximum assistance and deeper truths.

I do make small grammatical errors, and in some cases, I have said the wrong year. I have brain blips just like we all do, as we are living on a planet riddled with radio waves, microwaves, 5G technology and other artificial, other worldly technology that is as much a challenge for me as it is for others.

I am always inwardly guided to record the podcast once only because the urgency of getting the message out supersedes any imperfections in my wording.

Please be aware that the codes of remembrance contained within the messages are always perfectly given from the heart of Creation.

My role has been to help others to trust that they have all the tools inside themselves to surmount all challenges, and for those who wished to help humanity and to protect all precious life, my role has been to encourage you all to strengthen this heart connection — to get you all up and running for the final furlong of this arduous race.

The time is fast approaching when the race will be complete, and this is why I am being asked to share a final message for you

all to digest and explore, and hopefully, to help you make plans for your chosen future.

And this is where my heart is stepping in and I will move aside, so that the perfect codes of remembrance can reach you through your own heart and the heart of Creation.

If you ever have the need to question anything I share, please validate everything through your own heart intelligence who will be able to give you fullest truth and accurate advice.

Common sense tells us that these messages require a quiet room at home where we can lie down and safely relax with eyes closed.

Our bedroom is ideal and the recommended place.

Here is the message:

"Claire, it has come to pass that the time is nearly upon you all to make your final choices for your future.

The path has split. A change of direction has occurred for all life on Planet Earth and with that split comes new opportunities for growth.

A brief summary is as follows:

Over the last decade or so, planetary changes have been severely interfered with by outside forces: forces which have had humanity and all life that is trapped in the False Light Construct under their power and control.

This has now changed, and with that change of direction, a new set of possibilities have occurred.

Many of you perceive things from a deep level of inner exploration. Others are just starting to explore. Some are only now waking up after decades of being asleep.

The great awakening has begun in earnest and it is no small thanks to all those tiny frightened voices who called to LOVE at the Heart of Creation and asked for help.

This includes all manner of people, belief systems and inner perceptions. It is not one group or another. Simply put, enough in humanity care enough about their fellow humans and other life forms to speak out, to call out, and ask LOVE for help.

LOVE answered the call because sufficient numbers asked for help.

LOVE cannot impose. It is the law of Creation.

Not even LOVE can interfere with the free will choice to say nothing, to not even utter a cry for help whilst watching the worst genocide incident in history, nor while being aware that infants and children are being harmed and abused in the most awful way possible, by groups on your planet who masquerade as 'respectable' members of society.

LOVE can only come in equal measure to the calls for assistance, and so, it is why Claire has been putting out messages — to show you how powerful your heart calls are when enough care enough to ask for help.

LOVE does the rest. You were never expected to do any more than make requests for help.

The issues surrounding the delay in help reaching your door has been insufficient requests and lack of compassion at the sight of the many who were and are still suffering.

Even the holistic community, now only seen as a huge industrial complex of such magnitude, that any sentiment of compassion has been lost through lack of inner concern, inner questioning and lack of compassion for those who have suffered — when the holistic community chose, in the main, to ignore

LOVE's heart guidance to stop all external healing systems because they had become so badly contaminated with Lucifer frequencies, they had been rendered unusable as a meaningful way of healing self or others.

No, even this group, who can frequently hold themselves in high esteem, have failed to protect the souls they were sent here to protect, and it is only now that they will start to see the fall-out of their choices: the choice to carry on delivering systems of healing and energy which hold no fruits, from the heart of Creation's perspective, and this is leaving many humans and their souls injured in immeasurable ways: often, not visible, but there, none the less.

Then, we have the medical industry. A huge, profitable industrial complex inhabited by men and women who proclaim to be saving lives yet have, in the main, stood by and not questioned the safety of a vaccination program forced on the populace, with no safety data, no long term safety guarantees—a vaccine that was made very quickly if one is to believe the story, and when vaccines require normally 7-10 years of trials, one may like to ask the men and women in the hospitals why they did not stand firm and request more data, question the validity of mask wearing: a known cause of respiratory illness and of certain cancers, a mask with holes so big that any particle could enter and leave it....why did this group stand back and not protect the very public who they took an oath: to "first, do no harm"?

Claire, we could go on and on about the many groups who have allowed humanity to be harmed in this way, but we must keep this message as short as possible because it needs to go out urgently today, in order to time it with the other news which is presented now.

So far, the order of the day has been about laying out a few facts and truths, as seen from the heart of Creation.

What we wish to convey to you all now, because most who listen to this already understand why things are chaotic and why this is so...what we wish to share is that the time is upon you all to start creating your perfect reality, not 'in spite of' what has transpired on this current platform of learning.

We mean: it is time to start thinking in deeper ways about your 'future future' — meaning, it is time to prepare for your eventual departure from this platform and onto a place where you can truly flourish and grow, unrestricted by the chaos brought forth by those who could not or would not care about how their choices were harming yourselves and the vulnerable, the infants, children, elderly and homeless, and those who have not had a voice because they have been silenced, even after death, by Lucifer and other destroyer forces and those who were crushed by the ruthless choices of those who could not fulfil their promise to first do no harm.

This law of Creation, the first law: "Do no harm" has been broken by so many on the planet that if they have not asked for their errors to be remedied and the harm they have created, healed, then, they cannot leave this destroyer force space.

They will become trapped and hunted. That is their choice and they were warned many times that it would lead to this unless they had a change of mind and connected instead, to their hearts.

All is forgiven, yet, they cannot fulfil their true purpose because they have chosen to ignore what that is.

Your true purpose at this stage, is to prepare for departure and to ensure that you do everything in your power to abide

by the laws of Creation, meaning: do no harm, speak your truths, stand in your power, and above all these things and most urgently of all, the main advice of today is to not waste an ounce of your precious life force codes on anything, any topic, any issue that distracts you from your path.

You can ask for help for those who are in distress and suffering.

What we mean by not wasting energy is: if you ask your heart and LOVE for help, then ensure you use the help. To waste help at this stage is to entrap yourselves in this timeline which is in the process of being switched again, hence the urgency and the reminder.

All that you have here must come forward on your path.

You cannot allow others to take you away from your true path; your true purpose, which is: to get home to the Heart of Creation before the next Out Breath cycle of evolution — which is imminent.

The timeline switch is earmarked at a time of year when portals open and close. In the midst of the portal opening, the dark ones that are left have decided that the only way to secure enough life force of yours to live off is to create a timeline switch.

Timeline switches are deadly to a creative being.

Timeline switches are designed to steer humanity off one line of growth and onto a false line of learning and creation.

It causes distress at soul level and all the way along your conscious ladder as the parts of you that are more aware, more in tune with LOVE, see what the dark are doing and understand the consequences of that plan. The parts of your higher intelligence get distressed because, to them, it is like watching a murder and being powerless to stop it.

Those who have not asked for help cannot be interfered with. You must step back and focus on your own choices because to do otherwise will throw you all into the path of this oncoming train.

On this occasion it would break the Laws of Creation to interfere.

Others must use their own free will to ask LOVE for help. So far, this group have refused to be concerned about how their choices affect others. Many have shown no compassion for humanity, or the suffering caused by the vaccines. Many others have continued to cause harm even though it has been highlighted that their choices are harming at deep deep levels.

This group must make their own choices about their own future.

You must focus on your choices now, no one else's.

The other news is that LOVE and the Heart of Creation had previously created emergency purest light grids to assist all trapped souls and those in humanity who had called for help, because the Earth's grids had been completely destroyed by Yoga and Reiki practices, along with 5G, predominantly.

Humans have all made errors, and again, all is forgiven, however, this issue is explained to help all new listeners understand that many errors and many poor choices have lead to critical issues affecting the soul evolution of all living things and many choices have caused critical emergencies in the last few years.

The emergency purest light grids remained up and running until yesterday when they receded and returned to the heart of Creation.

These emergency escape grids have secured the safety of many trapped souls and those who had become powerless to evolve because of attack by Lucifer and destroyer force frequencies.

Many groups have called for help and the help has come in, only to be knocked down by those who were bent on harming and those who refused to stop harmful practices.

This has left the world's children exposed, also. The groups who understand this issue will be fully aware of how serious this issue is affecting millions of children and newborns, however, for those just joining us here, we wish you to know that when others remain fixated on their holiday planning and football fixtures, the TV and their mobile phones and social media, over and above raising their heads and being concerned about how bad this issue is on your planet, then the children have no one to defend them. The groups who like to harm children and who support child trafficking get away with murder, quite literally, and so, the effects of remaining ignorant to other's suffering holds very bad outcomes for those who could not care less about the children's plight.

Every time ignorance or selfishness is chosen — above looking at the the world around you and being concerned for the welfare of others especially the children, then, a huge karmic cycle is created and humanity are now being hit by their choice to ignore the plight of those who live in their towns, cities, and villages.

Claire has repeatedly shared that the councils and government, the military and armed forces all deal with child trafficking in various dark circles of these groups.

The drugs and children are easily trafficked because diplomatic immunity aids secrecy and hides the trafficking.

Many will take money and say nothing while these children are bartered for, like 'goods' in a warehouse.

That karmic cycle of learning is returned to all those who chose to look away from their suffering — which should be concerning you all.

The karma is returned to all those who killed, maimed, and injected lethal poison into the veins of billions of humans.

The harm brought about by the prejudice and hatred levelled toward any who objected is also returned to all those who segregated their friends and family members.

Your ignorance has cost lives, caused deaths and caused soul shock, soul fragmentation and soul death.

Many called for help and LOVE stepped in to deal with all issues because, more recently, in January 2024, two messages were placed in the emergency purest light grids and other grids, as it was witnessed that, not only was the Earth being destroyed energetically and the Earth grids, collapsed, but also, humanity's largest, shared grid of consciousness, which is trapped inside the False Light Construct, was also undergoing collapse.

The Cosmic Shield of Humanity held the codes of remembrance to exit the matrix and to return home safely, along a peaceful pathway to the heart of Creation.

The collapse of this shared grid of the family of humanity meant that even those of you who were trying to protect humanity, were now getting hit with attack by destroyer forces, because this Cosmic Shield was your most powerful defence.

Subsequently, those who were connecting to heart will have found things very challenging and disturbing, energetically.

Claire has spent a lot of her time trying to maintain a sense of balance, clearing the attack and settling it, only to experience an onslaught of satanic attack the next day, and the next...

One problem gets resolved by some, and the other groups knock down the help.

It has been a roller coaster ride and we are sure you are in agreement that from the start of the year, and up until yesterday, things have probably been tough for you all.

However, many of you have kept on asking for help and the help is always given.

In the last month or so, the Heart of Creation has surrounded this platform and space of learning.

The platform you are currently residing on energetically is provided by LOVE as an interim place to complete your growth until it is time to leave.

This does not mean that all on your planet are 'in heart'.

Some are still maliciously harming and intentionally harming, however, at some level, they have requested return. Perhaps not in the physical, but at some level on their ladder of consciousness, a part of them has asked for more time to try to change their ways.

This group are now planning the timeline switch.

There are less of them because many dark forces have been removed or deleted. The removed and deleted groups have had their powerful technologies obsoleted.

Therefore, the remaining groups have less power to wield against humanity and very few options, yet, they have not reached the stage of deciding to stop harming.

There are three groups who are harming the most: those who are maliciously harming; those who are intentionally harm-

ing, and those who are harming through ignorance, selfishness, greed, and wilful disregard for other's suffering.

While Claire writes, the hospitals are filling up with heart attack cases, cardiac issues, stroke cases and blood clotting.

The collapse of humanity's Cosmic Shield has become more serious, as the entire, protective ladder of consciousness which humanity shared, has been destroyed by those who still seek power and control over you all.

Therefore, when the Heart of Creation arrived to protect all precious life, the protection was put in place for those who had asked for help, but, for those who had not chosen to call for help, LOVE could not impose, and these are the groups who are now getting sick.

Illness always manifests in the Cosmic Shield of each human.

If humanity's Cosmic Shield is collapsed, and if a human has not asked their heart intelligence for the Heart of Creation to surround them, then, they will by default, get sick.

It is inevitable.

The level of sickness will depend on whether they acquiesced to the injected poison because 'acquiescence' allows Lucifer frequencies and destroyer forces free rein to walk into your energy fields and steal your life force codes.

It is with great sadness to report the knock-on effect: that if a human dies without asking LOVE for help at this late stage of their evolution, they will become trapped in this False Light Construct and will be unable to get home to the Heart of Creation because the destroyer forces steal these codes of remembrance.

What we are trying to impress upon you all is that: now is the time to give LOVE a call. Ask for help. Don't risk being trapped here, especially upon death.

All you have to do is ask your heart and LOVE for help. That is all that is required of you at this time.

LOVE will do the rest.

The timeline switch will throw many into chaos and the above explanation is shared in the hope that you will start to perceive that if all these issues above are occurring, then, what greater danger are humanity in if they fail to ask for help?

All errors and mistakes need to be repaired in the timeline you are on.

If others have failed at this stage to ask LOVE for help, then, the errors they have made in this timeline and previous timeline switches cannot be repaired and healed.

The dark execute these timeline switches to deliberately deprive the human of the opportunity to heal and repair any harm they have caused, and this leads to soul shock, soul fragmentation, soul death.

When a soul dies, the human self dies.

The collapse of the Cosmic Shield and lower rungs of the ladder of humanity's shared consciousness also leads to soul shock, soul fragmentation and soul death.

This is the true cause of the rise in death rates, currently.

It will lead to more deaths after the timeline switch.

Therefore, there is no time like the present to be focusing on the future you wish for, because you may not be able to interfere with the free will choices of others, however, you can create a reality of choice that is peaceful, loving and carefree where, perhaps, humanity does wake up in time to evolve home and,

perhaps, where all learn their lessons and stop harming before it is too late?

You cannot and must not interfere.

That does not mean that you must stop creating; dreaming; imagining your preferred future for your family of humanity.

We say: now is the time to focus with all your heart on the outcome you would *prefer* humanity to choose, as a group.

And perhaps, just perhaps, it will not be too late."

LINKS:

IMMENSE EMOTIONAL TRAUMA TO MOTHER EARTH —TOTAL GRID COLLAPSE | 4 JANUARY 2024
https://www.bitchute.com/video/gJl9grup5xcB/

HUMANITY'S COSMIC SHIELD — TOTAL COLLAPSE — PREPARE FOR AFTERSHOCKS | 6 JANUARY 2024 (URGENT SHARE)
https://www.bitchute.com/video/4OG9OFLOb1tm/

A PERFECT CIRCLE OF BLACK WILL TELL YOU ALL WHO TO AVOID AND WHO TO TURN AWAY FROM | 26 MARCH 2024|
https://www.bitchute.com/video/prjUscHSZ9wp/

SYNCHRONISE YOUR HEART WITH THE HEART OF CREATION — AVOID GROUNDING TO AVOID LOSING LIFE FORCE | 19 MARCH 2024 |
https://www.bitchute.com/video/5sBxS2AxppfR/

CLAIRE'S OTHER PLATFORMS:

Searching For The Evidence

on bitchute.com and TELEGRAM.COM,

LOVE'S HEART PLAN (FULL TRANSCRIPT) on SUB-
STACK.COM,

and @TRUELIGHTESSENCE DEEPER TRUTHS
ON ODYSEE.COM

Chapter Forty-Nine

PURE EVIL: THE CHILDREN'S FUTURE RESTS IN YOUR HANDS, "MAKE THE REQUEST, LOVE DOES THE REST"

Audio Link:

I call on my Infinite Self, Infinite LOVE and the Laws of Creation, which govern the whole of Creation, to advise me on how to help humanity and all precious life today.

It seems to me that an awakening of sorts is happening.

What advice do you wish me to share — to best serve all precious life in optimal ways?

"Claire, we say this:

It is true that an awakening of sorts is occurring in many.

It is not the awakening that was planned for them when they fell into this dark place of density.

Their true awakening was to use their gifts of Knowledge and Remembrance to form a safety barrier for those who were struggling in density and who were unable to leave.

Their role was to help the others who were injured and suffering soul damage, to gently raise the vibration, and in doing so, become a 'buoyancy chamber' of LOVE energies, to help raise them to a safer level of frequency bands, so that the weakened and injured could start to perceive their own divinity and true spiritual nature.

The 'Out Breath' is a huge event and is about to start very soon.

Humanity and many other life forms are presently stuck below decks on a sinking platform of learning that is descending on some days, and lifting up on others, according to each human's free will choice to either act lovingly to self and others, or, to serve the dark elite's plans of trans-humanism and servitude which is well in the making.

Sometimes, humans serve the dark's plans to overthrow humanity and enslave them simply by choosing to remain asleep; unaware; uneducated; deliberately blind, or too much in fear to be able to look with clear eyes at those who mean them harm.

This is called ignorance.

Ignorance is a very low vibrational action. It causes great harm to all precious life and it is this ignorance that is currently holding humanity back from moving forward.

There are many on the planet who have asked for rescue, meaning: they have prayed or called for help.

Their calls for help have been answered, and for many of you, your journey is about to become easier and more joyful.

The more you focus on your true nature and on reaching higher levels of consciousness through your heart centre, the more help comes for those who are struggling to remember that they fell into density and are trapped by their own choices — no one else's — to escape the 'End Game' here, which is enslavement, loss of freedom, darkness, and suffering.

Those who want to harm you serve Lucifer. Claire was advised to share about the Black Eyed Club and we wish you all to become aware of those who have perfect circles of BLACK around their eyes.

The Luciferians run your governments; banks; big corporations; the World Health Organisation; the United Nations; Big Pharma; and the World Economic Forum. The World Economic Forum serve as the 'payload' for what happens on your planet, meaning: they devise the plans for war, pandemics, flooding, weather manipulation, and poisoning of your planet.

They determine who gets into power and who does not.

They also own your media, and so, for many of you, you have remained in ignorance for the last four years about why a pandemic was so important to create by this group. They are truly evil.

You will have to come to terms with that quickly because you do not have long to help yourselves, and this group have their eye on you and the world's children.

Yesterday, Claire was inwardly guided by her heart to compile a short grouping of videos to help highlight your plight to those of you have have been unaware of the true deception affecting your planet.

The pandemic was a 'Black Swan' event. Make no mistake about that.

You have just two choices:

To remain in ignorance and denial about this group's motives — their plans to control and harm you and the world's children, or, you can choose to be in control of your own destiny by asking your heart and LOVE to help you.

Why is this so important? It is important because you are lacking many codes of Knowledge which have been stolen from you and weaponised against you.

5G, StarLink, Sky Net, microwave radiation and so forth is, really, all your heartache and the planet's heartache which has been stolen and weaponised against you.

How could this possibly be true, you might ask?

It is true because you are dealing with highly intelligent and highly evolved entities who understand how to manipulate energy and frequencies.

Heartache, fear, sorrow, anger, depression, grief, trauma, irritability and so forth are all low frequency emissions.

Low frequency emissions LOWER your protective shield.

Your protective shield was extensive and reached right back to the heart of Creation.

The planet also had a protective shield which did the same.

You also shared a protective shield with your family of humanity.

These three facets of protection have been destroyed in recent months, with the planet's protective shield destroyed by Reiki, Yoga and 5G users, predominantly.

Many calls have been put out in humanity's consciousness grids and planetary grids prior to their collapse and many messages have gone out on social media and other platforms to ask Yoga, Reiki and Energy healing groups such as Quantum Healing, Multidimensional Healing, Crystal Bowl Healing, Sound Healing, and all the holistic practices that transmit energy from outside a human into a human or other life form, to STOP their activities because the greater changes in the Greater Cosmos required different approaches to self healing and planetary healing.

There are mind control devices all around your planet — devices which transmit and receive information and which have the technological ability to affect your thoughts and influence behaviour.

With the activities of the Yoga, Reiki, and 5G user groups, and the satanic ritual practices of the Freemasons, many of whom have no understanding that they are in a group that purports to be a 'charity,' yet, at the higher levels, there is full knowledge that the more men that they can recruit, the more 'bodies on the ground' can be used to transmit Lucifer energies into your reality.

This may be a shock for many of you. You are going to have to digest this quickly because your safety is at risk currently, and all your lives hang in the balance, because the group who want control are plotting in real time — as Claire shares this message — on what scenario they can create that will throw you all into chaos and fear.

They are looking at many things...war, disease outbreaks, a bigger natural disaster than the others they have created, a nuclear explosion, another chemical train spillage, or collapsed bridge...

However, the main reason why Claire is being asked to put this message out today, is because it may be necessary for them to admit that the Covid 19 poison shot is killing many.

They may use this in order to cause more fear and confusion.

They may also advise you that behind the scenes, a new vaccine has been developed to cure the cancer, the illness and severe side effects caused by the previous 'poison' and we are asking Claire to warn you that at some point, you all have to make a decision about how much power of yours, you are willing to give to a group who are bent on harming you.

They love power and control, and for many, that 'power over' others stretches to the personal enjoyment of harming young children and infants.

This group plan to push for pedophilia to become 'acceptable'. It has been accepted as law in California and in parts of Europe.

Their 'agents' are setting up the opportunity for this in the UK and other countries.

How far will you allow the children to be exposed to these monsters?

It really is time to choose, because in May 2024, the World Health Organisation, led by Tedros — a known criminal in Ethiopia and wanted for crimes against humanity, who led a terrorist group called "The People's Liberation Front' which raped, burnt and tortured Ethiopians...this is the man leading the World Health Organisation, and in May, if you allow it to happen, the WHO are planning to strike a deal with all the players who serve the Lucifer Agenda to hand complete control to the WHO for any future pandemics, meaning: your government, your democratic voice will be silenced, and a total take-over of democracy will ensue as this group already have all their foot soldiers in position in your town councils.

They plan to penalise you for being human, and to impoverish you whilst using every and any opportunity to separate children from their families.

If you let the WHO get into power and if you choose to allow a Luciferian Agenda to ride rough-shod over you, you will regret the outcome of your choice to stand on the sidelines once again, and allow someone else to take your FREE WILL away.

Remember, you are a Sovereign Being. Nothing is unsolvable when you tap into your heart centre.

This is a war on your mind, body, and spirit, but you can overpower this group by calling on LOVE to shield you from all harm.

Under the Laws of Creation, those who have been actively calling for help are not permitted to interfere with your free will choices.

The outcome for the world's children rests with you.

The outcome of your choice to stand by and do nothing, when you could be using your heart intelligence to defeat this group, will carry severe outcomes for your own soul journey.

What you choose to do in this life affects your future soul journey...

Many will not be coming forward because they chose to remain in ignorance and would not protect the children.

The protective shields of your own ladder of Consciousness, the shield of Humanity and the shield of the planet are no longer in use.

LOVE can step in to protect you, but you have to decide — by using your free will — if you want help and protection.

Otherwise, you are leaving yourself exposed.

The signs are everywhere, now. You only have to talk briefly at the shops, and at hospitals, etc., to realise that many are getting sick from the poison shots.

Those who asked LOVE for help will be assisted to heal.

If you choose to do nothing, you are exposed.

Sky Net, StarLink and 5G technologies are all up in space and can read your temperature, see what you are doing in your home, and thanks to SMART meters and LED street lighting, SMART technology in your washing machine, fridge and tumble dryer, etc., you are already a target in your own home.

Some in humanity are partly aware, and many have been shouting from the roof tops to alert you.

You have not listened, and now, the children are also injected.

Many are dying. The nurses are seeing a rise in cardiac illness, the infants are being born with terrible defects, and perfectly healthy pregnant mothers are dying.

This is real data, not hearsay.

It is very frightening to think that there are others out there who could be so evil.

The sad fact is, they are evil to the core, and their hatred of you is very clear when you watch how they treated you during lock-downs.

They fear more of humanity awakening. It will mean that they are losing control.

What they fear the most is the emergence of this Black Eye, the circle of BLACK around the eye which will identify them as 'one who serves Lucifer.'

Why will they have a Black Eye?

Because those in your family of Humanity who love you, and care about your future and the children's safety, have been using their heart energy to peacefully ask LOVE: to gather up all malicious harm, all intentions to cause harm, and all harm caused by ignorance and to send it back to all those responsible for the harm.

Those who love you are using the Laws of Creation to send it all back to those who created, sent, perpetrated and brought the harm to your door.

It means that when those who have maliciously harmed you, lie on the TV about unexplained deaths and who stumble over their words, it is because they know that the Laws of Creation will send back all harm that they are causing and this harm is like lightening bolts.

It will knock some of them over, quite literally. Some have left the planet recently, some are getting cancer because the energy of hatred towards you has triggered a Karmic cycle of 'return.'

Whatever satanic rituals they chose to harm you with, is being returned to them.

Humans are very powerful when they lovingly ask for help to protect themselves and the vulnerable, and ask LOVE and the Laws of Creation to gather up and return all malicious harm to all those responsible. This is for their learning and must always be done with a peaceful heart, otherwise, it will not work.

So, in spite of things being terribly grim on your planet and quite a shock for many of you, you need to know, before it is too late.

All errors are forgiven when a heart seeks help for oneself and for others, and chooses to grow in LOVE to best help all.

LOVE and the Laws of Creation have the power to address all harm caused by these groups.

LOVE cannot impose. It comes when called upon. You have to ask LOVE for help to start the ball rolling and keep asking each day with a sincere heart, "for all precious life to be assisted."

This simple request brings much help to the children, many of whom were procured by Jimmy Saville, friend of King Charles, and those who favoured child-trafficking and abuse on Jeffrey Epstein's Island.

That list of visitors never fully made the public domain because all the child abusers did deals, had 'dinner' with Jeffrey, flew on his plane and harmed innocent life.

The Digital ID is also being forced on the populace in Australia.

Tony Blair is promoting it to 'keep us all safe.'

Tony Blair: a man who was fined for Importunity by police before he became Prime Minister, a man who was caught by undercover police when he approached an officer for sex in a man's toilet in LONDON, is now pushing the Digital ID because he also serves this group and that is why his Importunity activities were covered up by police, many of whom are Freemasons and serve the Lucifer agenda.

They prefer to keep each other's secrets, and it is becoming less of a secret now that many are leaving the planet, some have cancer, some are in hospital and some have disappeared for a while.

For those who use their hearts, please keep asking for all malicious harm to be gathered up and returned to help shield the children and this group who have chosen ignorance as a means to avoid looking at the world and concerning themselves with peacefully protecting those who are suffering.

How many dead babies is one too many?

Does it have to reach your own family or children before you look up?

You are all deeply loved. You are all free to choose.

We are saying, for one final time: you can come home, if you wish, and we are advising you that the doorway to this opportunity is closing.

Those who choose to do nothing will have no protection, not even from those who are protecting them now.

The children's future rests in your hands.

Your choice to ignore their suffering and their horrific future if this dark group have their way, will mean that you will be left all alone, without any defence to face your own demons because all harm is being returned, and if you are not protected by LOVE, if your errors have not been deleted, then, what future do you perceive is coming to meet you?

Take heart and listen to that still small voice within you, calling you to remember your true origins, your true reason for falling into this place and the promise made by LOVE that if you ever got into trouble, if you ever forgot who you were or why you were here, if you ever felt helpless, then, all you had to do was ASK LOVE to help you.

Remember this today, dear humanity:

All is easily resolved when enough love is generated by enough frightened voices, to call for help and end this war on your mind, body, and spirit:

"Make the request, LOVE does the rest.""

...

The most up-to-date Heart Connection is always the most recently dated on my online channels.

At the time of writing this "The Outer Waves of Infinite Possibilities" and the subsequent messages that follow contain the ever-upgrading Heart Connections.

Include links to the short movie I made highlighting the issues

and

Highly Recommended Documentary:

"Monopoly — Who Owns the World" By Tim Gielen:

"Less than a handful of megacorporations dominate every aspect of our lives. From the breakfast that's on the table in the morning, to the mattress we sleep on at night, and practically everything we do or consume in between contributes to the power of these corporations. In this video I show you how these corporations – or rather; their largest shareholders – are the protagonists in the play which we are currently witnessing, and the driving force behind "The Great Reset".

(Also shared on Searching For the Evidence Channel, Bitchute.c om.

"BY JUNE 2023 ALL WILL KNOW"

All of our choices are playing out. In June, the choices many made to look the other way started to collapse their outer 'Russian Doll' of protection. We are watching the fall out from these choices.

Chapter Fifty

FACIAL RECOGNITION CAMERAS — THE TRUE, NEFARIOUS AGENDA: PEDOPHILIA, CHILD ABUSE, CHILD TRAFFICKING

The Pedophile Agenda Is Child trafficking. If you fail to act, you expose the children.

Link to video: Bitchute.com:

I posted an important heart connection meditation yesterday, "HOW TO SAVE THE CHILDREN," which aims to help those who wish to protect humanity and all life here, to create peaceful opportunities for change, and to clear the darkness that is pervading our planet.

Today, I connected to my heart using the "How To Save The Children".

I received gifts of Knowledge and as I started to become aware of the room and my body, it dawned on me that the facial recognition cameras are being put in place as a ruse.

Their sole purpose is to hunt down, track and regulate the children in order to make it easier to abduct them and separate them from their parents, knowing where their parents are at all times — through number plate recognition, facial recognition in supermarkets and train stations.

This dark group who run the World Economic Forum, the World Health Organisation, King Charles and the Royals, the United Nations, the Big Corporation bosses of supermarkets, Amazon, Asda, DIY stores, big Bank bosses, Airline Bosses, the chairs of Airport planning and train travel...all have agreed to this, especially in London—the Satanic centre of the world, and the Vatican, who are also a corrupt group, and all are masquerading as 'respectable' organisations...these groups all have reputations for being linked to Jimmy Saville a prolific supplier of children to the rich and famous and Royal family.

Let us not forget Prince Andrew's recent escapades, nor the King's close friendship with Saville and his links to the BBC, another media corporation that serves the Pedophile Agenda.

And this agenda has been long in the making.

Here is what my heart wishes me to share:

"Claire, these groups (and there are many more not listed here) are bent on accessing the children.

The top players in all these corporate enclaves like to harm and kill children.

It may shock many to hear this, but you need to open your hearts to this information in order to understand that you are dealing with organised criminals here.

These criminals have already made a huge fortune out of frightening you into getting jabbed for a mild cold 'virus' which they have now admitted was not a threat to life.

The Bill and Melinda Gates Foundation, along with the Clinton Foundation, lead the way in the abduction and trafficking of children worldwide.

Bill Gates had a long standing relationship with Jeffrey Epstein. He denied this until it was proven that he met him many times and had flown on Jeffrey Epstein's plane. Bill Gates was pictured with Jeffrey Epstein and on this picture is a group of high up officials of the banking world and world of the elite puppets who serve a different 'god' than the ones with religious beliefs or spiritual beliefs.

The reason why Jeffrey Epstein was successful in harming children and young girls was because he was a high class pimp who procured and trafficked children for the world's rich and famous.

You think you can be famous and rich without a track record for child abuse?

All the top officials in your supplier companies have gone along with the plans for C40 cities, 15 Minute Neighbourhoods, Clean Air Zones and facial recognition cameras placed strategically in your towns and villages, your streets, your lamp posts, traffic lights, ULEZ cameras, shopping centres, etc., are there to track the children and identify the placement of their parents and family members.

You are all being fooled.

Isn't it obvious when boat loads of illegal immigrants who carry no ID, are not vaccinated, have criminal intentions and are beheading local residents, raping local women and causing mayhem in Ireland, the UK coastal areas, Europe, the USA and elsewhere...why do you seriously think that so many immigrants are flooding your country without any checks, and why are you being forced to be filmed wherever you go?

How does that correlate in any reasonable mind?

The answer is because this group love to maim and kill innocent lives. Many of you are already aware.

Many do not want to think about this topic. Many of you are parents.

You are going to have to grow and have courage.

Do you want your children exposed to a large group of Pedophiles and Satanists who have their eyes on your children?

Do you think protesting to your government and politicians who serve the Pedophile Agenda will work?

This group see child abuse as 'normal' behaviour.

It is why they plan to introduce pedophilia as the next 'descriptor' alongside other groups who may not wish to be associated with this type of behaviour.

Many men in these groups like to dress differently and they like to confuse children in this way. It makes children feel safer and they avoid seeing the true agenda.

That is why the politicians in various countries have pushed for the legalisation of Pedophilia.

They want everything legal and lawful so that they can access the children without redress.

It is a simple as that.

Claire found out recently that a local supermarket store, a smaller named outfit which uses a 'stretched-out Lion' as its symbol, but which has always been more discreet about its dark side, has installed facial recognition cameras in a town that has always served Lucifer, and this is clear by the Crown monument in its town centre.

Another nearby village has an obelisk with a black clock as its centre piece, and over the water, a huge black pyramid tower stands aside the busy main road, and yet, many locals have never noticed it.

The black tower is approximately 60 feet high. Provided by the Catholic Church and not seen by the local population...

No one questions. No one notices, and yet, the signs are all around you, if you care to take the time to look.

In June, D-Day celebrations are planned to celebrate humanity's freedom from Nazi domination and Hitler.

All those who died gave a lot to their country, and yet, the celebrations involve standing around an obelisk to remember the dead, and at other times, a ring of red flowers and poppies is used as a mark of remembrance.

A bonfire is going to be lit in each village or town across the UK to celebrate D-Day.

Aside from not being environmentally friendly or helping the fake "humans cause climate change crisis" — another hypocrisy right in front of your faces — the lighting of bonfires, standing around a satanic obelisk is all a ritual, and a ritual to serve satanic beliefs.

Those who organise these events know it is a Luciferian practice.

The bonfire on 'Bonfire night'— Guy Fawkes Night— in the UK is another example of satanic practices; wrapped up as a family outing, but burning a human body on a bonfire is satanic, as is 'Halloween', and we will get onto Halloween, shortly, because it is all tied in with this and it is partly why the Pedophile Agenda is in full swing.

The Pedophiles around the world in the top positions of your corporate companies, big, Pharma and big Banking, the CEO's of big Food, big DIY, big Airlines, Big Space projects all have dirty secrets.

Some are being blackmailed, some are protected by the power and money they wield.

There are many lackeys who serve them. They live in every town, village and city, and they operate in your area.

Some are in the police force. It is why many rape cases and child abuse cases get side- lined as, "insufficient evidence". The good cops are always pushed to one side by a senior officer who takes over the case that threatens to expose the pedophile ring, and it is happening in your military too.

There are links below, which Claire will share.

This is not hearsay. There is evidence galore, if you care to look.

What has satanism and pedophilia got in common, you may ask?

Fiona Barnett will tell you. She was abused by Nicole Kidman's father for many years, and her story of abuse is shocking. It is deeply upsetting, but her story needs to be told and the link to her story can be found here.

From Prime Ministers, to University Professors, Church communities, and parents of the children within these churches, police officers, royal family members, friends of Jimmy Saville, Jeffrey Epstein and Bill Gates, Tony Blair — who was fined for "Importunity" before he later became Prime Minister of Britain had approached an undercover police officer for sex in a man's toilet, was fined, but still protected from his past.

Claire has an MP in her vicinity with a similar penchant for importunity...yet, they are protected, even though many locals know.

It is happening right on the TV...all those faces who seem to be on telly everywhere...where are the new faces, new talent?

What do they have to do these days to keep on top of their game?

The FBI discovered the use of food descriptors — being used by these pedophile, child abusing, rich and famous...'pizza', 'ice cream', 'hotdog', all names used to depict the age and sex of the children they like to abuse.

Biden and Boris Johnson both like to be photographed licking Ice cream, as do others.

When the TV companies know about these things, don't you think an advisor would dissuade politicians and world leaders from doing this publicly — knowing it may cause suspicion?

The answer is: they do it in front of your faces because you are in ignorance about why they do these things.

They use satanic symbolism on you all the time — on TV and in interviews. Don't watch their faces — look at their hands — watch their 'secret' handshakes, the pyramid and diamond shapes they create with their hands.

In plain sight...

They are laughing at you.

And now, they are going to be laughing even louder as the facial recognition goes up — not for your safety, but to keep you tracked and watched, 24/7, and to keep tabs on where you are and where your kids are...the ones they plan to take from you, should they find a good enough excuse to do so.

And now, in the UK, the social services are not overseen by any government body, they are a private organisation and perfect for child abusers to gain access to.

The charities are awash with those who like to harm children.

You are all going to have to address this, and it can be done peacefully, because this war is on your mind, body, and ultimately, your soul.

Think of the facial recognition cameras as 'soul catchers', 'soul destroyers', 'soul harvesters', because the energy they transmit is Luciferian and satanic in nature.

The frequencies coming out of this technology is off-the-scale, in terms of the damage that it does to your natural protection from satanic energy.

These technologies beam radiation and microwaves at you.

They lower your protection, and they destroy the protection that new borns and infants naturally have.

Many children have also had their protection damaged by Wi-fi, 5G, SMART meters, SMART technologies in your washing machines and fridges. Your doorbell cameras transmit harmful frequencies.

All keep your brainwaves in an alpha state of dreamy wakefulness.

You do not notice. They have taken over your brain, and they have Artificial Intelligence that is so advanced, that your thoughts can be altered and monitored.

Those who have a strong mind get targeted to keep them dumbed down.

An active, questioning mind is a 'threat'.

It is why you must 'obey'.

You must not question their motives and you must stay dumb, so that when Biden licks his ice cream and others eat their pizza, you do not see the warning signs staring you in the face.

You do not see the 60 foot tower with a pyramid atop...you do not see, you do not care, and because many do not care, it is up to those who might care more, to do something creative and heart-centred to protect these children from the harm that is coming, if you don't do something to powerfully stop this satanic, cult agenda.

The World Economic Forum has spawned all the world leaders of the pandemic and all those pushing the 'Sustainability'/'Green' deal in your town councils, and the organisations who they have engaged to come out into your communities to 'groom' you all and make you feel that being trapped inside a 15 minute zone, having air travel taken away from you, and forced to drive an electric car, or nothing else if you want to be part of this dark society...this communist-style ruling of all peoples, facial recognition cameras — penalising you for every wrong move, and fining you for 'being human'.

How do these groups wield so much power?

How could anyone be so organised?

Their disheveled looks make you think they are stupid.

It is another clever 'ruse' to hide behind.

The grey suits, the weird dress of the Royal guards, the silly hats, and the snake energy wrapped around the lamp posts in London that no one notices, either...

And how do they do this?

They steal life force codes of DNA — Knowledge — that you possess.

They steal that Knowledge by lowering your protection. They break into your protective shield, and they steal the codes that enable you to live.

When enough codes are stolen, a human starts to die, but not before much Knowledge has been stolen — to support those off-worldly energies that live away from the light of LOVE; that break the Laws of Creation in order to exist.

The groups who worship satan and practice child-killing rituals do it to provide the 'fear' energy to the off-worldly energies — in exchange for money, power, wealth and off-worldly technologies to overthrow humanity.

8 Billion humans could easily overpower the few that make up this group.

They could if they used their heart energy and their power of Creativity...It is your most powerful defence, and the only way to weaken this group and help humanity fully awaken.

Until this is used by more, the children are being forced into a place of no escape.

Even the children cannot be awakened, and this is because of the blissful ignorance of parents who 'practice' satanic ritual, without ever knowing that is what they are doing, and they take their kids to these events.

Every time you take your kids to Halloween parties; Bonfire Night parties; every time you blindly turn your back on the agenda of those who rule your world, the children loose vital codes of Knowledge and their protection is weakened.

The stolen energy procured from Halloween, November 11 rituals, D-Day rituals, Poppy Day rituals around the obelisk, every time you accept that a star symbol is harmless and you clothe you infants in star-covered clothing, you are bringing in the off-worldly forces of Lucifer and satanic entities.

The children lost a lot of life force at the end of 2023, and they lost more over May Day, and will loose more during May Pole dancing, Beltane, and other satanic events: all designed to 'hook' your attention on them, and to steal your life force while you watch the event.

Your biggest failing is not noticing, and therefore, doing nothing to protect yourself or the children.

It is not pleasant to talk about these things, but it is hoped that those who do understand that the risks facing our children and newborns is so great, that any assistance is gladly accepted, and therefore, Claire will leave a powerful heart-connection exercise for all beliefs, all non-beliefs, essentially, this is all about your 'humanity' — your gift of Creativity — and the most powerful force of protection is your concern for the children's future.

When you care enough about others to want to help, all help is given.

No special skills are required.

Your compassion, your desire to peacefully address this is all that is required.

And please, remember this:

Peaceful, truly, is more powerful than force.

When you are facing a giant, you need a bigger giant to help you, and that giant is LOVE, together with the laws of Creation, and when called upon by a sincere, concerned heart, all help is given to weaken these plans, to highlight the true threats, and to find solutions that best serve all precious life.

Please set to work in earnest now, because you do not have much time to weaken these dark, nefarious plans.

'Be the change'. Create the children's brightest future.

The most powerful force is within you, not outside of you.

Use this force of goodness to help the children.

After all, it is the true reason why you are all

here."

Chapter Fifty-One

DIAMOND/PYRAMID HAND SHAPING —COLLAPSE THE SATANIC GRIDS— USE "THE OUTER WAVES OF INFINITE POSSIBILITIES"

"THE OUTER WAVES OF INFINITE POSSIBILITIES"

12 May 2024

Hello, this is Claire from LOVE's Heart Plan on substack.com and Searching For The Evidence on Bitchute.com, and my download channel, @truelightessence on odysee.com

A big thank you to each of you -all those who decided to use "The Outer Waves Of Infinite Possibilities" routine.

Much has been achieved in a very short time-scale thanks to all your efforts, and today, once again, I am being guided by my heart and Infinite LOVE to highlight the nefarious use of hand signalling by those who serve the Satanic Agenda — the ones who like to 'make shapes' with their hands while completing their media interviews, all in the arrogant knowledge that we won't notice or stir when we watch them doing pyramid shapes, eye pointing, finger pointing shapes and other 'knuckle grasping' hand-shakes.

The pyramid and the diamond shapes... What do they truly mean and why is it important, today, of all days to be highlighting this practice.

And this is where my heart and Infinite LOVE step in and I step out of the way to hear their words and type out deeper truths.

Please do listen because I sense that your help is being called upon today to help topple the grid systems that support many satanic practices of invisibility to help expose this group, and in doing so, help to raise awareness amongst those who do not see what this group are doing in plain sight, right in front of our faces, "as plain as day," as they say and yet, unseen by the masses who appear blind to pyramid shaping, and diamond hand shaping by TV journalists, actors, politicians, Royals, Priests, and Big Pharma companies.

If we can just wake them up a bit today, by collapsing some of these grid systems, then, much will be exposed and much less will be hidden from view.

The shape-shifters may not shape-shift as readily, the Black Eyed Club will be exposed, and those who harm the children will have no where to run and hide because the Mark of the Beast is coming their way: It is being *returned* by Infinite LOVE and the Laws of Creation, which govern all life including those who harm.

And the Laws of Creation operate to gather up all that has been *sent out* to maliciously harm innocent life, and *send it back* to those who created, sent, and perpetrated the harm received by those who are innocent, and therefore, it all must go back to those who intentionally harmed and that means all those in Big Pharma, including Astra Zenica, who have harmed many lives by causing blood clots and have now been sued and had to withdraw their product from the market, but not before the media downplayed the news and downplayed the lives ruined by a killer shot. Some children have lost their parents to the Astra Zenica clot-shot.

It was part of the plan and all harm must go back now to all who have deliberately taken part in this harm, including all those who looked the other way, in spite of knowing this clotting would occur.

From the Law of Creation's perspective, from the Laws of LOVE, this harm is called murder.

There is no other way to describe the harm done to innocent life.

To deliberately destroy the life and health of another carries many penalties, in the sense that those that have aided and abetted; to hide the harm originally; to mask the problem and to release the news quietly, so as not to cause alarm bells to ring is to cause murder; to assist with a genocide, and it is with regret that those who could have chosen to save lives, chose to aid the satanic cult, the diamond-shaping club, the Elon Musk and Macron Club, the Governor Green and his-minions-overseeing-the-cult-takeover-in-Maui Club.

They, and many of your politicians use this symbol prolifically and what does it really mean you may wonder? Why do they use it?

They use it to cause you all harm. The diamond shaping of the hands actually brings in satanic frequency from higher, more technologically advanced levels of consciousness and it brings this darker energy onto the Earth Plane.

Many healers are still foolishly connecting to diamond alignment energies.These frequencies are contaminated aspects of Purest Light codes which were stolen from the eleventh dimension when it existed. It collapsed when the Earth's grid systems collapsed into each other in 2018 onwards, and they are riddled with weaponised life force codes stolen from the Eleventh dimension.

The eleventh dimension of your conscious ladder also carried very advanced aspects of awareness which were attacked, and huge swathes of life force codes of Knowledge were stolen from that area.

The dark ones at higher levels of awareness who operate at higher and more advanced levels of consciousness, hold enough Knowledge to know how to strip a human of its life force codes — all the way down to the third dimensional level, and so, can you imagine how much life force has been stolen from humanity — from eight levels above their current ability to perceive?

You have to understand that the levels of consciousness that surround you like layers of a Russian Doll and which are meant to protect you have been broken into, over a long period of time, and all that has been stolen has been used to *fuel* the dark's existence, *fuel* the demonic realm, *fuel* the Annunaki and Draco energies and all other demonic frequencies, and all that *fuels* them is *your energy.*

The remaining *fuel* is converted into a weapon that can further destroy your protection; destroy those Russian Doll layers of protection from satanic forces, demonic entities and Lucifer frequencies.

When you see the politicians and Elon Musk pyramid shaping and diamond shaping with their hands, they are doing several things.

The first is signalling to their club members who they serve.

Secondly, they are intentionally — through deliberate focus on this hand-shaping — making a portal and through this portal of the diamond, or pyramid, they are bringing in the appropriate entities from the demonic realms.

When these entities enter this space we call Earth, they are free to attach themselves through frequencies to any human or pet who is watching those making the diamond hand shapes.

In effect, those who watch and who do not think to call from their hearts for protection for themselves and the innocent, including the children, are exposed to having their life force codes stolen by the entities who enter through the portals.

Your energy *goes* where your *attention* flows. And unless you are regularly protecting yourselves each day with a robust heart connection routine, you are exposed.

Elon Musk and Macron, Trudeau, Blair, King Charles, Klaus Schwab, Big Pharma CEO's, Bill Gates, et al., have no concern about your fate. They *know* it is causing you to have your life force stolen.

They *serve* the demonic realms and they are paid handsomely for their efforts, in the form of power, wealth, control and children.

Why do you think Jeffrey Epstein was 'friend to the rich and famous'.

You have to refrain from watching their faces so much as, watching their hand signalling.

They need to do it in order to be rewarded.

And *children are the currency* with this group which is why the facial recognition cameras are going up in your towns, country lanes, village squares, big food-chain supermarkets, and train stations.

The wealth of this group is off-the-scale and they can pay handsomely for all this technology in the form of bribery, but don't forget, you are funding your village square cameras — through your town councils — and if you care to look at the symbol used by your town councils, perhaps it may start to dawn on you that symbols are used prolifically by this satanic cult.

Look at your council's coat of arms, do you see the shield, the lion, the snaking ribbon, the cross, the snake, the crown and so forth?

Your whole world is riddled with satanic symbolism and all these symbols allow the demonic realm to enter your reality.

There are many who cannot see but those listening today *can* see that these combined practices of town council symbols, coats of arms, diamond and pyramid hand shaping, flag symbols, the star symbols, the snake around the pole medical symbols, the World Health Organisation symbol and the symbols used by Big Pharma are extremely dark and sinister, and together, these symbols form a grid system that is being weaponised against humanity and all precious life, and they need to be toppled...today, if possible, which is why Claire is asking for your kind help once more.

We are going to start with "The Outer Waves of Infinite Possibilities" recording which Claire is being asked to post here to save time.

What will follow is a short routine.

Please use your own discernment at all times.

Ensure you are at home and lying down on the bed that you sleep in at night.

Here is the recording of "The Outer Waves of Infinite Possibilities" which will prepare you.

...

[arriving at the outer waves: just before leaving...]

And here is a new routine to add to "The Outer Waves of Infinite Possibilities" that is enlisting your help should your heart discern that it is your path to help in this way.

You are standing at the edge of "The Outer Waves of Infinite Possibilities", having received specific gifts to help humanity and all precious life in their hour of need.

Your heart will guide you perfectly here.

It is suggested that the specific gifts needed to collapse these portals and symbols that are letting in demonic forces, including: through CERN, The Hadron Collider, and other toxic portals could be inwardly offered by yourselves, and if your heart guides you, placed carefully at the very edge of the outward, ever expanding and forward moving Waves of Infinite Possibilities,

[Allow One Minute]

and if you could ask the deepest part of your heart for any guidance on what vision you could create to best serve all precious life in optimal ways, in alignment with the laws of LOVE and the laws of Creation, to help collapse these portals once and for all, then it is hoped that your heart will lead the way on this.

[Allow One Minute]

Pause the recording if you need more time and take your time listening to your heart who will always guide you perfectly in peaceful ways that best serve all life.

Come back and join us once you are ready.

Thank you for protecting the world's children and the many who are suffering.

[Then enclose the ending of the meditation when you come back to the Cosmic libraries]

Chapter Fifty-Two

CLAIRE'S MESSAGE AND AUDIO LINKS AND TRANSCRIPTS:

Each one is shared with love from my heart to yours in hope, trust, and faith that you will start to see that all the answers truly are inside of you.

Remember the guidance:

"...no matter how high you hold others in high esteem, you will never really solve the Earth's problems when you look outside of yourself, to others who may appear to hold answers.

Your consciousness can rise above the twelve levels of awareness that are stuck inside this False Light Matrix.

Your mind cannot. Therefore, if your higher levels of awareness and consciousness hold the solutions and the answers, why would you continue to listen to others outside of self?

They do not hold the answers, but, your hearts do, and when a heart is willing to hear the truth above all, LOVE will escort that heart to beyond where the eye can see, to the Heart of Creation to secure the teachings that are held there, waiting for a soul with a heart and a care for others to make the request for help for all life.

You do not need intellect, academia, or degrees.

You need a heart that is filled with love and concern for all life.

When humanity overcomes this limited aspect of self: of 'the mind knows best' mentality, and starts to use heart, then, miracles happen because miracles are simply; the sincere request for help to come — from those who care.

No matter who you are, you can do this.

No matter how scared you are, you can do this.

You are all at the stage when you need to be making choices.

To stay in mind ignorance and cause death of the self, or to choose life and love and ask for help.

The choice is yours, and yours, alone."

Chapter Fifty-Three

LINKS FOR YOUR DISCERNMENT

"Regardless of who is self serving; who may have a hidden agenda, the following links provide insights into the danger we are facing if we decide to stand by and do nothing.

The Truth is that many who have positioned themselves in key places have hidden agendas; which serve the ***2030 TRANS-HUMAN AGENDA.***

They are very clever and highly plausible. They know how to manipulate. Many are pushing their wares for profit.

Try not to place anyone or anything outside of Self on a proverbial 'pedestal'.

They will fall off their pedestals in good time, however, they can do a lot of harm along the way.

When you ***hero worship another you lose your inner power*** *— power that is needed to climb your ladder.*

The links shared here are shared by Claire, through advice from her Infinite Self; to ***listen to the agenda, as portrayed through the characters in this story.***

When asked for Truth, your heart can work with the Laws of Creation to point you in the right direction; to help you to collate vital information and discern wisely.

What is Truth?

When an earnest heart wants the Truth; the fullest Truth above all, then, doorways open to higher learning to assist each soul to reach Truth.

Essentially, you cannot rely on another to give you the Truth.

You must seek it yourself.

The children need you to remember this because, as Claire writes this, new plans — terrible plans — are in the process of being unleashed on humanity.

The Beast system is now fully operational.

Your heart centre and LOVE is also fully operational.

The outcome for the world's children and all innocent life including the bee and chicken populations? They are facing ***a mass extermination event.***

You can stop this.

You all came here to stop this.

We are simply asking you to tap into your heart Knowledge, and make every peaceful attempt to try."

THE WARNING SIGNS:

FROM: Searching For The Evidence Channel, Bitchute.com

THE KILL GRID - MARK STEELE | TUNGSTEN IN VAX MAKES HUMANS 'DORMANT RADIATION TRANSMITTERS'

https://old.bitchute.com/video/qHXTgYC5b1xw/

or, if links broken as the site was sabotaged after I published these links:

old.bitchute.com

...

5TH GENERATION WARFARE THEY HAVE DECLARED WAR ON YOU

Channels: SAVEUSNOW, on SUBSTACK

TROLLCATCHERGENERALchannel, old.BITCHUTE.com

'MARK STEELE Channel', T.ME

Website: SAVEUSNOW. org.uk

...

CLASSIFIED - THE KILL SWITCH INSIDE YOU, STARLINK IS ACTIVATED. 4 AUGUST 2023 (SHARE)

SEARCHING FOR THE EVIDENCE, BITCHUTE.COM

https://old.bitchute.com/video/LIUGLktoamoI/

...

CERN CONFIRMS DEMONS FROM THE 4TH DIMENSION PRESENT AT ITS FACILITY...

Channels: ALIEN.WARS, old.BITCHUTE.COM

STRANGER THAN FICTION NEWS channel, BIOCOMPUTING, t.me:

STRANGER THAN FICTION NEWS, CONSCRIPTION IS COMING, T.ME

CYBORGS SHORTING-OUT LIVE ON TV | STRANGER THAN FICTION NEWS

SOURCE: STRANGER THAN FICTION NEWS channel, t. me:

MIRRORED BY SEARCHING FOR THE EVIDENCE: First published at 19:44 UTC on November 28th, 2022

https://old.bitchute.com/video/AYpBFkFv9mC3/

THE EVIDENCE:

MAUI FIRES

THE LUCIFER AGENDA IN PLAIN SIGHT - THE MAUI FIRES AND MORE, AS WITNESSED BY LOCAL RESIDENTS

0:20:24 NOTE: THE HAND-SHAPING CORRUPT STAFF; DEVIL HAND SIGNAGE BY THE TRANSLATOR FOR THE DEAF.

Channel: Searching For The Evidence, old.Bitchute.com

First published at 19:44 UTC on November 28th, 2022.

TRUTHFUL MEDIA?

FAKING THE NEWS:

CAN YOU FIND YOUR CRISIS ACTORS AT THESE MASS CASUALTY EVENTS?

MIRRORED: https://old.bitchute.com/video/IEZs2WOUaQxa/

SOURCE: https://x.com/AmericazOutlaw/status/1802756862166663461

old.bitchute.com

...

SKYNEWS.COM: FAKING THE NEWS - FAKE PROPS USED FOR WAR IN UKRAINE:

SKY NEWS | FAKE BUILDING COLLAPSE - SET CLEARED AND FAKE CONCRETE BLOCKS EASILY LIFTED BY ACTORS AS THE NEWS READERS WATCH, CAMERAS ROLL AND THE REPORTERS SAY NOTHING.

Channel: Searching For The Evidence, Bitchute.com

The site was sabotaged after I published these links, try

old.bitchute.com

...

FEMA IN HAWAII CAUGHT RED HANDED – FEMA FAKE THEIR OWN NEWS CONFERENCE

Channel: Searching For The Evidence: https://www.bitchute.com/video/417CxTxDvHrS/

or old.bitchute.com

Fake War News — Ukraine...'Dead' Body Replaces The Cover:
https://t.me/STFNREPORT/30605

THE WARNING SIGNS:

Dr Sean Brooks | BLOOD CLOTS D-DIMER TEST https://old..bitchute.com/video/DcajTwe29hsK/

...

COVID IS MAN-MADE VIRUS RELEASED TO ENSLAVE HUMANITY ACCORDING TO MEDIA

"The truth is coming out... COVID didn't originate at the "wet market" it came out of Fauci's lab with the support of Bill Gates and the "New World Order." And they released it just before the elections to thieve power from the people and put in place the current tyranny."

(CREDIT - ALIEN. WARS):

Channel: Alien Wars,

https://www.bitchute.com/channel/mse9ae9tQLqE/

UN AGENDA 2030: FOOD SHORTAGES AND CLOSURE OF FARMS

2 FARMERS FROM EASTERN IDAHO WHO HAVE JUST RECEIVED THEIR WATER SHUTOFF ORDERS

Mirrored: OHMYGOD Channel: bitchute.com https://old.bitchute.com/video/hlSM1exWbdgd

RESEARCH:

THE WORLD ECONOMIC FORUM AGENDA 2030:

...

BRILLIANT, DETAILED BREAKDOWN OF THE DYSTOPIAN '15 MINUTE CITY' AGENDA

Source: youtube.com | Coin Bureau

MIRRORED:

SEARCHING FOR THE EVIDENCE –

https://old.bitchute.com/video/FbIlbFNVScSp/

...

UNITED NATIONS AGENDA 2021 AND AGENDA 2030:

*CHECK OUT THE **PEDOPHILE** ART WORK AT THEIR HEAD QUARTERS, THE SATANIC CUBE, THE DARK MONUMENT PLACED OUTSIDE THESE BUILDINGS*

UNITED NATIONS SECURITY COUNCIL UNPACKING THE ART WORK

MIRRORED:

https://www.bitchute.com/video/DP2z0QEpyihm/

Do You Know About This? Research:

PROJECT 2045

...

THE WARNING SIGNS OF A 'ZOMBIE APOCALYPSE' STARTED WITH THE HOMELESS AND VULNERABLE MEMBERS OF OUR SOCIETY

HAVE THE COURAGE TO LOOK AT WHAT WE HAVE ALL CREATED: DO YOU LIKE THE 'AGENDA 2030 REALITY' WE HELPED TO CREATE FOR THE GLOBALISTS? THE HOMELESSNESS, THE POVERTY, THE CRIME, EXPOSING VULNERABLE CHILDREN TO THIS TYPE OF PREDATOR?

HAVE PITY ON THESE SOULS AND THE CHILDREN, AND DO SOMETHING PEACEFUL TO HELP CREATE CHANGE.

INTERESTINGLY, THERE WAS A LOT MORE INFORMATION ABOUT THIS HUGE PROBLEM SIX MONTHS AGO. I COULD NOT FIND AS MUCH ONLINE...IT APPEARS THAT THE VDIEOS ARE DISAPPEARING.

LOST SOULS, HOMELESS, TENT CITY, POVERTY, AND DRUG ABUSE INCREASES – TRANQ STATE – CITY OF ZOMBIES:

LIFESTYLE CHANNEL BITCHUTE.COM https://www.bitchute.com/video/uzAYQAT3a9LN/

ORCINY CHANNEL https://www.bitchute.com/video/6IVceUacJud0

@KENSINGTONDAILY, ODYSEE.COM https://odysee.com/@KensingtonDaily:8/the-reality-of-kensington-(documentary):e

...

WARNING SIGNS:

2021: SENIOR NURSE - "THE HOSPITALS ARE FULL OF VACCINATED PATIENTS." TEENS DROP DEAD, MYOCARDITIS

AUSTRALIA: *"HOSPITALS ARE FULL OF 'VACCINATED' PATIENTS"* - NURSES WARN HUMANITY ABOUT THE INCREASE IN C19 'VACCINE' RELATED DEATHS: HEART ATTACKS, BLOOD CLOTTING AND MYOCARDITIS — EVIDENT IN YOUNG ADULTS AND CHILDREN. "YOU WILL STILL GET COVID, STILL PASS IT ON, STILL DIE, STILL GET ADVERSE SIDE EFFECTS...."

"...serious adverse effects"... "Twenty year olds are dropping dead"..."the media need to start telling the truth" ... "Why vaccinate Australian children?"..."They're after our kids."

First published at 15:46 UTC on September 22nd, 2023:

MIRRORED:

Searching For The Evidence, Bitchute.com

THE EVIDENCE:

AUSTRALIA MEMORIAL DAY:

YOU MAY NEVER TRUST ANOTHER CELEBRITY AFTER WATCHING THIS VIDEO | 2021 — DOCTORS WARN OF THE DANGERS,

MIRRORED:

SEARCHING FOR THE EVIDENCE BITCHUTE.COM

WEEPING PARENTS - "MY SON IS DEAD. HE TOOK THE VACCINE"

MIRRORED:

Channel: DarknessToLight.111, Bitchute.com,

https://www.bitchute.com/channel/F8nnw2tnXp9t/

MORE EVIDENCE FROM SENIOR DOCTORS AND THE VACCINE INJURED:

Covid Deaths After Vaccine: https://t.me/covidbc

Sudden Adult Death Signal :

DR JEYANTHI KUNADHASAN TESTIFIES BEFORE AN AUSTRALIAN SENATE COMMITTEE ON PFIZER TRIAL DEATHS

The Daily Clout, mirrored by: LavaFox, Bitchute.com

JAPAN'S MOST SENIOR ONCOLOGIST, PROF. FUKUSHIMA CONDEMNS MRNA VACCINES AS 'EVIL PRACTICES OF SCIENCE

JAPAN: SENIOR ONCOLOGIST | SEARCHING FOR THE EVIDENCE:

First published at 15:19 UTC on April 29th, 2024 —

https://www.bitchute.com/video/0qMp6lEgdos7/

...

JAPAN — DOCTORS OUTRAGED C.VAX DEATHS 100/110 TIMES HIGHER: "THE CURRENT ISSUE IS PEOPLE ARE DYING"

First published at 14:54 UTC on May 28th, 2024 | Searching For The Evidence https://www.bitchute.com/video/4Wtm9aAaegp5/

...

MALAYSIANS UNITE AGAINST WHO, MRNA VAX DEATHS — DOCTORS EXPRESS REMORSE AND SHAME FOR MISTAKES MADE

First published at 13:27 UTC on May 28th, 2024 | Searching For The Evidence: https://www.bitchute.com/video/YBBZjW0vgXKC/

...

IS THE “SPEED OF SCIENCE” SAFE AND EFFECTIVE?

INFORMED CONSENT REQUIRES FULL DISCLOSURE:

IF YOU RECEIVED THE "TRIAL PHASE THREE, GENE THERAPY INJECTION", WERE YOU INFORMED IT WAS IN TRIAL? WERE YOU WARNED ABOUT THE RISKS OF:

TURBO CANCER, HEART ATTACK, STROKE, BLOOD CLOTTING, DEATH, DISABILITY, FIBROMYALGIA, CHRONIC FATIGUE, GUILLAIN BARRE SYNDROME, AIDS, HIV, LONG TERM HEALTH ISSUES, PERICARDITIS, VIOLENT SEIZURES?

IF NOT, CAN YOU PRIVATELY SUE THE INDIVIDUALS WHO INJECTED YOU?

...

MURDERED: DR ANDREAS NOACK 2021 - GRAPHENE HYDROXIDE 'RAZOR BLADES' CUT BLOOD CELLS (RE: FINAL DAYS)|

SEARCHING FOR THE EVIDENCE | T.ME

https://odysee.com/@Adverse:c/AndreasNoack:a

MANY DOCTORS AND SCIENTISTS WERE WARNING ABOUT THE MRNA GENE THERAPY HARMS FROM 2020 ONWARDS. A QUICK SEARCH ONLINE OF THE ALTERNATIVE MEDIA SUPPLIED A WEALTH OF INFORMATION: MANY DOCTORS AND SCIENTISTS APPROACHED THE ALT. MEDIA BECAUSE THE MAINSTREAM MEDIA WOULD NOT REPORT THEIR SCIENTIFIC WARNINGS.

Dr Sucharit Bhakdi - THE VACCINES WERE DESIGNED TO FAIL:

https://doctors4covidethics.org/

...

LONE VOICES IN THE WILDERNESS:

LONE VOICES IN THE WILDERNESS, WHO HAVE BEEN BRAVE ENOUGH TO SPEAK THEIR TRUTHS, DILIGENTLY FOUND AND SHARED LINKS HIGHLIGHTING THE EVIDENCE OF THE AGENDA AND THOSE WHO ARE PLAYING THEIR PART IN HARMING HUMANITY.

WHILE OTHERS SAT ON THE FENCE, THESE SOULS AND MANY OTHER FRIGHTENED VOICES FOUND COURAGE TO STAND FIRM AND SET TO WORK.

THESE SOULS HAVE NOT STOPPED: AND MANY OTHERS LIKE THEM ARE THE TRUE HEROES, QUIETLY GETTING ON WITH THEIR ROLE HERE, UNLIKE THE DOCTORS WITH THEIR 'SAVIOUR' AGENDAS. MEANWHILE THE NEWS THAT THE C19 VACCINES ARE, INDEED, CAUSING SEVERE ADVERSE SIDE EFFECTS GATHERS SPEED, BUT DON'T WORRY, THE 'SAVIOURS' ARE ALL IN POSITION TO OFFER THEIR 'SNAKE OIL ANTIDOTE', TO ANY ONE WHO IS FOOLISH ENOUGH TO LISTEN.

ACKNOWLEDGING:

SIXTH SENSE, BITCHUTE, ODYSEE

OH MY GOD, BITCHUTE.COM |

OH MY GOD, 153NEWS.NET

AND MANY THANKS TO OH MY GOD CHANNEL FOR HELPING ME TO LOCATE VITAL LINKS!

THE WARNING SIGNS

WATCH MONOPOLY WHO OWNS THE WORLD? | Tim Gielin

(FOR A CONDENSED AND CONCISE PRESENTATION OF THE WIDESPREAD MAFIA STYLE CORRUPTION AND EVIDENCE TO CORROBORATE THE ISSUES PRESENTED: IT IS SELF EVIDENT).

LAST BIT OF EVIDENCE

FINALLY, THEY DID TELL YOU WHAT THEY WERE PLANNING...

FAUCI AND HIS COHORTS; GAINING YOUR ACQUIESCENCE TO THEIR AGENDA, WHICH WAS ALREADY IN PLACE. IT JUST NEEDED HUMANITY TO *IGNORE THE THREAT AND 'SIGN IT OFF'.*

2019 - THIS WAS PREMEDITATED MURDER / DEMOCIDE VIA INJECTION

MIRRORED: SIXTH SENSE CHANNEL – https://www.bitchute.com/video/RhzslQKCgRyT/

The Pedophile Agenda; You think the globalists don't like children to abuse? The Pedophile Agenda — the one that your 'free world' politicians won't be promoting, pre-election, but will be imposing on the children, post election...?

Evidence of child trafficking and abuse: WOW - RUSSIAN TV JUST AIRED THIS - HUNTER BIDEN WITH KIDS, CRACK AND WHORES

Channel: DarknesstoLight111: https://www.bitchute.com/video/WhBw64jxAIEm/

"Schools must equip children to have sexual partners" - say the UN and WHO

This evidence report reveals how the World Health Organization and United Nations are sexualizing little children in primary education worldwide, for the purpose of normalizing pedophilia.

Source: https://stopworldcontrol.com/children/

FOR THOSE JUST WAKING UP: A BRIEF SUMMARY OF 2020-2024 — HOW YOU CAN HELP YOURSELVES (SHARE)

SEARCHING FOR THE EVIDENCE: https://www.bitchute.com/video/1Patgf372PUG/

BILL GATES | DELETED DOCUMENTARY | "20:1 RETURN" | WHY HE SWITCHED FROM MICROSOFT TO VACCINES,

including The Children Killed In India By The Gates Foundation Vaccines,

Channel, Searching For The Evidence:

https://www.bitchute.com/video/4csKILgH4sEA/

WHAT ARE THE GLOBALIST'S GOALS?

Source: Rumble.com — https://rumble.com/v27sc5r-iclei-the-wef-and-un-in-your-local-councils..-research-learn-share-kate-mas.html

Bitchute.com:

ICLEI , THE WEF & UN IN YOUR LOCAL COUNCILS.. RESEARCH LEARN SHARE - KATE MASON

Kate advises (upon wide research) to learn to recognise the TERMS that ARTICULATE the 'GLOBAL AGENDA'.

In other words, GLOBAL MEASURES in LOCAL AREAS. THE - ICLEI -

This may be via the 'W.E.F STRATEGIC INTELLIGENCE' (See: link below).

Search 'TRANSFORMATION MAPS',
then 'AUSTRALIA'.

Kate, also, made the point of articulating some of these 'terms'.

RESEARCH:

• ICLEI

• 'Smart Cities'. S.M.A.R.T = Self-Monitoring And Reporting Technology

• 'Digital I.D'

• 'Metaverse'

• 'Digital' infrastructure, such as 'lighting' & 'surveillance' (they the same thing!)

• 'Data collection/storage'

• 'Digital currency'

• 'E.S.G Scores'

- 'Carbon credits'
- 'Food/agricultural transformations'
- 'Synthetic biology'

Other TERMS that ARTICULATE the 'GLOBAL AGENDA', include:

- 'Transformations'
- 'Sustainable'
- 'Disruption'
- 'Inclusive/Inclusion'
- 'Climate change'
- 'Equitable'
- 'One Health'

ICLEI: https://iclei.org/

Search ICLEI for local council areas: https://iclei.org/iclei-members/

LINKS TO 'W.E.F STRATEGIC INTELLIGENCE'

https://www.weforum.org/biodivercities-by-2030/transformation-map

https://www.weforum.org/strategic-intelligence/

https://www.climatechangeauthority.gov.au/sites

Source: https://rumble.com/v27sc5r-iclei-the-wef-and-un-in-your-local-councils..-research-learn-share-kate-mas.html

Mirrored: https://www.bitchute.com/video/zIOlgM2cl1SY/

DIGITAL ID SHUT DOWN IN L.A: THE LAWYER WHO SHUT IT DOWN EXPLAINS HOW HE DID IT:

https://old.bitchute.com/video/538m59NlfnIL/

Planetlockdown:

https://planetlockdownfilm.com/documentary/
https://rumble.com/vsw5gf-planet-lockdown-a-documentary.html

Interview with Michael Yeadon, former VICE President and Chief Science Officer of PFIZER, where he worked for 16 years:

https://rumble.com/vg4inv-michael-yeadon-full-interview-planet-lockdown.html

...

IN MEMORY OF DR ARNE BURKHARDT:

HOW ARE VACCINE ADVERSE EVENTS DETERMINED? DR ARNE BURKHARDT, RENOWNED PATHOLOGIST GIVES DETAILED ACCOUNT OF HIS WORK AND FINDINGS:

FINAL INTERVIEW WITH PATHOLOGIST ARNE BURKHARDT:

Channel: POINTOFATTENTION, https://www.bitchute.com/video/SDumGPj8CM1V/

...

Some of these links became temporarily unavailable on

www.bitchute.com recently and were transferred over by Bitchute to the

old.bitchute.com server.

I recommend you always visit my other channels, as listed, in order to find any links; which may be removed in the future as the censorship increases.

@Loves Heart Plan substack.com

Searching For The Evidence, bitchute.com

@truelightessence, odysee.com

Remember the children.

Remember, their future rests in your ability to create a world free from suffering.

It can be done and must be done because without your efforts, the gift of Creativity is wasted.

An opportunity lost.

Creativity is the most powerful defence, the most powerful protection. It has the power to change the game.

You have the power to end the game, to end the suffering and bring about peace.

Create, imagine, dream.

Chapter Fifty-Four

ACQUIESCENCE: DEFINITION

acquiescence | ˌakwɪˈɛsns |

noun *[mass noun]*

the acceptance of something without protest: *in silent acquiescence, she rose to her feet.*

Chapter Fifty-Five

"THE WINDS OF CHANGE," FREEDOM FROM FEAR, Claire Hastain © 2014

What message have you for those who share my concerns for Planet Earth?

"It is time to open your hearts and your Divine minds to the reality of this dimension, and the reality of those who are intent on causing you harm.

Untold suffering is happening across your planet.

You sit in your armchairs each evening, whilst the horrors of the world are displayed across your TV screens.

Many of you are so disconnected from your hearts and Higher Self, that you have become numb to the atrocities facing your family of humanity.

Others have become drawn into the deliberate ploy, by the elite: to keep you in fear; to believe that this is the only reality.

It is not.

This is the reality of choice, made by humanity, because they choose to remain asleep.

Those who came in with more Divine remembrance, who were given the opportunity to use their gifts with the intention of protecting the vulnerable, are themselves locked into the Mind Control Programs.

This does not serve The Whole.

It is easy to get lost in the dramas of your day to day living, and the challenges that you are experiencing are two-fold:

Partly they are happening as a result of your decision to stay asleep. The new Light codes are unpicking your clenched hands from the sinking ship: your refusal to let go is what is causing you the most pain. Our guidance, therefore, is to LET GO, and allow Divine Light to guide you away from this place.

The second issue affecting humanity's suffering, is their passive acceptance that it is OK for others on their planet to be murdered; shot; blown up ... as long as it doesn't come to their village.

Open your hearts to those who are suffering.

You all have the ability within your heart centres, to access all the tools that you need, to counterbalance all that the elite are doing to cause harm.

You are many. They are few. They have simply learned how to manipulate your Divine connection to Source, and to hold you in a place of limitation, but this is all an illusion.

If you choose to, you can stay in this illusion, but why would you choose suffering over Joy, Happiness, and Peace?

Each soul has the ability to generate Peace on this planet.

Peace in the world starts with Peace within the Self, by simply building a ladder on a firm foundation, that gets you past the rogue cowboys on the various decks, and into the lifeboats, and eventually, beyond the rocks.

Each soul is being invited to learn how to get beyond the rocks, and to uncover their puzzle pieces, so that humanity has a chance of reaching its highest Ascension potential.

All have a huge part to play in this sweep-up operation.

All are honoured for all they have done to assist thus far.

The Winds of Change are blowing your way.

They are calling to you all to awaken: to become the Divine Light that you truly are; to help transmute and purify the distortions that are causing so much harm to all life; and to step into your mastery.

Who amongst you will unclench your fists from the sinking ship, and allow yourselves to be guided perfectly, to help your beautiful planet become the shining jewel of the Greater Cosmos?

For this is the future of humanity that was written in the stars, aeons ago.

The miracle of Peace is a heartbeat away.

Hear the Winds of Change that are calling you to awaken to these Truths, and have courage that your being here, is for a higher purpose.

You were always part of this Plan, and you are being called to choose what type of ending you wish for yourselves, your children, and your children's children.

Mother Earth has fulfilled her side of the mission.

The outcome of this Plan now rests with you."

From: ***FREEDOM FROM FEAR,*** *Claire Hastain © 2014*

Printed in Great Britain
by Amazon

43977816R00435